Ultimate SQL for Relational Database Design

Design and Build Robust Relational Databases with SQL to Power Modern Analytics

Gregory Thomas Hay

www.orangeava.com

First Published: February 2026

Published By: Orange Education Pvt Ltd, AVA®

Address: 9, Daryaganj, Delhi, 110002, India

275 New North Road Islington Suite 1314 London,
N1 7AA, United Kingdom

ISBN (PBK): 978-93-49887-47-3
ISBN (E-BOOK): 978-93-49887-48-0

Scan the QR code to explore our entire catalogue

www.orangeava.com

Get a Free eBook

We hope you're enjoying your recent book purchase! Your feedback is incredibly valuable to us and helps other readers discover books that truly make a difference.

If you found this book useful or enjoyable, we'd greatly appreciate it if you could leave a short review with a 5-star rating on Amazon. Your review supports our work and allows us to reach more learners worldwide.

As a thank-you, we're happy to offer you a **free digital copy of this book** plus a **30% discount code** for your next purchase on our official websites:

www.orangeava.com

www.orangeava.in (For the Indian Subcontinent).

☑ How it works:

Leave your review on Amazon, take a screenshot of the confirmation or use the following link to submit the claim and email it to **info@orangeava.com.** Once received the required detail, we will send your rewards within 24 hours, **along with one month free subcription to the book on AVA SkillShelf!**

Claim Form
https://rebrand.ly/4d2477

Thank you for your support–it truly means a lot to us.

Downloading the code bundles and colored images

Please follow the links or scan the QR codes to download the ***Code Bundles and Images*** of the book:

https://github.com/ava-orange-education/Ultimate-SQL-for-Relational-Database-Design

The code bundles and images of the book are also hosted on ***https://rebrand.ly/87b3fa***

In case there's an update to the code, it will be updated on the existing GitHub repository.

Errata

We take immense pride in our work at **Orange Education Pvt Ltd,** and follow the best practices to ensure the accuracy of our content to provide an indulging reading experience to our subscribers. Our readers are our mirrors, and we use their inputs to reflect and improve upon human errors, if any, that may have occurred during the publishing processes involved. To let us maintain the quality and help us reach out to any readers who might be having difficulties due to any unforeseen errors, please write to us at:

errata@orangeava.com

Your support, suggestions, and feedback are highly appreciated.

Dedicated To

My wonderful siblings, from whom I learned much about hard work, loyalty, dedication, commitment, and teamwork:

Jeff Hay

Dan Hay

Kate Heino

Ann Nykamp

And also two lifelong buddies, Mitch Gilbert and John Husby as well as my dear friend of more than 37 years, Suzi Ibach, along with all the fantastic people I met through my two years of traveling, teaching, and writing in Central Asia (Kazakhstan, Uzbekistan, Tajikistan, and Kyrgyzstan).

About the Author

Gregory Thomas Hay holds a master's degree in Information Management from the University of Washington, and has earned a range of technical certifications since 1992. His professional career spans more than 26 years, and includes work as both an employee and a contractor for several prominent organizations in the greater Seattle area, including Microsoft, the Walt Disney Internet Group, and the Bill & Melinda Gates Foundation. Throughout his career, Greg has specialized in data, technology, and systems that support large and complex organizations.

From the 1990s through approximately 2014, Greg devoted significant time to community service as a volunteer math tutor and youth mentor with Community for Youth. As part of that work, he produced a short documentary fundraising film highlighting the experiences of six students and four mentors in the program. Though now dated, the film remains available online and reflects his long-standing commitment to education and mentorship.

In 2008, Greg began a second academic career as a university instructor. He has served as a Senior Lecturer at the University of Washington, the University of Chicago, Northeastern University, and most recently at Suleyman Demirel University in Kaskelen, Kazakhstan. Across nearly 130 courses, Greg has personally taught more than 3,500 students, many of whom now work at leading technology companies around the world.

Alongside his academic and technical work, Greg maintained a parallel career as a basketball official from the mid-1980s through 2010. He officiated men's and women's games at levels ranging from youth leagues to high school, NCAA, Pro-Am, and NBA/WNBA practice scrimmages for the Seattle Supersonics and Seattle Storm.

About the Technical Reviewers

Umar Adam Ibrahim is a Ph.D. in Artificial Intelligence (AI), and has extensive experience in software development, academia, and AI research. He began his career as a software developer, building robust and scalable systems before transitioning into academia, where he taught a range of computing courses, including machine learning, data science, and programming.

In addition to teaching, Umar has been deeply involved in student innovation and entrepreneurship, serving as a startup advisor and mentor for emerging technologists.

His research focuses on the application of Artificial Intelligence in education, healthcare, climate, and energy, with a passion for using intelligent systems to drive social and economic impact. Umar is dedicated to advancing the responsible adoption of AI technologies, and empowering the next generation of innovators through hands-on learning and applied research.

Jacqueline Hsu is a technical reviewer currently working at a FinTech company as a data scientist. She earned her bachelor's degree from the University of Washington, and her master's degree from the Carnegie Mellon University. Jacqueline's SQL journey began in a class with Greg, and she has since built on that foundation, applying and expanding her expertise across a range of professional roles.

Acknowledgments

There are a few people I want to acknowledge for keeping this book moving forward through endless distractions.

Dr. Matthew Saxton was a part of the search committee at the University of Washington that took a chance on me in 2008 when I was an inexperienced instructor.

Dr. Umar Adam is one of the best thinkers I have had the pleasure of collaborating (and traveling) with. We share an office at SDU, and frequently riff on project ideas as well as frame potential features for our common AI project, Smash-Index.

Nurbol Aidarbayevl is the Program Coordinator in the School of Education and Humanities at SDU, and my boss at work. He has helped me navigate through various cultural differences, halfway around the world and connected me with outstanding students for numerous projects.

Karen L. Watterson (and her husband Fred) had an incredible impact on my life, when I was a 19-year-old freshman at Shoreline Community College. She hired me as a teaching assistant, and helped guide me to Microsoft, when I was just beginning my career in this industry.

Dr. Solland inspired me in 1985 to explore my interest in learning when I took her 100-level Anthropology class.

Robert 'Bobby' Herrold was an accomplished collegiate basketball referee that was a true guardian of the game. He was a fantastic and inspiring leader.

David Libbey is also an accomplished basketball referee with a passion for teaching and a strong commitment to youth development.

James Marshall Hendrix: Everyone should have a hero; someone who inspires and guides us through many of the challenges we face in life. The difficulties I experienced as an adolescent were blunted by my inspiration from the genius in Jimi.

Preface

The author is not an economist, sociologist, or anthropologist, though he admits to occasionally pretending at expertise outside his lane. By his own account, he is mediocre at many pursuits—including golf, guitar, and probably poker. He has, however, achieved professional mastery in relational database design and SQL, building a long and successful career working with production data for several large, well-known organizations. This book represents his attempt to help the next generation of data professionals develop a broader awareness of the context in which data exists throughout its finite lifecycle. He believes future professionals will be more effective if they understand organizational data needs, establish learning objectives, design appropriate storage structures, and write efficient data retrieval processes using Structured Query Language (SQL).

His nearly 40-year career in data began accidentally in the 1980s, when database technology was still in its early days. At the time, he had no intention of pursuing a technical career; his ambition was to become a professional basketball referee. Although he never reached the NBA as a full-time official, he officiated hundreds of closed practice scrimmages for the Seattle Super Sonics and Seattle Storm over eight seasons. As a college freshman at Shoreline Community College in 1986, he enrolled on a whim in a five-credit course titled *Business Computers*. It became a turning point, earning him the only 4.0 grade of his academic life. His instructor, Karen L. Watterson, was impressed enough to invite him to serve as her teaching assistant and later encouraged him to apply as a software tester at a new company near Seattle—Microsoft.

As an instructor, he has consistently sought to understand his students' backgrounds, technical experience, motivations, and career goals. Before each course, students' complete surveys and participate in brief one-on-one interviews, generating hundreds of data points each year. This information helps him tailor course content, examples, and datasets to better engage students and address broader trends in higher education and technology.

One recurring question he asks is where students see themselves professionally in five years. Across nearly 3,000 responses, not a single student has named a job title containing the word "database

This book is designed to present these topics not in isolation, but within a broader, practical context. The author aims to provide readers with a solid professional understanding of the data layer and the design decisions behind it, whether for a simple household application or a system serving millions of users. While some material may require rereading and further research, his goal is that readers finish the book better prepared to face professional challenges with greater skill and confidence.

DID YOU KNOW

Did you know that Orange Education Pvt Ltd offers eBook versions of every book published, with PDF and ePub files available? You can upgrade to the eBook version at **www.orangeava.com** and as a print book customer, you are entitled to a discount on the eBook copy. Get in touch with us at: **info@orangeava.com** for more details.

At **www.orangeava.com**, you can also read a collection of free technical articles, sign up for a range of free newsletters, and receive exclusive discounts and offers on Print Books and eBooks.

PIRACY

If you come across any illegal copies of our works in any form on the internet, we would be grateful if you would provide us with the location address or website name. Please contact us at **info@orangeava.com** with a link to the material.

ARE YOU INTERESTED IN AUTHORING WITH US?

If there is a topic that you have expertise in, and you are interested in either writing or contributing to a book, please write to us at **business@orangeava.com**. We are on a journey to help developers and tech professionals to gain insights on the present technological advancements and innovations happening across the globe and build a community that believes Knowledge is best acquired by sharing and learning with others. Please reach out to us to learn what our audience demands and how you can be part of this educational reform. We also welcome ideas from tech experts and help them build learning and development content for their domains.

REVIEWS

Please leave a review. Once you have read and used this book, why not leave a review on the site that you purchased it from? Potential readers can then see and use your unbiased opinion to make purchase decisions. We at Orange Education would love to know what you think about our products, and our authors can learn from your feedback. Thank you!

For more information about Orange Education, please visit **www.orangeava.com**.

Table of Contents

CHAPTER 1
Organize or Die: Learning from Data

Introduction

Hello, and welcome to Ultimate Introduction to SQL for Data Analytics! While data is practically omnipresent in today's vast technological landscape, few of us understand how to effectively establish the systems that answer complex questions through thorough analyses. This lesson will be our introduction to the history of data as well as the best practices of modern data collection and retrieval. We will also review the organizational and structured processes that allow for extended learning for any individual or many enterprises from around the world. This book aims to introduce relational theory, database design, and the Structured Query Language (SQL) to prepare readers for their respective professional journeys as an elite analyst or data scientist.

By the end of this chapter, readers will be equipped with several key thoughts that will frame how and when they seek additional data. These include an understanding of the progress advanced societies have made with organized learning and computerized databases as well as a better grasp of the limitations of data by itself and how most organizations need the context of data to color the information they rely on.

As this approach is presented, consider artifacts we use today that are evidence of learning by previous generations. For example, standard processes like the Systems Development Life Cycle (SDLC) are widely used today for a very good reason: they work!

Please also recognize the human passion to learn about and understand almost everything around us combined with making every day activities more efficient. We try to innovate and optimize repetitive tasks across all industries and cultures. Finally, apply this attitude of leveraging data to optimize performance as you develop database skills. Harnessing learning at tremendous scale, speed, and breadth will be the greatest asset of your future.

Structure

In this chapter, we will explore the following topics:

- Organize or Die
- Information Ladder: The DIKW Pyramid
- Data in Ancient Societies
- System Development Life Cycle (SDLC)
- Historical Database Systems
- Flaws and Limitations of Modern-Day Spreadsheets

Organize or Die

It is a human streak observed through history that we aim for personal recognition as well as when aligned as a team in professional organizations. However, we also seek better ways to get similar or greater output with the same or less effort. This has been proven many times during the evolution of ancient civilizations, inventions across industry, as well as in mundane activities like team sports.

People have often sought a competitive advantage in repetitive daily activities through the innovation of tools and optimization of processes. This is the reason that we use the adage of 'organize or die' to reflect the urgency of leveraging for innovation, while dwelling on the human zeal of increasing efficiency, productivity, and profit in professional undertakings. Although this might be daunting, the terms illustrate the roadmap for being assertive in making improvements to data organization and management processes.

To explain further, the 'organize or die adage' also finds a place in Charles Darwin's concept of 'natural selection' (*On the Origin of Species*, 1859). To simplify it, Darwinism postulates that each environment has a set of consistent conditions that define it. For instance, a desert in South Africa is different from the frozen tundra of Siberia or a dense rainforest in Brazil. Since the material and geographical conditions of each area are different, it only makes sense that the endemic species of flora and fauna will be different as well. These species are able to survive through specialized adaptation occurring over many years.

Furthermore, as conditions change in any environment, some characteristics determine a higher probability for survival moving forward. Over time, all the species must adapt via mutation or willful adoption of competitive practices to propagate to their progeny.

However, this book is not about human evolution as these examples are intended to get readers to recognize the following aspects, which will be instrumental in understanding why we manage data in the ways we do:

- Competition for resources is fierce.
- Not everyone "wins" or gains control of a limited resource; we must learn how to position ourselves and our organizations to be better suited and prepared for the conditions that determine success in obtaining control of the resources we desire.
- Business and market conditions are always changing; therefore, we must re-learn how to win.
- New competitive characteristics will prevail as market conditions evolve.
- Data has been leveraged to determine competitive actions for a long time.
- The modern economy relies heavily on data to get ahead on new opportunities.
- 'Organize or die' is knowing when and how to adapt to changing market conditions.

It can be argued that our common interests control the factors in our lives and allow us to succeed. When stripped down to its most basic elements, individuals and our collective societies have two simple goals: producing the goods or services that enable us to provide for ourselves and our closest associates, increasing the probability of survival.

This is a strong parallel between ancient human development and survival in exceptionally harsh environments with current corporations of today; each has to compete for limited resources, adapt to uncaring conditions, and react to adversity by inventing tools on the fly. We can learn more about dealing with competition in the current economy if we can understand how to leverage collective resilience to make processes efficient.

There are several objectives or motivations that entice organizations to follow the principles of the philosophy of Organize or Die. These include gaining control of resources to solve immediate or short-term needs, as well as building a set of repeatable processes that allow for improved outcomes and ongoing optimization over time. This has a focus on longer-term opportunities and future achievements. Let's take a closer look at each.

Short-Term or Immediate Needs

The first motivation of most ventures is to define and meet short-term or immediate obligations. The concepts of Organize or Die is paramount as

According to Founders Forum Group (*The Ultimate Startup Guide With Statistics* (2024-2025) | Founders Forum Group), almost 70% of start-ups fail before reaching year five as they are not able to meet short-term production or revenue demands. While the reasons for professional failure can be many, it comes with a stark realization that not being able to build systems or processes to tackle immediate goals does not guarantee survival in a competitive data ecosystem.

Long-Term or Continuous Success

While majority of enterprises fail due to not being able to meet immediate goals, the remaining examples exist as they also cater to long-term goals, and plan for continuous success besides immediate goals.

The pattern has been observed through history and highlights the presence of intrinsic features that allow only a few enterprises to achieve long-term success. Some of these features include the following:

- Efficient spoken and written communication between organizational units
- Presence of organized codes of behavior
- Diversified skills spanning multiple domains
- Generic training as well as special expertise in production methodologies
- A vision prioritizing the goals of the organization
- Adapting through learning and incorporating effective and efficient processes

While competition has always been present in the society, it has prompted organizations and individuals to innovate and succeed. Those with specialized skills demanded by the market will have a distinct advantage over others as they can stay relevant.

Moreover, for thousands of years, societies had to run on limited resources and tedious organizational processes of handwritten notes, oral traditions, and first-hand observations.

As a result, the scope of analyses was limited when compared to modern systems and processes that can assess copious amounts of data. Consider for a moment how brilliant the innovations from just a few generations ago given the limitations they had with communication and technology!

It is important to recognize that today's economy rewards organizations (and by extension the individuals) that can learn and act before others. This means being able to become predictive and quickly learn from massive amounts of data to find the critical patterns, trends, outliers, and anomalies. Successfully adapting to trends can result in higher productivity, profit, and prosperity. Essentially, being in control of data is now akin to being in control of our environment and success.

The next few sections will explain the process of innovation and the DIKW pyramid. We will also consider parallel examples from history to reinforce how using data to achieve goals has been a constant feature of humanity, despite rudimentary processes.

Information Ladder: DIKW Pyramid

Numerous academic models have defined the differences between data, information, knowledge, and wisdom. These conversations have provided clarity about finding and tackling imperfections within communication as well as helping systems engineers and information architects develop effective reporting dashboards. It benefits prospective data science professionals immensely as it illustrates how analysis fits into a larger system of processes.

The common components in this information hierarchy represent the acronym DIKW, which stands for:

- Data
- Information
- Knowledge
- Wisdom

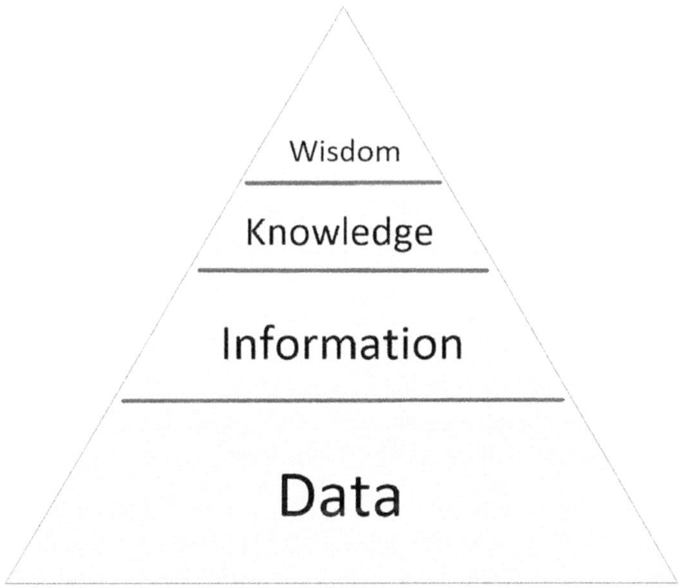

Figure 1.1: *The DIKW pyramid*

These components are ordered as a hierarchy because the subsequent components rely on the previous block. Simply put, wisdom is the result of having broad prior knowledge, and knowledge does not exist without appropriate information. You may also observe that the pyramid is predominantly occupied by data and the other components get increasingly smaller in scale as we move up.

Most systems operate on enormous amounts of data; however, many users might not be aware of how to translate it into actionable insights. The process of learning begins with data but requires adequate documentation and commitment by users to with it, while paying attention to nuanced indicators, patterns, and trends to gain full awareness of a given scenario. You can look up 'DIKW Pyramid' on the web for more background and perspective.

Data

Data conveys everything we hear, see, feel, and use to document experiences and trends. However, data by itself cannot help us effectively envision the larger picture as these individual packets of information lack perspective and depth without analysis and application. Raw data lacks purpose, definition, or even problem space. This missing context discourages a person from taking any action on raw data.

Think about our reaction in a situation where we are on a city bus and the stranger next to us starts spouting random words all of a sudden (like 'red', 'A24', 'LAX', 'Martha', 'Tuesday', and 'Argentina'). We might decide to avert our eyes or move away from them. If the gibberish continues, we might even exit the ride. This example illustrates how without a relation to broader concepts, we cannot connect disparate data bits into a cohesive idea. This is often frustrating as we struggle to comprehend the intentions of the person we are communicating with.

Consider how the vast amount of data present in the world might frustrate an organization that lacks professional expertise in data management. How will executives and prominent stakeholders react to a similar presence of 'gibberish' as they seek to solve real issues? Therefore, you must realize that data by itself does not provide direction on how to react or which action should be a priority.

Information

Data that has definition or context allows people to act on it. Let us use the raw data elements from the preceding example ('red', 'A24', 'LAX', 'Martha', 'Tuesday', and 'Argentina') and add context to make them coherent.

It can be, 'My neighbor is Martha; she is arriving at Los Angeles International airport ('LAX') on Tuesday from Argentina at gate A24. She will be carrying a red backpack.' Note the increased context about the previously unrelated elements of data, which us to visualize the scenario. While you might be less anxious with this information, there may still be a few questions, such as 'So...*do you want me to pick her up from the airport? If so, when is she expected to arrive*?' It indicates how despite having more context, one may not know how to react on it. This is where knowledge comes in.

Knowledge

To many people, knowledge is the accumulation of several pieces of information from a variety of mechanisms and acts such as reading, listening to conversations, and observations from living our lives while engaging with others. It can be argued that knowledge is earned through diligently processing the available information. Much of the valuable knowledge people obtain is created through purposeful investigation and discovery; it is not guaranteed by mere listening or knowing.

Knowledge includes understanding the context of how information is produced, processed, and the purpose for which it is presented. This can be phrased as knowing the 'meaning' of the information. From the earlier example, being told that 'Martha is coming into LAX on Tuesday at gate A24' might refer to a specific meeting for which you are coordinating with someone. Previous information from conversations, meetings, or news might be relevant to their understanding of any expected reactions to the new information. Their knowledge of the context of this information aids any decision-making about the situation. As a result, a person may check the itinerary for exact details of Martha's flight and create a spot in their calendar to pick her up.

As people gain more knowledge in a specific area or topic, they become more effective at processing it. As we gain expertise in a process we are able to break down the sequential steps and even be able to train or instruct others on the nuances of how each component fits in with the whole. Additionally, being knowledgeable about a topic or a process means that we can easily detect inefficiencies in a given process. This is perhaps the most critical for advancing the collective knowledge of a team about a task. By identifying inefficiencies, we can conduct controlled experiments and adapt to challenges and demands. This aspect has propelled markets, industries, organizations and societies towards success.

However, having knowledge does not guarantee any particular outcome. It is important to realize that it is possible to make mistakes even with accurate information and considerable experience.

Wisdom

Finally, we get to the last letter of the DIKW acronym: wisdom. As we know, wisdom lies at the top of the DIKW pyramid. Therefore, it is not only rare, but is the most valuable part of organizing data.

Drawing from the previous example, a person's knowledge of previous trips to LAX might be to contact Martha directly and arrange a meeting spot near the baggage claim. A person scheduled to pick her up will most likely make sure that she has their phone number in case there are any issues. Moreover, you would like to check the traffic reports while heading to LAX and select the most appropriate temporary parking space based on real-time information. Ultimately, the wisest decision to make in this situation might be to get an Uber ride-share for her.

Data in Ancient Societies

The story of data does not begin with the advent of modern technologies, but some 40,000 years ago. While this text does not deal with cultural anthropology, history, or sociology, it elaborates that recording data and pandering to the 'organize or die' adage has been a constant feature of humanity and its tryst for data collection.

As we know, the urge to be competitive and control our environment to 'win' has been a known trait observed in every civilization. Each of such civilizations relied on various forms of data to learn and optimize processes for easing hardships and ensuring survival.

The astonishing success of each civilization mentioned here depended on how they discovered better methods of doing repetitive tasks as well as using infrastructure to reduce risks, enhance protection, and provide for basic short-term and long-term goals. These efforts are akin to the concerns faced by many organizations and practitioners in data science today.

Try to imagine the world and harsh conditions early humans had to cope with; no internet, no organized manufacturing, zero engineering schools or elaborate global supply chains. While it was admirable to survive back then, many innovations of the era are considered extremely basic in the face of the modern developments we have now. However, it will not be wise to ignore these fundamentals that still inform our efforts at organizing data today:

- Written and Spoken Language
- Division of Labor
- Detailed Administrative Structures
- Organizational Learning
- Common Defense Architectures

Out of these, language has been the single greatest invention ever. The power to communicate effectively is not only practical for getting tasks completed, but also allows for better emotional connection and establishment of clans or common groups. Consider the power of collaboration; being able to coordinate effort significantly reduces duplication of tasks and needless competition.

Language enabled the quick transfer of information as well as organized and prescribed knowledge. This means people could begin to understand the world beyond their limited lived experience. They were able to gain insight into the best practices for diet, healthcare, and trade. Additionally, language fostered generational learning of specific skills like farming, woodworking, animal husbandry, and hunting. Younger clan members were able to become artisans much earlier by understanding the mistakes and the valuable experience of their predecessors. Their ability to subsequently innovate and build on the knowledge of their mentors propelled each civilization further in being successful.

Specialized skills allowed for nomadic groups to establish permanent settlements near fertile river floodplains. These flood plains were rich in minerals and produced a range of edible vegetation, which reduced the need to forage. Having control of a stable food source by domesticating animals and establishing farming practices thousands of years ago allowed civilizations to further concentrate on the division of labor.

When it comes to the division of labor, individuals were able to gain specialization in a skill as opposed to being trained for generic tasks. In a way, developing expertise helped people deconstruct technical processes and determine which steps are inefficient. Understanding flaws and inefficiencies led to experimentation and continuous optimization. These principles are still relevant in the world of data and technology. With the help of computers and Artificial Intelligence (AI), we can complete several cycles of development, analyses, and optimization more quickly.

Once these early civilizations became sedentary, developed a surplus of food, and specialized skills, they expanded their collective capabilities even more. They each developed other aspects that strengthened their core, including formal administration (creating laws and rules), organized education, and common defense. Each of these structures was intended to improve the outcomes of the collective civilization and increase their strength and resilience.

Societies with these characteristics were able to reduce the risks associated with survival and ultimately prospered. This is important to consider as database design draws from the same principles of constant learning and innovation. Each civilization captured data, processed it into relevant information, and created several best practices that provided a blueprint for efficiency and success. All of this expanded the collective body of knowledge and made each society exceptionally well-equipped to embrace their unique challenges.

Systems

Now that we have established the timeline of human innovation and the drive to excel, we are ready to dive into database design, SQL, and analytics. No database or SQL discussion is complete without knowing how 'systems' tie everything together. Briefly put, a system is an established structure that has a desired outcome; it is a set of processes that are organized sequentially to achieve a goal. These sequences of events, tasks, and steps collectively act as a larger cohesive unit. The purpose of a system is to provide efficiency in a repetitive process to generate better outputs with limited input resources. More sophisticated systems have built-in steps to measure progress, validate status, gauge the effectiveness of the work completed, and verify if the desired outcome is still viable.

Ultimately, the value of any system is how well it can simplify or organize a repetitive process. Again, this is achieved by breaking down each process into many smaller tasks or steps that are connected to provide a solution that saves time and money. Perhaps the biggest benefit of implementing a system is learning. To illustrate these points, let us explore some examples of simple and complex systems.

Example System/Repetitive Process #1: Farming

Agriculture perhaps is a fine example of a complex system that benefits from having a sequential structure of organized steps.

Desired Outcome: Produce a crop of edible vegetables like to feed family and/or sell at a market if there is any surplus.

Sequential Steps:

1. Locate available arable land.
2. Decide on appropriate crop(s).
3. Plant seeds in the ground and tend to them.
4. Harvest the produce after it has grown.

In this example, farming is a complex process that has been refined over thousands of years with many processes, sequential steps, dependent tasks, and analytical measurements that are critical to produce viable crops. The steps however are very simplified and many innovations must be learned through conversations, observation, and lived experience. Essentially, any sophisticated process like farming can be reduced to an unrealistic and simple form by an uninformed analyst.

Let us see another process that may be more familiar to people:

Example System/Repetitive Process #2: Commuting to Work

A common repetitive task for many people is traveling to-and-from a place of employment. We are programmed to experiment while defining routine or repetitive processes, finding inefficient steps, innovating, and measuring outcomes to obtain 'better' results. As such, driving to and from work every day is a good example for analysis and optimization.

Desired outcome: Getting to work in a predictable timeframe efficiently.

Sequential Steps:

1. Find quickest route to commute destination according to the GPS.
2. Drive as aggressively as traffic permits without being reckless.

3. Locate the closest parking lot to destination.
4. Try different routes, departure times, and parking lots for maybe a week or two.
5. Review/evaluate for time, cost, and overall convenience for some time.
6. Settle into optimal routine with modification only as conditions change.

Many of us spend an inordinate amount of time and effort during our commute to reach at our workplace. When we assume a normal 30-minute commute each way, we might end up spending hundreds of hours each year on a high-stress activity with insufficient planning.

We might consider the following questions when evaluating the two example systems here:

- Is example #1 (farming) any less complex than example #2 (driving to work) simply because it has fewer steps?
- How does writing down the sequence of steps for any system affect the probability of successfully achieving our desired objectives?
- What might happen as these processes mature and we complete the processes several times?

Is example #1 (farming) any less complex than example #2 (driving to work) simply because it has fewer steps?

While the number of steps might be an indicator of the complexity of any process, farming is incredibly complicated with many factors and conditions that span a cycle that is several months long. The number of steps, tasks, and considerations for producing a viable crop can be even more, despite planting resilient crops. On the other hand, while the inputs for driving during a commute are dynamic and can occur multiple times, it can be argued the complexity of farming far exceeds that of driving.

The system of farming represents generational knowledge spread over thousands of years and is complex and sophisticated. Yet, many of us might be tempted to minimize it. This may be the ultimate instance of 'Organize or Die'.

Let us now compare the system for farming to the system many of us follow to get to work each day. Maybe we can assume that driving to work has little 'deep' analysis and relies mostly on emotion and impulsive reactions to perception every few seconds.

According to a simple search on the internet, the average duration for an American citizen to commute to work is 27 minutes. For illustrative purposes, let us round off this number to 30 minutes. We often drive aggressively during a typical day to save minutes; however, the 'saved' minutes from our commute are lost during a typical work day. Consider that even one missed elevator, canceled meeting, or being placed on hold during a phone call negates everything we have saved during the commute.

Aggressive driving is an example of the innate desire to 'win' and might also include:

- Choosing alternate routes to avoid paying tolls
- Switching lanes numerous times to 'win' even just a few car-lengths
- Cutting in the line 'unfairly' during a merging scenario
- Driving through parking lots or residential neighborhoods to get past slower traffic

The above characteristics do not include exceeding the speed limit, driving in High-Occupancy Vehicle (HOV) lanes with no passengers, or perhaps running red-lights, tailgating, or passing on the shoulder.

As our commute is not complete until we park and exit our vehicle, the 'winning' behavior includes aggressive parking tactics such as:

- Double-parking in a turn lane
- Truck loading zone
- Someone else's reserved parking
- Disabled parking

If most commuters conducted a deep analysis of how much time, money, and aggression we invest into getting to work, most of us would soon realize that perhaps the most-efficient behavior is taking public transit instead.

How does writing down the sequence of steps for any system affect the probability of successfully achieving our desired objectives?

Writing down the sequence of steps is a great way to improve the probability of success.

Some of the important goals of most systems are to increase efficiency, improve predictability, and ensuring the reliability of outcomes. Many factors will change over the lifetime of a system, such as our knowledge, the capabilities of technology, legal requirements, competitive forces, and perhaps even the weather. This means that as we learn more about each process over multiple cycles of the system, we must make updates. These updates are not just limited to what the written or documented steps are; they may also include facilities, equipment, personnel, and training. A system is quite often a work in progress. To be most effective, it should represent the best-known steps and reflect the current operational knowledge based on evidence.

This is both logical and practical; it not only helps us visualize the process in a cohesive arc, but also allows the transfer of knowledge to someone else unfamiliar with the process.

In the case of the steps for farming that are included in example #1 above, it is woefully inadequate to understand a complex process. Extra steps such as scientific evaluation of the mineral content of the soil, a reasonable amount of fertilization, and validation steps to indicate progress such as weekly measurements and surveys from customers can be added to enrich the process.

What might happen as these processes mature and we complete the processes dozens of times?

A system is about improving efficiency, reliability, quality, and predictability. As there is no such thing as a perfect system, each cycle is an opportunity to reflect on the collective steps to assess whether it has any obvious flaws and is still providing value. We know that repetition allows for familiarity and emergence of people with potential expertise. The ability for experienced personnel to suggest innovations can be evaluated. Some of society's greatest inventions were born as workarounds, band-aid experiments, and lucky guesses in the middle of well-established processes.

Again, a system can be complex or simple. While we can recognize that whatever works for a particular situation is often the rule, we can acknowledge that no system is perfect and every system has a lifespan of effectiveness. The window might only last several months or perhaps centuries. This means that every system can be improved or optimized. While there may be a slight inefficiency at any stage, it may not be a sound investment of time, money or other resources. We usually avoid taking on system improvement projects until the benefit of spending resources on the overhaul is significantly greater than the cost of maintenance.

The point of these examples is twofold:

- People are always innovating or seeking new ways to gain efficiency (often based on impulse or flawed perception).
- Inefficiencies can be discovered in nearly any process by analyzing data.

Like data, systems exist at various levels of complexity. Data science is a system too, however, it should be viewed as a critical component in several larger and more complex systems.

Systems Analysis

No system is perfect! Each system might have inefficient steps; the only question is whether the cost of inefficiency exceeds the cost of fixing it. In other words, after spending time and money to make a process more efficient, do we get our investment back through greater competitive advantages achieved in the future?

Every generation, civilization, and organization has benefited from analyzing their systems of production and making improvements. It is related to our need to be efficient and maintain a competitive advantage. Let us take a quick look into this process of innovation.

Process of Innovation

For every innovation, tool, or process that was ultimately adopted, there have been several that were attempted and tried, that failed to provide value. Consider coffee; someone thousands of years ago in Ethiopia figured out that the red berries of a particular plant held light green beans. This person peeled the beans, roasted and crushed them into a fine powder before soaking them in hot water and drinking the concoction. While this discovery was a success, consider how many other hundreds of people became sick (or worse) when experimenting with other plants that happened to be poisonous.

When Greek philosopher Plato stated that 'necessity is the mother of invention'; it meant that when faced with an otherwise insurmountable obstacle or deadline, we become desperately creative in search of a solution. Any new tool to reduce the effort required to accomplish a common task represents somebody trying to gain efficiency. Think about it: throughout human history, there might have been millions of tools developed to make a process quicker, easier, or more effective. Just looking around a work desk at 2:00 in the morning on this random Tuesday, dozens of tools are visible: speakers, coffee cups, stapler, batteries, cell phone, cat tree, pens and paper. Each of these items was 'invented' at some point to create a benefit that did not exist previously.

In our modern lives, examples of innovation are determining the quickest way to get to the freeway through side streets on the way to work. We may try many different combinations trying to avoid red lights, tolls, or heavy traffic before figuring out a regular path. Our victory may only result in saving just a few minutes or dollars, but we work hard to determine it nonetheless.

In today's competitive economy, finding a definitive "better way" often requires a plethora of documentation to support analyses. Gone are the days of investing millions of dollars on a 'new approach' based on a hunch. We must be able to point to a precise pattern or correlation based on actual findings from analyses. This begins with identifying the exact step of a process that either takes the most time, resources, or perhaps has significant variance in outcomes that affect an organization's ability to predict or control costs. Identifying the biggest problem step in a complicated process is not easy, but let us assume that with enough experience of engaging any process we can break down each separate component by sequence and dependency.

The simplest processes involving data include a record of what was attempted for a particularly flawed process as well as the ensuing results that were deemed inefficient or undesirable. Prior to recorded history, these observations had to be shared orally. Today, we might categorize the documentation into smaller chunks by establishing end-result goals, articulating step-by-step processes, analyzing each step, determining inefficiencies or flaws, experimenting with alternative steps, and finally implementing the best step after observing the impact.

We will build further concepts on your existing understanding of data and the mechanism that is used to contain and characterize it. The following diagram is a rough estimation of the steps people go through when learning about a process with a goal to make it better. Note that the entire collection of steps outlined is iterative and leads to continual process improvement.

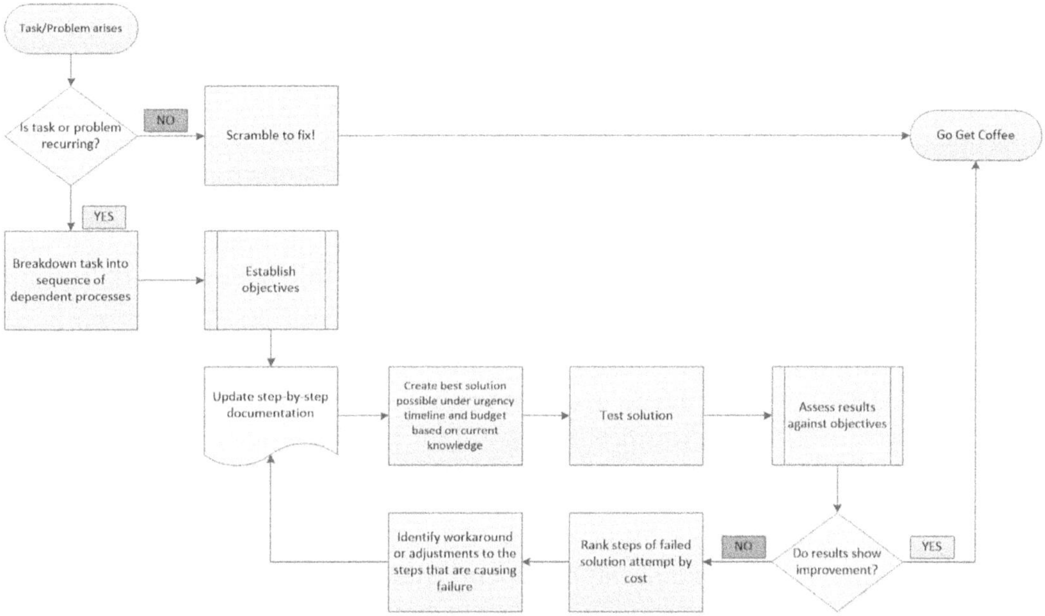

Figure 1.2: *Innovation as a workflow diagram*

Documentation of Steps in a Process: To simplify the diagram, a system is made up of components or steps that are sequential. If we are to analyze an existing process, the first challenge is to document the big steps of how things are done. The next few tasks are to determine the sequence of these steps. We will then document how and when it is known that a step is completed or is ready to transition to the next one. If possible, write these details of requirements, dependencies, and expected outcomes down.

Key Performance Indicators (KPIs): Each step most likely has desired outcomes; establish these as precisely as possible. It is important to define the metrics as well as Key Performance Indicators (KPIs) to recognize that a step is successful. More important is knowing quickly when a particular step is failing or even just lagging 'normal' or expected behavior.

Observation of Real-Life Behavior: After completing the first pass of documenting a process, we might want to observe an actual execution of the process running in real-life, while paying attention to how the steps are being completed. Measure the outcomes of each step according to the predetermined Key Performance Indicators (KPI); note which steps achieved the desired objective and which did not. During this observation, expect that there will be variance from what is documented and the behavior of people and machines. When there is a discrepancy from the expected behavior, make a note and either modify the documentation or process of execution so that they align. Additionally, document the amount of time and resources such as people, money, and the equipment each step might require.

Identify Least Efficient and Costly Steps: After a few cycles of going through a particular process completely, we can measure which step is taking up most resources. Again, resource consumption can be measured in time, people, expenses, or equipment. We will want to rank the steps in order of resource consumption from highest to lowest. Also, our goal should be to determine the steps that had the highest variance in terms of resources required. Try and identify the root cause of the variance and determine if additional controls, training, or sub-tasks are required to level out the cost of executing this step. The steps at the top of this list are candidates for redesigning to gain better consistency of outcomes.

Experiment with Alternatives: After a few cycles of going through a particular process completely, we can begin measuring the effectiveness of replacement or alternative processes within the problematic step. This experimentation may be as simple as adding additional steps, changing the order of execution, adopting new tools, or experimenting with new materials or technology. If the results provide better consistent outcomes, the innovation may be formally adopted as a standard. If the results do not provide consistent improvement, then they may be discarded for the next experiment.

Formally Adopt Innovation as a New Step: Throughout human history, our predecessors have followed standard systems and process improvements very similar to modern ones for centuries. While continuous improvement does not guarantee long-term success or profitability, it certainly provides a competitive advantage in most business scenarios. Storing data allows for immediate as well as long-term analyses and introduces the opportunity for investigation. Organizations that have structured the documentation of their processes can continually improve the quality of goods and services they provide.

Hence, this practical learning adequately captures the complexity of human behavior and our common need for winning control of scarce resources. It could be argued that nearly every single discovery, invention, or optimization in history was the result of innovation. While I am sure more than a few significant innovations have happened by pure accident, most are from someone thinking about a better way to do things.

As we search for a competitive advantage through innovation or optimization, we must realize that we might end up with many discoveries from the data we are collecting.

Innovation does not end; there is much more coming up in several industries. In other words, in an intensely competitive world, experts and professionals with specialized skills will have a formidable and distinct competitive advantage over those who lack them.

We will conclude this section with some thoughts on recognizing how critical systems have existed throughout human history. Firstly, systems continue to be as critical as before in our data-driven economy. While the advent of electronic systems has been pretty recent, the amount of data captured and used in analyses has been growing exponentially ever since. The human need for learning and 'winning' through innovative problem-solving has only become more reliant on valuable insights from data. As a result, data lies at the heart of most industries.

Essentially every company is investing in learning from data analyses. This includes understanding our collective behaviors and impulses. Examples include customer preferences and satisfaction with brands, supply chain and distribution efficiencies, as well as product manufacturing and materials procurement. No industry is untouched by strategists learning from historical data.

System Development Life Cycle (SDLC)

The **systems development life cycle (SDLC) is an important framework that provides a** high-level overview of the various phases encountered by development teams as they construct a system from scratch.

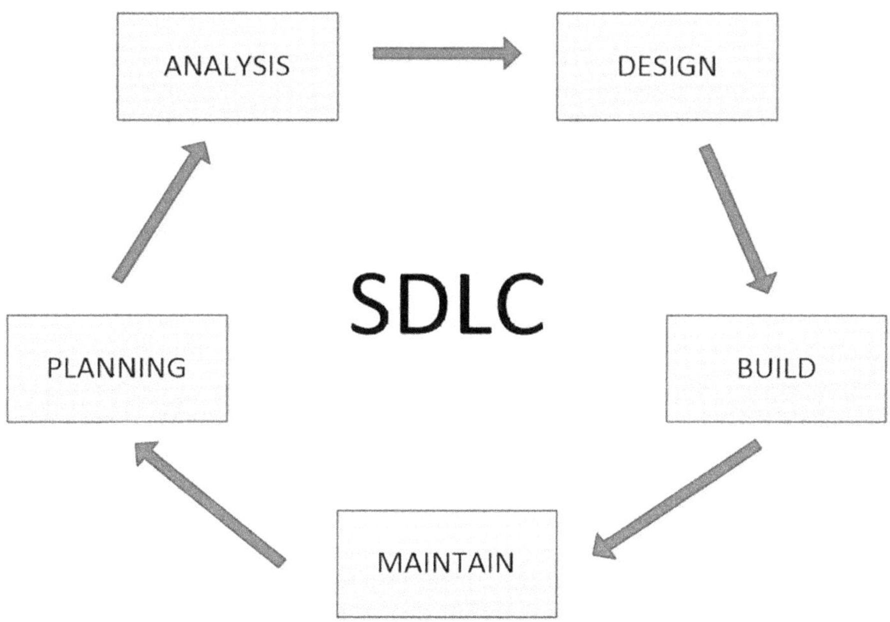

Figure 1.3: *Iterative phases in SDLC*

Therefore, it is important to understand why we use it, how it is followed, and how it is different from a methodology. Firstly, we use SDLC as a template to increase the probability of the success by the end of a project. Success refers to the timely delivery of features addressing user requirements within budget. This is known as the 'scope' of a project.

Having a set of well-defined phases allows a distributed team to coordinate efforts, track progress, communicate, and be prepared to tackle hurdles when the project hits delays. Basically, this template of steps when building a system provides better information and leads to more opportunities for learning. This means that as a team iterates through multiple projects and therefore has multiple cycles of traversing the SDLC framework; this results in improved experience and anticipation of challenges. Due to SDLC, professionals become more flexible and confident in tackling invariable project glitches.

The SDLC is a template of phases, and consists of planning, analysis, design, implementation, and maintenance. In many common methodologies, the SDLC is iterative and a single project may include several complete cycles of the framework depending on the project needs. Many projects initiate in the planning phase as this is where an organization sets priorities and assigns budgets. Once a potential project has been identified, it must be investigated for viability from a cost/benefit perspective. It is important to remember that only a handful of projects are funded. Each organization must make sure that a project is going to eventually pay for itself by generating additional revenue or reducing expenses.

Once a project is approved, the analysis phase begins. This phase is where the current system is explored and details around the problem space are defined. Users are interviewed and research is conducted to determine a set of requirements. Potential solutions are considered here as well. During the design phase, individual components like computer hardware, data models, database structures, cloud architecture, and other software aspects are explored as an integrated system. The implementation phase is where the code for each component is generated by developers. This includes testing system performance against benchmarks and training users. If the solution is a replacement of an existing system, the older system is phased out.

The final phase in the SDLC is maintenance. From a high level, this is the phase where a staff of operations engineers monitor the overall system performance and conduct the daily tasks that keep the system working. Tweaks and relatively small changes are made as necessary during the immediate post-implementation period. This phase may be several years (or even decades) in length and exceed the duration of all other phases combined, depending on the life of the system.

Again, the SDLC is a framework that can be implemented in thousands of different methods. The specific routine of implementation is called a methodology. The selection of an appropriate methodology almost always aligns with industry best practices and norms established by market leaders. For example, the construction industry defined the waterfall methodology because it has been proven over many decades that successful projects in this industry benefit greatly from the controls completing entire phases sequentially. The prominent factors in the construction industry are the reluctance at issuing changes due to high risk and incurring the subsequent cost associated with them.

Methodology

A methodology is simply the method through which the SDLC is implemented. There can be thousands of distinct methodologies across dozens of industries. Several common characteristics usually define each methodology such as an emphasis on thorough documentation, measurements of success at key points (called 'Key Performance Indicators' or KPIs), as well as iterating sequential phases.

Perhaps, the biggest indicator of which methodology is preferred for SDLC is the industry in which the project is being conducted. The most common methodologies and their associated industry are outlined as follows:

Methodology #1: Waterfall (Construction)

This methodology gets its name from the visual of water cascading down and filling up a series of buckets completely before the excess water falls from one full bucket into a lower downstream bucket. This methodology is known for being exhaustive, thorough, and somewhat slow. However, it is good for implementing the SDLC framework for industries that have many inflexible, deliberate, and dependent requirements which need approval or validation. This methodology is also good for industries that do not need nimbleness around rapid customer interaction; this means that once a set of project requirements are agreed upon, they rarely ever change.

Waterfall is perhaps the most popular and common methodology for construction. The reasons behind it are the changes that are exceptionally expensive or even prohibited. Imagine having built the third floor of a new apartment building designed to be four stories in height. A customer then decides that they instead want to build an office park with a little league football stadium on the site. Any work conducted in the planning, analysis, or implementation phases is then rendered moot as the construction team must reverse pivot and essentially start-over. Much of the permitting, foundational work and infrastructure must be scratched as well. Changes are exceptionally expensive in the land use and construction industries, therefore the methodology implemented to improve success needs to reflect that.

Methodology #2: Lean/Kanban (Repetitive Manufacturing)

This methodology was introduced by Toyota way back in the late 1940s and revolutionized the repetitive manufacturing of heavy equipment that traversed assembly lines. It essentially breaks down each critical job (such as putting doors on a half-built car) and makes that a specialized task. This means that a person was trained and became an expert over thousands of repetitions of doing the same task. This acquired expertise enabled the experts to redefine the process, develop specialized tools, schedule a delivery of parts that was more efficient, as well as shared validation of quality. Moreover, quality became a shared experience, with each specialist being allowed to 'shut down the line' if they see any defect or suspect workmanship in any aspect of the manufacturing process.

The effectiveness of Kanban has not only dramatically improved the quality and lifespan of personal vehicles, but also nearly every appliance and electronic system that hits an assembly line. Cars in the 1970s, for example, had a life that would end after 50,000 miles of use. Vehicles engineered in the 2020s often exceed 200,000 miles with fewer surprises and failures. Kanban is a very interesting study of continuous improvement and is worth considering for anyone who is interested in creating a culture of efficiency and quality.

Methodology #3: Scrum/Agile (Software Development)

The Agile methodology took hold in the late 1990s and early 2000s after colossal failures of large companies in the technology sector. Before Agile, software development teams often managed projects through the waterfall methodology, which was deliberate, precise, and slow. Moreover, changes to agreed-upon features are difficult to incorporate and customer interaction is diminished. The process often took three years to complete a single product release. Unfortunately, the problems being addressed when the project began are no longer relevant either or the customers no longer needed the solution.

Agile emphasizes rapid 'sprints' that deliver only a handful of features in a span of mere weeks. Customers often attend daily 'scrum' meetings, with eager engagement. Changes and updates are more easily included frequently with little concern or fanfare. This methodology understands the dynamic nature of software and builds a process that makes these beneficial to getting a high-quality product in the hands of customers very quickly. Customers win because they feel listened to, and they have functional products in a matter of months. Development companies win because they have happier customers and generate revenue quickly, with less bloat and risk. The coders win because they can specialize, while finding interesting and challenging work that makes them feel valued.

Thus, Agile is the dominant methodology in the technology industry. Take the time to become familiar with this methodology if you intend on becoming a data science professional.

Key Takeaways

Companies and their customers benefit when projects get completed on time. Having flexible and customizable methodologies that align with the unique culture of each different industry allows an organization to adopt a set of processes to improve their learning about how to create their product or service. The companies learn over time the specific way of delivering their goods (be it construction, manufacturing, or coding) while identifying mistakes as well as successful corrections. This repetitive reflection over time allows each interested company better insight and accuracy in the following domains:

- Planning (Budgeting)
- Spending
- Task Management (Recognition of Dependencies, Prioritization)
- Avoiding Problematic Situations
- Troubleshooting
- Reacting Quickly and Efficiently to Emerging Issues

Again, each industry (and to a lesser extent, each organization) can develop a unique methodology tailored to their culture and approach to delivering their goods. This is accomplished by capturing data throughout the lifecycle of many projects and building a body of knowledge which analysts can learn from. This repetitive experience allows for continual improvement, establishing 'best practices', nurturing of specialists for each process, as well as being better able to on-board or train new employees with little disruption. Customers benefit because the quality of the product or service purchased is predictable with less variance.

Perhaps, the greatest benefit of developing a methodology is when a project schedule begins to slip or something occurs that was unplanned. This introduces risk to the overall project scope. With a proper methodology, the risk is often mitigated as mistakes and corrections are anticipated for the process. The sooner a risk is identified; the sooner it can be corrected. Future projects can be informed from the work and projects done previously, which allows the organization to make budgetary and timeline estimates more accurately.

This is an opportunity to iron out any confusion you may have about the relevance and application of SDLC in the realm of database management. Before we can begin working with real data, we need a methodology and framework to contain our ideas and ground our innovation.

Comparing SDLC with Organize or Die

Now that we have been exposed to "Organize or Die", as well as SDLC, let us compare the two. Organize or Die is an overriding philosophy that affects an individual society's evolution or an individual person or organization's approach to a position, problem, or career.

The SDLC is a framework that responds to "Organize or Die"; it is a method for becoming more effective and efficient in a competitive environment through repetition, evaluation/analyses, and continuous innovation.

Data is at the core of all learning; being able to quickly, effectively, and strategically build and implement well-designed databases will support any organization seeking to learn. Again, in the modern economy, every organization understands they must learn at a rapid rate if they want to compete for customers, manufacturing efficiencies, or other insight into their operations.

In this section, we have established a foundational need for data and information to support the never-ending quest humans must improve. The next section covers the methods of data management people employed throughout history to learn and improve efficiencies to gain a competitive advantage.

Database History: Paper-Based, Hierarchical, and Network

We have used paper-based systems for centuries to keep track of things. After World War II, the overreaching industrial goal was to automate a lot of paper processes. With the advent of **relational theory in the 1970s**, we have come a long way.

Thus, new data analysts need to put data collection into context to gain competitive advantage and foster a culture of innovation. Data is at the core of all these motivations and thus needs extensive documentation of goals and objectives, step-by-step processes of each objective task, the results of these processes, as well as our observations and analyses of outcomes in relation to envisioned goals.

As we saw previously, for thousands of years, data had been managed manually with pen and paper. While this was easy to implement, it had obvious limitations in security, durability, and the ability to digest at any valuable scale.

These limitations when combined with the competitive nature of post-World War II enterprises led to the emergence of opportunities to gain significant advantages through computerizing processes. The primary objectives at this stage were to gain efficiency in production and distribution, and increase the output of goods and services to reach the burgeoning middle class.

The hierarchical model was the *de facto* standard with paper because there was essentially no other way to manually organize physical items. We had to group physical items in similar clusters all the time.

Computers were effectively a new tool in midst of long-standing and standardized business processes that had existed for centuries, such as order processing, supply chain management, and inventory control. Obviously, these processes were optimized around manual data collection and reading, which was structured in a top-down or hierarchical manner. As many companies had whole departments and processes organized around paper-based systems, there was no apparent need to change "how" data was being processed. This led to the first computers mimicking the hierarchical model by default as it simplified the time and expense of adopting computers.

Early computerized systems had flaws, as hierarchical design has limitations that were previously less noticeable in manual paper-based systems. The hierarchical model has a rigid top-down structure where each level has only one "parent" that controls access to the lower level. We realized that this rigid structure was difficult in operation when applied to real-world business scenarios. Not every relationship was hierarchical (strictly defined as one-parent only), especially when tracked over a fifty-year period. Most businesses engage in complex markets, where flexibility and reactions to change or fluctuations require speed and agility to remain competitive.

Also, to save time and resources, hierarchies are essentially designed as if people are reading the data 'in place on disk' directly from the hierarchy. This line of thinking caused designers to organize the hierarchy in the shape of an instantly readable report with all the data included in the structure of the hierarchy. Taking this report-design problem one step further, each hierarchy must have its own copy of common data.

Multiple hierarchies in a database require many copies of similar data to artificially inflate the overall size and time for processing simple inserts in multiple locations, as well as the costs for maintaining the extra storage. You may have heard analysts complain of 'duplicate data' or 'data redundancy' previously; there are reasons why it happens.

Insertion/Deletion Anomalies

The hierarchical model has insertion and deletion anomalies, which are caused by the rigid design structure that requires a record to have only one single parent. The insertion anomaly becomes visible when a company receives a record of data, yet a parent record does not exist to attach it. Similarly, a deletion anomaly occurs when a parent record is set to be deleted, but there exist one or more child/dependent records underneath it that are still considered valuable, and not desired to be deleted.

These challenges are difficult and often affect how companies conducted business operations. Many times, companies force their practices into a rigid hierarchical model.

An example can be how a delivery driver working at a pizza chain cannot work a shift at a different store in the same area, despite the outlet being operated by the same enterprise. In the pizza chain's hierarchical database system for payroll, employees are hired at a store and not by the company itself. It often means that the company would have to hire the same worker again if they are asked to cover a shift at a different location than their home store. This would also mean that the company will file official paperwork with the State of Washington and Internal Revenue Service (IRS). Since this was considered too much of a hassle to do things the right way back in the '80s, managers loaned their cars to workers for covering the shifts. These workarounds were common at that time as many companies struggled with inflexible database systems that did not align easily with the demands of real-life business operations.

Another detailed example of a hierarchy is a bus transit system where a database is organized in a collection of several hierarchies. When we look at these hierarchies, we must consider that they follow a cabinet filing system of order forms, invoices, and paper receipts. In paper-based systems, each original record is run through a copy-machine for each folder where a duplicate is needed. The data stored in these transit hierarchies may be centered around a few common areas of management, as shown here:

- **`Neighborhoods`**
- **`Drivers`**
- **`Vehicles`**
- **`Routes`**
- **`TRIPS/SCHEDULES`**

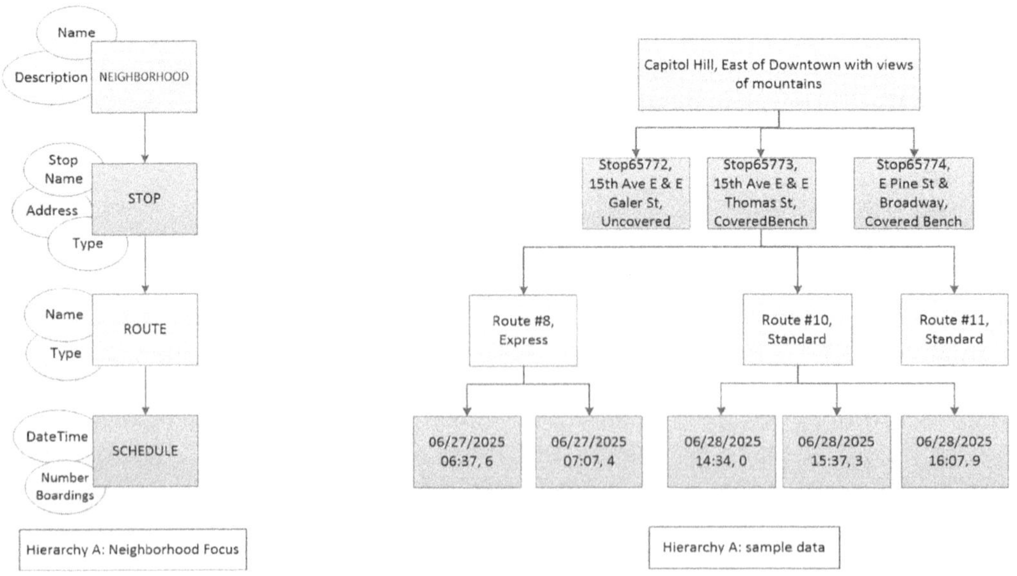

Figure 1.4: *A hierarchy of neighborhood trips for* METRO_TRANSIT

Let us see another example from **METRO_TRANSIT**:

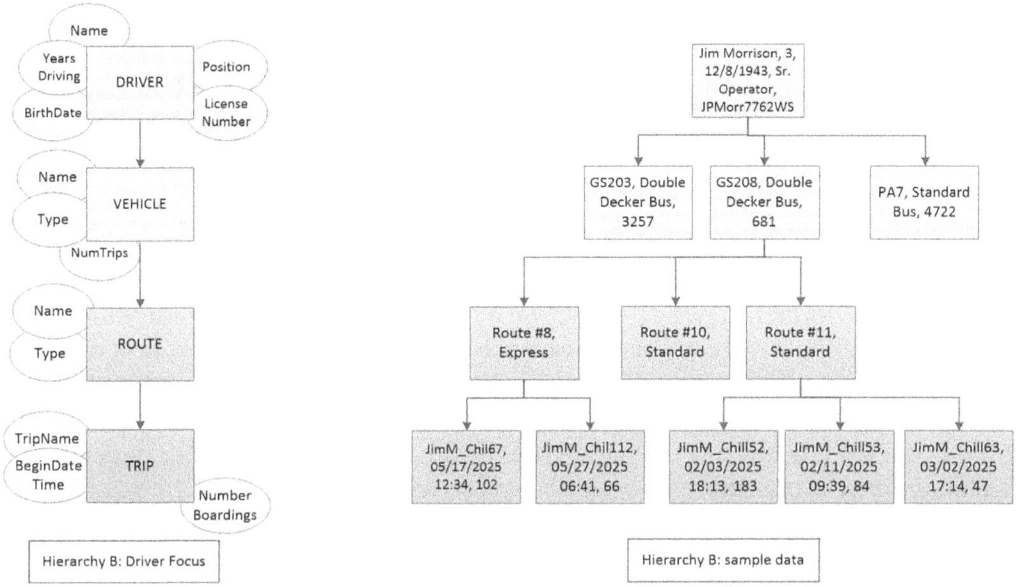

Figure 1.5: *Hierarchy of driver-centric data for* ***METRO_TRANSIT***

Inefficiencies with Hierarchical Model

There are several inefficiencies associated with the data stored in the hierarchies above. First, words for the types of bus stop and route are used to provide clarity. These words are necessary in this design because users will want to know if they should bring an umbrella if the bus stop is uncovered in case of rain. Also, the type of route (express or standard) may be important for the passenger in a hurry. The use of words for these values is of concern because they take up more storage space than reference and how they introduce the possibility for typos or misspellings.

A second inefficiency with the **NEIGHBORHOOD** hierarchy is having a summary of number of boardings at the base of the hierarchy. While these values are easy and convenient for a user to read if they are seeking data regarding a single route, they are difficult to include in aggregations across multiple routes as a full traverse through the hierarchy is required to obtain additional values. Also, an update is required each time a bus completes a scheduled route to make sure that boarding at each stop is properly recorded.

Please note that the driver-centric hierarchy is an entirely different structure from the first one focused on neighborhoods, yet it is filled with similar data. There are similar inefficiencies as before with using words to describe 'type' values for vehicle and route, but since these entire hierarchies have duplicate values, any insert, update, or delete will need to be written in both structures. This means that basic transactions will take longer to process even for simple statements. Any slight mistake will introduce discrepancies where different values are returned for the same question depending upon which hierarchy is engaged.

The final inefficiency is the math of 'Number of Boardings' recorded at the base of the hierarchy under **`TRIP`**. This value just might be the result of a human calculation adding up the values either as they happen or by tallying values from the neighborhood hierarchy. Either way, integrity and consistency of these values across hierarchies are exceptionally vulnerable and at risk of being accidentally misrepresented. Our ability to make decisions based on accurate data is in jeopardy.

Again, imagine this hierarchy as a collection of paper that is placed in folders and stored in a steel file cabinet. When a person wants to learn from the data, they first recognize which perspective or focus they need to adopt, such as **`DRIVER`** or **`NEIGHBORHOOD`**, as this will determine the hierarchy (or file cabinet) they will search. The same data is stored in each hierarchy but the path to the desired data will be shorter depending on which hierarchy is chosen.

Another example of a hierarchical structure could be how we track music from an online streaming service (services such as Amazon Music, Spotify, and Pandora come to mind). We may want to retrieve songs and play them from a certain artist, genre, or perhaps from another person's playlist. How might this be organized in a hierarchical structure? The short answer is a different hierarchy for each! This is shown as follows:

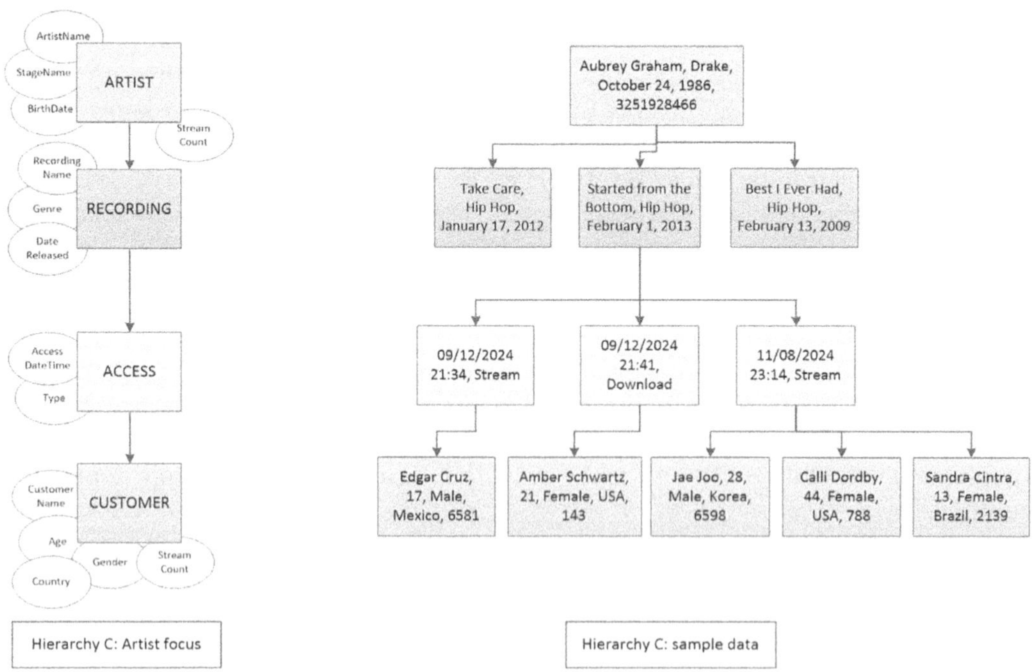

Figure 1.6: *Example hierarchy of artist-centric data for* `MUSIC_STREAM`

Once again there are challenges for efficiency and maintaining data integrity with the example hierarchy above for a music streaming service. Please note the duplicate words for genre, access type, gender, and country. These will be problematic as the subscription base increases and the number of users and overall streaming activity builds and any typos or abbreviations become more impactful.

The most notable flaws of trying to query data from a hierarchical model were when the exact hierarchy to start the query was unknown. Imagine trying to locate the details about a specific TRIP when none of the higher-level facts are known (such as **`ROUTE`**, **`BUS`**, or **`DRIVER`**). Locating the TRIP data would require significant time to traverse each possible combination of the higher-level values, perhaps with hundreds or even thousands of iterations. Please notice the following inefficiencies associated with a hierarchical data storage structure:

- Redundant copies of data are written to several hierarchies on each transaction, which increases the time required to process a single transaction (writing to three or four hierarchies equals three- or four-times the usual duration).
- Redundant data requires detailed understanding of all hierarchies as well as a manual process to validate integrity throughout the group.
- A mistake of either missing an update or deletion can result in inaccurate data; this means that different answers are returned from the system depending on where the question is searched.

These alternate structures create redundant values that effectively double or triple data storage demands. More than being bloated, slow, and expensive, these duplicate structures require extra care to maintain accuracy. Again, each insert, update, and/or delete has to be performed in each hierarchy, which significantly slows each operation. Unfortunately, over a period of months and years, many operations are not completed in each hierarchy as required, which introduce several inaccuracies. The inaccurate data can lead to mistrust about retrievable data, which results in many people resorting to managing data offline and even retreating to paper-based systems.

Additional flaws of the hierarchical database model are effectively having computer systems dictate limitations to the business, where tasks or actions that did not fit neatly into the established set of hierarchies are not allowed. An example of this frustrating restriction is when a driver "covers a shift" of a second driver in either another route or with a different bus. The rigid hierarchical database designs of the 1980s did not allow drivers to be assigned a bus, route, or trip dynamically. The result was that a business had to rehire the driver for a single trip, thereby duplicating their personal data and creating downstream confusion or misinformation when it was not cleaned up properly in the computer system.

These flaws led to the creation of the network database model that was still hierarchical in structure but allowed a workaround or band-aid for records to be "owned" by more than one parent (basically an object higher in the hierarchy such as **DRIVER** to **TRIP**). While the network database model better aligned with the navigation processes, it did not address the major issues of duplicate data and resulted in error-prone inconsistencies over time.

Breakthrough to a New Data Model

There was a breakthrough in database management around 1970. The relational model was articulated in late 1970 by Dr. Edgar Codd, a data scientist working for IBM. As we will see, the relational model effectively solved all the previous flaws for collection and retrieval of large data sets and remained unchanged for over 50 years. We have seen so far that database design history follows human history as each civilization had their own methods for communicating, record-keeping, and learning. Each civilization sought to lessen the burden of survival by the innovation of essential processes such as farming, carpentry, healthcare, and basic education. As a global society, we continue to search for efficiency via innovation every single day. As data is at the center of all learning, the major development in the relational model cannot be overstated as it has allowed for massive increases in learning. This has changed every aspect of our lives from how goods and services are manufactured, delivered, and consumed throughout the world.

Flaws and Limitations of Spreadsheets

This topic explains when we can think of data management in terms of an easy-to-use spreadsheet and when to embrace more complicated relational theory. Simply put, early in the data management process, while capturing the creation of original transactional data for long-term storage, we will not work with it like we do with a spreadsheet. A spreadsheet is best for 'last mile' analysis of data and perhaps making projections or visualizations of potential scenarios. When designing robust data storage systems with millions of rows of data, it is important to not treat data as lines of text; instead, we need to treat it as the input for machines that will be processed and stored with great sophistication.

While Excel might be the most popular software application ever, we need to curb our excitement around using it to solve every data-related problem we encounter. Excel has its place, but it is time to venture into the realm of relational theory while being aware of its limitations.

Spreadsheets are perhaps the single most common computer application in use across the world after internet browsing and email. While they are tremendously valuable to organize simple tasks, estimate costs, or calculate future values, there are significant limitations that curtail their effectiveness in most high-volume, data-intensive mission-critical business scenarios. These include security, consistency, scalability/automation, and querying data at volume.

Security

One of the benefits of working with spreadsheets is the ease of access and manipulation of data. They are often available to modify either by over-writing with new values or changing the underlying formulas that do the math. This great flexibility is part of the power and attraction to spreadsheets being one of the world's most popular applications. With this flexibility, there may be insufficient protections and security concerns for data. Many times, there are no restrictions for users to access a spreadsheet at the file-level or the cell level. This often means that we must be diligent about how and when we share sensitive data. Additionally, not all data in a spreadsheet can be transactionally sound.

Consistency

The brilliance of spreadsheets lies in their flexibility and ease of use. Unfortunately, the integrity associated with transactional data is difficult to enforce in a spreadsheet. This ability to overwrite data on a whim may be considered a feature for ease of use when we are exploring data with 'what if' projections, but it introduces data anomalies and inconsistencies. The hallmark of relational theory and the role of database management systems to maintain consistency across hundreds of tables and many hundreds of columns is therefore, paramount.

Scalability/Automation

As stated previously, spreadsheets are fantastic analytical tools, but are not well-suited for managing high volume transactions. This is a significant limitation of spreadsheets. People frequently try to store transactional data in a spreadsheet because it is a tool they are comfortable with. They end up 'copy and pasting' chunks of data into their spreadsheets in a manual process because they are unfamiliar with more robust methods of capturing transactions such as relational systems.

Querying Data

As we shall see shortly, transactional details are difficult to query in a spreadsheet beyond basic aggregates, like average, maximum, and minimum. This is because a spreadsheet works best with summarized or aggregated data, and not the details of thousands or millions of individual transactions. Better methods exist to engage transactional data without losing the ability to conduct complex queries across millions of rows.

Understanding the purpose and limitations of a spreadsheet will help align your expectations, simplify your search for tools, reduce frustrations, and increase productivity and effectiveness. In the next section, you will unpack the relevance of a book club in the database management sphere.

`METRO_TRANSIT` as a Spreadsheet Example

Here is an example of a transportation system in the form of a table that that contains example data which specifically tracks passengers who have boarded various vehicles and paid fares.

While reviewing the data in the spreadsheet, consider if it will be easy to read and learn from it.

DateTime	Passenger	RouteName	RouteNumber	RouteType	Driver	StopName	StopType	Destination	BusType	Fare	Neighborhood
2/13/25 7:36	Ivey Hazekamp	Capitol Hill-Downtown	32	Regular	Jimi Hendrix	Broadway Avenue and Cherry Street	Covered	Downtown	Articulated	$4.50	Capitol Hill
2/13/25 9:36	Darcel Eustache	Fremont-Waterfront-Downtown	78-S	Special	Meryl Streep	Hwy 99-N 36th	Covered	Downtown	Extra-long	$2.75	Fremont
2/14/25 6:36	Darcie Eustache	Fremont-Waterfront-Downtown	78-E	XP	Bruce Lee	Elliott Avenue and Mercer Street	Covered	Downtown	Extra-long	$2.75	Interbay
2/16/25 6:32	Kenyetta Terron	Sodo-Downtown Express	42-E	Express	Meryl Streep	First Avenue and Terry Street	Covered	Downtown	Doub	$2.75	SODO
2/19/25 15:39	Kenny Terron	Sodo-Downtown Express	42-E	Express	Bruce Lee	First Avenue and Terry Street	Uncovered	Fremont	Doubled	$4.50	South Downtown
2/21/25 6:13	Darcel Eustache	Fremont-Waterfront-Downtown	78-S	Special	Jimmy Hendricks	Elliott Avenue and Mercer Street	Cvd	Downtown	Extra-long	$2.75	Interbay
2/21/25 7:36	Kenyetta Terron	Sodo-Downtown Express	42-E	Express	Bruce Lee	First Avenue and Terry Street	UC	Downtown	Doubled	$4.50	South Downtown
2/22/25 8:32	Ivey Hazekamp	Capitol Hill-Downtown	32	Regular	Jim Morrison	Broadway Avenue and Cherry Street	Covered	Downtown	Articulated	$4.50	Capitol Hill
3/1/25 6:33	Ivey Hazekamp	Capitol Hill-Downtown	32	Regular	Bruce Lee	Broadway Avenue and Cherry Street	Covered	Downtown	Articulated	$4.50	Capitol Hill
3/1/25 6:36	Ivey Hazekamp	Capitol Hill-Downtown	32	Regular	Meryl Streep	Broadway Avenue and Cherry Street	Covered	Downtown	Articulated	$4.50	Capitol Hill
3/3/25 6:42	Darcel Eustache	Fremont-Downtown Commuter	78	Commute	Jim Morrison	Sixth Avenue and Battery Street	Regular	Fremont	Doubled	$4.50	Downtown
3/5/25 6:32	Darcel Eustache	Fremont-Waterfront-Downtown	78-E	XP	Meryl Streep	Elliott Avenue and Mercer Street	Covered	Downtown	Extra-long	$2.75	Interbay
3/9/25 7:52	Kenyetta Terron	Sodo-Downtown Express	42-E	Express	Jimi Hendrix	First Avenue and Terry Street	UC	Downtown	Doubled	$4.50	South Downtown
3/10/25 6:33	Darcel Eustache	Fremont-Downtown Commuter	78	Commute	Jim	Elliott Avenue and Mercer Street	Covered	Downtown	Extra-long	$2.75	Interbay
3/11/25 6:32	Kenyetta Terron	Sodo-Downtown Express	42-E	Express	Bruce Lee	First Avenue and Terry Street	Uncovered	Downtown	Doubled	$4.50	South Downtown
3/13/25 8:32	Ivey Hazekamp	Capitol Hill-Downtown	32	Regular	Bruce Lee	Broadway Avenue and Cherry Street	Covered	Downtown	Articulated	$4.50	Capitol Hill
3/14/25 6:32	Ivey Hazekamp	Capitol Hill-Downtown	32	Express	Bruce Lee	Broadway Avenue and Cherry Street	Covered	Downtown	Articulated	$4.50	Capitol Hill
3/15/25 1:36	Janey Lundgren	Capitol Hill-Downtown	32	Reg	Jimmy Hendricks	Broadway Avenue and Cherry Street	Covered	Downtown	2 Decks	$2.75	Capitol Hill
3/16/25 6:32	Darcel Eustache	Fremont-Downtown Commuter	78	Commute	Jim Morrison	Sixth Avenue and Battery Street	Regular	Fremont	Doubled	$4.50	Downtown
3/17/25 11:33	Ivey Hazekamp	Capitol Hill-Downtown	32	Regular	Jimi Hendrix	Fourth Avenue and Seneca Street	Covered	Capitol Hill	Doubled	$2.75	Downtown
3/18/25 16:13	Jane Lundgran	Capitol Hill-Downtown	32	Reg	Meryl Streep	Fourth Avenue and Seneca Street	Covered	CH	2 Decks	$2.75	Downtown
3/19/25 6:32	Janey Lundgren	Capitol Hill-Downtown	32	Reg	Meryl Streep	Broadway Avenue and Cherry Street	Covered	Downtown	2 Decks	$2.75	Capitol Hill
3/21/25 6:32	Darcel Eustache	Fremont-Downtown Commuter	78	Commute	Meryl Streep	Sixth Avenue and Battery Street	Regular	Fremont	Doubled	$4.50	Downtown
3/26/25 9:04	Janie Lundgren	Capitol Hill-Downtown	32	Regular	Jimmy Hendricks	Broadway Avenue and Cherry Street	Covered	Downtown	2 Decks	$2.75	Capitol Hill
4/18/25 5:23	Darcie Eustache	Fremont-Downtown Commuter	78	Commute	Jimi Hendrix	Fourth Avenue and Seneca Street	Regular	Fremont	Doubled	$4.50	Downtown

Figure 1.7: *Example `METRO_TRANSIT` data in a spreadsheet*

Please note that the spreadsheet is flawed in the sense that it is not normalized and is written for people as opposed to a database application. While using a spreadsheet to track this data might be relatively easy to get started with, it will be eventually difficult and cumbersome as we add more and more data.

After considering this data for a few minutes, consider the following questions:

- Which route generated the most revenue from fares?
- Which driver had the most trips?
- Which passengers took the most trips to Capitol Hill?

If these questions cause frustration, you are beginning to see why merely eyeballing data is a losing proposition these days. Perhaps, the single-greatest reason companies transitioned from paper-based systems to computers was that organizational learning was severely restricted under a manual process. The few questions that could have been answered by manually looking at transactional data are so simple that the effort is almost not even worth it.

Each of the questions above requires reading each row (perhaps, multiple times) and handwriting notes. Obviously, manual processing is slow, cumbersome, dependent on secondary note-taking, and prone to human error. There is probably not enough value or timely insight to discover patterns or trends in behavior, and make competitive decisions.

The important part of the spreadsheet example is to recognize the limitations of managing high-volume, transactional data that includes millions of rows. We must break free of our reliance on 'eyeballing' data, and embrace the power of relational theory to support data-driven decision making.

Therefore, the crux of this book is to help each reader recognize how data is the core of modern economy. There is simply no learning of any kind without data. There will be 'winners' and 'losers' in this upcoming era. Those who are skilled at consuming data, and recognizing patterns, trends, outliers, and effectiveness of innovations will be in a better position to excel than those who do not.

Conclusion

It is a human urge to prioritize efficiency and seek competitive advantages while performing the most mundane tasks. We are habituated to improve processes, produce more, save time, and prosper. The core of all innovation, discovery, and gains in product quality has always been based on data.

For centuries, innovations were slowly adopted because of manual processes and could only be shared with limited number of people. Nowadays, not only can problem-solving issues include anyone with access to the internet, but learnings can be shared across the globe in mere minutes. Collaboration, experimentation, and learning can occur at lightning speed through digital databases. Anyone with the right technical skills can participate in this exercise and help shape the future.

Next, we will become more familiar with the structure of relational databases and other concepts in this book. Relational databases are the birthplace of data meant for analytical processing. Virtually, every organization creates original data from many daily operations such as manufacturing products or providing services. Additionally, secondary data from customer purchasing preferences can be combined with data from other businesses in unrelated industries to determine complex relationships and behavioral patterns. When done correctly (and ethically), learning across industries can be truly groundbreaking.

Post-Chapter Challenges

Here are a few challenges for you to try based on the objectives stated in the chapter.

Track 1 (THINK): Data Tourist Seeking Ancillary Awareness

You must spend a total of 10 minutes reviewing the following questions and exploring your thoughts. These questions and your responses will capture the essence of this chapter.

- How important are data systems for societies, organizations, and individuals? Why?
- What are some breakthroughs of innovation throughout human history that can be attributed to a sense of "Organize or Die"? What is the significance of these innovations in people's everyday lives?
- Which contemporary companies or organizations are executing "Organize or Die" well? Which companies/organizations did you choose? Why?
- How come something as simple as scheduling a bus trip explodes in complexity?
- Why/How is the use of a spreadsheet to manage data problematic or flawed?

Track 2 (WRITE): Dedicated Student or Recent Graduate:

Write a few paragraphs in response to each of the following questions:

- Which data is required to track a passenger's travel habits and preferences from the perspectives of the passengers, drivers, and the municipal management office?
- What are the questions a typical passenger may want to ask while selecting an appropriate route to their workplace?
- What are the metrics/measurements to determine whether a route, driver, or stop is 'successful'? How frequently can these metrics be reviewed? Why?
- Reflect on the presence of misspellings in the spreadsheet; how might it be best to manage the typos and/or abbreviations out of the spreadsheet?

Track 3 (BUILD): Full Speed Learner Seeking Job

This track targets readers of this book who want to develop professional skills in data science. Let us begin with a challenge to structure data collection to keep track of a large-scale metropolitan transit system:

- Copy the column headers (as well as some of the data from *Figure 1.3*) into an Excel spreadsheet to track the metropolitan transit system.
- Assume that the users of your data set want to learn about route safety; begin tracking data on incidents of injuries, assaults, or aggressive panhandling. Which data needs to be captured? Give reasons for your answer.

CHAPTER 2
Brief Overview of Relational Model

Introduction

The first chapter provided a foundational understanding of why humans capture data in order to be efficient competitors who "learn to win". We also reviewed how data has been captured throughout history via oral traditions and paper-based systems for the past 40,000 years and hierarchical systems that began with the first electronic computers post-World War 2. Remember, hierarchical database systems were designed to imitate the paper-based systems used for thousands of years, but these soon became bloated from duplicate data being stored in multiple hierarchies. Like an old-school filing cabinet, hierarchical data structures arrange important data in perspectives that are useful for only a small percentage of queries.

The benefits of relational theory are massive. This chapter explores the details and helps each aspiring data scientist understand the science beneath the basic structures many people take for granted. Learnings from this chapter will provide analysts with the ability to become functionally independent from infrastructure engineers and develop their design skills capable of building a robust database in third normal form (3NF) within hours.

Structure

In this chapter, we will explore the following topics:

- Quick review of hierarchical databases
- High-level overview of relational model
- Introduction of objects Primary Keys (PK) and Foreign Keys (FK)
- Defining relations between entities and the use of Crow's Foot notation
- Articulate the range of data types used in relational model with their best uses

Hierarchical Database: A Quick Review

Hierarchical databases must read and assemble all data from the underlying file one-by-one and then evaluate whether the record is desirable based on the logic of a query. This process also often ends up casting away more than 99% of records for each query after reading everything! This design is inefficient, especially in the 1960s, when a single megabyte of memory cost about the same as a brand-new car.

Back in the mid-20th century, when companies did not have internet or digital databases, they managed their entire business with paper-based systems and rudimentary equipment. Events such as registration for classes took days, while ordering material from a catalog often took weeks.

Everything changed for the better with the emergence of the relational model in 1969, when Dr. E.F. Codd from IBM proposed a novel design based on relational theory. In relational theory, each object is represented as a table and an entire database becomes a collection of related tables as opposed to multiple hierarchical structures based on a perspective. Instead of having to duplicate data, relational databases have the concept of 'keys' that join tables together, while forming the same wider collection of data with significantly less effort and no redundancy. This design has been effectively unchanged in the 56 years since it was first defined in the late 1960s.

By design, a hierarchy has a top-level object by which all the remaining data is assembled underneath. Let us remind ourselves of one hierarchy each from **METRO_TRANSIT** (*Figure* 2.1) and **MUSIC_STREAM** (*Figure* 2.2)from the previous chapter:

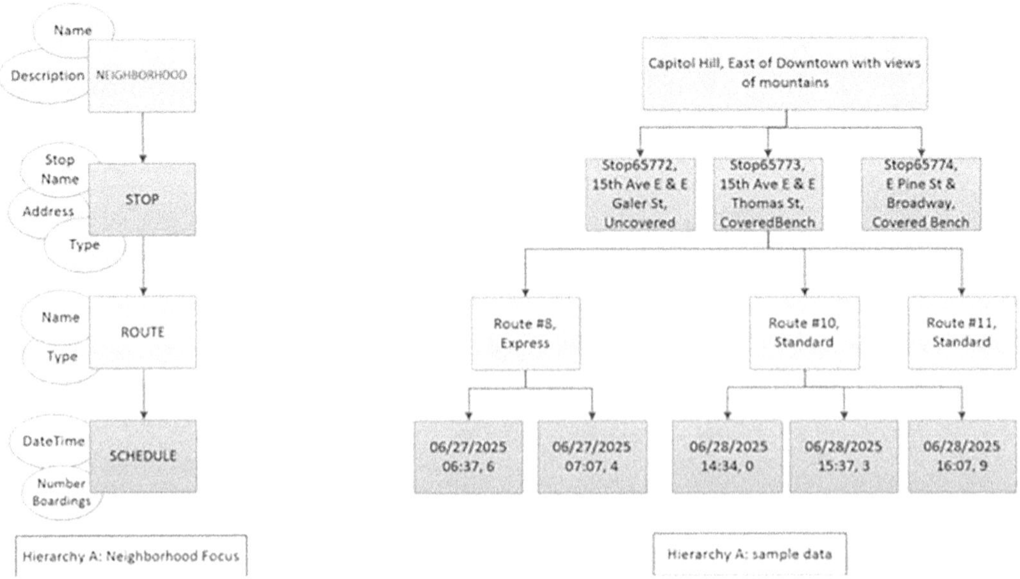

Figure 2.1: *Example hierarchy of neighborhood trips for* `METRO_TRANSIT`

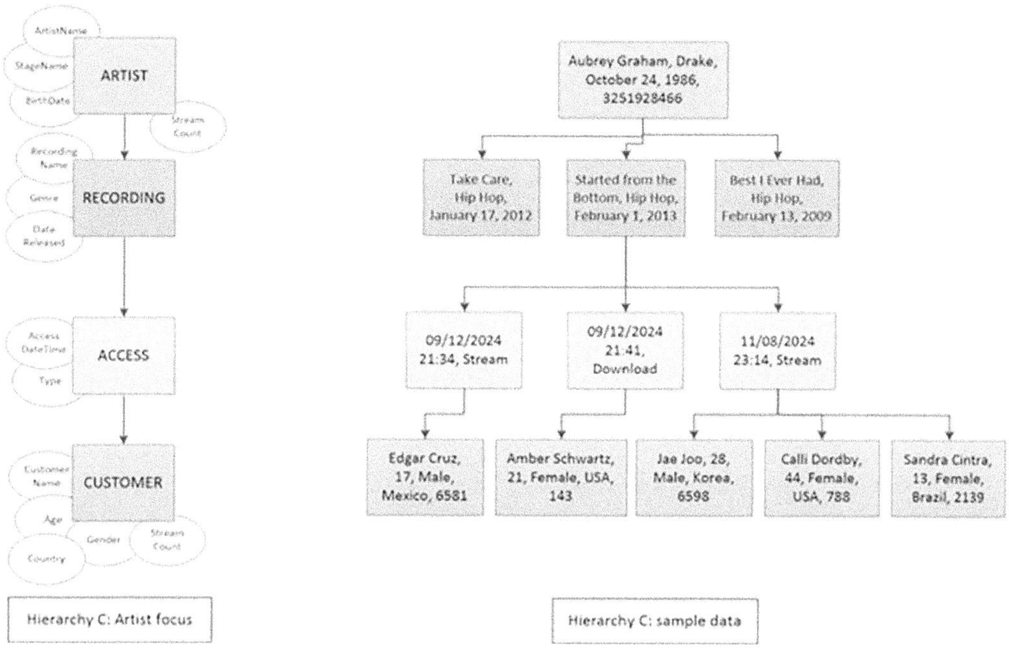

***Figure 2.2**: Example hierarchy of artist-centric data for MUSIC_STREAM*

Relational Models: `METRO_TRANSIT` and `MUSIC_STREAM`

Even though we have not yet learned how to construct or read a relational model, we will consider several designs for comparison with hierarchical models. We will now see what finished relational models for **`METRO_TRANSIT`** and **`MUSIC_STREAMING`** databases might look like, as shown here:

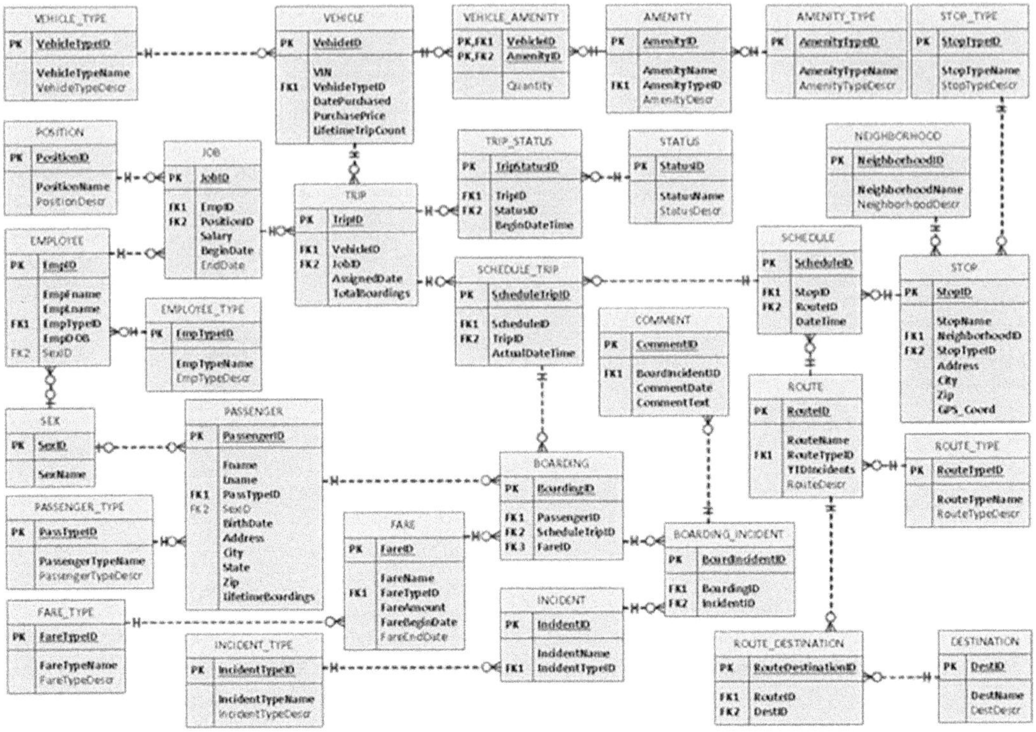

Figure 2.3: *Example relational data model of METRO_TRANSIT*

Initial Explanation

If this is the first time you have looked at an ERD, do not worry; these concepts will be explored in greater depth in this chapter. The above example in *Figure* 2.3 for **`METRO_TRANSIT`** has 31 boxes, while *Figure* 2.4 for **`MUSIC_STREAM`** has 30. These boxes are referred to as entities and will eventually be called 'tables' once the design is coded and installed within a database management system, such as Oracle, Postgres, or Microsoft SQL Server.

An entity should represent or align with a 'real-world' object that business users require data from. Take a quick minute and review some of the objects included in this design; they should be familiar to you.

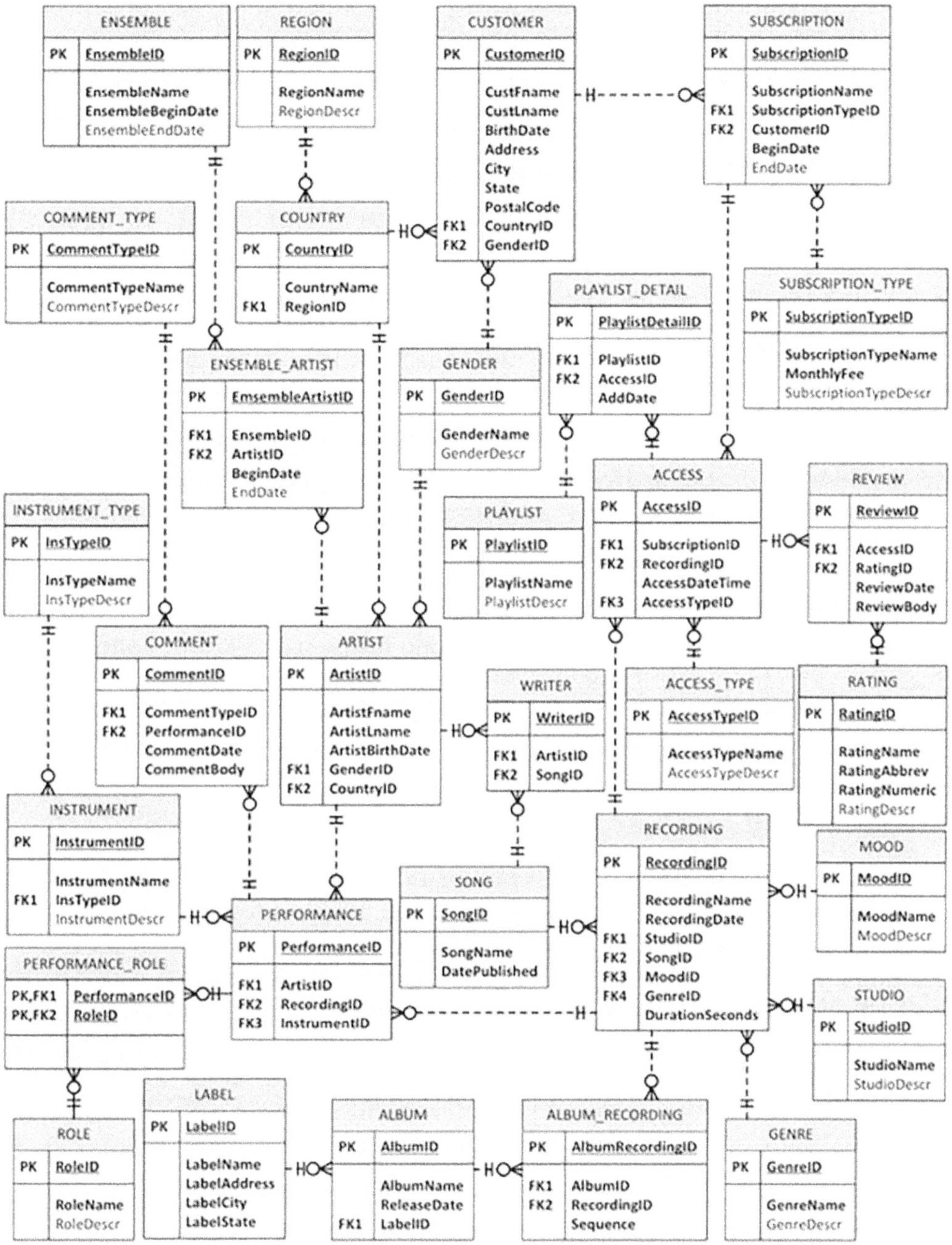

Figure 2.4: *Example relational data model of* MUSIC_STREAM

The perforated lines between each entity represents a relationship, while the arrow-shaped markings, also called the crow's foot notation, provide clarity about the type of relationship that exists. We will learn about more aspects of ERD later in this book.

Investigating a relational model starts with the introduction of the concept of keys, including the Primary Key (PK) and Foreign Keys (FK). The rule to follow with keys is that every table should have a PK to uniquely identify each row. An FK is a reference of a PK placed on a different table and acts as a link between the two. This ability to reference every column of a different table by simply having a copy of the unique identifier is an example of the ease of use of relational theory.

With the relational model, we no longer design data on disk as reports; there is now a separation between the storage of data and the reading of data. Since the rigid hierarchical structure that defined how data was stored is absent, the relational model stores each object such as **`VEHICLE`**, **`EMPLOYEE`**, **`ROUTE`** or **`ARTIST`**, **`RECORDING`**, and **`SUBSCRIPTION`** as a 'stand-alone' table that can be referenced from any other object.

An entity/table represents a single business object that is essential for the operations of the business. We list out attributes of each object that provide the details necessary to make decisions about that object, such as names and birthdays of employees or the exact vehicles that were used on specific trips in a day. Recognize that the attributes of each entity are focused on the data that relates directly to the business object which bears the name of the entity. If we think that additional data from another object is required, it is a sign to create another entity and bring in an FK that connects all the additional data from a related object. This design significantly reduces the amount of duplicate data required as well as limits the possibilities for typos and abbreviations (also known as 'bad data') to enter the system.

Primary Key

A Primary Key (PK) is a column or a combination of columns that is guaranteed to be unique when compared to every row in a table. This is a foundational concept for relational theory. We all have ID values such as driver's license, Student ID, Employee ID, Account ID for phone, electric bill, and a passport. Colleges, governments and utilities all need to make sure our account is unique; our payments are sorted and applied based on our activities. Every purchase we make at any store has a unique Product ID for each item we buy as well as a unique Order ID for the same reason; businesses must be able to track which items are being sold to manage their operations efficiently.

We know that there must be a unique identifier for the relational design to work well. Each of the tables from the TRANSIT example above have surrogate PKs (even the 'bad design' examples). Technically, a PK does not have to be a standalone surrogate key whose sole purpose is to be unique. In fact, a PK can be any combination of columns that are part of the table already, such as first name, last name, and zip code.

Despite academic arguments about the use of keys, it is strongly suggested to design all tables with surrogate keys whenever possible. It is because a surrogate key has several performance benefits that are otherwise not available with a composite primary key constructed from multiple columns.

- The integer data type is narrow (only 4 bytes), which means that we can fit more rows in memory than the combined key of several columns of names. Basic calculations tell us that the more food in our fridge exists (memory), the fewer trips we will need to make to the store (disk or cloud). The only difference in this metaphor is that in the case of databases, the 'store' is not just down the street in our immediate neighborhood; it is the equivalent of being 200 times further away as opposed to a neighborhood store!
- The integer data type can quickly have an 'auto-increment' or Identity feature enabled. This means that the assignment of primary key values is automated without manual intervention. This speeds up insert transactions to the point that millions of rows of data can be processed in an hour. Additionally, the auto-increment is *sequential* (this is secretly very impactful to tables where read/write activity are both busy). As you might be aware, the write activity (insert, update, and delete statements) require exclusive control of the rows affected by the statement logic; if the auto-increment feature is enabled on the PK, then all of the affected rows for the insert statement are at the very top of the table, which leaves the rest of the rows open for read activity (SELECT statements only need a shared lock).
- The default index on the primary key is a clustered index. This means that the data is placed on disk in a physical order of the sequential auto-incremented integer. As we might know, having similar data located physically close together on disk allows for range-searches at the root level of an index (these are like flipping through a dictionary trying to find a particular word and not having to validate the actual words on a page; we trust the index at the top. We can very quickly scan the top-level of the index until we locate the sought-after value. Additional explanations on both data types, locks, and indexes will be provided later in this book.

Foreign Key

A Foreign Key (FK) is part of the brilliance of relational theory. As mentioned previously, it allows for the referencing of data held in other tables by having a copy of the other table's PK. We then define that the entire contents of the referenced table can be read when the PK/FK values align. As we have seen, this is much more efficient than copying the related data in other tables throughout the database. Understanding how PK/FK work is the central point of relational theory and data analytics. However, it is usually not clear until users start writing queries with JOIN statements.

Assuming that we have followed proper data modeling techniques of normalization (covered in greater depth in Chapter 3), all appropriate relationships have been determined and the PK/FK exchange is moving in the right direction. While this is perhaps one of the most common mistakes from amateur designers, even seasoned engineers can make a mistake in this situation if not paying close attention.

Relationships

In a database, tables sometimes have direct relationships where one table contains values that help describe the values in another table. Examples are '**TYPE**' tables that help categorize the data in a second table. Consider the **ERD** earlier in this chapter; transit organizations in large cities may have more than several thousand vehicles in their version of the **VEHICLE** table (one row for each physical vehicle they operate). The **VEHICLE_TYPE** table, however, may have fewer than ten rows! The reason is that the **VEHICLE_TYPE** table simply provides context and clarity as a look-up table. Again, it is intended to prevent typos/abbreviations and allow for fast processing of both reading data to create reports as well as writing new data into the system by avoiding manual data entry of existing categorical data.

Every relationship is established when the PK from one table is placed in a second table as an FK. This connects values on a row-by-row basis and effectively extends the reach of one table into the other where the PK and FK columns align.

Cardinality

Cardinality is a label designers use when defining a relationship between entities. We can go further and say cardinality is the definition of the number of occurrences between rows from one table and rows in the other table that participates in the relationship. The most common relationship definitions will be one-to-many (1:M), one-to-one (1:1), and many-to-many (M:M). Please note that relational theory does not allow M:M relationships to be coded into a finished database! This means that once we identify a relationship as M:M, we have more work to resolve it into multiple 1:M relationships by creating a bridge table in the middle, which is called an 'associative entity'.

Crow's Foot Notation

There are two directions for each relationship thus established, which are 'right-to-left' and 'left-to-right'. Accordingly, there are symbols for each relationship, with some appearing at each endpoint of the line that connects entities. These symbols have an inner and an outer part; one for participation (either mandatory or optional) and the other for multiplicity, which indicates the number of occurrences on a row-by-row basis for the relationship.

The values for multiplicity will be either '1' (symbolized with a vertical line) or 'many' (symbolized with a crow's foot like a 3-pronged fork). There are only four possible combinations for each direction. Let us see some diagrammatic representations of these definitions:

Figure 2.5: *Example 'Optional Zero to One' relationship read left-to-right*

Figure 2.6: *Example 'Optional Zero to One' relationship read right-to-left*

The relationship of 'optional one' is not uncommon in a fully normalized database unless a foreign key is determined to not be mandatory or is often unknown. Outside of having a NULL value for a foreign key, having an 'optional zero-to-one' relationship indicates an opportunity to continue exploring whether there might be a 'many-to-many' (M:M) relationship between the participating entities over a longer period.

This relationship definition only exists in **`METRO_TRANSIT`** regarding the **`SexID`** for **`EMPLOYEE`** and **`PASSENGER`**. In **`MUSIC_STREAM`**, there exists a relationship for **`GenderID`** for **`CUSTOMER`** as well as **`MoodID`** in **`RECORDING`** (which is subjective). While it could be advantageous to capture this data if it were available, it might not be relevant in many instances.

Consider the following definition of a PK-FK relationship:

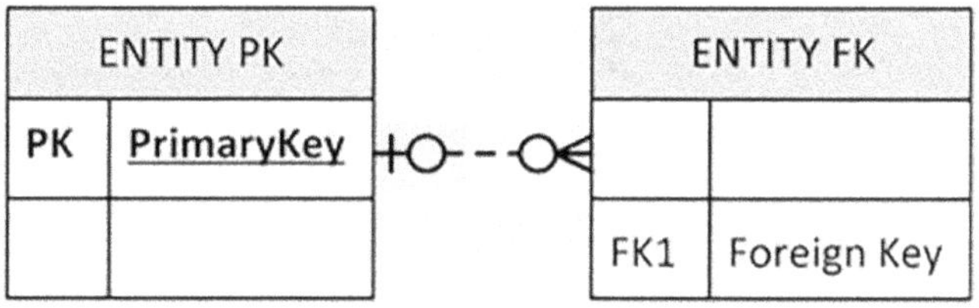

Figure 2.7: *Example 'Optional Zero-to-Many' relationship when read left-to-right and 'Optional Zero-to One' when read right-to-left*

As per *Figure* 2.7, the FKis 'optional', as indicated in the entity on the right with FK1 in regular font that is not in **bold**. The yellow highlights the changing symbol that shows 'optional' (the 'O' or zero) versus 'mandatory' (the vertical line) in *Figure* 2.8.

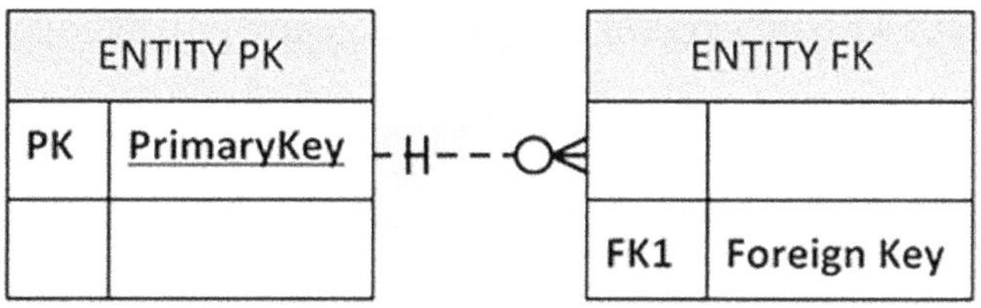

Figure 2.8: *Example 'Optional Zero-to-Many' relationship read left-to-right and 'Mandatory One-and-Only One' when read right-to-left*

An example where the relationships can be re-interpreted to match an 'optional zero-to-one' could be between a **BOARDING** and **INCIDENT**. Defining this relationship as 'optional zero-to-one' means that for any single boarding (defined as a passenger getting onto a vehicle at a specific stop on a specified trip with a precise date and time) there can be zero or only a single incident recorded in the database.

While this may make sense at first, it can be argued that one person can have many incidents on a single boarding. Imagine if a passenger tries to evade a fare (incident#1), then gets into a verbal exchange with the driver over incident #1 (making incident #2), and then proceeds to fight a second passenger who intervenes in incident #2 (creating incident #3 and #4 because a second boarding is now involved) before causing an accident (incident #5). This depends on how detailed the database needs to be and whether everything just described needs to be tracked as details or just one single incident.

Chances are high if more than 5% of the relationships defined so are 'optional zero to one' as you are not evaluating the relationship over a long enough perspective of time. Spend a few more minutes to see if these relationships can be better labeled as 'optional zero-to-many' when considering a broader range of time.

Figure 2.9: *Example 'Optional Zero to Many' relationship read right-to-left*

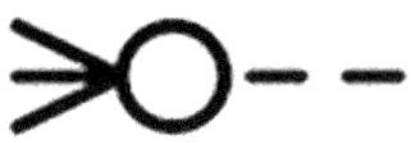

Figure 2.10: *Example 'Optional Zero to Many' relationship read right-to-left*

The relationship of 'optional zero-to-many' is very common in relational database design and represents the 'many' sides of nearly every 1:M relationship. In the examples like **METRO_TRANSIT** and **MUSIC_STREAM**, this relationship is prominent. We will see that in most fully normalized designs, majority of relationships between objects will evaluate to 1:M when accounting for an assessment over many years.

We learned about the relationship in both directions and considered the duration to be the lifetime of a relationship. For example, in the **TRANSIT ERD** we can read the relationship between the entities **NEIGHBORHOOD** and **STOP** (seen in the upper-right of the ERD in *Figure* 2.3 with an excerpt included in *Figure* 2.11) as follows:

"A **NEIGHBORHOOD** can have between zero and many **STOP**s, and the same **STOP** can be of one and only **NEIGHBORHOOD** for the lifetime of the database". This is defined as a 'one-to-many' relationship and written as 1:M.

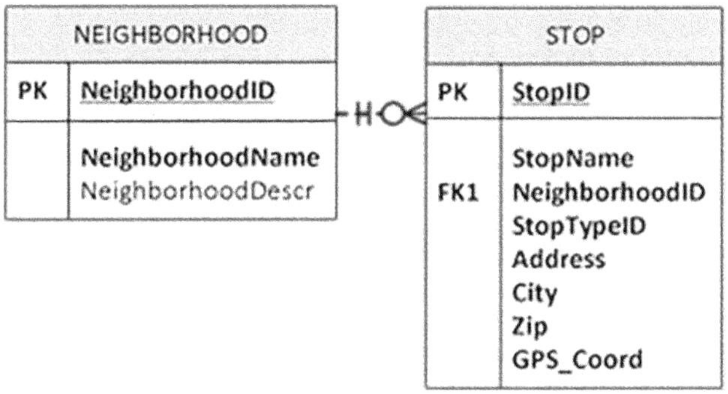

Figure 2.11: *Example depicting 1:M relationship*

Again, when we articulate the relationship between two entities, we read both left-to-right and right-to-left punctuating the symbol opposite from whichever entity we start with. For example, reading left-to-right will describe the relationship **NEIGHBORHOOD** has with **STOP**. This is articulated as "One neighborhood has optionally zero to many stops". Please note we look past the two vertical lines immediately next to **NEIGHBORHOOD** as they describe the relationship in the other direction.

The two vertical lines mean 'mandatory one' and describe the relationship a stop has with a row in **NEIGHBORHOOD**. It is articulated when the relationship is read right-to-left.

It is also possible that a city will rename neighborhoods. In that case, we probably will not need to maintain the history of the previous neighborhood name and will just simply update the **NeighborhoodName** in the entity **NEIGHBORHOOD** if the previous name is changed, or possibly the **NeighborhoodID FK** value in the entity **STOP** if the boundaries of an existing neighborhood have expanded.

PK/FK is how all tables are joined together in a multi-table query. The exact syntax will be seen in significant detail in *Chapter* 5.

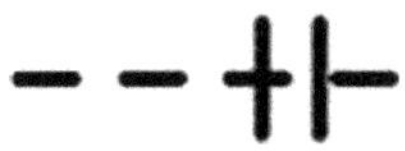

Figure 2.12: *Example 'Mandatory One and Only One' relationship read left-to-right*

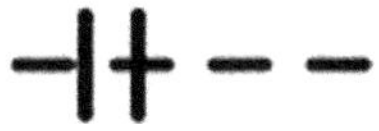

Figure 2.13: *Example 'Mandatory One and Only One' relationship read right-to-left*

The relationship definition of "*mandatory one and only one*" is also very common in a fully normalized relational database. This represents the primary key side of a relationship that sends a value as a foreign key to the other entity. Whenever we establish a relationship (and are therefore bringing in a foreign key value to one of the entities), there should only ever be one foreign key value for the lifetime of the relationship. This includes an FK value that changes over time.

Looking at the two diagrams we have seen so far in *Figure* 2.3 **METRO_TRANSIT** and *Figure* 2.4 **MUSIC_STREAM**, there are dozens of relationships with the 'mandatory one and only one' foreign key value. In my mind, a foreign key value should rarely (if ever) change if it was correctly defined in the first place. An example is correctly an obvious mistake such as erroneously placing the home country of musician Drake as United States, when he is from Canada.

If we find ourselves changing a foreign key value more than once due to changes in the underlying data (like **STATUS** of a single **TRIP**), we most likely made a mistake in the relationship definition. Frequently updating a value such as **StatusID** is very impactful for performance due to the need to gain exclusive access to the data. We will try to avoid forced updates whenever possible.

Using **StatusID** as an example, if we mistakenly define the relationship between **TRIP** and **STATUS** 1:M as opposed to M:M, it will look as follows:

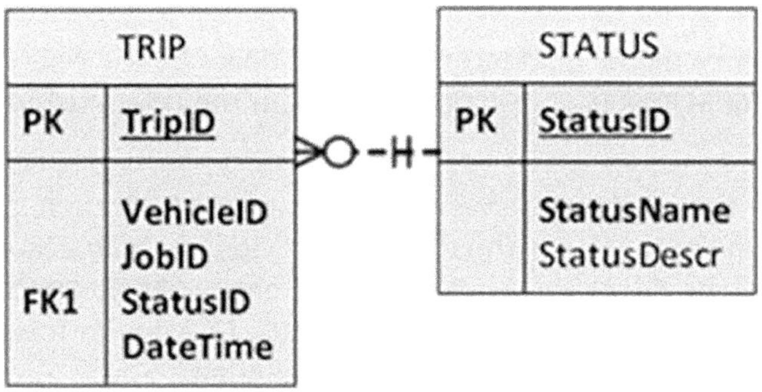

***Figure 2.14**: Mistake in defining TRIP and STATUS relationship as 1:M instead of M:M*

When we define the relationship between **TRIP** and **STATUS** as 1:M, we are overwriting the **StatusID** for a **TRIP** each time the value changes. We are effectively destroying the previous record of its previous status. You may argue that the previous value for **StatusID** is no longer relevant since no one should care if the bus *that was late* is now on time. When we destroy data, we lose the opportunity to analyze the change. Think about what we can investigate like the frequency or duration of each different status, potential causes, patterns of occurrence and other critical components. Any data that was important enough to capture should be held for analytical purposes later.

Please note that one single **TRIP** with 12 scheduled **STOP**s may in fact be on time for most stops but either early or late for a handful of others. A better design interpretation is to define the relationship as M:M and capture the exact time the status changed. With this design choice, we can eliminate the invasive updates that require exclusive locks, as well as preserve previous values, which allow analysis of the root cause of why the status changed.

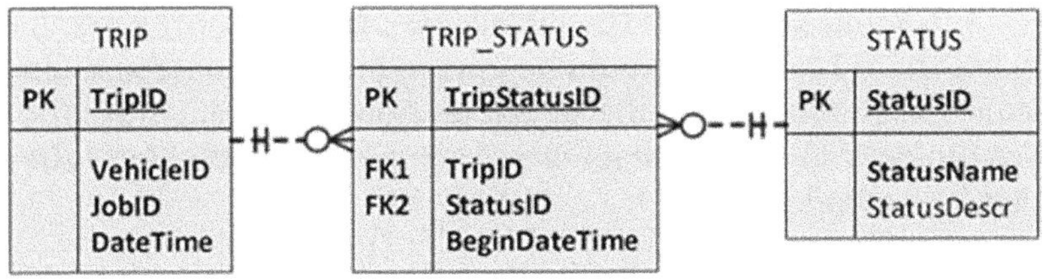

Figure 2.15: *Correct Definition of* **TRIP** *and* **STATUS** *Relationship as M:M with* **TRIP_STATUS** *Included as Resolving Associative Entity*

Please note that the true relationship between **TRIP** and **STATUS** is M:M; one **TRIP** can have many statuses over its lifetime and the same **STATUS** (such as on-track, early, or late) can be held by any number of trips. We will see in Chapter 3 how to resolve M:M relationships into two that are 1:M by creating a middle table, which is also called an associative entity.

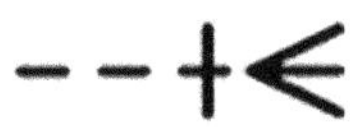

Figure 2.16: *Example 'Mandatory Many' relationship read left-to-right*

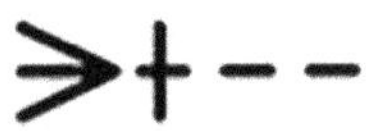

Figure 2.17: *Example 'Mandatory Many' relationship read right-to-left*

The relationship definition of 'mandatory many' is relatively uncommon in relational database design. In the two diagrams presented so far, there are no occurrences of this definition in any of the relationships.

While it may seem that this definition should be frequently used, it is reserved for complex relationships where we must have values from all participating entities for a record to be captured. For example, let us imagine **METRO_TRANSIT** with a requirement that each boarding is for two or more people. This requires a new entity called **RESERVATION** to be added to the diagram. See *Figure* 2.18 here:

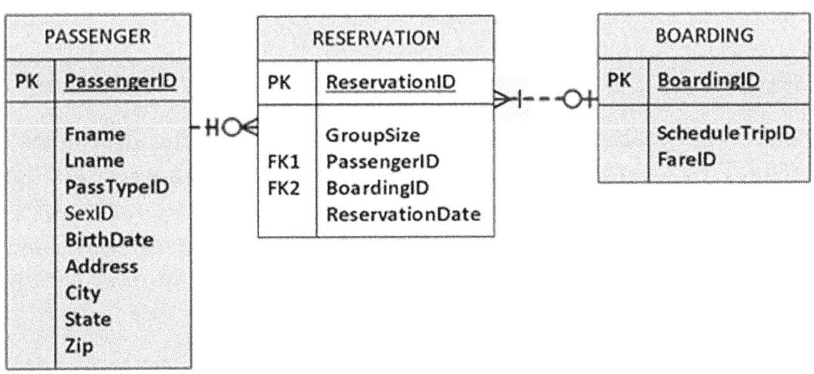

Figure 2.18: *An example relationship of 'Mandatory Many' between* **BOARDING** *and* **PASSENGER** *by adding new entity* **RESERVATION**

This example shows that all rows in the **BOARDING** table may only exist in conjunction with a row in **RESERVATION**; these would be entered into the database simultaneously within the same transaction. Since this is just an example to illustrate the 'mandatory many' relationship definition, please ignore the presence of **RESERVATION** as an entity in **METRO_TRANSIT** moving forward.

Data Types

Somewhere between understanding the basics of the relational data model and constructing one on your own is having clarity on what makes up data types. This section is intended to prepare readers for forthcoming chapters on data modeling and writing SQL code. This overview is relatively brief as it is not intended to be a definitive resource on each of the dozens of data types available. Please continue researching online if there are questions unanswered here.

Anytime a relational database is being considered for development, all stakeholders must understand the purpose, intent, and primary uses the data will provide. Therefore, you must consider the following questions:

- Who is going to use this database?
- What decisions are they going to make from the data?

We will learn about normalization in *Chapter* 3, but before we get there, we need to develop a basic understanding of data types. These are the definitions of the 'shape' of data for each column of a table. We will also see that it is not enough to just come up with a list of objects and call them entities; we must know the element and their characteristics as we are creating the design. This requires that engineers know how the data will be read or included in queries for dashboards and reports fed to key decision-makers.

Data types are one of the most critical decisions engineers make when designing a new database. Not only can they prevent any number of unintentional human errors, but data types also keep the collection of data in each table structured. This presentation can be better used in an intentional manner when it comes time to write queries and display reports.

Across all relational database products, data types provide the first layer of security against 'bad data' by establishing a pre-set shape for all values in a single column. Along with establishing maximum length of characters and range of permissible values, we can say that a data type supports the 'domain' of a column. Having control at the domain level can prevent having 'January' as a phone number for example or a 300-word paragraph as someone's last name.

Beyond the obvious 'clean data' restrictions everyone wants, there are often nuanced controls that each industry or application designer needs. Examples may include the number of decimals for columns defined as numeric values for engineering or scientific research. Columns defined with currency ('money') data types frequently provide benefits by allowing greater programmatic controls by a larger number of financial applications. Obviously, global exchange rates are volatile, and precise controls are required to avoid rounding or truncation.

We can even create our own custom data type to keep up with any situation mandated by our organization or industry. An example might be mandatory formats for driver's licenses which often are a set pattern that includes a mixed combination of letters and numbers in a sequence. Many industries have their own patterns and sequences for data values that may appear to be impossible to control through an application, but become much easier when defined as a data type.

Categories of Data Types

In life, there are many different types of data beyond the written word. These include obviously audio files, photographs, and other visual artifacts like maps, charts, and diagrams of any kind. The point I want to convey is, not only are there many kinds of data, but we need to label them correctly to learn quickly.

Relational databases have a 'sweet spot' of tracking data from repetitive events we call transactions. These transactions are very common such as 'badging in' at a locked door at work, texting someone from our phone, or crossing a toll bridge. While many of these transactions may also include corroborating data like a picture, the core of these events are words and numbers.

With this delineation in mind, let us take a quick look at the range of data types most common in relational databases. These include the following:

- Numeric (whole, exact, and approximate)
- Date and Time
- String (letters and numbers without intention of 'doing math')
- Other Data Types

Numeric Data Types

There are many reasons to capture numbers with each transaction recorded into a relational database. These include the price of a product, the date and time that it was ordered, as well as the cost. Many factors will determine which data type is most appropriate; perhaps the most important being whether a user is ever going to include the value in any math equation. This may seem like a strange condition, until we evaluate all columns that hold numeric values; consider the following intentionally absurd and silly math questions from a classroom of students:

- What is the average phone number?

- What is the result of adding three dorm room numbers together?
- What is the result of multiplying everyone's zip code?

Obviously, while we may be able to calculate an answer to each of the questions above, none of the results may be useful for any effective learning. One of the validation steps when assigning a data type to any column is determining how often there will be any math applied to its values. Surprisingly, perhaps, very few columns will be involved with math being applied to its values. Looking at the data model for **METRO_TRANSIT** in *Figure* 2.3 there are only four columns in the entire database (outside of date, time or computed columns) that will have frequent math.

- **FARE.FareAmount**
- **JOB.Salary**
- **VEHICLE.PurchasePrice**
- **VEHICLE_AMENITY.Quantity**

In the **MUSIC_STREAM** model in *Figure* 2.4, there are also only four columns that are 'math-friendly' that are not computed columns or date/time centric:

- **SUBSCRIPTION_TYPE.MonthlyFee**
- **RATING.RatingNumeric**
- **RECORDING.DurationSeconds**
- **ALBUM_RECORDING.Sequence** (maybe...just maybe)

An additional four columns each in **METRO_TRANSIT** and **MUSIC_STREAM** are computed columns and cannot be edited by users. These are intended to speed up reporting and have a high demand or frequency of calculations by customers or management for a reporting dashboard somewhere. Computed columns, user-defined functions and stored procedures are considered advanced SQL topics, and are beyond the scope of this textbook.

METRO_TRANSIT

- **VEHICLE.LifetimeTripCount**
- **PASSENGER.LifetimeBoardings**
- **TRIP.TotalBoardings**
- **ROUTE.YTDIncidents**

MUSIC_STREAM

- **SUBSCRIPTION.LifetimeAccessCount**
- **RECORDING.TotalAccessCount**
- **RECORDING.AverageRating**
- **ARTIST.TotalAccessCount**

So, assuming that we have identified the columns that have the probability of being included in math like the columns above, the most appropriate data types to assign depend on the range of expected values. Let us roll through the choices, and see the best use for each.

Whole Numbers and Integers

Integer data type might be the most common choice for capturing numbers inside a relational database. Many real-world items are counted in whole numbers such as the number of passengers who board a bus or the number times that same bus has traveled across a bridge for example. All that is left to determine for these columns are the highest expected volume of occurrences that could be stored in the database. Here are the choices we have:

TINYINT

TinyINT has a finite range of 256 whole numbers from the value of 0 through 255. Please note this does not include values less than zero. This range also matches some common restrictions with early versions of Excel spreadsheets that included the maximum number of columns or allowable characters in a single cell. While these limitations are no longer present in more recent versions of Excel, it may be a factor in the decision-making process as you determine the range of data to be placed in a column, which is defined as TinyINT.

The best uses for TinyINT are for columns that are tracking values that will never exceed 255. Examples from either design presented earlier include the PK values for most of the look-up or type tables that provide FK values and the context to other tables. These include the following from the previous examples:

METRO_TRANSIT

- **EMPLOYEE_TYPE**
- **AMENITY_TYPE**
- **STATUS**

MUSIC_SUBSCRIPTION

- **ACCESS_TYPE**
- **SUBSCRIPTION_TYPE**
- **REGION**

Projecting columns that do not yet exist in either database may include a column that tracks the number of hours per week a driver is scheduled to work, or the number of incidents that occurred in relation to a single **BOARDING**.

Unfortunately, TinyINT is not very common for practical use; many designers will opt for a more flexible data type like **INTEGER** to avoid surprises of unforeseen values not fitting into their database years after it was originally designed.

SMALLINT

SmallINT has a finite range of whole numbers from the value of -32,768 through 32,767. Like **TinyINT**, **SmallINT** can be used for situations where the values of a column will never reach the tens of thousands. Examples from the database designs we have explored may include **TotalBoardings** for a single **TRIP** in **METRO_TRANSIT** as well as **DurationSeconds** for a single **RECORDING** in **MUSIC_STREAM**.

INTEGER

Integer has a finite range of whole numbers from the value of -2,147,483,648 through 2,147,483,647. This data type may be the most common for use as a primary key and foreign key definition as we can very easily make the values automatically increment in a sequential manner without any manual intervention.

INTEGER data type is also a solid choice for many columns that track measurements of cumulative events such as recordings a single person has streamed over the life of their **MUSIC_STREAM** subscription. Please consider that more than two billion is a large number; most databases will never have any values that reach this figure.

Very few non-scientific measurements will exceed the limits of an integer at 2.147 billion, but they have occurred. For example, there are numerous real-life artists who have individual songs that have exceeded this number for total streams.

BIGINT

BigINT has a finite range of whole numbers from the value of -9,223,372,036,854,775,808 through 9,223,372,036,854,775,807. This is a very large number and is intended to capture extremely large data values like primary key values for authentication into busy social media or email systems. Some of these applications are used by more than a third of the people on earth and can see multiple billions of transactions on a normal day. Most organizations will never exhaust the values in this data type.

Numbers with Decimals

Not every column that tracks numbers is correctly represented with a whole number; we need to track data with greater detail. This may include values that track weight, partial consumption of a household utility (such as a water or energy bill), or anything that might be shared. Some columns can handle rounding or truncation of the values they contain while others will not. Some columns will require significant total digits for large numbers (called precision) while others may require many digits beyond the decimal point (called scale). We have several data types that each offer significant uses, including 'exact' data types and approximate data types.

Exact Data Types

Two data types that are exact include **`NUMERIC()`** and **`DECIMAL()`**. The best use for exact data types is when a column of values has a set pattern such as grades for high school and college students as well as nutrient information (like calories, percentage of daily protein per serving) on packaged food items. Exact data types allow the engineer to specify the total number of digits allowed in a column value as well as the total amount of digit after the decimal point. The first of these two settings that appear inside the parentheses are precision and the second is scale.

The best use of these data types is when there will be calculations to be applied to columns or values. This will include determining average or cumulative values for weight, dimensions, percentages, duration of expense and similar data. In these cases, accuracy is considered critical.

`NUMERIC()` and **`DECIMAL()`** are essentially interchangeable in use; both allow for flexibility in designing a column that controls the range of acceptable values up to 19 digits combined between precision and scale settings. One slight difference between these exact data types is that NUMERIC data type is rigid in the enforcement of its definition while DECIMAL data type will allow values that exceed the limitations of how it was defined. Frequently, designers will use exact data types for columns that are tracking money or whole numbers that may be better defined as either INTEGER or one of the money data types.

This section on data types is an overview to establish a basic understanding for readers heading into the further chapters on design and coding. You can augment your understanding with additional research online. Before exploring the various data types for money and currency, let us quickly review approximate data types for numbers.

Approximate Data Types

Within SQL, there are two different data types that are considered approximate, which are **`FLOAT()`** and **`REAL()`**. These are often used in scientific calculations when significant digits are greater than two (or vary from measurement to measurement) and where the decimal point is not always in the same position.

Here are the differences between **`FLOAT`** and **`REAL`**:

- **`FLOAT`** has a broader range of values when compared to REAL.
- **`FLOAT`** is a 64-bit number, while **`REAL`** is 32-bit (the range of possible values is not 'twice as much'; the bit difference is the space of the memory occupied).
- **`REAL`** data type is 'single-precision', while **`FLOAT`** is 'double-precision'.
- Each float value is also a real number.

- Not every real number can be stored with **FLOAT**.

In the databases **METRO_TRANSIT** and **MUSIC_STREAM**, there are no columns that are assigned a **FLOAT** or **REAL** data type. This is because other numeric data types (like **INTEGER AND NUMERIC**) suffice for the ranges of each domain. Examples of potential columns that can be included in these database designs that would benefit from a **FLOAT** would be as follows:

METRO_TRANSIT

- Revolutions per minute for a **VEHICLE** engine during a specific **TRIP**
- Average weight per person on a **VEHICLE** with passengers at each **STOP**

MUSIC_STREAM

- Sound frequency for an instrument or vocal performance on a recording
- Streaming bandwidth for a recording as it is being accessed

The measurements mentioned above are not included in the database design because they are not critical for answering the most pressing questions for database users. If we adopt the perspective of engineers concerned about infrastructure, performance, maintenance, and operations, then perhaps measurements like these would become a higher priority.

Money Data Types

People often are doubtful when it comes to tracking what people or organizations owe us or what we have been charged for products, services and fees. Therefore, data types that identify money or currency to the database system are critical to presenting data efficiently, as nearly every database has at least one column designed to store financial data. In the two database designs we have seen so far, there are the following columns that store data on money:

METRO_TRANSIT

- **FARE.FareAmount**
- **EMPLOYEE.Salary**
- **VEHICLE.PurchasePrice**

MUSIC_STREAM

- **SUBSCRIPTION_TYPE.MonthlyFee**

Besides providing transparency to users, other benefits of defining columns storing financial data with 'money' data types are better able to leverage other measurements that track exchange or conversion rates, annual inflation, and taxes.

smallmoney

smallmoney is a data type with a range of values from negative 214,748.3648 through positive 214,748.3647. While this range is significant, it should be limited for columns that are in the low double or perhaps triple digits, such as individual food items in a grocery store. In the database designs we have seen, there are several columns where **smallmoney** would be appropriate. These are:

METRO_TRANSIT

- **FARE.FareAmount**

MUSIC_STREAM

- **SUBSCRIPTION_TYPE.MonthlyFee**

When we look at **EMPLOYEE.Salary**, many positions could easily fit under $214,000 per year, but obviously not all of them, such as in 2045. Additionally, not all databases are tracking money as USD; if the local currency is in Japanese Yen, Korean Won, or Kazakhstani Tenge, then the range of numbers in **smallmoney** data type can be severely limited.

Likewise, while most subscription types for the MUSIC_STREAM database can be perhaps $20 to $30 USD a month, consider the possibility of having a subscription type of 'Major University' or 'Corporate Partner' that may have 150,000 users. Is it possible that the monthly fee amount might exceed $214,000? How about in 25 years or after a major technology breakthrough? The best design choice in this case will be to include a data type that does not cause any hassles later just to save a few bytes of memory today.

money

The money data type has a range of values from negative 922,337,203,685,477.5808 through positive 922,337,203,685,477.5807. This range is significant and covers a vast range of data needs for tracking money (probably even for many countries). In the database designs we have seen there are several columns where the money data type is appropriate:

METRO_TRANSIT

- **EMPLOYEE.Salary**
- **VEHICLE.PurchasePrice**

MUSIC_STREAM

- **SUBSCRIPTION_TYPE.MonthlyFee**

The range for most columns that are tracking money are a good fit for this data type. This includes different countries as mentioned previously where the exchange rate is multiple hundreds or even thousands to 1 USD or EUR.

Date and Time Data Types

There are many times in nearly every relational database where the transaction details require the time context to provide the most information. Occasionally, the context just needs to be a simple date such as the date that a person was born, married, got hired for a job or purchased a house. Sometimes, we might need more detail and the time of day becomes important, such as when an online purchase was made or when a tolled bridge was crossed.

Most relational database management systems have a collection of data types to address the context that individual columns need to provide the most appropriate context across cultures and the different formats that dates and times are presented. Most importantly, we need to let the system know which columns are holding date and time values as we can change the format on the fly as needed.

`date`: When just the date is required for a column, the data type '**`date`**' has sufficient range to capture most values ever needed. It has a range of values from January 1 from the year '0001' through the year '9999' ending on December 31 with a default format of YYYY-MM-DD. An example is 1942-11-27.

`time`: When the time of an event is best stored separately from the date, the data type '**`time`**' is used. This has a very precise measurement down to a nano-second with a format of of HH:MM:SS[.NNNNNNN]. The range of values for the time data type is 00:00:00.0000000 through 23:59:59.9999999. The need to measure seven digits after each second is found in infrequent commercial business scenarios. There might be a need for flexibility if there are billions of transactions and a sorted order of sequence.

`smalldatetime`: It captures both simple date and time data with a range from the years 1900 to 2079. It has a detailed measurement of hours and minutes. Quick analysis is this data type could suffice for most columns in almost all databases in the world. Columns that include time values where 'down to the minute' is acceptable are at toll billings, point-of-sale retail purchases, as well as badging-in at work.

The biggest potential problem here is the granularity of values being shared across many rows of data. With the lack of smaller, more detailed measurements, it will become increasingly difficult to determine the order or sequence of events with this data type in high-volume tables.

`datetime`: When both date and time are desired for a transaction, the combination data type datetime is used. This stores a range of values from the year 1753, through 9999. The granularity is as small as three-hundredths of a second (3.33 milliseconds). The format is presented as YYYY-MM-DD HH:MM:SS[.NNN]. An example value is 2025-09-28 17:24:01.110.

Usually, the datetime format will suffice for greater than 90% of date and time requirements and is effectively a default value in many data modeling and database management systems.

In the database diagrams presented so far, there are several columns of date or time values as seen:

METRO_TRANSIT (columns that need just date without any mention of time)

- **VEHICLE.PurchasedDate**
- **JOB.BeginDate**
- **JOB.EndDate**
- **COMMENT.CommentDate**
- **TRIP.AssignedDate**
- **EMPLOYEE.EmpDOB**
- **PASSENGER.BirthDate**
- **FARE.FareBeginDate**
- **FARE.FareEndDate**

METRO_TRANSIT (columns that need both date and time)

- **TRIP_STATUS.BeginDateTime**
- **SCHEDULE.DateTime**
- **SCHEDULE_TRIP.ActualDateTime**

MUSIC_STREAM has 15 columns that track dates (from birthdates to when certain events occurred, like recording date and release date) and only one that requires the specific time (**ACCESS.AccessDateTime**). Usually, this 15:1 ratio of dates-only to the time of an event is accurate.

It is important to know what the potential queries will be when designing a database, especially around dates and times. With a column defined as 'datetime' for example, an analyst can explore what time of the day events are occurring and adjust staffing or other resources accordingly.

datetime2: There are additional data types for the occasional column that holds data with the need for greater granularity of time. **datetime2** provides precise measurements down to 100 nanoseconds while keeping the same date range as '**datetime**'.

datetime2 has the format of YYYY-MM-DD HH:MM:SS[.NNNNNNN]

Datetimeoffset: Occasionally, larger companies are tracking events across the globe and find it important to know the local time in addition to the difference from Greenwich Mean time. The data type '**datetimeoffset**' has the same format as datetime2 and includes a measurement to distinguish the local time zone difference from GMT (also known as Coordinated Universal Time/UTC).

`Datetimeoffset` has a format of YYYY-MM-DD HH:MM:SS[.NNNNNNN] [+|-]HH:MM

`timestamp`: This data type gives columns the ability to automatically capture the current date and time whenever a row is inserted or updated. This column is added to the schema (maximum one per table) to record when a row was last modified. A timestamp datatype captures a unique number generated by the system that gets re-written every time a row is created or updated.

The format for timestamp is YYYY-MM-DD[HH:MM:SS].

Hopefully, by now you must have realized the importance of being able to work with data and correctly define the context of time, often both from a calendar and clock perspective. We will discuss retrieving date and time values with date functions in Chapter 6 more elaborately.

String Data Types

The most-common data types in my experience are those that store essentially any character found on a computer keyboard. These are known as string data types although sometimes people say 'alpha-numeric'. Since string data types are open to all characters, many inexperienced database designers will misuse string data types, while trying to capture all values that may be better assigned a numeric, datetime, or money data type.

When assigned appropriately, string values can be very legible to people when we are reading data output, as they include names, emails, and phone numbers of customers, the name and address of the store we shopped at plus a list by name of the products we purchased. The string data type even includes the names of the employees that assisted us with our order.

The flexibility of string data types allows us to place characters up to 8,000 bytes per value. This means that we can store data in Unicode characters which allows many different languages (especially East Asian languages like Chinese, Japanese, and Korean) to be included in the database.

Let us take a quick look at the different string data types available. There are fixed-length and variable-length string data types within the relational model.

Fixed-Length and Variable-Length

String data types are available in finite or fixed length when the size and shape of the data in a column are the same for each value as well as variable when they are not. Examples for fixed-length values include a 10-character postal code, 2-character state abbreviation, or a 10-digit phone number. These values are known to be an exact length, and have the same shape for each row.

When observing the two databases we have seen already, **METRO_TRANSIT** and **MUSIC_STREAM**, the only columns that are fixed length are **PASSENGER.Zip**, **STOP.Zip**, **STOP.GPS_Coord** and **CUSTOMER.PostalCode**. If phone numbers, country codes or perhaps, driver license data were being stored, there is a possibility that these might also have a fixed length.

Variable-length values are essentially names, addresses, and descriptions for most objects in the database. Looking at the **METRO_TRANSIT** design in *Figures* 2.3 as well as the design for **MUSIC_STREAM** in *Figure* 2.4, there are more than 40 columns of 'names, addresses, or descriptions' in each database that are defined as variable character (usually as varchar(50) for names and cities and varchar(500) for description columns). Obviously, most names and addresses are inconsistent in length.

There are string data types for non-Unicode data as well as for Unicode. In each case with string data types, the number of bytes to be assigned to each value is placed in the parentheses of the data type definition. The fixed-length Unicode character data type is written with the letter 'n' in front of the data type with the number of bytes assigned to each value up to 8,000 enclosed in the parentheses. The difference between these is that non-Unicode string data type takes a single byte per character stored, while Unicode requires 2 bytes per character. Quick math suggests the maximum number of bytes for non-Unicode string data types is 8,000 while Unicode string data types can only go to a maximum of 4,000 as there are two bytes per character.

Name	Fixed-Length	Data Type	Range
char(n)	Yes	Non-Unicode	0 to 8,000 bytes
nchar(n)	Yes	Unicode	0 to 4,000 characters
binary(n)	Yes	Non-Unicode	1 to 8,000 bytes
varchar(n)	No	Non-Unicode	0 - 8,000 bytes
nvarchar(n)	No	Unicode	0 to 4,000 characters
varbinary(n)	No	Non-Unicode	1 - 8,000 bytes
varchar(max)	No	Non-Unicode	0 - 2 GB
nvarchar(max)	No	Unicode	0 - 2 GB
varbinary(max)	No	Non-Unicode	0 - 2 GB

Table 2.1: *A list of both Fixed-Length and Variable-Length data types*

The data commonly assigned binary data type are diagrams, photographic images or audio files such as those with JPEG, PNG, GIF, or mp3 extensions. Data that is encrypted or compressed is frequently assigned the binary data type.

Other Data Types

Beyond the standard data types that have been presented so far, there are more that are available in relational database management systems. These include XML, cursor, timestamp and even custom-designed data types. These are going to be dependent on whichever database platform you are using and are outside the scope of this text. If you find that the data types that have been introduced are not able to accommodate the specific size or shape of the data you are working with, search them online to find about the respective data types for the product platform you have installed.

Like many products with flexibility in design, databases have potential conflicts when deciding exact data types. If we make the shape too restrictive, we may inadvertently cause a burden on users having to re-enter data several times. This may unnecessarily cause application performance to suffer and possibly shatter the fragile goodwill companies have with their customers. Similarly, if the data type restrictions we select are too broad, we may introduce other problems such as too much unnecessary data creating search and performance issues, besides raising storage costs.

There is a balance between protecting the data and eventually using it in queries or dashboard reports. Be considerate towards your end-users by keeping their work and overhead to a minimum by thinking how the data is going to be queried. There will be different uses and fundamental conflicts regarding the shape of data across an enterprise. Do your best to ensure that the data is protected and is accurate for ease of use.

Now that we have been exposed to a broad overview of the relational model, let us take a moment to reflect on the key takeaways for this chapter with a summary of advantages and disadvantages of the structure.

Advantages of Relational Model

There are many advantages and features of a relational model that can be used for storing data. These include the following:

- The relational model is very good at creating records based on original transactional events in large volumes with millions of new rows per day.
- Repetitive processes like customer orders can be effectively automated with exceptional accuracy.
- The relational model and its vast set of tools are very stable with little variation from the model introduced in 1969.

- The most popular tools for creating and managing relational databases (data modeling, data storage, and reporting) have been built by very large and prominent companies like Oracle, IBM, Amazon, and Microsoft.
- The standard manipulation language (SQL) is relatively easy to learn which allows even non-technical managers the ability to directly engage with data.
- The relational model is flexible to be customized to the unique methods of a company, as well as to adapt as data needs evolve during an organization's operational lifetime.

Disadvantages of Relational Model

There are several disadvantages when using a relational data model as a platform for storing data. These include the following:

- Engineers need to be aware of and follow the industry standards to get the best results, which requires intensive training and experience.
- Users will need basic training to write SQL as it is the lingua franca of relational databases.
- The protections of transactional processing (known as ACID principles) will become an impediment to developers who are not savvy or sophisticated in relational design principles. Again, there is a fundamental baseline of basic operational skill required to design and implement a relational database.

Conclusion

A relational model has the ability to create massive amounts of data that can be retrieved to encourage large-scale organizational learning. The speed and volume of data we can capture has increased exponentially from when the relational model was first introduced in the late 1960's. In the days before it, the written word dominated every process at large organizations.

The relational model had a direct impact on several industries. Organizations can now create, capture, analyze, and learn at immensely faster speeds. For this reason, many organizations refer to this model for optimizing costs and making learning accessible.

In *Chapter* 3, readers will explore how to take a problem (or 'learning' space) and develop a corresponding relational database in a step-by-step manner. This database development will include 'normalization', which might be tedious initially, but is eventually important in building robust relational data structures. Mastering this skill will earn you significant dividends going forward.

Post-Chapter Challenges

Based on your objectives and intentions on learnings from this book, please approach the following challenges as appropriate for your personal objectives.

Track 1 (THINK): Data Tourist Seeking Ancillary Awareness

Review the following questions:

- How has the relational model helped societies, organizations, and people evolve in terms of learning?
- What aspects of your life would become better if you had more relevant and accessible information to assist you in decision-making?
- Find examples of the spreadsheets you have designed or worked with frequently in both your career; how are they designed in accordance with (or against) the principles of the relational model?
- How can you elect to track data in the future with the fundamentals of a relational model, either with a spreadsheet, text files, or other methods?

Track 2 (WRITE): Dedicated Student or Recent Graduate

Based on your comprehension of this chapter, respond to the following questions:

- Which industries (besides technology) were improved with the technological breakthroughs since relational theory was articulated in 1969 and how?
- How has the world economy become more robust, resilient, and efficient due to the ability to create billions of transactions digitally? Provide several specific examples of exact industries and/or companies.
- After reviewing the example database models for **`METRO_TRANSIT`** and **`MUSIC_STREAM`** in *Figures* 2.3 and 2.4, what do you think of the way the designs store data when compared to how you may have approached it prior to reading this chapter?

Track 3 (BUILD): Professional Aspirants

This track targets aspirants who wish to craft a successful career in data science. Let us continue with the challenge from the last chapter where you were asked to structure a data collection in a spreadsheet to track a large-scale metropolitan transit system.

- Review the different objects in the example relational model for **`METRO_TRANSIT`** in *Figure* 2.3; how is the perspective of the database in the example different from yours?

- While comparing the objects in your spreadsheet to the **METRO_TRANSIT** database, what elements of data do you find are present/missing in your spreadsheet?
- Think about a hobby or interest that might be similar to designing an original database. See if you can build an original database drawing from the examples in this chapter.

CHAPTER 3
Data Modeling and Normalization

Introduction

In this third chapter, we will explore effective data modeling. Readers so far are familiar with database history and relational theory. Now, we will explore the complexity of normalization and gain advanced skills in database design, while preparing the path to master analytical skills with SQL.

After observing historical categorization and classification systems that are hierarchical in design, the previous chapter introduced the relational model, and explained how to read a completed logical data model with the crow's foot notation. From this foundation, you will now be introduced to creating your own unique database, and become a skilled data analyst without relying on additional guidance.

This chapter reinforces the symbols and vernaculars involved in data modeling, which includes normalization. These steps provide insight into the inner workings of creating a relational database from initial research through to a physical database schema. We will also learn about two methods of creating a professional Entity-Relationship Diagram (ERD), which is a read-to-code blueprint like the Third Normal Form (3NF). These skills will help you become fluent in database design and gain functional independence.

Structure

In this chapter, we will explore the following topics:

- Systems Development Lifecycle (SDLC)
- Basics of data modeling
- Normalization
- Example demonstration of creating a fully normalized data model

Systems Development Lifecycle

The Systems Development Lifecycle (SDLC) provides a structure through which developers, users, and stakeholders in any system can learn about the requirements and the desired outcomes of a project. We can become more efficient at our jobs after each iteration (or "build cycle") of the SDLC as we document each step, and measure the results.

We can embellish the SDLC model slightly by expanding the DESIGN phase to include two sub-phases as illustrated in the following figure:

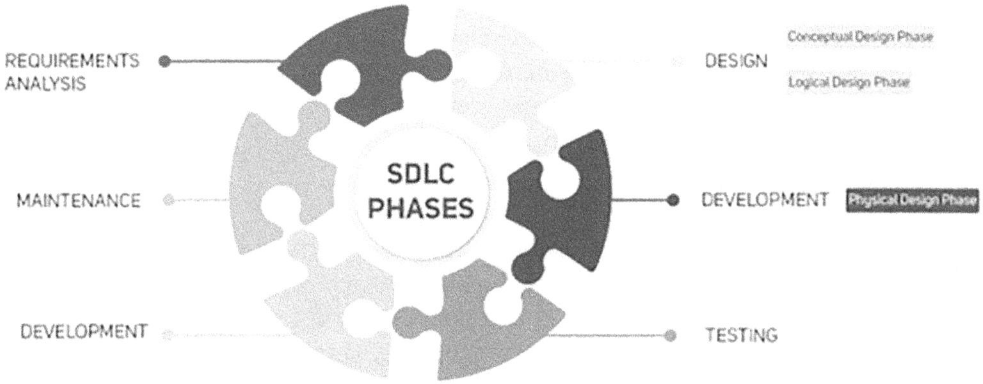

Figure 3.1: *Iterative phases in SDLC*

These sub-phases are the Conceptual Design Phase and the Logical Design Phase. In the section titled *Development, you will also see a* Physical Design Phase. We will explore these sub-phases in greater detail coming up.

The important part is to be aware of the location where database design and development occurs within the wider scope of software application development. Much of the effort to construct and code databases will occur in the DESIGN phase of the SDLC.

As we study data modeling, it is important to see it as an opportunity to articulate the guts of an organization and decide the elements that end up being recorded perhaps thousands and thousands of times each day. This opportunity can establish the key objects that are critical to learning throughout an organization whereby the entire mission of the business can continuously improve year after year. If you skip this factor by cutting corners, it will ultimately limit the specific data that is being captured and therefore curtail the scope of data that can be analyzed. Shortcuts during the data modeling phase can be the difference between an organization having an exceptional presence in an industry or becoming irrelevant and leading to its premature death. Organizations that can learn over time will outperform others that do not; it all starts with analyzing the effectiveness of the resources and delivery processes within an organization.

One of the best methods to understand these complex processes is to see demonstrations of a real-life database in a step-by-step manner. In this chapter, an incremental construction of two databases will be shown starting with brainstorming business nouns and finishing with an Entity-Relationship Diagram (ERD) in at least Third Normal Form.

Where Do Databases Come From?

Let us start from exploring the occasion and location where databases are created. In terms of a project, a relational database is a supporting component to an application that is intended to either solve an existing problem or address a new market opportunity. This simply means that many companies will start with an application focused on engaging people to address a data problem and afterwards consider designing a database to support the application.

Solving an Existing Problem

Problems are endemic in most organizations; most members answer that their average day could be improved if there was better access to data or higher quality information. This internal data strife is often the driving force behind establishing a project that provides a fix. This fix could be relatively simple (such as a new dashboard drawing on existing data) or it could be more complicated (like designing and building out an application to support a new process that captures data that does not currently exist).

New Market Opportunity

Companies are encouraged to be aware of new opportunities to grow and expand their businesses to generate additional revenue. These opportunities frequently require new applications and processes to manage people and control the execution of processes or manufacture and delivery of products and services. Much of these efforts mandate brand new applications and supporting databases. Basically, databases are built to store and provide access to the data required for an application that many people use to get their work completed, shop, organize their activities, or communicate with one another.

To simplify, problems and opportunities are brought to the attention of executives from all the departments in a company. This includes operations/manufacturing, sales and marketing, legal, human resources, accounting and even the IT department. Each of these departments need to track events and associated costs with specific tools.

Popular commercial products such as Salesforce for customer relationship management and QuickBooks for accounting are available as a subscription for a relatively low cost. Buying a ready-made product or service like these effectively reduces the risk and technical resource requirements of building new software from the ground-up. Aside from entering data into these commercial systems, they can be ready to go live almost immediately.

Other times, a company has a very specific problem or opportunity, and decides that a commercial product or service is not going to be a good fit or cost-effective in the long term. These companies usually have the technical staff and resources to build a custom solution. The trade-off of spending more time and money on a custom application is essentially owning a technical asset which is a better fit for the problem or opportunity being addressed.

Moreover, departments are usually provided with an annual budget for payroll, facilities, office furniture, computers, and software tools. Common software tools include personal productivity applications like email, spreadsheets, and job specific applications like diagram architecture projects or the ones that perform engineering costing drawing from measurements.

Prior to budget allocation, departments often review priorities, known issues, outstanding or ongoing development projects and make a list of projects prioritized for funding. However, not every project receives funding.

According to estimates, one out of every four proposals end up getting funding. Even the best proposals must be well-researched and come up with alternatives in addition to feasibility studies and cost-benefit/risk analyses to get to the final round of consideration. Again, it is not always the most important project that gets funded, as it often comes down to which project has the most compelling argument from a sponsor.

Some of the research for making a funding request occurs in the planning or analysis phases of the SDLC. The following diagram is a very simplified flowchart illustrating the cyclical nature and sequence of decisions that frequently occurs with the creation of software application projects:

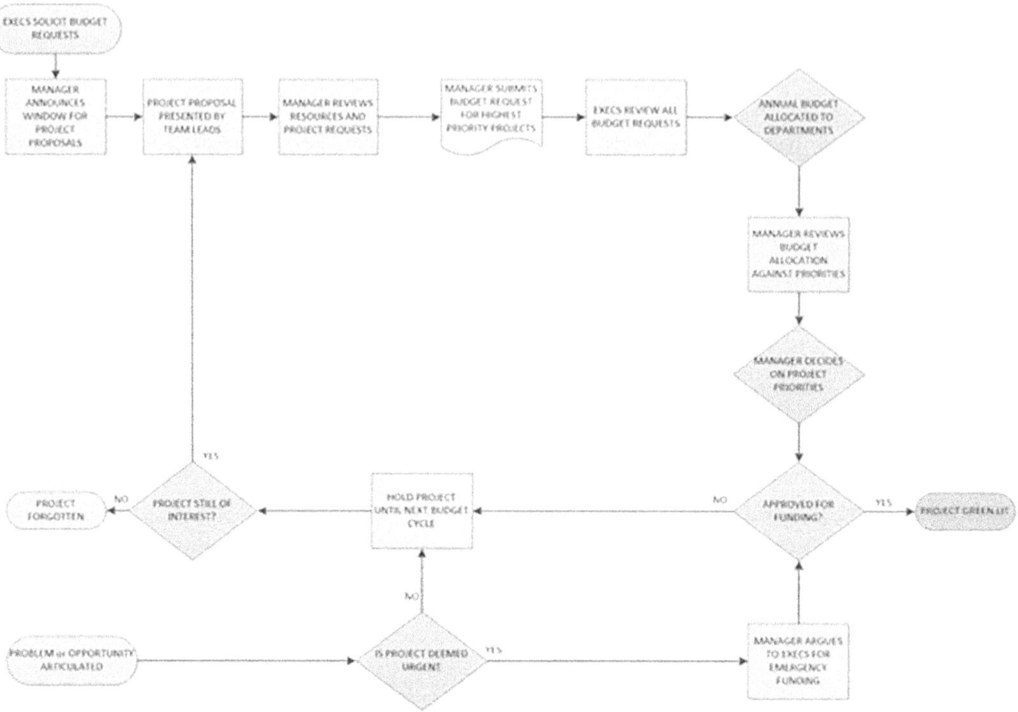

Figure 3.2: *Example process flow for project funding*

Please note that the flow chart depicted in *Figure* 3.2 begins with either a scheduled review of many budgetary concerns that are all-encompassing and not limited to technology applications. The standard budget process often includes opportunities for many different projects to submit funding requests. Individual projects must be researched, documented, and argued for based on ROI and timeline for impact. Again, most requests are denied.

Once a project has been green lit and allocated funding, the real work has just begun. Assuming that preliminary research has occurred in developing the material to request money, additional data-centric research must be conducted. We often refer to this sub-process as defining requirements, which entails observing how employees conduct business during regular operations of live activity, researching industry-centric best practices, as well as interviewing stakeholders and vendors. Once a body of knowledge has been assembled to get a new application, we are ready to design the database, starting with a robust data model that will address the stakeholder features that are required to be included in the application.

The process of designing a database has conceptual and logical phases; normalization occurs in the logical design phase after we have completed a consolidated conceptual diagram which includes all entities and attributes pieces of a puzzle.

Overview of `METRO_TRANSIT`

Many cities have an organized, formal, and publicly funded transportation system. This is fantastic and useful for getting people of all incomes and mobile abilities around town in a safe and predictable manner.

The effective ubiquitousness of these systems is why we have chosen **`METRO_TRANSIT`** as one of the working database examples going forward. While the data in **`METRO_TRANSIT`** is mostly fabricated, the structure and sophistication of the database allows learners to practice.

Let us consider a fictitious **`METRO_TRANSIT`** system that is struggling to manage operations with data held in a spreadsheet. They need a new relational database design, which is as follows:

DateTime	Passenger	RouteName	Type	Driver	StopName	Type	Destination	Type	Fare	Neighborhood
2/13/2025 7:36:00 AM (delayed)	Ivey Hazekamp	32 Capitol Hill-Downtown	Regular	Jimi Hendrix, 206555-7661	Broadway Ave. Cherry St	Covered	Convention Center	Articulated	$ 4.50	Capitol Hill
2/13/2025 9:36	Darcel Eustache	78 Fremont Waterfront Downt	Special	Meryl Streep	Hwy 99 N 30th	Covered	Fremont, Space Needle, P70	Extra Long	$ 2.75	Fremont
2/14/2025 6:38		78 Fremont Waterfront Downt	XP	Bruce Lee	Elliott Avenue and Mercer St	Covered	Downtown	Extra Long	$ 2.75	Interbay
2/16/2025 6:32	Kenyetta Tenon	42 Sodo Downtown Express	Express	Meryl Streep	First Avenue and Terry Street	Covered	Fremont, Space Needle, P70	Doub	$ 2.75	SODO
2/19/2025 15:39	Kenny Tenon	42 - E Sodo-Downtown Express	Express	Bruce Lee	First Avenue and Terry Street	Uncovered	SoDo, DT	Doubled	$ 4.50	South Downtown
2/21/2025 6:13	Darcel Eustache	78-S Fremont Waterfront-Down	Special	Jimmy Hendricks, 206 555 7661	Elliott Avenue and Mercer St	Cvd	Fremont, Space Needle, P70	Extra long	$ 2.75	Interbay
2/21/2025 7:36	Kenyetta Tenon	Sodo-Downtown Express	Express	Bruce Lee	First Avenue and Terry Street	UC	Downtown	Doubled	$ 4.50	South Downtown
2/22/2025 8:32	Ivey Hazekamp	32 Capitol Hill-Downtown	Regular	Jim Morrison	Broadway Ave and Cherry St	Covered	CCntr,	Articulated	$ 4.50	Capitol Hill
3/1/2025 6:33			Regular	Bruce Lee, 425 6109225	Broadway Ave and Cherry St	Covered	Downtown	Articulated	$ 4.50	Capitol Hill
3/1/2025 6:36:00 AM (Blocked)			Regular	Mary Streep (mstreep@metrotransit.org)	Broadway Ave and Cherry St	Covered	Downtown	Articulated	$ 4.50	Capitol Hill
3/3/2025 6:42	Darcel Eustache	78 Fremont Downtown Comm	Commute	Jim Morrison	Sixth Avenue and Battery	Regular	Fremont, Space Needle, P70	Doubled	$ 4.50	Downtown
3/5/2025 6:32			XP	Meryl Streep	Elliott Avenue and Mercer St	Covered	Downtown	Extra Long	$ 2.75	Interbay
3/6/2025 7:52	Kenyetta Tenon	42 Sodo Downtown Express	Express	Jimi Hendrix	First Avenue and Terry Street	UC	Downtown	Doubled	$ 4.50	South Downtown
3/10/2025 6:33	Darcel Eustache	78 Fremont Downtown Comm	Commute	Jim	Elliott Avenue and Mercer St	Covered	Downtown	Extra long	$ 2.75	Interbay
3/11/2025 6:32	Kenyetta Tenon	Sodo Downtown Express	Express	Bruce Lee, [illegible]@metrotransit.org	First Avenue and Terry Street	Uncovered	Downtown	Doubled	$ 4.50	South Downtown
3/13/2025 8:32:00 AM (Late)	Ivey Hazekamp	32 Capitol Hill Downtown	Regular	Bruce Lee	Broadway Ave and Cherry St	Covered	Convention Center	Articulated	$ 4.50	Capitol Hill
3/14/2025 6:32			Express	Bruce Lee	Broadway Ave and Cherry St	Covered	Downtown	Articulated	$ 4.50	C Hill
3/15/2025 1:36	Janey Lundgren	32 Capitol Hill Downtown	Reg	Jimmy Hendricks	Broadway Ave and Cherry St	Covered	Convention Center	2 Decks	$ 2.75	Capitol Hill
3/16/2025 6:32	Darcel Eustache	78 Fremont Waterfront Downt	Commute	Jim Morrison	Sixth Ave and Battery Street	Regular	Fremont, Space Needle	Doubled	$ 4.50	Downtown
3/17/2025 11:33	Ivey Hazekamp	32 Capitol Hill Downtown	Regular	Jimi Hendrix	Fourth Avenue and Seneca	Covered	Capitol Hill	Doubled	$ 2.75	Downtown
3/18/2025 16:13	Jane Lundigan	32 Capitol Hill Downtown	Reg	Meryl Streep	Fourth Avenue and Seneca St	Covered	CH	2 Decks	$ 2.75	DT
3/19/2025 6:32	Janey Lundgren	32 Capitol Hill Downtown	Reg	Meryl Streep	Broadway and Cherry St	Covered	Downtown	2 Decks	$ 2.75	Capitol Hill
3/21/2025 6:32	Darcel Eustache	78 Fremont Waterfront Downt	Commute	Meryl Streep	Sixth Avenue and Battery	Regular	Fremont, Space Needle, P70	Doubled	$ 4.50	Downtown
3/26/2025 9:04	Janey Lundgren	32 Capitol Hill Downtown	Regular	Jimmy Hendricks, 206 555 7661	Broadway and Cherry St	Covered	Downtown	2 Decks	$ 2.75	CHill
4/18/2025 5:23	Darcel Eustache	78 Fremont Waterfront Downt	Commute	Jimi Hendrix	Fourth Avenue and Seneca	Regular	Fremont, Pier 70, Needle	Doubled	$ 4.50	Downtown

Figure 3.3: *Example of `METRO_TRANSIT` data held in a spreadsheet*

While this data is fabricated and fictitious, the design it represents is an amalgamation of several common design errors we encounter frequently. Review the data in *Figure* 3.3 and determine which flaws are present. You might wonder about the reason these data issues are not controlled. As we attempt to build an original database design from scratch, we may return to *Figure* 3.3 to see what it was like as a raw and untrained view. We will learn about two approaches to designing a new relational database, that start with gaining a full understanding of stakeholder requirements.

Method 1: Focus on Each Object with a Vertical Design Approach

The first method is a more traditional academic process that focuses on identifying objects involved in the business as well as the core characteristics and attributes of each object critical for the business. After these objects and their attributes are listed, we will evaluate their relationships and patch together the finished design. Students are thus instructed to visualize this 'vertical' approach with emphasis on an exhaustive exploration of each database object. After each object has been fully explored, we will move on to other objects before putting the pieces together.

Method 2: Focus on the Puzzle with a Horizontal Design Approach

The alternative method has a simple set of characteristics (ID, Name, and Description) that will by default become the beginning columns. These are assigned to each business 'noun' that is identified during brainstorming efforts. The initial focus of this method is getting each object placed in their own entity and immediately defining relationships with other objects. Students are often instructed to visualize a 'horizontal' approach with an initial shallow definition of each database object and instead focus on how the puzzle of objects fit together. After the relationships are defined with a frame of the puzzle clear, designers then circle back and build out the characteristics of each object.

This second alternative method of building an original relational database model will be explored in greater depth in *Chapter 4*.

Stakeholder Requirements

Any building process should begin with knowing the user needs. For a database, it is critical to answer the following questions *before* brainstorming, diagramming or writing code:

- Who is going to use the database?
- What are the decisions that the database users might make?
- Which data elements need to be stored in the database?

For the basis of **`METRO_TRANSIT`**, we can make broad assumptions from a simple view learned from transit systems in North America, Europe, and Asia. The points of view and interests will include both management operations and consumers that we elicited from our research efforts during the early phases of the SDLC. Each of these needs listed as follows should be validated with the project sponsor and primary stakeholders.

- **MANAGEMENT/OPERATIONS**
    - Which routes are the busiest?
    - Which destinations are most popular?
    - Which routes have the most incidents?
    - Which neighborhoods need coverage?
    - Which drivers are most reliable?
    - When are riders taking trips?

    - Is the capacity sufficient?
- **CONSUMER**
    - Which routes are best suited for getting to a specific destination?
    - What times are the best to travel?
    - What concerns should I have regarding safety?
    - What are the costs for traveling to my destination?

Once the data needs are validated, we will brainstorm our primary stakeholders present and actively participating. Stakeholders are critical to creating a well-designed database by helping clear up any ambiguities we might encounter as well as identify terms and objects considered out of scope.

BRAINSTORMING

The act of brainstorming occurs during the Conceptual Design Phase to determine an exhaustive list of business objects required to meet the objectives listed in the data needs provided by stakeholders. This meeting to define objects for the database includes members from across the company, including web developers, a project manager, infrastructure engineers, and database designers, in addition to people from the business side of the company. Collectively, they will have a broad understanding to address the application problem space.

The meeting starts with one person writing all the suggestions on a whiteboard. Then, the teams filter and eliminate some objects during a specific clean-up process to understand everyone's thoughts regarding the problem space.

For the next section, you can pause here for and spend about 15 minutes brainstorming over the data required to manage a public transit system that includes employees, buses, passengers, stops, boardings and fares. Compare your notes from your thoughts and see where you align.

Remember, there are no wrong answers or suggestions! With even just a few participants, duplicate words or objects are bound to occur; simply write down each thought and look to trim or edit later.

The following table represents the results from a brief brainstorming session looking to identify the objects to facilitate a database supporting the operations of a typical urban transit system:

VEHICLE	DRIVER	CUSTOMER
DESTINATION	OIL CHANGE	TRAFFIC
FARE	ROUTE	CANCELED
STREET	STOP	LATE

TIRE ROTATION	SEAT	INCIDENT
FIGHT	SECURITY CAMERA	GARBAGE SPILL
TRANSFER	ELDERLY	DISABLED
SHUTTLE	EXPRESS	CAPACITY
WI FI	AIR CONDITIONING	WHEELCHAIR LIFT
DELAYED	NEIGHBORHOOD	PASSENGER
YOUTH	TRAIN	BUS
SECURITY OFFICER	INCLEMENT WEATHER	ENGINEER

Table 3.1: *Example of initial brainstorming session for* `METRO_TRANSIT`

In *Table* 3.1, there are several objects related to the management and use of a common metropolitan transportation system. While this list is relatively simple and was constructed in about 20 minutes, it is a simplified representation of what might be produced in a single session. In a more realistic situation at a company, the list may be closer to 100 objects created in over 90 minutes.

The next step of our data model evolution is to review the brainstorming output and do a bit of editing and clean-up. Our goal here is to validate strong objects and find others that may survive as columns or rows.

During this clean-up process, we do not want to throw away any values; while we may cross-off more than half of the suggestions, we can still return to revisit a suggestion upon further review.

We then review the list of suggestions and highlight the 'keepers' by making them bold red. Also, we will strike through the suggestions that are not strong candidates:

VEHICLE	~~DRIVER~~	~~CUSTOMER~~
DESTINATION	~~OIL CHANGE~~	~~TRAFFIC~~
~~FARE~~	**ROUTE**	~~CANCELED~~
~~STREET~~	**STOP**	~~LATE~~
~~TIRE ROTATION~~	~~SEAT~~	**INCIDENT**
~~FIGHT~~	~~SECURITY CAMERA~~	~~GARBAGE SPILL~~
~~TRANSFER~~	~~ELDERLY~~	~~DISABLED~~
~~SHUTTLE~~	~~EXPRESS~~	~~CAPACITY~~
~~WI FI~~	~~AIR CONDITIONING~~	~~WHEELCHAIR LIFT~~
~~DELAYED~~	**NEIGHBORHOOD**	**PASSENGER**
~~YOUTH~~	~~TRAIN~~	~~BUS~~
~~SECURITY OFFICER~~	~~INCLEMENT WEATHER~~	~~ENGINEER~~

Table 3.2: *Clean-up of initial brainstorming*

Our initial clean-up has yielded seven candidate entities, including VEHICLE, DESTINATION, ROUTE, STOP, INCIDENT, NEIGHBORHOOD, and PASSENGER. As different regions of the world may use different words to describe the same objects (such as 'STOP' instead of 'STATION' and 'ROUTE' in place of 'LINE'), we are consciously choosing terms that are a good fit for a mixed-use or combined bus and rail system.

Next, let us take a closer look at why suggestions got crossed out.

Common Parent

Nearly every database brainstorming session ends up with several similar suggestions that can be consolidated as rows underneath a more abstract title. For example, consider the suggestions AIR CONDITIONING, WIFI, WHEELCHAIR LIFT and SECURITY CAMERA; these are possibly better labeled as instances or values of a noun like AMENITY. There may even be a category above AMENITY with an entity named **`AMENITY_TYPE`**, which we will explore later.

Consider other combinations of suggestions that might have a common parent:

- **`STATUS`**
  - Late
  - Delayed
  - Canceled
- **`EMPLOYEE_TYPE`**
  - Driver
  - Security Officer
  - Engineer
- **`VEHICLE_TYPE`**
  - Heavy Rail Train
  - Light Rail Train
  - Shuttle
  - Double-Decker Bus
  - Regular/Standard Bus
- **`ROUTE_TYPE`**
  - Express
  - Inclement Weather
- **`MAINTENANCE`**
  - Oil Change

  - Tire Rotation
- **PASSENGER_TYPE**
  - Elderly
  - Youth
  - Disabled
- **INCIDENT_TYPE**
  - Fight
  - Garbage Spill

Now, we have established several new entities above that were not present on our brainstorming, including **STATUS**, **EMPLOYEE_TYPE**, **VEHICLE_TYPE**, **ROUTE_TYPE**, **MAINTENANCE**, **PASSENGER_TYPE**, **INCIDENT_TYPE**, and **AMENITY_TYPE**.

The next step is to explore these new entities for any values beyond the ones we have already. The objects that have more values are going to be better candidates for entities.

We want to quickly continue brainstorming and explore these entities for any additional data values that may exist:

- **INCIDENT_TYPE**
  - Fight, Garbage Spill
  - Medical
  - Collision
  - Fare Evasion
  - Drug Use
  - Verbal Abuse
- **MAINTENANCE_TYPE**
  - Oil Change, Tire Rotation
  - Vacuum
  - Steam Clean
  - Garbage Collection
- **AMENITY_TYPE**
  - Security
  - Safety
  - Comfort
  - Legal Mobility Accommodation

Additional entities might be found by exploring potential 'TYPE' values for the remaining base entities that were considered strong and marked in red.

Consider the following brainstorming around various 'types' of values:

- `DESTINATION_TYPE`
  - Tourist
  - Employment
  - Shopping
  - Educational
  - Social Hub
  - Arts
- `FARE_TYPE`
  - Unlimited Monthly/Daily Pass
  - Youth
  - Anonymous
  - Disabled/Elderly

We have taken an initial 20-minute brainstorming session that started with 7 entities and have come up with another 15 or so. We are still in the conceptual design phase and are not stuck with keeping any of these objects. We will now take each of our candidate entities and explore their attributes. These attributes will eventually be called 'columns' when the code for the database is built.

The following list represents a vetted beginning point to constructing a data model. There are two methods that are popular among database designers, like a formal method with symbols that includes an exhaustive definition of each object in isolation, followed by defining relationships before consolidating everything in a single diagram. This method will be demonstrated first, followed by a second step-by-step example of the 'ironing' method.

Hopefully, one of the two methods will be more comfortable for the way your brain works!

Method 1: Focus on Each Object with a Vertical Design Approach

Again, the first method has a more traditional, academic approach with many benefits; we gain a significant depth of understanding of the conditions of business objects that generate data and how that data will be used. As it will require more formal documentation for a larger audience, this method will take longer. This is probably the preferred method when the business processes are being invented or designed at the same time as the database.

Regardless of which process ends up being the better alternative, it is important to be flexible as we go through a design process. Therefore, knowing both processes is going to be valuable. Let us start this exploration with an introduction to the standard terms and symbols with the more academic process.

Common Data Modeling Symbols: Boxes, Orbs, and Diamonds

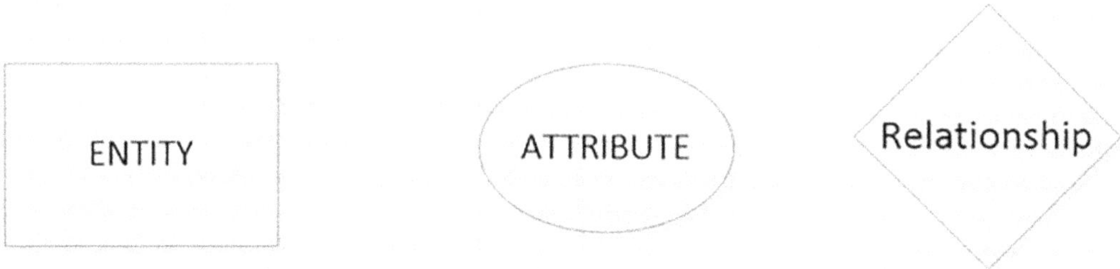

Figure 3.4: *Common data modeling symbols*

The next steps to define the relational database **METRO_TRANSIT** following the first method involve using the standard set of symbols to visually represent the entities (soon to be called 'table') and the various attributes of each (again, soon to be called 'columns'). This process involves more brainstorming as we engage our stakeholders, review the application requirements, and possibly conduct additional research.

We start this process by evaluating the critical characteristics for each potential entity by itself, without considering any relationship it may have with other entities.

Starting with the most obvious objects of **EMPLOYEE**, **VEHICLE**, and **PASSENGER**, we will explore the characteristics (formally named 'attributes'). These are the actual elements of data that will be critical for users of the database to leverage when writing queries or viewing a dashboard. This should still be considered brainstorming as we can always add or drop elements as we progress through the design process. Observe Figure 3.5 as shown here:

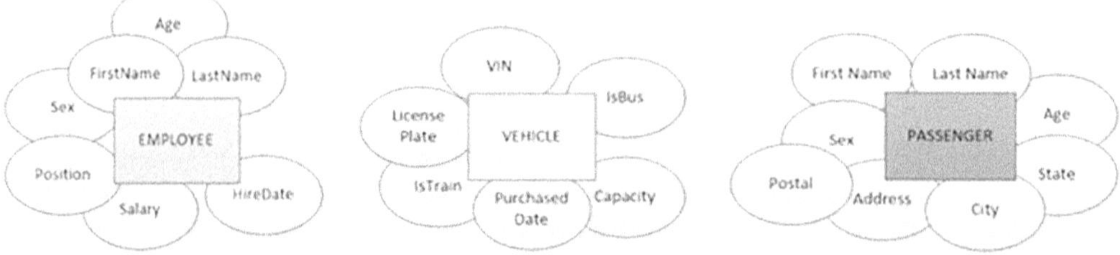

Figure 3.5: *Brainstorming attributes for* EMPLOYEE, VEHICLE, *and* PASSENGER

Next, the brainstorming of attributes continues by vetting the details for objects **INCIDENT**, **DESTINATION**, and **NEIGHBORHOOD** as seen in *Figure* 3.6:

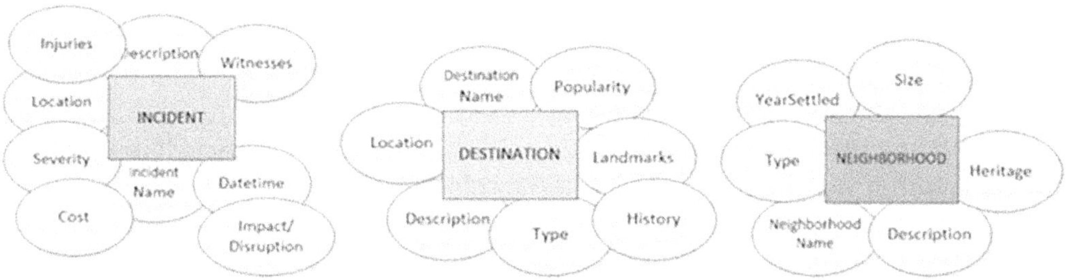

***Figure 3.6**: Brainstorming attributes of INCIDENT, DESTINATION and NEIGHBORHOOD*

Further brainstorming includes **STOP**, **AMENITY**, and **ROUTE**, as shown in *Figure* 3.7:

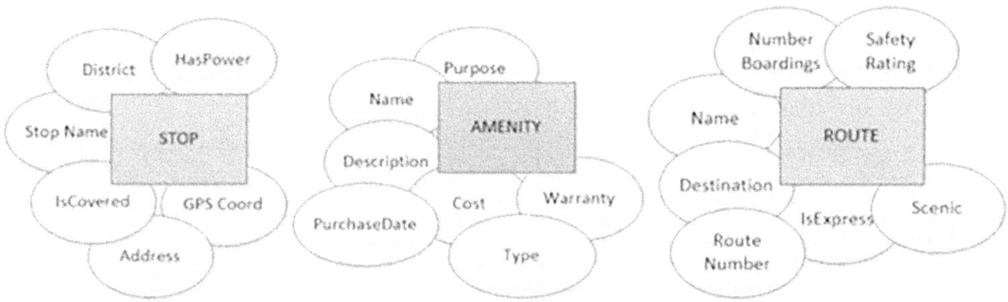

***Figure 3.7**: Brainstorming attributes for STOP, AMENITY and ROUTE*

The process of coming up with various attributes for each entity should be based on the knowledge and research conducted prior to the funding approval. Our goal is to identify every descriptor, element, or characteristic of the entity object that will be relevant for the organization while presenting reports, measuring performance or otherwise learning about how well the company is doing. It is encouraged to be exhaustive as we can always trim attributes later.

Defining Relationships

Next, we can begin articulating the relationships these attributes have with each other entity. Recognize that while exploring relationships between entities, we may discover attributes (or even new entities) that were missed previously.

Defining relationships between entities might be more difficult than coming up with their attributes, as it requires having a deeper understanding of the business. Many times, database designers are dependent on other employees within the company with a stronger awareness of the operations of the organization. This means interviewing people from different departments like marketing, accounting, and human resources among others.

Defining relationships between entities can be described as putting a puzzle together, not only because there are dozens of pieces that need to be placed in a physical position, but we also need to decrypt the relationship in two directions. We might be confused about these for the first couple of attempts, however, most students get a good handle on defining relationships after a few examples. A quick reminder of the object names that will be evaluated for initial relationships is provided here:

EMPLOYEE	NEIGHBORHOOD	INCIDENT	STATUS
VEHICLE	AMENITY	DESTINATION	FARE
PASSENGER	MAINTENANCE	STOP	ROUTE

Table 3.3: *List of initial base entity objects to be evaluated for direct relationships*

The nouns or objects held in Table 3.3 represent those that most likely will have demand for more details. This may include dates, addresses, categories, associated fees, or other characteristics. Therefore, we need to explore making TYPE tables for each as follows in *Table* 3.4:

`AMENITY_TYPE`	`FARE_TYPE`
`INCIDENT_TYPE`	`EMPLOYEE_TYPE`
`STOP_TYPE`	`PASSENGER_TYPE`
`MAINTENANCE_TYPE`	`ROUTE_TYPE`
`DESTINATION_TYPE`	`VEHICLE_TYPE`

Table 3.4: *List of initial type entities to be evaluated for direct relationships*

Deciding which entities have a direct relationship with others is not easy. A *direct* relationship can be assigned if there is clear demand for data each time the two objects interact, while *indirect can be assigned* if the answer is 'maybe'. If there is no clear or obvious data connection between the entities, then we should label the relationship as *incidental*.

Base Entity Name	Relationship With EMPLOYEE
NEIGHBORHOOD	This relationship is defined as ***incidental*** unless the company needs to track where an employee lives.
INCIDENT	At this time, we will say there is a ***direct*** relationship between INCIDENT and EMPLOYEE. There will be a need to track which employee was involved in certain incidents. We will see later that other entities will be discovered during the normalization process to remove the need for this direct relationship.

STATUS	This relationship is defined as ***incidental*** unless the company needs to track the employment status (such as good standing, suspended, on leave, or perhaps retired).
VEHICLE	At this time, we will say there is a ***direct*** relationship between VEHICLE and EMPLOYEE as there will need to be a record of which person was the driver or maintenance person who provided service. Normalization may change our definition of this relationship.
AMENITY	This relationship is defined as ***incidental*** unless the company needs to track which amenities a particular employee needs as accommodation (unlikely).
DESTINATION	This relationship is defined as ***incidental*** as no clear or relationship exists between DESTINATION and EMPLOYEE.
FARE	This relationship is defined as ***incidental*** as no clear or relationship exists between FARE and EMPLOYEE.
PASSENGER	This is an ***indirect*** relationship between PASSENGER and EMPLOYEE, as there is most likely a need to know when drivers and passengers were on the same vehicle.
MAINTENANCE	This is a ***direct*** relationship between MAINTENANCE and EMPLOYEE. Normalization may change this relationship if we determine this later as M:M.
STOP	This relationship is ***indirect***. There is probably critical data required to know when the `EMPLOYEE_TYPE` 'driver' was at a STOP, it can be seen as M:M. Normalization will resolve this relationship.
ROUTE	This relationship is defined as ***indirect***. Again, there is probably data required for each time a driver is assigned a ROUTE. We will learn that this is a M:M relationship that will be resolved during normalization.

Table 3.5: *List of initial base entities with brief description*

Multiplicity

In addition to having words in the middle of the diamond to describe the relationship between two entities, we have numbers that identify the range of permissible occurrences. This is known as multiplicity with the following choices:

Name	**Symbols**	**Description**
Zero-to-Many	(0..*) or (0:M)	Most-common relationship with perhaps ⅔ of all relationships meeting this definition. Nearly each relationship from a TYPE table will meet this definition (such as a PRODUCT_TYPE can have zero to many products of their type)

One-to-One	**(1..1) or (1:1)**	Most-common with super class and sub class
One-to-Many	**(1..*) or (1:M)**	Very common relationship; here the 'One' side means there is a mandatory existence ('participation') of a value. Examples include a product must have a product type
Many-to-Many	(*..*) or (M:M)	Many-to-many is a common definition when we are discovering relationships between entities (such as one student can take many classes and the same class can have many students). Many-to-Many relationships are not allowed to linger under the rules of normalization. Every *..* relationship must be resolved to include an associative entity and resulting 1..* relationships before building the database

Table 3.6: *List of symbols and definition for relationship multiplicity*

Let us see what a first draft of including relationships looks like by evaluating many combinations of entities. You must know that not every entity will have a direct relationship with others. Our job is to check out each combination of identity-relationships to determine the ones that have direct relationships. It does not really matter which entities are evaluated first, but we can start with EMPLOYEE.

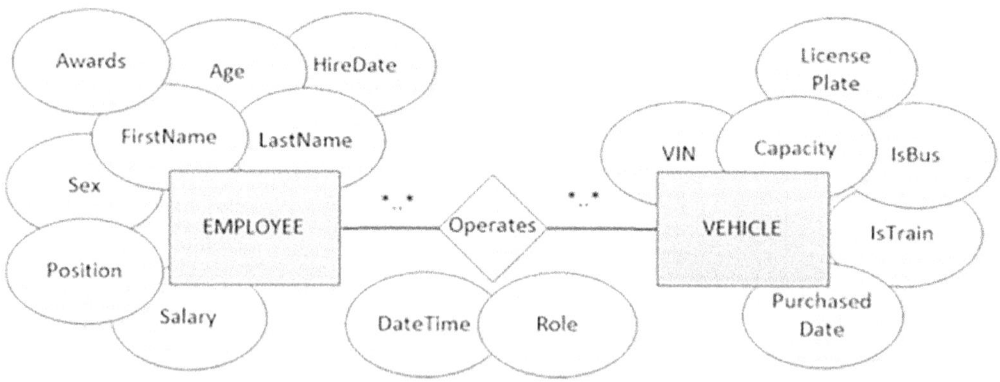

Figure 3.8: *Relationship* `EMPLOYEE : VEHICLE`

The relationship in *Figure* 3.8 is read many-to-many in both directions as one employee can operate many vehicles over time. One vehicle can also be operated by many employees. As relational theory does not allow M:M relationships to be coded, the relationship of **`EMPLOYEE : VEHICLE`** must be resolved to multiple 1:M relationships.

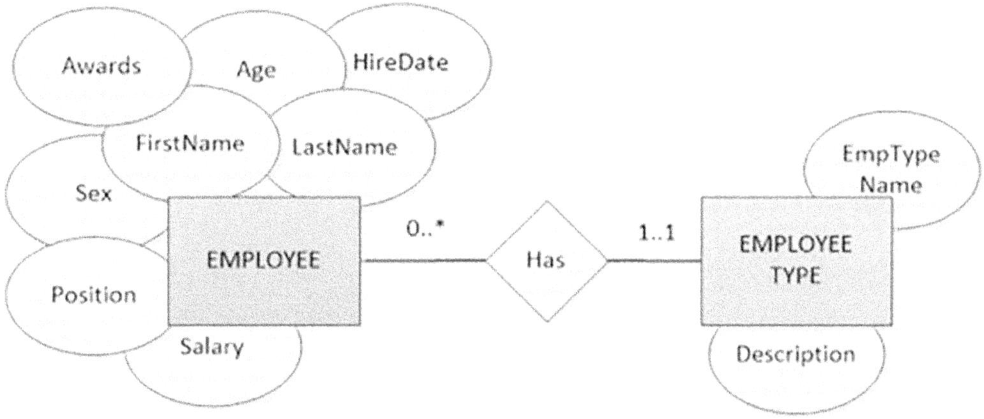

Figure 3.9: *Relationship* EMPLOYEE : EMPLOYEE_TYPE

The relationship shown in *Figure* 3.9 is an example of a 'type' entity and the base table, which is perhaps the most common ones in database designing. There may be as many as half of all such relationships on an average in a relational database. The relationship in *Figure* 3.9 is read as 'one employee can have one and only one employee type' and an employee type is defined as between zero and many employees. The multiplicity is included in the diagram, while the cardinality is spoken as 'one to many' and is written as 1:M.

There is a common confusion about the differences between multiplicity and cardinality. Multiplicity defines the range of possible occurrences, while cardinality describes the relationship that a single row in one entity has to the second entity.

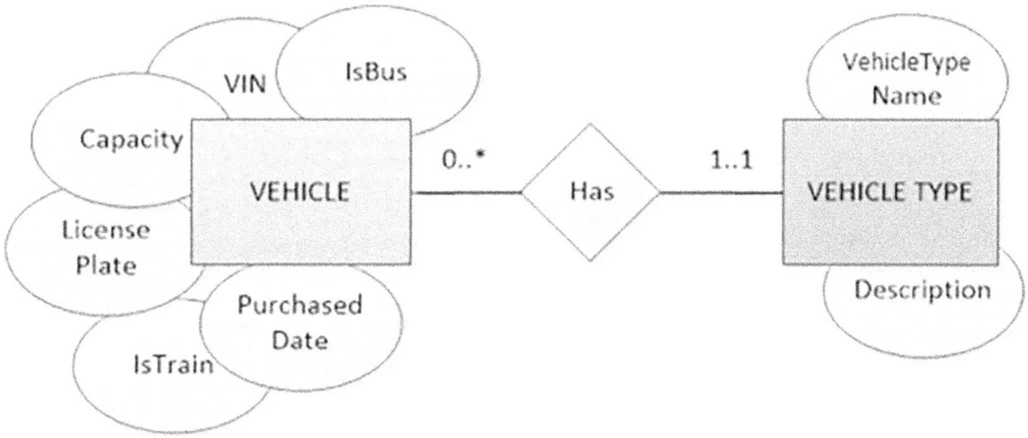

Figure 3.10: *Relationship* VEHICLE : VEHICLE_TYPE

The relationship in *Figure* 3.10 between VEHICLE and VEHICLE_TYPE is a classic 1:M relationship. The way to configure the relationship is for the base table (which in *Figure* 3.10 is VEHICLE) to receive the primary key from the type of entity as a foreign key. This means the primary key in **VEHICLE_TYPE** (**VehicleTypeID**) will become the foreign key of the same name in VEHICLE.

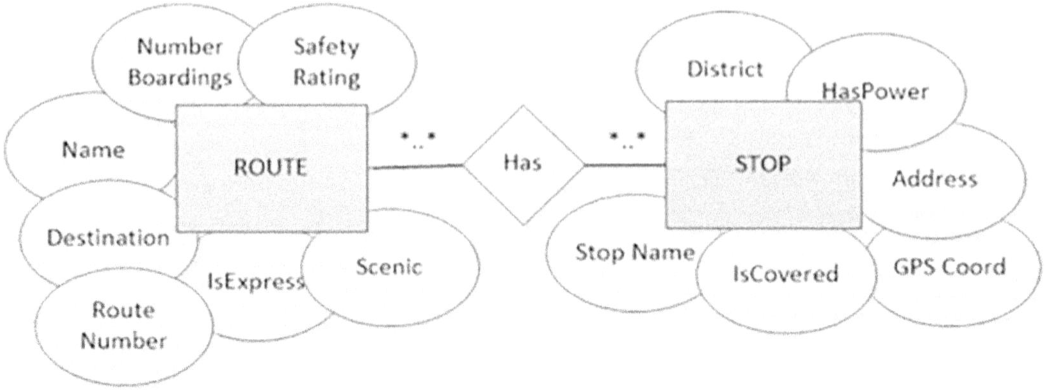

Figure 3.11: *Relationship ROUTE : STOP*

The relationship above between ROUTE and STOP is M:M and must be resolved with an associative entity before coding. It is read as 'one route has between zero and many stops while the same stop can have between zero and many routes that use it'. The associative entity can be temporarily called **ROUTE_STOP**, before being re-titled something more consistent with the popular corporate vernacular, like TIME_SCHEDULE or just SCHEDULE.

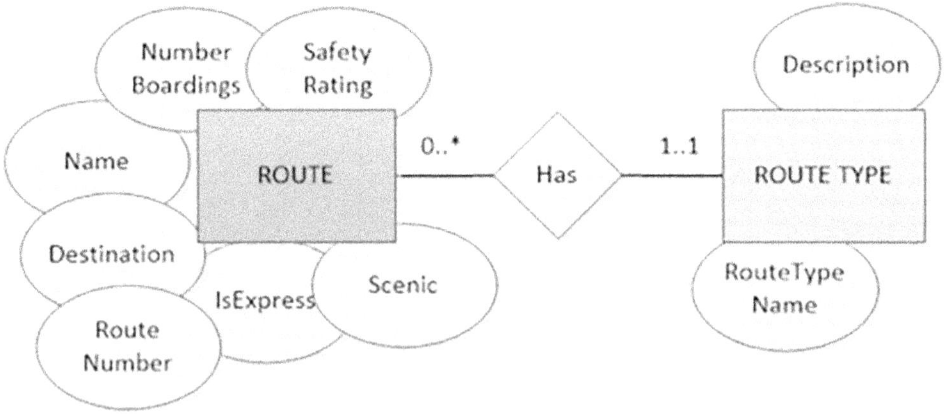

Figure 3.12: *Relationship ROUTE : ROUTE_TYPE*

This relationship and the next few examples are probably all 1:M and are very typical of how a base table relates to its 'type'. In each case, we will want to think about the different values of the parent table (the one that provides the foreign key to the other) and whether or not the child table will ever have multiple values of the parent. Many times organizations will say 'pick one' type for each row in the child entity and move on; other times it may really be important to capture all labels. If it turns out that capturing all labels for each row in the child entity is important, then the relationship is actually many-to-many (M:M) and must be resolved with an associative entity. Let's see these up close:

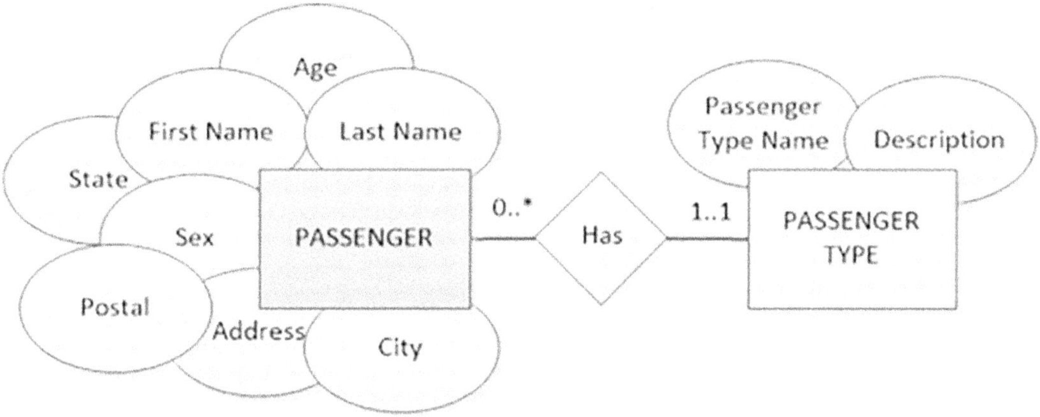

Figure 3.13: *Relationship PASSENGER : PASSENGER_TYPE*

The relationship between PASSENGER and PASSENGER_TYPE in Figure 3.13 can be validated by thinking about the values of different types of passengers in our heads; we might come up with 'commuter', 'regular', 'student' or perhaps 'mobility impaired'. Each of these types can have many passengers that have that label while each passenger usually only has a single type that describes them. The next step in design is to place the primary key from the TYPE entity into the base entity as a foreign key.

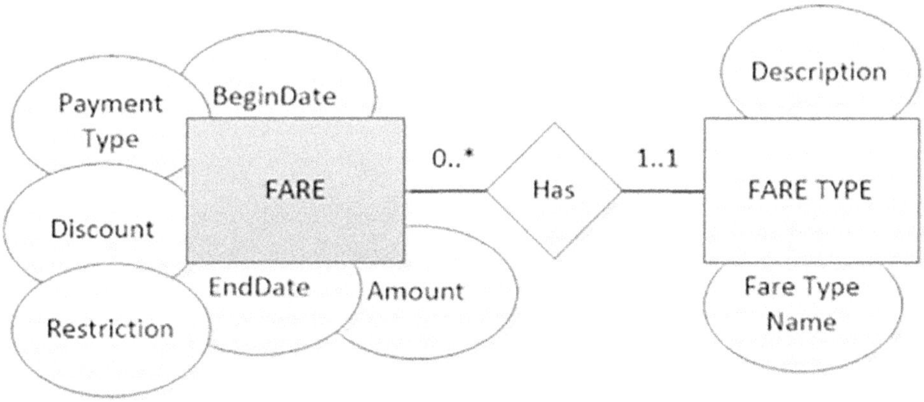

Figure 3.14: *Relationship FARE : FARE_TYPE*

Again, validation of the relationship between FARE and FARE_TYPE in Figure 3.14 will follow a similar process as before. Think about the values of the FARE_TYPE table, such as 'Peak', 'Senior', 'Employee', 'Monthly Pass', or 'Youth' and explore whether or not a single fare will ever need to have multiple types. This is most-often defined as a standard 1:M relationship.

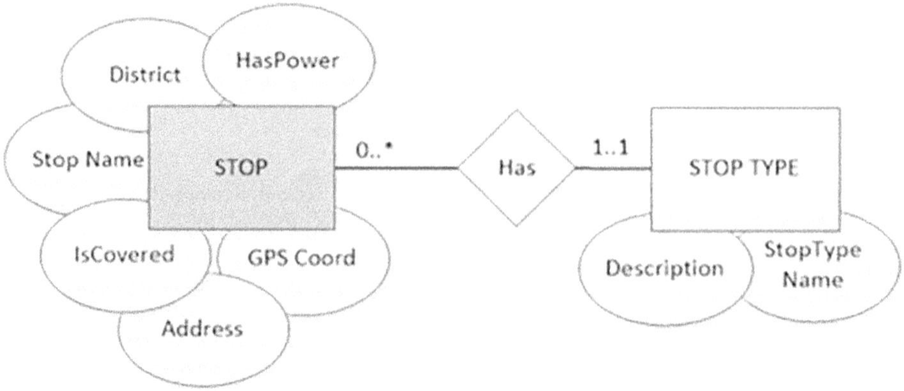

Figure 3.15: *Relationship* `STOP : STOP_TYPE`

The relationship between STOP and STOP_TYPE in Figure 3.15 will be easier than many others. We think about the values of the STOP_TYPE table, such as 'Covered', 'Un-Covered', or perhaps 'Full Service', before exploring whether or not a single stop will ever need to have multiple types. Chances are high that it is going to be a 1:M relationship.

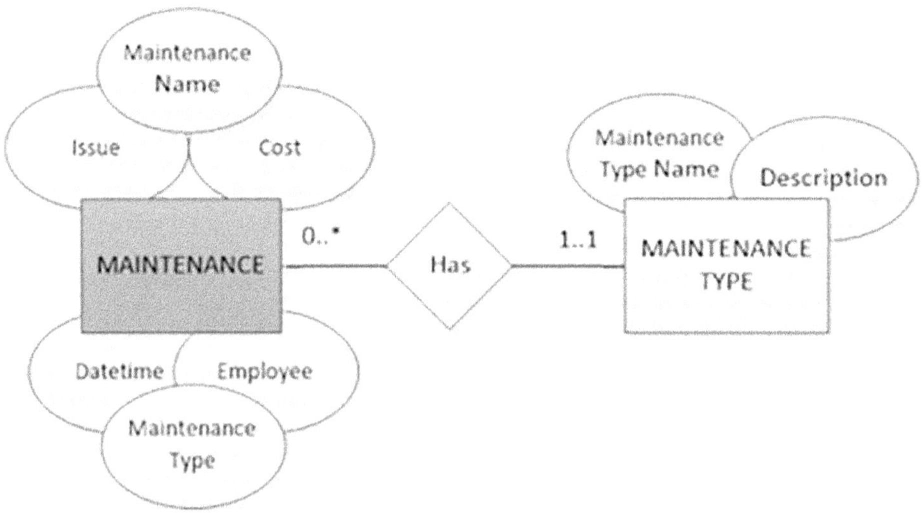

Figure 3.16: *Relationship* `MAINTENANCE : MAINTENANCE_TYPE`

The relationship between MAINTENANCE and MAINTENANCE_TYPE in Figure 3.16 is more complex as there are potentially many labels for a single maintenance task. Is sweeping the coach of a bus or train considered 'routine', 'mandatory', 'safety', or 'hygienic'? What about changing the oil or checking the air pressure in the tires? For many reasons, designers need to meet with the users and be certain to understand how the business side of the organization classifies these tasks. Aim to keep things functional and simple, if possible.

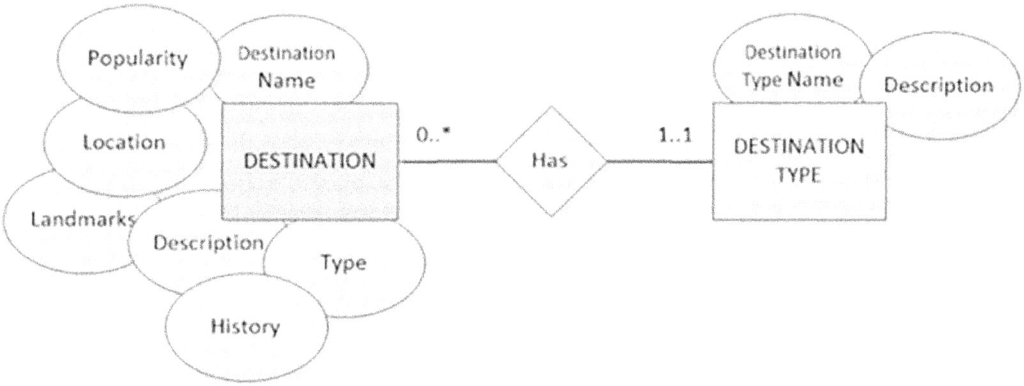

Figure 3.17: *Relationship* `DESTINATION : DESTINATION_TYPE`

The relationship between DESTINATION and DESTINATION_TYPE in Figure 3.17 is again complex as there are obviously many labels for a single destination. Consider again the different values that can be applied to a single destination such as 'downtown' for any major city. This destination can have many labels, including 'employment center', 'shopping district', 'tourist', 'entertainment', or even 'education'. While the truth will be determined by the organization sponsoring the database project, the best label might be 'multi-purpose' or 'high commercial activity'.

Depending on the needs of the organization that will be using the database, this may be an example of a complex relationship that needs many labels for a single child entity. This means the relationship is 'many-to-many' and requires many labels for a single destination.

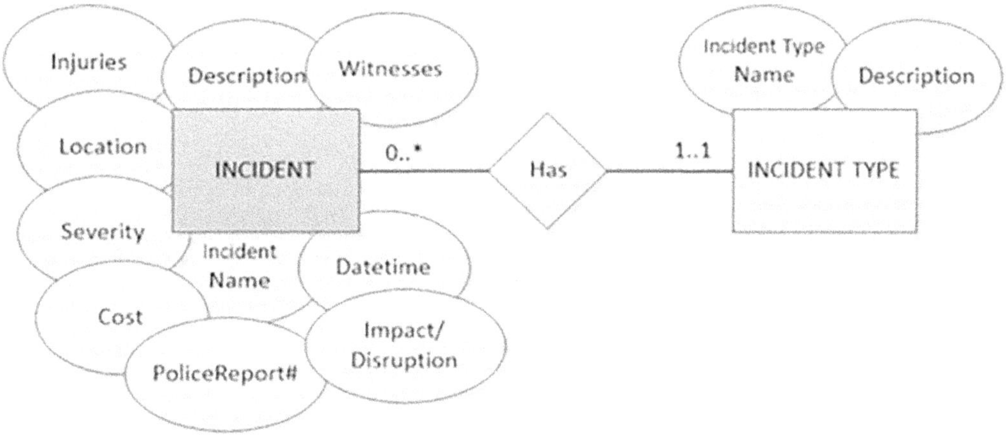

Figure 3.18: *Relationship* `INCIDENT : INCIDENT_TYPE`

The relationship between INCIDENT and INCIDENT_TYPE in Figure 3.18 is again complex as evidenced by the details included from brainstorming. The attributes of

'PoliceReport#', 'Witness', 'Impact/Disruption', 'Cost', and 'Severity' point to this object being significant.

Chances are high that a separate database focused solely on issues and incidents is in order as there may be a dozen or so entities required to handle all of these details. Perhaps, the definition of 'INCIDENT' is narrowed to be only those with scheduling staff or operating a vehicle during a trip, and everything else is beyond the scope of this database.

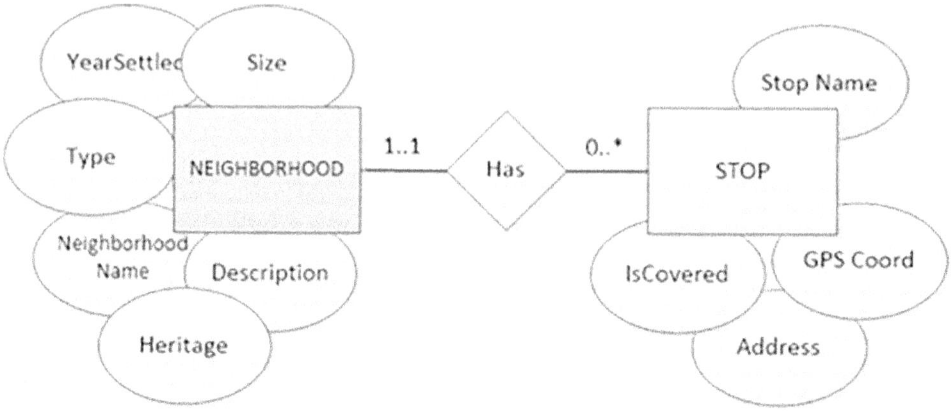

Figure 3.19: *Relationship* `NEIGHBORHOOD : STOP`

Next, we observe the relationship between NEIGHBORHOOD and STOP in Figure 3.19. We consider the values in our head, starting perhaps with a single familiar neighborhood name like the 'university district' or 'Capital Hill'. We recognize that a single neighborhood may have zero or many transit stops. The same stop is in one and only one neighborhood.

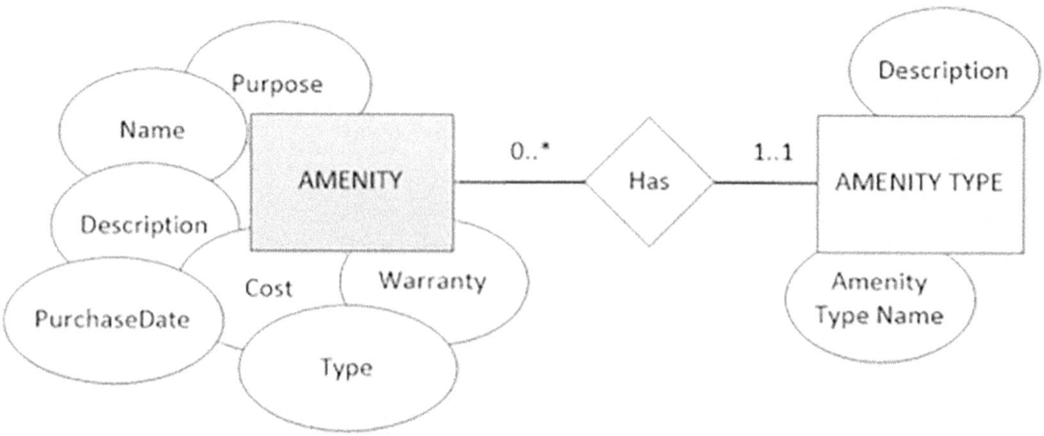

Figure 3.20: *Relationship* `AMENITY : AMENITY_TYPE`

Finally, we observe the relationship between AMENITY and AMENITY_TYPE in Figure 3.20. Follow the same process of listing the potential values of the type entity in our head, followed by questioning whether the business organization needs to capture multiple values for a single row in the base entity (in this case, AMENITY). There is a good chance we can keep this as a 1:M and move on.

The previous eight relationships probably each had a cardinality of 1:M and similar multiplicity, depending on our interpretation of business needs. We want to review the process by which we evaluate and label relationships (especially between a base table and a related type table). These tend to follow a similar pattern with a simple 1:M relationship in most cases. Be able to quickly see the relationship and know immediately how to construct the tables involved assigning the foreign key correctly.

Consolidate All Relationships into One Large Conceptual Diagram

When we consolidate relationships into a single, large diagram, it is important to review each entity and relationship to reaffirm each is contributing to the purpose of the application and database. It is never too late to drop or add entities based on a shift in priorities or market conditions. Let us see an example of dropping an entity or two.

In the `METRO_TRANSIT` database example, it makes sense to DROP the entity MAINTENANCE, as well as the M:M resolution entity `VEHICLE_MAINTENANCE` in the consolidated design to illustrate this point. In real life, there are many reasons to drop a previously selected and validated entity; redundant systems are one of the most common reasons to do so. Now, let us imagine that `VEHICLE_MAINTENANCE` is already being tracked in a database specifically tied to manufacturer's warranties and union payroll systems. For the sake of simplicity, it has been removed from the diagram.

As we will see, there are several M:M relationships that must be resolved with an associative entity. The M:M relationships are indicated in the consolidated conceptual diagram below with a YELLOW highlight as well as a designation of 'MANY' in the relationship diamond.

These include the following relationships:

- `ROUTE : STOP`
- `ROUTE : STATUS`
- `VEHICLE : ROUTE`
- `PASSENGER : VEHICLE : ROUTE : FARE`

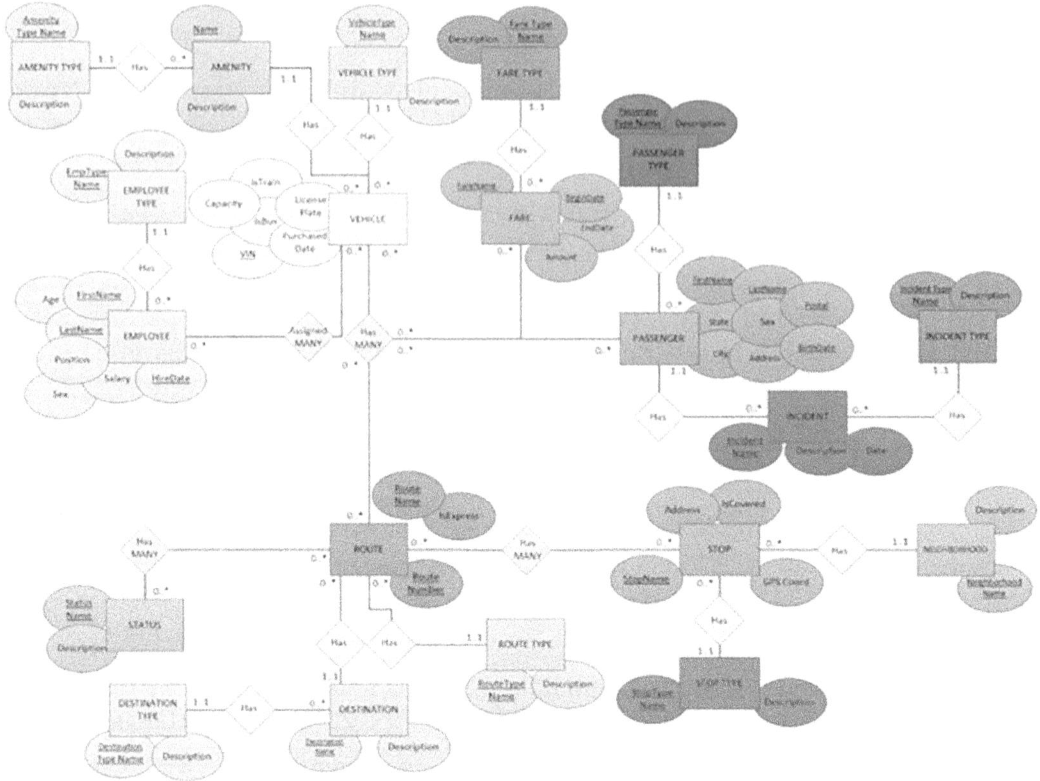

***Figure 3.21:** Consolidated conceptual diagram with four M:M relationships*

The next steps are to work closer with the M:M relationships that we have initially identified. We need to redefine and diagram these relationships and possibly rename them because relational theory does not allow us to code an M:M relationship inside a finished database.

Thus, in each case of a M:M relationship, we will create a new entity in between the entities participating in the relationship. We have created them in the following figure for TRIP, BOARDING, TRIP_STATUS and ROUTE_STOP:

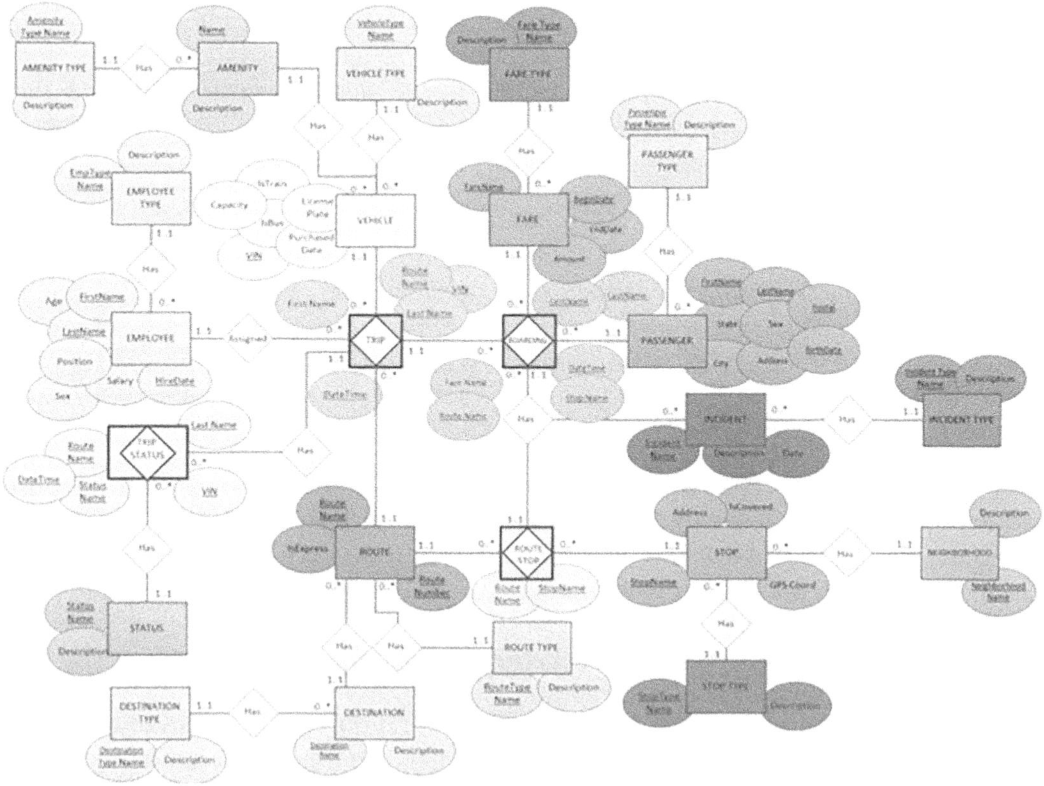

Figure 3.22: *Consolidated conceptual diagram with four associative entities*

Figure 3.22 is a great step towards building a relational database in Third Normal Form (3NF). There are four M:M relationships resolved with associative entities. These are given new names and placed in an entity with a diamond as follows:

- TRIP
- BOARDING
- TRIP_STATUS
- ROUTE_STOP

The TRIP seems like a decent name to record the occurrence of an EMPLOYEE, who is assigned to drive a VEHICLE on a specific ROUTE on a specific date and time.

Additionally, BOARDING is an accurate descriptive name for the resolution of the M:M relationships between PASSENGER, FARE, STOP and then ROUTE and VEHICLE (which has been renamed as TRIP). Hopefully, we can see how this consolidation was made.

Hence, both **TRIP_STATUS** and **ROUTE_STOP** have been created to resolve two simple M:M and are named literally.

While *Figure* 3.22 represents a significant amount of work, we must acknowledge there are several fundamental flaws in the current design. These flaws include some awkward primary keys for most entities, in addition to having several yes/no questions as columns.

Awkward Primary Keys

Many database designs have a collection of columns that are combined to create a primary key; this is known as a 'natural' key. As mentioned previously, this is fine for many database designs but creates some awkward situations in managing foreign keys (which we have learned are the primary keys of one entity that are placed in another entity to cement the relationship). To address this, let us first assign a surrogate primary key for each entity.

With surrogate keys, designers are better able to define relationships with other entities and bring over the primary key as a foreign key as warranted. For an example of a clogged mess for a primary key, look at the TRIP and BOARDING entities; these have four and five attributes respectively that have to be assembled just to find uniqueness.

Yes/No Questions as Column Names

Now, we might want to take the entities with 'yes/no questions' as column headers, and replace them with a TYPE table. When we remove the 'yes/no' columns, we reduce the burden on the base table to account for every possible 'type' value. In some cases, there could be a dozen potential 'yes/no' options to choose from, which means that 12 columns are required. Additionally, the query writing burden is significantly reduced as a query writer does not need to be aware of all permutations before writing any code.

Moreover, **`EMPLOYEE`** had an attribute of Position in *Figure* 3.22. Upon further evaluation, a single employee can have many positions during their career at **`METRO_TRANSIT`**. Also, the same position, such as 'Senior Coach Operator' may describe many employees, each with a different **`BeginDate`**, **`EndDate`**, and **`Salary`**.

Upon re-evaluation, this relationship is better defined as M:M and must be resolved with an associative entity. The new entity can be called **`EMPLOYEE_POSITION`** or perhaps JOB. For simplicity, it is probably easier to use JOB.

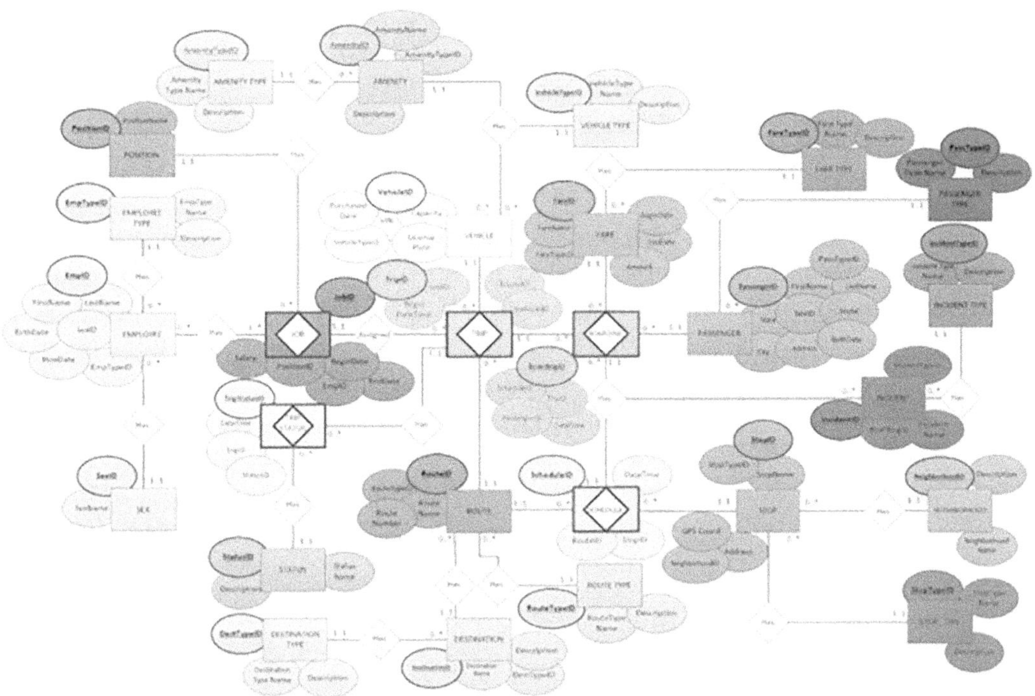

Figure 3.23: *Consolidated conceptual diagram with PK/FK and five associative entities*

In *Figure* 3.23, notice that each entity has a proper primary key (unique identifier). These are referred to as *surrogate* keys as they are not a direct part of the entity except to provide uniqueness. These are auto incremented in a sequential manner by the computer system, which eliminates the need for people to get involved in determining any values (imagine trying to find 'the next value' when there are millions of new records each day).

While there are arguments to find a combination of existing columns in a table to provide an enforceable uniqueness (and be used as a primary key), many experienced database designers advocate for using surrogate keys whenever possible.

Figure 3.23 also shows the evolution of the design to include foreign keys, as well as substituting out difficult columns, including those that ask 'yes/no' questions, and those with a fixed 'age' with a birthdate.

Another update here is that ROUTE_STOP had a composite primary key of RouteID and StopID, which has been changed to a surrogate key. Having a composite primary key is fine in most cases, however when BOARDING needs a foreign key value from ROUTE_STOP, it is a challenge to send two columns (since RouteID and StopID make up a single primary key) over as a foreign key. Thus, it is better to establish a single surrogate primary key of the newly re-named entity of SCHEDULE in order to manage the surrogate key ScheduleID as a foreign key in BOARDING.

Final Steps: Re-Evaluating Relationships Looking for M:M

Lastly, we will review all relationships now that a proper primary key has been assigned to each entity. Specifically, we are looking for entities that are M:M over a period that may not have been recognized yet. This is due to having re-defined four relationships already which may have unwittingly impacted other relationships.

Upon doing so, we will confer with our stakeholders to validate our interpretation and their urgency to capture outliers or other low-probability occurrences. We end up with the following relationships that are in fact M:M:

- `AMENITY : VEHICLE`
- `ROUTE : DESTINATION`
- `BOARDING : INCIDENT`

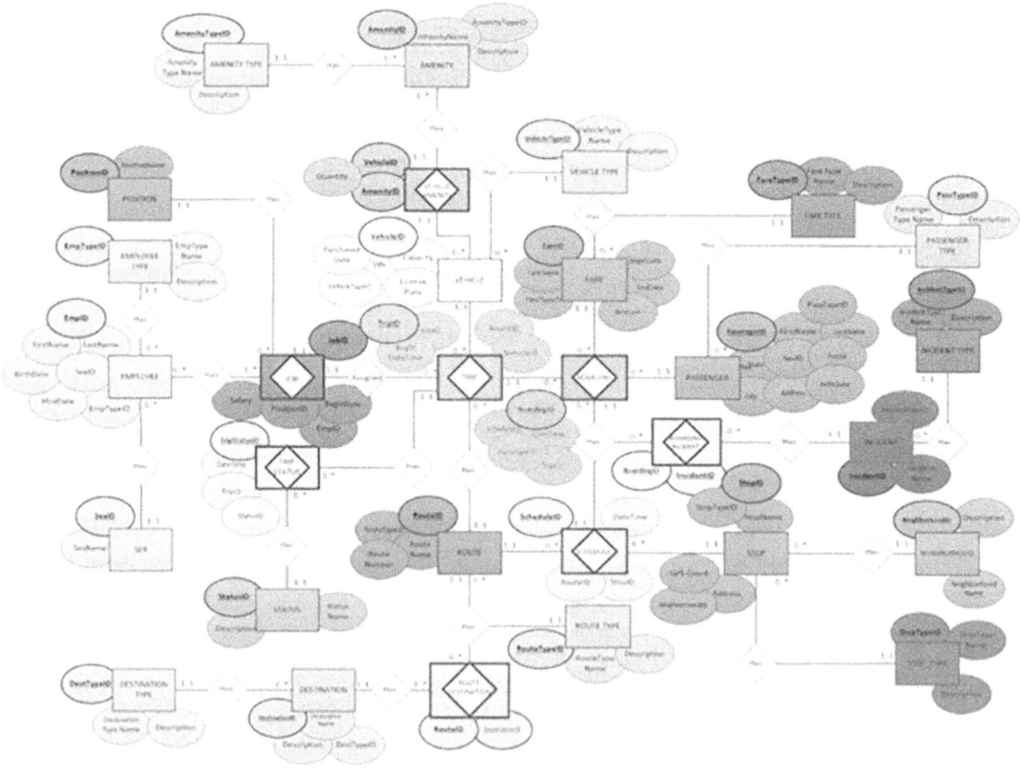

Figure 3.24: *Near final ERD with three additional M:M relationships resolved*

This latest rendering might be as accurate as it can be. It represents 'one-way' to get a decent data model without having to worry about the details of the normalization process. Before we meet for one final review with the business folks and primary stakeholders, we may want to at least understand the different normalization forms and defend many of our decisions. Additionally, if we have a better than average comprehension of the different forms, we may discover that some of our design logic is flawed or perhaps missing other attributes or even entities.

Quick Review of How We Got Here

Here is a brief summary of the steps we have seen in a standard process for building a data model:

- Conducting Research: This includes requirements of the company, industry best practices, seeking clarity in the problem space, interviewing stakeholders, and observing production operations.
- Validating findings and interpretations with project sponsors
- Conducting brainstorming with active participation from stakeholders
- Cleaning up brainstorming results in a filtered set of objects aligned as entities
- Further exploring potential characteristics or attributes relevant for each entity
- Defining relationships between the entities including cardinality and multiplicity
- Assigning surrogate primary key values for each entity (making 2NF)
- Resolving four many-to-many (M:M) relationships into several one-to-many (1:M)
- Reviewing priorities of data and determined that maintenance was outside the scope of the data needs and dropped the entity from the diagram
- Re-evaluating relationships and determining that there were a total of 8 M:M relationships that needed to be resolved instead of the four we thought (making 3NF) about
- Creating the consolidation diagram in Figure 3.24, which reflects the current state of the design using an exhaustive entity-by-entity approach

Database design can be complex and tedious, and is hence often beyond the interest and learning objectives of most people. Hang in there! One of the goals of this textbook is to prepare the readers with the skills to quickly construct a well-formed relational database.

The final touches of understanding data modeling are having basic comprehension of normalization. Normalization can be very complex and confusing; it seems that very few people can explain the detailed engineering or the calculations behind the decisions that are made during the normalization process. So far, we have explained a simpler approach that will enable readers to make better design choices without having to delve into the calculation aspect.

Conclusion

Data modeling is a refined skill that is instrumental for building robust relational transactional database systems. A well-defined model not only provides a repository of critical organizational data that is trustworthy, but which is readily available and secure. A well-designed database also allows organized learning via assembling a series of reports drawn from a database (we call this read activity) without intruding on or slowing down the process of creating or collecting new data (we call this write activity).

Ultimately, a database is intended to provide organizational learning that enhances the capabilities and competitive strength of an organization as it evolves. Proper analytics with truthful data allow for high-speed learning, which makes companies nimbler and responsive to customer and market demands. Their investments will gradually become deliberate and intentional as they envision long-term impact. Therefore, professionals and organizations who know how to design these structures are effectively independent and capable of conducting their own systems without relying on others for infrastructure or transactional data.

Going forward, we will delve into the specifics of the normalization process. This is a key component of building data layer structures which ensure that the data is secure, reliable, and trustworthy.

Post-Chapter Challenges

You can approach the following challenges based on what you have learned so far:

Track 1: Data Tourist Seeking Ancillary Awareness (THINK ~10 minutes)

Review the following questions to test your grasp of the concepts laid out in this chapter:

- How well did you grasp this initial exploration into data modeling concepts and processes now that you have seen a step-by-step review of a database build with method 1? What is not clear?
- If you have experience being a passenger on public transit systems, how close does the proposed data model in this chapter align with your understanding? What data might be missing?
- What other topics or business scenarios might you find interesting in creating a data model? This may include hobbies or interests you have currently or areas of your life that could benefit from a better analysis.

Track 2: Dedicated Student or Recent Graduate (WRITE ~ 45 minutes)

Respond to the following questions and state your reasons for the answers given:

- Reflect on misspellings in the spreadsheet of data in Figure 3.3; what are the challenges associated with allowing typos and abbreviations in any collection of data? How might it be best to eliminate or manage the typos and/or abbreviations out of any data set?
- Write down the basic core nouns for one of the following business topics:
    - A retail store that sells second-hand or used clothing.
    - A five-person operation that offers private and guided tours of a major city including historic landmarks, museums, and major scenic outlooks.
    - A house-repair contractor who has a seasonal team of six workers.

Track 3: Aspiring Professional (BUILD ~3 hours)

This track targets those readers who envision a career in data science:

- Let us find a topic or business scenario that is interesting to you; your challenge is to create a data model that is the same level and depth as the METRO_TRANSIT model presented in this chapter. Consider any aspect of your life for a repetitive process lacking clear data and explore it via a database.
- Start with raw brainstorming, clean it up as needed, and then finish this task by consolidating into a single, cohesive data model. The finished design should be similar to the examples provided in this chapter.

CHAPTER 4
Learning About Normalization

Introduction

In this chapter, we will go beyond effective data modeling to include a new perspective on the normalization process. Normalization can be overwrought with rules and formulas; hence, the goal in this chapter is to simplify this critical process and introduce a better method for designing effective data structures that can scale without the burden of having to learn arcane rules.

During this chapter, we will dwell on the horizontal design approach introduced in the previous chapter and reinforce the need to recognize relationship patterns. By the end of the chapter, readers will gain the insight and confidence to construct fully-normalized database structures quickly by using the standard practice elaborated here.

Structure

In this chapter, we will explore the following topics:

- Two Methods of Normalization Process
- Basics of Rules that Define a Relation
- Example Normalization from UNF to 4NF
- Common Database Design Patterns

A Closer Look at Normalization

It will be apt to envision that designing a data model resembles producing music; while there is the science of scales and key signatures behind every hit song, but many people with zero formal musical training can still recognize good music by ear. Most people can recognize dissonant notes because they are jarring. Similarly, during the normalization process, we can easily see columns that are misplaced while viewing a model.

The purpose of normalization is to construct a repository that not only holds the data necessary for an organization to capture and analyze ("learn"), but also to do so while keeping the data pristine and trustworthy. Thus, constructing an effective data model from knowledge requires more than a passing awareness of the normalization process. It is imperative that professionals recognize poor database designs on-site and also be aware of the common mistakes in many flawed databases. If a database is not fully normalized, there are several complications that arise and lead to poor performance and inconsistent data.

Two Methods of Conducting Normalization Process

While the science behind a 'well-designed' database seems complicated and theoretical, it is far from how the best designers think. Professionals usually advocate for a more intuitive approach as compared to a highly calculative one.

Therefore, the two methods of normalization referred to in this textbook are as follows:

- Relational Calculus (calculative)
- Ironing (intuitive)

Ironing resembles the adage of "ironing out the wrinkles" and tweaking a design where columns approved during brainstorming are temporarily located in the wrong entity. This ironing process is the preferred method for many data science students when creating original structures. This method will be explained shortly as a step-by-step process while designing the **`METRO_TRANSIT`** database.

Method 1: Relational Calculus

Now, let us get into the specific definitions of the different normal forms and corresponding examples. However, we must start with defining a *relation*. In relational theory, a relation is defined as a collection of values that have the same characteristics. We have several names for a relation, such as entity or a table. You can have a look at the table here to know more:

Phase	Name for the Data Collection	Name for an Element of a Collection	Name for a Single Instance of Values
Conceptual	Relation	Field	Record
Logical	Entity	Attribute	Tuple

Physical	Table	Column	Row

***Table 4.1**: Labels used for the names of objects based on the design phase*

While many professionals might be confused about the names of objects in the list above, it is important for all technicians to be aware of the formal names for each object and when to refer to them. Most developers will refer to objects by the name associated with them during the physical design phase.

Basic Rules for Normalization

However, before acquainting ourselves with the various normal forms, we must address the following violations that prevent the establishment of a relation (also known as a '`table`'):

Violation	**Description**
Non-Unique Relation Name	The name of the relation must be unique within the database.
Non-Unique attribute Name	Each attribute must have a unique name within a relation.
Non-Unique Row	Each row must be unique within a relation (we solve this with primary key).
Multi-Valued Attribute	Each cell of an attribute can contain only a single value.
Inconsistent Domain Value	Each attribute must have a single data type and a range of values.
Row-Dependency	The order of rows shall not matter (unlike when people make lists).

***Table 4.2**: Violations that can cause a design to be labeled as Unnormalized Form (UNF)*

Unnormalized Form (UNF)

Unnormalized form is the state of an entire relational database when the definition of a relation faces any violation. It can also be said that if any object in the database that will hopefully become a table has any violations from *Table* 4.2, the entire database will be termed as UNF.

Let us see an example of UNF with sample data in a spreadsheet/table from **`METRO_TRANSIT`**; this example has many issues that violate the definition of a relation, as shown here:

DateTime	Passenger	RouteNumber/Name	Type	Driver	StopName	Type	Destination	Type	Fare	Neighborhood
2/13/2025 7:36:00 AM (delayed)	Ivey Hazekamp	32 Capitol Hill-Downtown	Regular	Jimi Hendrix, 206555-7661	Broadway Ave Cherry St	Covered	Convention Center	Articulated	$ 4.50	Capitol Hill
2/13/2025 9:36	Darcel Eustache	78 Fremont-Waterfront-Downtown	Special	Meryl Streep	Hwy 99-N 36th	Covered	Fremont, Space Needle, P70	Extra-long	$ 2.75	Fremont
2/14/2025 6:36		78 Fremont-Waterfront-Downtown	XP	Bruce Lee	Elliott Avenue and Mercer St	Covered	Downtown	Extra-long	$ 2.75	Interbay
2/16/2025 6:32	Kenyetta Terron	42 Sodo-Downtown Express	Express	Meryl Streep	First Avenue and Terry Street	Covered	Fremont, Space Needle, P70	Doub	$ 2.75	SODO
2/19/2025 15:39	Kenny Terron	42 - E Sodo-Downtown Express	Espress	Bruce Lee	First Avenue and Terry Street	Uncovered	SoDo, DT	Doubled	$ 4.50	South Downtown
2/21/2025 6:13	Darcel Eustache	78-S Fremont-Waterfront-Downtown	Special	Jimmy Hendricks, 206 5557661	Elliott Avenue and Mercer St	Cvd	Fremont, Space Needle, P70	Extra-long	$ 2.75	Interbay
2/21/2025 6:13	Darcel Eustache	78-S Fremont-Waterfront-Downtown	Special	Jimmy Hendricks, 206 5557661	Elliott Avenue and Mercer St	Cvd	Fremont, Space Needle, P70	Extra-long	$ 2.75	Interbay
2/21/2025 7:36	Kenyetta Terron	Sodo Downtown Express	Express	Bruce Lee	First Avenue and Terry Street	UC	Downtown	Doubled	$ 4.50	South Downtown
2/22/2025 8:32	Ivey Hazekamp	32 Capitol Hill-Downtown	Regular	Jim Morrison	Broadway Ave and Cherry St	Covered	CCntr.	Articulated	$ 4.50	Capital Hill
3/1/2025 6:33			Regular	Bruce Lee, 425 6109225	Broadway Ave and Cherry St	Covered	Downtown	Articulated	$ 4.50	Capitol Hill
3/1/2025 6:36:00 AM (Blocked)			Regular	Mary Streep (mstre@mtransit.org)	Broadway Ave and Cherry St	Covered	Downtown	Articulated	$ 4.50	Capitol Hill
3/3/2025 6:42	Darcel Eustache	78 Fremont-Downtown Commuter	Commute	Jim Morrison	Sixth Avenue and Battery	Regular	Fremont, Space Needle, P70	Doubled	$ 4.50	Downtown
3/6/2025 6:32			XP	Meryl Streep	Elliott Avenue and Mercer St	Covered	Downtown	Extra-long	$ 2.75	Interbay
3/9/2025 7:52	Kenyetta Terron	42 Sodo-Downtown Express	Express	Jimi Hendrix	First Avenue and Terry Street	UC	Downtown	Doubled	$ 4.50	South Downtown
3/10/2025 6:33	Darcel Eustache	78 Fremont-Downtown Commuter	Commute	jim	Elliott Avenue and Mercer St	Covered	Downtown	Extra-long	$ 2.75	Interbay
3/11/2025 6:32	Kenyetta Terron	Sodo-Downtown Express	Express	Bruce Lee; blee@metrotran.org	First Avenue and Terry Street	Uncovered	Downtown	Doubled	$ 4.50	South Downtown
3/13/2025 8:32:00 AM (Late)	Ivey Hazekamp	32 Capitol Hill-Downtown	Regular	Bruce Lee	Broadway Ave and Cherry St	Covered	Convention Center	Articulated	$ 4.50	Capitol Hill
3/14/2025 6:32			Express	Bruce Lee	Broadway Ave and Cherry St	Covered	Downtown	Articulated	$ 4.50	C Hill
3/15/2025 1:36	Janey Lundgren	32 Capitol Hill-Downtown	Reg	Jimmy Hendricks	Broadway Ave and Cherry St	Covered	Convention Center	2 Decks	$ 2.75	Capitol Hill
3/16/2025 6:32	Darcel Eustache	78 Fremont-Waterfront-Downtown	Commute	Jim Morrison	Sixth Ave and Battery Street	Regular	Fremont, Space Needle	Doubled	$ 4.50	Downtown
3/17/2025 11:33	Ivey Hazekamp	32 Capitol Hill-Downtown	Regular	Jimi Hendrix	Fourth Avenue and Seneca	Covered	Capitol Hill	Doubled	$ 2.75	Downtown
3/18/2025 16:13	Jane Lundgran	32 Capitol Hill-Downtown	Reg	Meryl Streep	Fourth Avenue and Seneca St	Covered	CH	2 Decks	$ 2.75	DT
3/19/2025 6:32	Janey Lundgren	32 Capitol Hill-Downtown	Reg	Meryl Streep	Broadway and Cherry St	Covered	Downtown	2 Decks	$ 2.75	Capitol Hill
3/21/2025 6:32	Darcel Eustache	78 Fremont-Waterfront-Downtown	Commute	Meryl Streep	Sixth Avenue and Battery	Regular	Fremont, Space Needle, P70	Doubled	$ 4.50	Downtown
3/26/2025 9:04	Jame Lundgren	32 Capitol Hill-Downtown	Regular	Jimmy Hendricks, 206 5557661	Broadway and Cherry St	Covered	Downtown	2 Decks	$ 2.75	CHill
4/18/2025 5:23	Darcie Eustache	78 Fremont-Waterfront-Downtown	Commute	Jimi Hendrix	Fourth Avenue and Seneca	Regular	Fremont, Pier 70, Needle	Doubled	$ 4.50	Downtown

Figure 4.1: *Example of data on `METRO_TRANSIT` tracking* BOARDINGS *in* UNF

The data in *Figure 4.1* shows how a person might track **`METRO_TRANSIT`** in a spreadsheet; this is considered an UNF for reasons that are explained further in this chapter. While this is a very common method of organizing data, it is highly flawed.

Many people will try to capture data in the form of how they will be reading it. While this reflects the human zeal for organizing or categorizing objects, the design and structure of storing data (on disk or in the cloud) is different from how it will be read by people.

Violation of Relation #1: Non-Unique Relation/Entity Name

For the first violation, having two relations ('tables') with the same name is like having duplicate files in the same folder on a computer. Thus, designers have to ensure that each entity must be uniquely named to be coded into a relational database management system.

Violation of Relation #2: Non-Unique Attribute Name

DateTime	Passenger	RouteNumber/Name	Type	Driver	StopName	Type	Destination	Type	Fare	Neighborhood
2/13/2025 7:36:00 AM (delayed)	Ivey Hazekamp	32 Capitol Hill-Downtown	Regular	Jimi Hendrix, 206555-7861	Broadway Ave Cherry St	Covered	Convention Center	Articulated	$ 4.50	Capitol Hill
2/13/2025 9:36	Darcel Eustache	78 Fremont-Waterfront-Downtown	Special	Meryl Streep	Hwy 99-N 36th	Covered	Fremont, Space Needle, P70	Extra-long	$ 2.75	Fremont
2/14/2025 6:36		78 Fremont-Waterfront-Downtown	XP	Bruce Lee	Elliott Avenue and Mercer St	Covered	Downtown	Extra-long	$ 2.75	Interbay
2/16/2025 6:32	Kenyetta Terron	42 Sodo-Downtown Express	Express	Meryl Streep	First Avenue and Terry Street	Covered	Fremont, Space Needle, P70	Doub	$ 2.75	SODO
2/19/2025 15:39	Kenny Terron	42 - E Sodo-Downtown Express	Espress	Bruce Lee	First Avenue and Terry Street	Uncovered	SoDo, DT	Doubled	$ 4.50	South Downtown
2/21/2025 6:13	Darcel Eustache	78-S Fremont-Waterfront-Downtown	Special	Jimmy Hendricks, 206 5557661	Elliott Avenue and Mercer St	Cvd	Fremont, Space Needle, P70	Extra-long	$ 2.75	Interbay
2/21/2025 6:13	Darcel Eustache	78-S Fremont-Waterfront-Downtown	Special	Jimmy Hendricks, 206 5557661	Elliott Avenue and Mercer St	Cvd	Fremont, Space Needle, P70	Extra-long	$ 2.75	Interbay
2/21/2025 7:36	Kenyetta Terron	Sodo-Downtown Express	Express	Bruce Lee	First Avenue and Terry Street	UC	Downtown	Doubled	$ 4.50	South Downtown
2/22/2025 8:32	Ivey Hazekamp	32 Capitol Hill-Downtown	Regular	Jim Morrison	Broadway Ave and Cherry St	Covered	CCntr.	Articulated	$ 4.50	Capital Hill
3/1/2025 6:33			Regular	Bruce Lee, 425 6109225	Broadway Ave and Cherry St	Covered	Downtown	Articulated	$ 4.50	Capitol Hill
3/1/2025 6:36:00 AM (Blocked)			Regular	Mary Streep (mstre@mtransit.org)	Broadway Ave and Cherry St	Covered	Downtown	Articulated	$ 4.50	Capitol Hill
3/3/2025 6:42	Darcel Eustache	78 Fremont-Downtown Commuter	Commute	Jim Morrison	Sixth Avenue and Battery	Regular	Fremont, Space Needle, P70	Doubled	$ 4.50	Downtown
3/5/2025 6:32			XP	Meryl Streep	Elliott Avenue and Mercer St	Covered	Downtown	Extra-long	$ 2.75	Interbay
3/9/2025 7:52	Kenyetta Terron	42 Sodo-Downtown Express	Express	Jimi Hendrix	First Avenue and Terry Street	UC	Downtown	Doubled	$ 4.50	South Downtown
3/10/2025 6:33	Darcel Eustache	78 Fremont-Downtown Commuter	Commute	jim	Elliott Avenue and Mercer St	Covered	Downtown	Extra-long	$ 2.75	Interbay
3/11/2025 6:32	Kenyetta Terron	Sodo-Downtown Express	Express	Bruce Lee; blee@metrotran.org	First Avenue and Terry Street	Uncovered	Downtown	Doubled	$ 4.50	South Downtown
3/13/2025 8:32:00 AM (Late)	Ivey Hazekamp	32 Capitol Hill-Downtown	Regular	Bruce Lee	Broadway Ave and Cherry St	Covered	Convention Center	Articulated	$ 4.50	Capitol Hill
3/14/2025 6:32			Express	Bruce Lee	Broadway Ave and Cherry St	Covered	Downtown	Articulated	$ 4.50	C Hill
3/15/2025 1:36	Janey Lundgren	32 Capitol Hill-Downtown	Reg	Jimmy Hendricks	Broadway Ave and Cherry St	Covered	Convention Center	2 Decks	$ 2.75	Capitol Hill
3/16/2025 6:32	Darcel Eustache	78 Fremont-Waterfront-Downtown	Commute	Jim Morrison	Sixth Ave and Battery Street	Regular	Fremont, Space Needle	Doubled	$ 4.50	Downtown
3/17/2025 11:33	Ivey Hazekamp	32 Capitol Hill-Downtown	Regular	Jimi Hendrix	Fourth Avenue and Seneca	Covered	Capitol Hill	Doubled	$ 2.75	Downtown
3/18/2025 16:13	Jane Lundgran	32 Capitol Hill-Downtown	Reg	Meryl Streep	Fourth Avenue and Seneca St	Covered	CH	2 Decks	$ 2.75	DT
3/19/2025 6:32	Janey Lundgren	32 Capitol Hill-Downtown	Reg	Meryl Streep	Broadway and Cherry St	Covered	Downtown	2 Decks	$ 2.75	Capitol Hill
3/21/2025 6:32	Darcel Eustache	78 Fremont-Waterfront-Downtown	Commute	Meryl Streep	Sixth Avenue and Battery	Regular	Fremont, Space Needle, P70	Doubled	$ 4.50	Downtown
3/26/2025 9:04	Janie Lundgren	32 Capitol Hill-Downtown	Regular	Jimmy Hendricks, 206 5557861	Broadway and Cherry St	Covered	Downtown	2 Decks	$ 2.75	CHill
4/18/2025 5:23	Darcie Eustache	78 Fremont-Waterfront-Downtown	Commute	Jimi Hendrix	Fourth Avenue and Seneca	Regular	Fremont, Pier 70, Needle	Doubled	$ 4.50	Downtown

Figure 4.2: *Example violation of a relation with non-unique attributes in a spreadsheet*

In *Figure* 4.2, observe how there are three different columns with an identical name of **`TYPE`**; it appears that these are intended to track types for **`ROUTE`**, **`STOP`**, and **`DESTINATION`**. A relational database management system will not admit these duplications as it is a violation.

While a human might be able to decipher this flaw in labeling manually, a database management system on the other hand will interpret labels in a literal fashion, and will not be able to discern the subtle difference shown in *Figure* 4.2.

Violation of Relation #3: Non-Unique Row

DateTime	Passenger	RouteNumber/Name	Type	Driver	StopName	Type	Destination	Type	Fare	Neighborhood
2/13/2025 7:38:00 AM (delayed)	Ivey Hazekamp	32 Capitol Hill-Downtown	Regular	Jimi Hendrix, 206555-7661	Broadway Ave Cherry St	Covered	Convention Center	Articulated	$ 4.50	Capitol Hill
2/13/2025 9:36	Darcel Eustache	78 Fremont-Waterfront-Downtown	Special	Meryl Streep	Hwy 99-N 36th	Covered	Fremont, Space Needle, P70	Extra-long	$ 2.75	Fremont
2/14/2025 6:36		78 Fremont-Waterfront-Downtown	XP	Bruce Lee	Elliott Avenue and Mercer St	Covered	Downtown	Extra-long	$ 2.75	Interbay
2/16/2025 6:32	Kenyetta Terron	42 Sodo-Downtown Express	Express	Meryl Streep	First Avenue and Terry Street	Covered	Fremont, Space Needle, P70	Doub	$ 2.75	SODO
2/19/2025 15:39	Kenny Terron	42 - E Sodo-Downtown Express	Espress	Bruce Lee	First Avenue and Terry Street	Uncovered	SoDo, DT	Doubled	$ 4.50	South Downtown
2/21/2025 6:13	Darcel Eustache	78-S Fremont-Waterfront-Downtown	Special	Jimmy Hendricks, 206 5557661	Elliott Avenue and Mercer St	Cvd	Fremont, Space Needle, P70	Extra-long	$ 2.75	Interbay
2/21/2025 6:13	Darcel Eustache	78-S Fremont-Waterfront-Downtown	Special	Jimmy Hendricks, 206 5557661	Elliott Avenue and Mercer St	Cvd	Fremont, Space Needle, P70	Extra-long	$ 2.75	Interbay
2/21/2025 7:36	Kenyetta Terron	Sodo-Downtown Express	Express	Bruce Lee	First Avenue and Terry Street	UC	Downtown	Doubled	$ 4.50	South Downtown
2/22/2025 8:32	Ivey Hazekamp	32 Capitol Hill-Downtown	Regular	Jim Morrison	Broadway Ave and Cherry St	Covered	CCntr,	Articulated	$ 4.50	Capital Hill
3/1/2025 6:33			Regular	Bruce Lee, 425 6109225	Broadway Ave and Cherry St	Covered	Downtown	Articulated	$ 4.50	Capitol Hill
3/1/2025 6:36:00 AM (Blocked)			Regular	Mary Streep (mstre@mtransit.org)	Broadway Ave and Cherry St	Covered	Downtown	Articulated	$ 4.50	Capitol Hill
3/3/2025 6:42	Darcel Eustache	78 Fremont-Downtown Commuter	Commute	Jim Morrison	Sixth Avenue and Battery	Regular	Fremont, Space Needle, P70	Doubled	$ 4.50	Downtown
3/5/2025 6:32			XP	Meryl Streep	Elliott Avenue and Mercer St	Covered	Downtown	Extra-long	$ 2.75	Interbay
3/9/2025 7:52	Kenyetta Terron	42 Sodo-Downtown Express	Express	Jimi Hendrix	First Avenue and Terry Street	UC	Downtown	Doubled	$ 4.50	South Downtown
3/10/2025 6:33	Darcel Eustache	78 Fremont-Downtown Commuter	Commute	jim	Elliott Avenue and Mercer St	Covered	Downtown	Extra-long	$ 2.75	Interbay
3/11/2025 6:32	Kenyetta Terron	Sodo-Downtown Express	Express	Bruce Lee; blee@metrotran.org	First Avenue and Terry Street	Uncovered	Downtown	Doubled	$ 4.50	South Downtown
3/13/2025 8:32:00 AM (Late)	Ivey Hazekamp	32 Capitol Hill-Downtown	Regular	Bruce Lee	Broadway Ave and Cherry St	Covered	Convention Center	Articulated	$ 4.50	Capitol Hill
3/14/2025 6:32			Express	Bruce Lee	Broadway Ave and Cherry St	Covered	Downtown	Articulated	$ 4.50	C Hill
3/15/2025 1:38	Janey Lundgren	32 Capitol Hill-Downtown	Reg	Jimmy Hendricks	Broadway Ave and Cherry St	Covered	Convention Center	2 Decks	$ 2.75	Capitol Hill
3/16/2025 6:32	Darcel Eustache	78 Fremont-Waterfront-Downtown	Commute	Jim Morrison	Sixth Ave and Battery Street	Regular	Fremont, Space Needle	Doubled	$ 4.50	Downtown
3/17/2025 11:33	Ivey Hazekamp	32 Capitol Hill-Downtown	Regular	Jimi Hendrix	Fourth Avenue and Seneca	Covered	Capitol Hill	Doubled	$ 2.75	Downtown
3/18/2025 16:13	Jane Lundgran	32 Capitol Hill-Downtown	Reg	Meryl Streep	Fourth Avenue and Seneca St	Covered	CH	2 Decks	$ 2.75	DT
3/19/2025 6:32	Janey Lundgren	32 Capitol Hill-Downtown	Reg	Meryl Streep	Broadway and Cherry St	Covered	Downtown	2 Decks	$ 2.75	Capitol Hill
3/21/2025 6:32	Darcel Eustache	78 Fremont-Waterfront-Downtown	Commute	Meryl Streep	Sixth Avenue and Battery	Regular	Fremont, Space Needle, P70	Doubled	$ 4.50	Downtown
3/26/2025 9:04	Janie Lundgren	32 Capitol Hill-Downtown	Regular	Jimmy Hendricks, 206 5557661	Broadway and Cherry St	Covered	Downtown	2 Decks	$ 2.75	CHill
4/18/2025 5:23	Darcie Eustache	78 Fremont-Waterfront-Downtown	Commute	Jimi Hendrix	Fourth Avenue and Seneca	Regular	Fremont, Pier 70, Needle	Doubled	$ 4.50	Downtown

***Figure 4.3:** Example violation of a relation with non-unique rows*

The second example of a violation that causes a database relation to be labeled as UNF is having duplicate rows in a single relation. In *Figure 4.3*, there are two identical rows highlighted in yellow. While these can be assumed to be erroneous, they can be recorded in a spreadsheet because it does not reject duplicate rows by default. This is a violation as it would be impossible to determine which row is being queried or referenced in a relational database.

A relational database management system prevents duplicates because at least one column (the primary key) is guaranteed to be unique. The data shown in *Figure 4.3* is by definition UNF because there are two or more rows that are duplicated and cannot be uniquely identified.

Violation of Relation #4: Multi-Valued Attribute

Here, we will see an example that shows a common violation of a relation with multiple values in a single cell. Note that this error resembles violation #5. However, it is different.

DateTime	Passenger	RouteNumber/Name	Type	Driver	StopName	Type	Destination	Type	Fare	Neighborhood
2/13/2025 7:36:00 AM (delayed)	Ivey Hazekamp	32 Capitol Hill-Downtown	Regular	Jimi Hendrix, 206555-7681	Broadway Ave Cherry St	Covered	Convention Center	Articulated	$ 4.50	Capitol Hill
2/13/2025 9:36	Darcel Eustache	78 Fremont-Waterfront-Downtown	Special	Meryl Streep	Hwy 99-N 36th	Covered	Fremont, Space Needle, P70	Extra-long	$ 2.75	Fremont
2/14/2025 6:36		78 Fremont-Waterfront-Downtown	XP	Bruce Lee	Elliott Avenue and Mercer St	Covered	Downtown	Extra-long	$ 2.75	Interbay
2/16/2025 6:32	Kenyetta Terron	42 Sodo-Downtown Express	Express	Meryl Streep	First Avenue and Terry Street	Covered	Fremont, Space Needle, P70	Doub	$ 2.75	SODO
2/19/2025 16:30	Kenny Terron	42 - E Sodo-Downtown Express	Espress	Bruce Lee	First Avenue and Terry Street	Uncovered	SoDo, DT	Doubled	$ 4.50	South Downtown
2/21/2025 6:13	Darcel Eustache	78-S Fremont-Waterfront-Downtown	Special	Jimmy Hendricks, 206 5557661	Elliott Avenue and Mercer St	Cvd	Fremont, Space Needle, P70	Extra-long	$ 2.75	Interbay
2/21/2025 6:13	Darcel Eustache	78-S Fremont-Waterfront-Downtown	Special	Jimmy Hendricks, 206 5557661	Elliott Avenue and Mercer St	Cvd	Fremont, Space Needle, P70	Extra-long	$ 2.75	Interbay
2/21/2025 7:36	Kenyetta Terron	Sodo-Downtown Express	Express	Bruce Lee	First Avenue and Terry Street	UC	Downtown	Doubled	$ 4.50	South Downtown
2/22/2025 8:32	Ivey Hazekamp	32 Capitol Hill-Downtown	Regular	Jim Morrison	Broadway Ave and Cherry St	Covered	CCntr.	Articulated	$ 4.50	Capital Hill
3/1/2025 6:33			Regular	Bruce Lee, 425-6109225	Broadway Ave and Cherry St	Covered	Downtown	Articulated	$ 4.50	Capitol Hill
3/1/2025 6:36:00 AM (Blocked)			Regular	Mary Streep (mstre@mtransit.org)	Broadway Ave and Cherry St	Covered	Downtown	Articulated	$ 4.50	Capitol Hill
3/3/2025 6:42	Darcel Eustache	78 Fremont-Downtown Commuter	Commute	Jim Morrison	Sixth Avenue and Battery	Regular	Fremont, Space Needle, P70	Doubled	$ 4.50	Downtown
3/5/2025 6:32			XP	Meryl Streep	Elliott Avenue and Mercer St	Covered	Downtown	Extra-long	$ 2.75	Interbay
3/9/2025 7:52	Kenyetta Terron	42 Sodo-Downtown Express	Express	Jimi Hendrix	First Avenue and Terry Street	UC	Downtown	Doubled	$ 4.50	South Downtown
3/10/2025 6:33	Darcel Eustache	78 Fremont-Downtown Commuter	Commute	Jim	Elliott Avenue and Mercer St	Covered	Downtown	Extra-long	$ 2.75	Interbay
3/11/2025 6:32	Kenyetta Terron	Sodo-Downtown Express	Express	Bruce Lee; blee@metrotran.org	First Avenue and Terry Street	Uncovered	Downtown	Doubled	$ 4.50	South Downtown
3/13/2025 8:32:00 AM (Late)	Ivey Hazekamp	32 Capitol Hill-Downtown	Regular	Bruce Lee	Broadway Ave and Cherry St	Covered	Convention Center	Articulated	$ 4.50	Capitol Hill
3/14/2025 6:32			Express	Bruce Lee	Broadway Ave and Cherry St	Covered	Downtown	Articulated	$ 4.50	C Hill
3/15/2025 1:36	Janey Lundgren	32 Capitol Hill-Downtown	Reg	Jimmy Hendricks	Broadway Ave and Cherry St	Covered	Convention Center	2 Decks	$ 2.75	Capitol Hill
3/16/2025 6:32	Darcel Eustache	78 Fremont-Waterfront-Downtown	Commute	Jim Morrison	Sixth Ave and Battery Street	Regular	Fremont, Space Needle	Doubled	$ 4.50	Downtown
3/17/2025 11:33	Ivey Hazekamp	32 Capitol Hill-Downtown	Regular	Jimi Hendrix	Fourth Avenue and Seneca	Covered	Capitol Hill	Doubled	$ 2.75	Downtown
3/18/2025 16:13	Jane Lundgran	32 Capitol Hill-Downtown	Reg	Meryl Streep	Fourth Avenue and Seneca St	Covered	CH	2 Decks	$ 2.75	DT
3/19/2025 6:32	Janey Lundgren	32 Capitol Hill-Downtown	Reg	Meryl Streep	Broadway and Cherry St	Covered	Downtown	2 Decks	$ 2.75	Capitol Hill
3/21/2025 6:32	Darcel Eustache	78 Fremont-Waterfront-Downtown	Commute	Meryl Streep	Sixth Avenue and Battery	Regular	Fremont, Space Needle, P70	Doubled	$ 4.50	Downtown
3/26/2025 9:04	Janie Lundgren	32 Capitol Hill-Downtown	Regular	Jimmy Hendricks, 206 5557661	Broadway and Cherry St	Covered	Downtown	2 Decks	$ 2.75	CHill
4/18/2025 5:23	Darcie Eustache	78 Fremont-Waterfront-Downtown	Commute	Jimi Hendrix	Fourth Avenue and Seneca	Regular	Fremont, Pier 70, Needle	Doubled	$ 4.50	Downtown

Figure 4.4: *Example violation of a relation with multi-valued attributes*

The fourth violation for avoiding UNF is known as a multi-valued attribute. In *Figure* 4.4, the highlighted data represents multiple destinations listed in a single cell. For instance, in the yellow highlighted cells, there are multiple values in each cell, with **`DateTime`** (column 1) having descriptions of status as well as date and time data.

The column of **`RouteNumber/Name`** (column 3) not only has multiple values in a single cell, it also has multiple bits of different data (**`RouteNumber`** like '32', as well as the Name of the Route, 'Capital Hill-Downtown'. Driver (column 5) has multiple values that are also of different ranges, with names and contact information).

Please note these examples are of two different violations which are:

- Multiple values in any cell
- Having different types/ranges of data in the same column

Additional violations of having multiple values in a single cell that are highlighted in yellow in *Figure* 4.4 include **`DESTINATION`**.

While people can read these values and deduce that there are two or three distinct values in a single cell, a database management system is going to read this as a single value that has a few more characters in its name. You may notice multiple typos and misspellings; creating additional entities to manage these values will go a long way towards preventing alternate spellings of all values.

Objects that have multiple values per relationship are very common in life and we need to accommodate them in our database designs. These are almost always a 'many-to-many' relationship and the best solution is creating two new entities, one for the column that has multiple values and a second for the associative entity between these two entities.

Violation of Relation #5: Inconsistent Domain Value Range

DateTime	Passenger	RouteNumber/Name	Type	Driver	StopName	Type	Destination	Type	Fare	Neighborhood
2/13/2025 7:36:00 AM (delayed)	Ivey Hazekamp	32 Capitol Hill-Downtown	Regular	Jimi Hendrix, 206555-7661	Broadway Ave Cherry St	Covered	Convention Center	Articulated	$ 4.50	Capitol Hill
2/13/2025 9:36	Darcel Eustache	78 Fremont-Waterfront-Downtown	Special	Meryl Streep	Hwy 99 N 36th	Covered	Fremont, Space Needle, P70	Extra-long	$ 2.75	Fremont
2/14/2025 6:36		78 Fremont-Waterfront-Downtown	XP	Bruce Lee	Elliott Avenue and Mercer St	Covered	Downtown	Extra-long	$ 2.75	Interbay
2/16/2025 6:32	Kenyetta Terron	42 Sodo-Downtown Express	Express	Meryl Streep	First Avenue and Terry Street	Covered	Fremont, Space Needle, P70	Doub	$ 2.75	SODO
2/19/2025 15:39	Kenny Terron	42 E Sodo-Downtown Express	Espress	Bruce Lee	First Avenue and Terry Street	Uncovered	SoDo, DT	Doubled	$ 4.50	South Downtown
2/21/2025 6:13	Darcel Eustache	78 S Fremont-Waterfront-Downtown	Special	Jimmy Hendricks, 206 5557661	Elliott Avenue and Mercer St	Cvd	Fremont, Space Needle, P70	Extra-long	$ 2.75	Interbay
2/21/2025 6:13	Darcel Eustache	78-S Fremont-Waterfront-Downtown	Special	Jimmy Hendricks, 206 5557661	Elliott Avenue and Mercer St	Cvd	Fremont, Space Needle, P70	Extra-long	$ 2.75	Interbay
2/21/2025 7:36	Kenyetta Terron	Sodo-Downtown Express	Express	Bruce Lee	First Avenue and Terry Street	UC	Downtown	Doubled	$ 4.50	South Downtown
2/22/2025 8:32	Ivey Hazekamp	32 Capitol Hill-Downtown	Regular	Jim Morrison	Broadway Ave and Cherry St	Covered	CCntr.	Articulated	$ 4.50	Capital Hill
3/1/2025 6:33			Regular	Bruce Lee, 425 6109225	Broadway Ave and Cherry St	Covered	Downtown	Articulated	$ 4.50	Capitol Hill
3/1/2025 6:36:00 AM (Blocked)			Regular	Mary Streep (mstre@mtransit.org)	Broadway Ave and Cherry St	Covered	Downtown	Articulated	$ 4.50	Capitol Hill
3/3/2025 6:42	Darcel Eustache	78 Fremont-Downtown Commuter	Commute	Jim Morrison	Sixth Avenue and Battery	Regular	Fremont, Space Needle, P70	Doubled	$ 4.50	Downtown
3/5/2025 6:32			XP	Meryl Streep	Elliott Avenue and Mercer St	Covered	Downtown	Extra-long	$ 2.75	Interbay
3/9/2025 7:52	Kenyetta Terron	42 Sodo-Downtown Express	Express	Jimi Hendrix	First Avenue and Terry Street	UC	Downtown	Doubled	$ 4.50	South Downtown
3/10/2025 6:33	Darcel Eustache	78 Fremont-Downtown Commuter	Commute	jim	Elliott Avenue and Mercer St	Covered	Downtown	Extra-long	$ 2.75	Interbay
3/11/2025 6:32	Kenyetta Terron	Sodo-Downtown Express	Express	Bruce Lee; blee@metrotran.org	First Avenue and Terry Street	Uncovered	Downtown	Doubled	$ 4.50	South Downtown
3/13/2025 8:32:00 AM (Late)	Ivey Hazekamp	32 Capitol Hill-Downtown	Regular	Bruce Lee	Broadway Ave and Cherry St	Covered	Convention Center	Articulated	$ 4.50	Capitol Hill
3/14/2025 6:32			Express	Bruce Lee	Broadway Ave and Cherry St	Covered	Downtown	Articulated	$ 4.50	C Hill
3/15/2025 1:36	Janey Lundgren	32 Capitol Hill-Downtown	Reg	Jimmy Hendricks	Broadway Ave and Cherry St	Covered	Convention Center	2 Decks	$ 2.75	Capitol Hill
3/16/2025 6:32	Darcel Eustache	78 Fremont-Waterfront-Downtown	Commute	Jim Morrison	Sixth Ave and Battery Street	Regular	Fremont, Space Needle	Doubled	$ 4.50	Downtown
3/17/2025 11:33	Ivey Hazekamp	32 Capitol Hill-Downtown	Regular	Jimi Hendrix	Fourth Avenue and Seneca	Covered	Capitol Hill	Doubled	$ 2.75	Downtown
3/18/2025 16:13	Jane Lundgran	32 Capitol Hill-Downtown	Reg	Meryl Streep	Fourth Avenue and Seneca St	Covered	CH	2 Decks	$ 2.75	DT
3/19/2025 6:32	Janey Lundgren	32 Capitol Hill-Downtown	Reg	Meryl Streep	Broadway and Cherry St	Covered	Downtown	2 Decks	$ 2.75	Capitol Hill
3/21/2025 6:32	Darcel Eustache	78 Fremont-Waterfront-Downtown	Commute	Meryl Streep	Sixth Avenue and Battery	Regular	Fremont, Space Needle, P70	Doubled	$ 4.50	Downtown
3/26/2025 9:04	Janie Lundgren	32 Capitol Hill-Downtown	Regular	Jimmy Hendricks, 206 5557661	Broadway and Cherry St	Covered	Downtown	2 Decks	$ 2.75	CHill
4/18/2025 5:23	Darcie Eustache	78 Fremont-Waterfront-Downtown	Commute	Jimi Hendrix	Fourth Avenue and Seneca	Regular	Fremont, Pier 70, Needle	Doubled	$ 4.50	Downtown

Figure 4.5: *Example violation of a relation with domain violations in two columns*

In *Figure* 4.5, the yellow-highlighted cells represent three columns with different kinds of data; this is problematic for database systems to try and decipher. Under column '**DateTime**' there are at least two data ranges; the first is the **datetime** values, while the second range of values appears to indicate status. '**Delayed**', '**Blocked**', and '**Late**' are values that are distinct from **DateTime**. While this could be understood by a human, it will not be included in a relational database. Data stored in this manner cannot be stored in a database as different data types and objects are being referenced.

As mentioned previously, in the column titled 'Driver', there are several distinct ranges of values that are not a name. In fact, there are phone numbers and email data along with combined first and last names. Again, while people are used to interpreting multiple ranges in columns like these, database management systems might not.

We will consider solutions to tackle this flaw and see how to improve the database design so that it can be accommodated in a relational system.

Violation of Relation #6: Row-Dependency

DateTime	Passenger	RouteNumber/Name	Type	Driver	StopName	Type	Destination	Type	Fare	Neighborhood
2/13/2025 7:36:00 AM (delayed)	Ivey Hazekamp	32 Capitol Hill-Downtown	Regular	Jimi Hendrix, 206555-7661	Broadway Ave Cherry St	Covered	Convention Center	Articulated	$ 4.50	Capitol Hill
2/13/2025 9:36	Darcel Eustache	78 Fremont-Waterfront-Downtown	Special	Meryl Streep	Hwy 99 N 36th	Covered	Fremont, Space Needle, P70	Extra-long	$ 2.75	Fremont
2/14/2025 6:36		78 Fremont-Waterfront-Downtown	XP	Bruce Lee	Elliott Avenue and Mercer St	Covered	Downtown	Extra-long	$ 2.75	Interbay
2/16/2025 6:32	Kenyetta Terron	42 Sodo-Downtown Express	Express	Meryl Streep	First Avenue and Terry Street	Covered	Fremont, Space Needle, P70	Doub	$ 2.75	SODO
2/19/2025 15:39	Kenny Terron	42 - E Sodo-Downtown Express	Espress	Bruce Lee	First Avenue and Terry Street	Uncovered	SoDo, DT	Doubled	$ 4.50	South Downtown
2/21/2025 6:13	Darcel Eustache	78-S Fremont-Waterfront-Downtown	Special	Jimmy Hendricks, 206 5557661	Elliott Avenue and Mercer St	Cvd	Fremont, Space Needle, P70	Extra-long	$ 2.75	Interbay
2/21/2025 6:13	Darcel Eustache	78-S Fremont-Waterfront-Downtown	Special	Jimmy Hendricks, 206 5557661	Elliott Avenue and Mercer St	Cvd	Fremont, Space Needle, P70	Extra-long	$ 2.75	Interbay
2/21/2025 7:36	Kenyetta Terron	Sodo-Downtown Express	Express	Bruce Lee	First Avenue and Terry Street	UC	Downtown	Doubled	$ 4.50	South Downtown
2/22/2025 8:32	Ivey Hazekamp	32 Capitol Hill-Downtown	Regular	Jim Morrison	Broadway Ave and Cherry St	Covered	CCntr.	Articulated	$ 4.30	Capital Hill
3/1/2025 6:33			Regular	Bruce Lee, 425 6109225	Broadway Ave and Cherry St	Covered	Downtown	Articulated	$ 4.50	Capitol Hill
3/1/2025 6:38:00 AM (Blocked)			Regular	Mary Streep (mstre@mtransit.org)	Broadway Ave and Cherry St	Covered	Downtown	Articulated	$ 4.50	Capitol Hill
3/3/2025 6:42	Darcel Eustache	78 Fremont-Downtown Commuter	Commute	Jim Morrison	Sixth Avenue and Battery	Regular	Fremont, Space Needle, P70	Doubled	$ 4.50	Downtown
3/5/2025 6:32			XP	Meryl Streep	Elliott Avenue and Mercer St	Covered	Downtown	Extra-long	$ 2.75	Interbay
3/9/2025 7:52	Kenyetta Terron	42 Sodo-Downtown Express	Express	Jimi Hendrix	First Avenue and Terry Street	UC	Downtown	Doubled	$ 4.50	South Downtown
3/10/2025 6:33	Darcel Eustache	78 Fremont-Downtown Commuter	Commute	Jim	Elliott Avenue and Mercer St	Covered	Downtown	Extra-long	$ 2.75	Interbay
3/11/2025 6:32	Kenyetta Terron	Sodo-Downtown Express	Express	Bruce Lee, blee@metrotran.org	First Avenue and Terry Street	Uncovered	Downtown	Doubled	$ 4.50	South Downtown
3/13/2025 8:32:00 AM (Late)	Ivey Hazekamp	32 Capitol Hill-Downtown	Regular	Bruce Lee	Broadway Ave and Cherry St	Covered	Convention Center	Articulated	$ 4.50	Capitol Hill
3/14/2025 6:32			Express	Bruce Lee	Broadway Ave and Cherry St	Covered	Downtown	Articulated	$ 4.50	C Hill
3/15/2025 1:36	Janey Lundgren	32 Capitol Hill-Downtown	Reg	Jimmy Hendricks	Broadway Ave and Cherry St	Covered	Convention Center	2 Decks	$ 2.75	Capitol Hill
3/16/2025 6:32	Darcel Eustache	78 Fremont-Waterfront-Downtown	Commute	Jim Morrison	Sixth Ave and Battery Street	Regular	Fremont, Space Needle	Doubled	$ 4.50	Downtown
3/17/2025 11:33	Ivey Hazekamp	32 Capitol Hill-Downtown	Regular	Jimi Hendrix	Fourth Avenue and Seneca	Covered	Capitol Hill	Doubled	$ 2.75	Downtown
3/18/2025 16:13	Jane Lundgran	32 Capitol Hill-Downtown	Reg	Meryl Streep	Fourth Avenue and Seneca St	Covered	CH	2 Decks	$ 2.75	DT
3/19/2025 6:32	Janey Lundgren	32 Capitol Hill-Downtown	Reg	Meryl Streep	Broadway and Cherry St	Covered	Downtown	2 Decks	$ 2.75	Capitol Hill
3/21/2025 6:32	Darcel Eustache	78 Fremont-Waterfront-Downtown	Commute	Meryl Streep	Sixth Avenue and Battery	Regular	Fremont, Space Needle, P70	Doubled	$ 4.50	Downtown
3/26/2025 9:04	Janie Lundgren	32 Capitol Hill-Downtown	Regular	Jimmy Hendricks, 206 5557661	Broadway and Cherry St	Covered	Downtown	2 Decks	$ 2.75	CHill
4/18/2025 5:23	Darcie Eustache	78 Fremont-Waterfront-Downtown	Commute	Jimi Hendrix	Fourth Avenue and Seneca	Regular	Fremont, Pier 70, Needle	Doubled	$ 4.50	Downtown

Figure 4.6: *Example violation of a relation with row dependencies*

This violation of rules for constructing a relation is called a 'row dependency' as highlighted in *Figure* 4.6. A row dependency is where a row in a table requires an adjacent row (usually the row above) to provide context or values to be fully understood. For example, in *Figure* 4.6, we can see several examples of the passenger and **`RouteName`** columns being empty with no values. When looking at this spreadsheet, a person may deduce that the blank cells are relying on the rows immediately preceding the empty cells for context. Looking at the second and third rows, we can read that the passenger 'Darcel Eustache' is the intended value for the third row, which is blank.

While the third-row value for '**`Passenger`**' may have been left blank on purpose, a computer is not going to know which other surrounding rows or values should be used for describing them. This technique may work when you are writing notes on the fridge for your roommates, but it fails when you are trying to construct a relational data model and deems the entire database as UNF.

Example Normalization: Going from UNF to 1NF

Now that we have a high-level understanding of what makes a relation, let us consider a systematic approach of converting the non-normalized design of **`METRO_TRANSIT`** to the design of a relational database in 1NF.

As mentioned earlier, the basic requirements for relation are as follows:

- Each entity within a database must have a unique name.
- Each attribute (column) within an entity must also have a unique name.
- No row may depend on any other row for its existence ("row dependency").
- Each cell must contain at most one value (known as a "multivalued attribute").
- Each cell in a column must adhere to a single range of values (known as a "domain").

We are assuming that each element of data present as column headers is critical for the organization; we will now find a more appropriate location for the values instead of just dropping it from the database.

First Normal Form (1NF)

A database design is automatically in First Normal Form (1NF) if it meets all the conditions for being a relation. This should be an initial goal though; as some of the worst database designs can be at least 1NF and still completely ineffective. We will get an opportunity to see **`METRO_TRANSIT`** progress from UNF to 3NF after considering all the normal forms.

Second Normal Form (2NF)

A database design is automatically in Second Normal Form (2NF) if it meets all the conditions for being in 1NF and does not have what are called "partial dependencies". This is where attributes in an entity are describing 'part' of the primary key. Partial dependencies occur when designers try to combine several attributes to establish a "natural" primary key without resorting to a surrogate key (this is another argument for assigning surrogate keys).

Here is an example of a partial dependency and a design in 2NF using the entity **`EMPLOYEE`** from **`METRO_TRANSIT`** with several other attributes added:

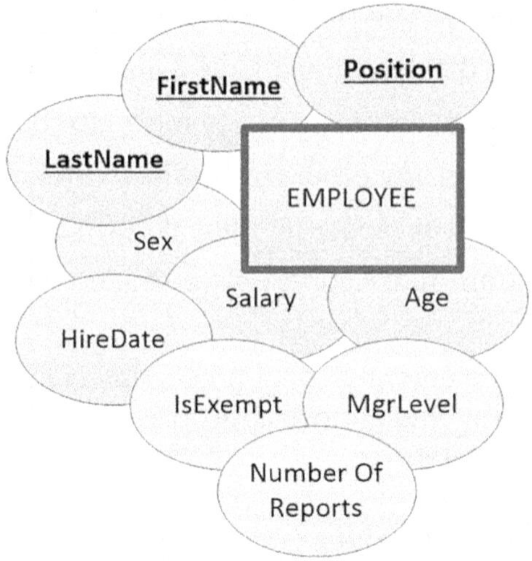

***Figure* 4.7:** *Example of a relation with partial dependencies*

The entity **`EMPLOYEE`** in *Figure* 4.7 has three attributes underlined with bold type to indicate the composite primary key. The attributes are **`IsExempt`**, **`MgrLevel`**, and **`NumberOfReports`**. The new attributes **`IsExempt`** and **`MgrLevel`** both describe the attribute '**`Position`**', which is a part of the primary key. The attribute **`NumberOfReports`** describes only the combined attributes of **`FirstName`** and **`LastName`**, which are other parts of the primary key. Here are two different partial dependencies in a single example.

This design, which includes a partial dependency, renders the entire database to First Normal Form or 1NF. The following image in *Figure* 4.8 is the design fix that places the same entity in 2NF, as it does not have any partial dependencies:

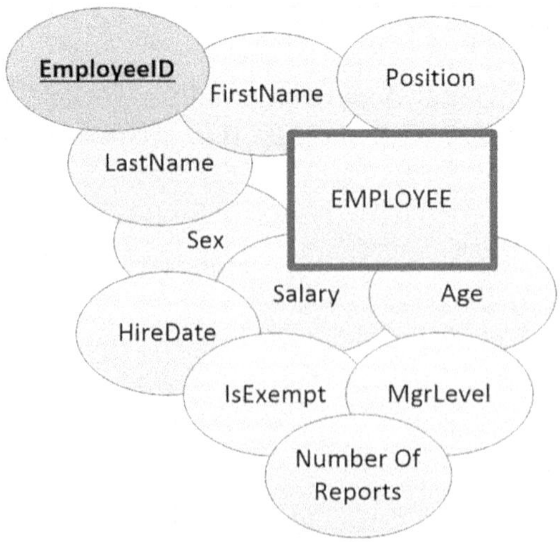

***Figure* 4.8:** *Example of a relation without a partial dependency*

In *Figure* 4.8, a surrogate primary key has been added instead of having three attributes as a composite primary key. With this slight change, the attributes **IsExempt**, **MgrLevel**, and **NumberOfReports** are not described as parts of the primary key. While **IsExempt** and **MgrLevel** still both describe the attribute Position, since there is a surrogate key, this is called a transitive dependency as opposed to partial dependency.

Since **NumberOfReports** describes **EmployeeID** (the primary key), it is no longer problematic or a cause of concern. Briefly, a transitive dependency is when an attribute is describing a non-key attribute. We will break this down to a math formula of "A > B > C", where:

- 'A' represents the primary key.
- 'B' represents a non-key attribute.
- 'C' represents another attribute that is dependent on the value of the non-key.

In *Figure* 4.8, 'A' is **EmployeeID**, 'B' is **Position**, and 'C' is both **IsExempt** and **MgrLevel** by itself (two instances of a transitive dependency). We often describe a transitive dependency as "when A defines B and B defines C, then A transitively defines C". This is commonly written as "A > B > C". This table in *Figure* 4.8 is in second normal form or 2NF because it has two transitive dependencies.

Third Normal Form (3NF)

A design is defined as being in 3NF if it meets all the requirements for 2NF and does not have any transitive dependencies. The resolution of the example in *Figure* 4.9 requires several new entities, including **POSITION**, **POSITION_TYPE**, and **JOB**, as shown here:

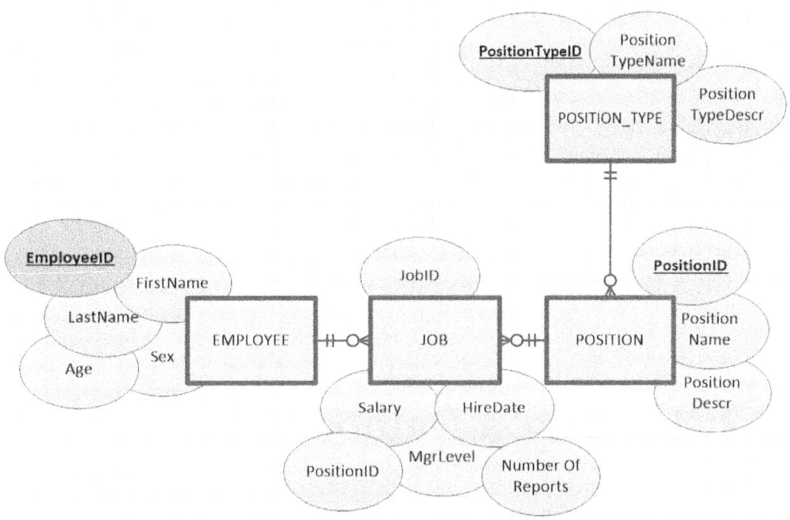

Figure 4.9: *Example of a set of relations without a transitive dependency*

In *Figure* 4.9, there are no transitive dependencies unlike in *Figure* 4.8. Here, **`JOB`** is an associative entity resolving the M:M relationship between **`POSITION`** and **`EMPLOYEE`** as one employee can hold many positions within the same company or organization. Conversely, the same position (such as 'Shift Manager') can be held by many people over the lifetime of the database.

Since an instance of **`JOB`** is one person and one position coming together, we can attach the attributes that were misplaced previously, as they describe the position in the context of the person doing the job. This provides flexibility in having a range of values, for instance in **`MgrLevel`**, where a new hire in the position of Shift Manager may have a Mgr Level of '1' while someone else with more experience will have a **`MgrLevel`** of '3', even though the **`PositionName`** is the same. As for the attribute '**`IsExempt`**', it can be placed as a value under the new entity **`POSITION_TYPE`** and the attribute of **`PositionTypeName`**.

Fourth Normal Form (4NF)

A relational database design is defined as being in 4NF if it meets all the requirements for 3NF and does not have any multi-valued dependencies. Multi-valued dependencies are found in the relationships that have not been fully articulated to be M:M even in rare cases. In *Chapter 3, Data Modeling and Normalization*, we saw several examples of a consolidated conceptual diagram data model for **`METRO_TRANSIT`**. In the chapter, when we look at *Figure* 3.23, there are only five associative entities defined.

In *Figure* 3.24, there were three extra associative entities that were defined for a total of eight. It can be argued that *Figure* 3.23 is in Third Normal Form and *Figure* 3.24 is in Fourth Normal Form because all potential multi-valued dependencies were resolved. We will see more examples of the differences between 3NF and 4NF soon.

Hopefully, this brief foray into normalization has not made your interest in data science wane. It caters to one of the objectives of this book, which is to enable readers to be entirely independent of other data professionals and not rely on someone else to design a database for them.

Normalization is a difficult concept to understand. However, practice with hands-on examples and further sections will allay your concerns and help you strengthen your expertise. Now, we will move to the next section to conduct the normalization process using a method that combines aspects of conceptual and logical design phases as we 'iron' the database into 3NF.

Method 2: 'Ironing' a Database from UNF to 4NF

The ironing method of building an Entity Relationship Diagram (ERD) has a 'horizontal' nature as we emphasize a quick and shallow definition of entities while defining relationships as we add more entities. This process might be more common if we have pre-existing systems, are in a hurry, or we are not as committed to proper documentation as in the first method. We will end up in the same spot as the first method eventually, so the preferred method depends on particular organizational objectives.

We have seen what a UNF version of **`METRO_TRANSIT`** looks like in *Figure 4.1* (which is shown again for quick reference):

DateTime	Passenger	RouteNumber/Name	Type	Driver	StopName	Type	Destination	Type	Fare	Neighborhood
2/13/2025 7:36:00 AM (delayed)	Ivey Hazekamp	32 Capitol Hill-Downtown	Regular	Jimi Hendrix, 206555-7661	Broadway Ave Cherry St	Covered	Convention Center	Articulated	$ 4.50	Capitol Hill
2/13/2025 9:36	Darcel Eustache	78 Fremont-Waterfront-Downtown	Special	Meryl Streep	Hwy 99-N 36th	Covered	Fremont, Space Needle, P70	Extra-long	$ 2.75	Fremont
2/14/2025 8:36		78 Fremont-Waterfront-Downtown	XP	Bruce Lee	Elliott Avenue and Mercer St	Covered	Downtown	Extra-long	$ 2.75	Interbay
2/16/2025 6:32	Kenyetta Terron	42 Sodo-Downtown Express	Express	Meryl Streep	First Avenue and Terry Street	Covered	Fremont, Space Needle, P70	Doub	$ 2.75	SODO
2/19/2025 15:39	Kenny Terron	42 - E Sodo-Downtown Express	Espress	Bruce Lee	First Avenue and Terry Street	Uncovered	SoDo, DT	Doubled	$ 4.50	South Downtown
2/21/2025 6:13	Darcel Eustache	78-S Fremont-Waterfront-Downtown	Special	Jimmy Hendricks, 206 5557661	Elliott Avenue and Mercer St	Cvd	Fremont, Space Needle, P70	Extra-long	$ 2.75	Interbay
2/21/2025 6:13	Darcel Eustache	78-S Fremont-Waterfront-Downtown	Special	Jimmy Hendricks, 206 5557661	Elliott Avenue and Mercer St	Cvd	Fremont, Space Needle, P70	Extra-long	$ 2.75	Interbay
2/21/2025 7:36	Kenyetta Terron	Sodo-Downtown Express	Express	Bruce Lee	First Avenue and Terry Street	UC	Downtown	Doubled	$ 4.50	South Downtown
2/22/2025 8:32	Ivey Hazekamp	32 Capitol Hill-Downtown	Regular	Jim Morrison	Broadway Ave and Cherry St	Covered	CCntr,	Articulated	$ 4.50	Capital Hill
3/1/2025 6:33			Regular	Bruce Lee, 425 6109225	Broadway Ave and Cherry St	Covered	Downtown	Articulated	$ 4.50	Capitol Hill
3/1/2025 6:36:00 AM (Blocked)			Regular	Mary Streep (mstre@mtransit.org)	Broadway Ave and Cherry St	Covered	Downtown	Articulated	$ 4.50	Capitol Hill
3/3/2025 6:42	Darcel Eustache	78 Fremont-Downtown Commuter	Commute	Jim Morrison	Sixth Avenue and Battery	Regular	Fremont, Space Needle, P70	Doubled	$ 4.50	Downtown
3/5/2025 6:32			XP	Meryl Streep	Elliott Avenue and Mercer St	Covered	Downtown	Extra-long	$ 2.75	Interbay
3/9/2025 7:52	Kenyetta Terron	42 Sodo-Downtown Express	Express	Jimi Hendrix	First Avenue and Terry Street	UC	Downtown	Doubled	$ 4.50	South Downtown
3/10/2025 6:33	Darcel Eustache	78 Fremont-Downtown Commuter	Commute	jim	Elliott Avenue and Mercer St	Covered	Downtown	Extra-long	$ 2.75	Interbay
3/11/2025 6:32	Kenyetta Terron	Sodo-Downtown Express	Express	Bruce Lee; blee@metrotran.org	First Avenue and Terry Street	Uncovered	Downtown	Doubled	$ 4.50	South Downtown
3/13/2025 8:32:00 AM (Late)	Ivey Hazekamp	32 Capitol Hill-Downtown	Regular	Bruce Lee	Broadway Ave and Cherry St	Covered	Convention Center	Articulated	$ 4.50	Capitol Hill
3/14/2025 6:32			Express	Bruce Lee	Broadway Ave and Cherry St	Covered	Downtown	Articulated	$ 4.50	C Hill
3/15/2025 1:36	Janey Lundgren	32 Capitol Hill-Downtown	Reg	Jimmy Hendricks	Broadway Ave and Cherry St	Covered	Convention Center	2 Decks	$ 2.75	Capitol Hill
3/16/2025 6:32	Darcel Eustache	78 Fremont-Waterfront-Downtown	Commute	Jim Morrison	Sixth Ave and Battery Street	Regular	Fremont, Space Needle	Doubled	$ 4.50	Downtown
3/17/2025 11:33	Ivey Hazekamp	32 Capitol Hill-Downtown	Regular	Jimi Hendrix	Fourth Avenue and Seneca	Covered	Capitol Hill	Doubled	$ 2.75	Downtown
3/18/2025 16:13	Jane Lundgran	32 Capitol Hill-Downtown	Reg	Meryl Streep	Fourth Avenue and Seneca St	Covered	CH	2 Decks	$ 2.75	DT
3/19/2025 6:32	Janey Lundgren	32 Capitol Hill-Downtown	Reg	Meryl Streep	Broadway and Cherry St	Covered	Downtown	2 Decks	$ 2.75	Capitol Hill
3/21/2025 6:32	Darcel Eustache	78 Fremont-Waterfront-Downtown	Commute	Meryl Streep	Sixth Avenue and Battery	Regular	Fremont, Space Needle, P70	Doubled	$ 4.50	Downtown
3/26/2025 9:04	Jame Lundgren	32 Capitol Hill-Downtown	Regular	Jimmy Hendricks, 206 5557661	Broadway and Cherry St	Covered	Downtown	2 Decks	$ 2.75	CHill
4/18/2025 5:23	Darcie Eustache	78 Fremont-Waterfront-Downtown	Commute	Jimi Hendrix	Fourth Avenue and Seneca	Regular	Fremont, Pier 70, Needle	Doubled	$ 4.50	Downtown

Figure 4.10: *Review of `METRO_TRANSIT` in UNF*

To continue taking data from UNF to 3NF involves using a data modeling tool.

Let us take the spreadsheet dataset from *Figure 4.10* and place it in a data modeling tool to begin ironing. The dataset will look like *Figure 4.11*:

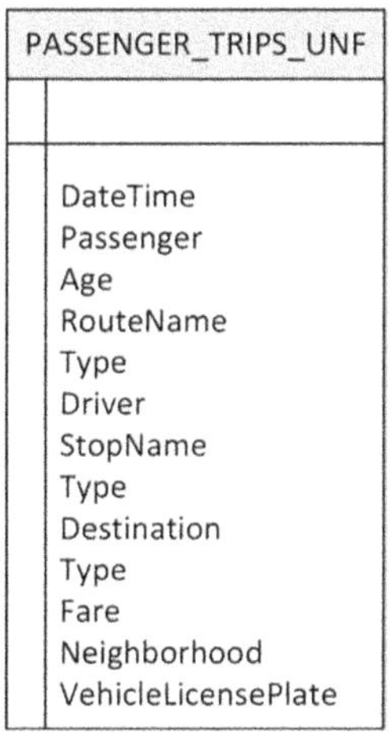

Figure 4.11: *Example design of `METRO_TRANSIT` in UNF*

There may be several reasons why this image is considered UNF, as it includes all violations of what makes a 'relation'. Please refer to the images in *Figure* 4.2 through *Figure* 4.9 earlier in this chapter for reminders on the following violations:

- Non-Unique Column Names
- Row Dependency
- Domain Violation
- Multivalued Attribute

Next, let us consider what the fixes to the violations will do to the design in *Figure* 4.1 (which again is in UNF). These fixes will need to address each of the violations specified in *Table* 4.2 to create a relation in 1NF. Consider the design in *Figure* 4.12 which no longer has any violations outlined for a basic relation.

PASSENGER_TRIPS_1NF	
PK	**DateTime**
PK	**Passenger**
PK	**RouteName**
PK	**VehicleLicensePlate**
PK	**Driver**
	RouteType
	Age
	StopName
	StopType
	Destination1
	Destination2
	Destination3
	VehicleType
	Fare
	Neighborhood
	Status
	DriverPhone
	DriverEmail

Figure 4.12: *Example design of* `METRO_TRANSIT` *in* 1NF

Remember, the First Normal Form has met the requirements of a relation as none of the six violations are present. However, there are instances of other violations that keep the design in 1NF. These include what has been defined as 'partial dependencies'.

In *Figure* 4.12, **`RouteType`** describes the attribute of **`RouteName`**, which is part of the three attributes that comprise the primary key. Likewise, all three destination attributes also are describing only **`RouteName`**.

Other partial dependencies found in *Figure* 4.12 include the following:

- **`Age`** describing **`Passenger`**
- **`VehicleTypeID`** describing **`VehicleLicensePlate`**

- **DriverPhone** and **DriverEmail** both describing Driver

The presence of these attributes keeps *Figure* 4.12 in 1NF. Next, let us address the partial dependency issue and see if we can get the design into Second Normal Form (2NF). We can quickly substitute the composite primary key with a surrogate key that will provide a unique value for each row, as shown here:

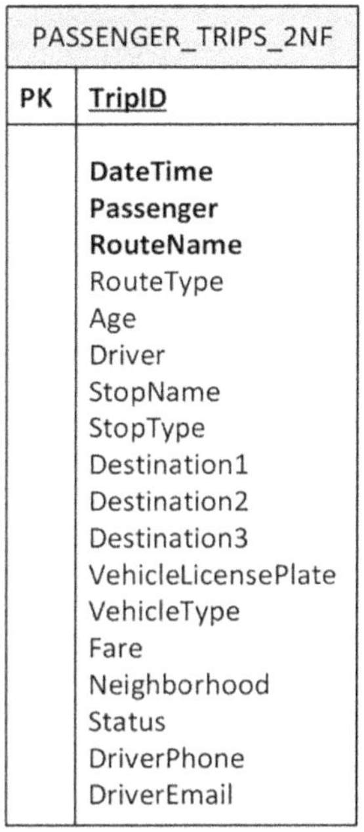

Figure 4.13: *Example design of* ***METRO_TRANSIT*** *in* 2NF

Figure 4.13 has a surrogate primary key that has replaced the previous natural composite primary key that had five attributes. Nothing else has changed in this design and it is now in 2NF. This is still a rough design, but it meets the conditions of 2NF for this example. Each of the previous partial dependencies that made the design 1NF are now considered 'transitive' dependencies. As we have read previously, the presence of these transitive dependencies prevents the design from being in 3NF.

The next step involves taking this design in 2NF into 3NF. Therefore, we must identify each attribute that can survive independently as an entity. This will take a few concerted steps and includes more brainstorming.

Consider the diagram in *Figure* 4.14, which shows an extraction of rows from the single-table design in *Figure* 4.13 into an initial collection of 13 entities:

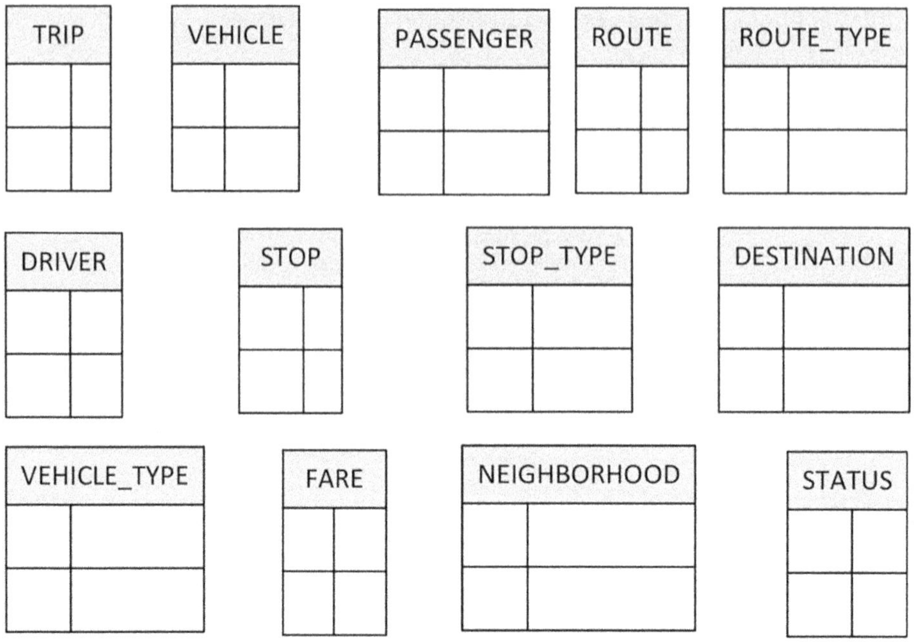

Figure 4.14: *Identifying potential new entities based on columns that are nouns*

In *Figure* 4.14, we can see that twelve new entities are created based on the attributes specified in **`PASSENGER_TRIPS_2NF`**, which takes the total to thirteen. The next step in the ironing process includes adding surrogate primary keys to each entity.

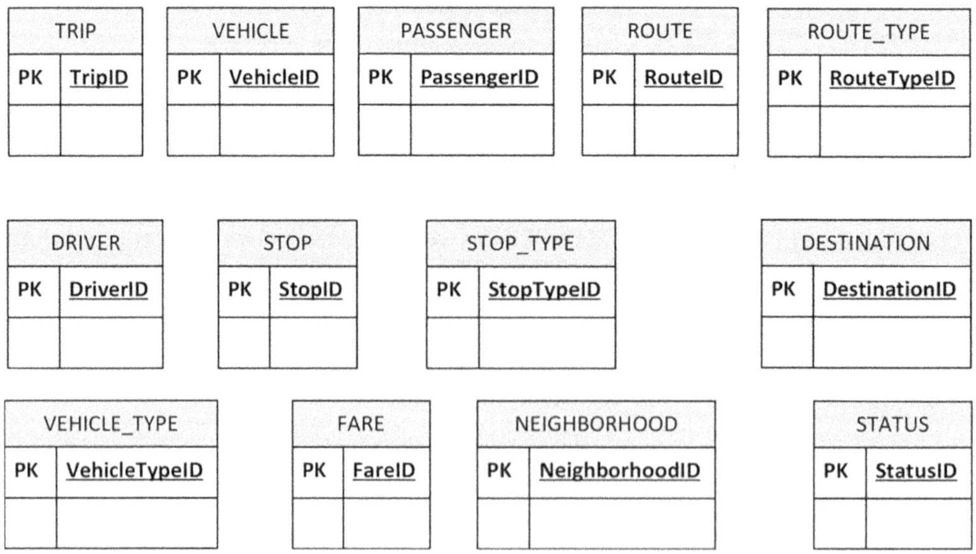

Figure 4.15: *Adding surrogate PK values following tablename + ID*

For now, a good choice is to follow 'tablename + ID' as the default name of the new primary key columns for each entity with a data type of INTEGER. This design provides flexibility for many different scenarios and allows best-practices such as auto-incrementing PK and physical indexes.

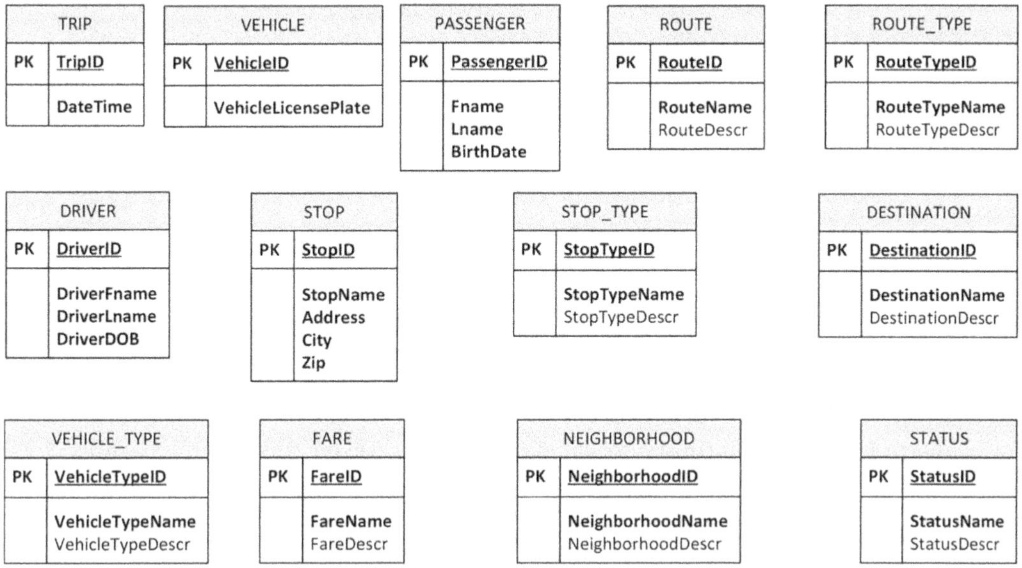

***Figure 4.16**: Adding name, description, and other columns*

Database Design Patterns

There are certain patterns that occur when following the 'ironing' method. These include establishing surrogate primary keys as well as both a 'name' and 'description' attribute almost by default. There may be modification of this pattern on a case-by-case basis, but when we follow this template, it reduces the mistakes that are easily made when designers get in a hurry trying to over-burden an entity with attributes that belong somewhere else.

For now, the process of ironing a database design provides a straight-forward direction that leads to better-than-average outcomes with completed database designs that are fully normalized and scale well.

The next step in the design process is to take a high-level view of the entire diagram and see which objects or entities are related to each other. Positioning related entities together at this stage will go a long way towards establishing a readable ERD. This provides designers with a clear picture as they continue with the normalization process by adding relationships.

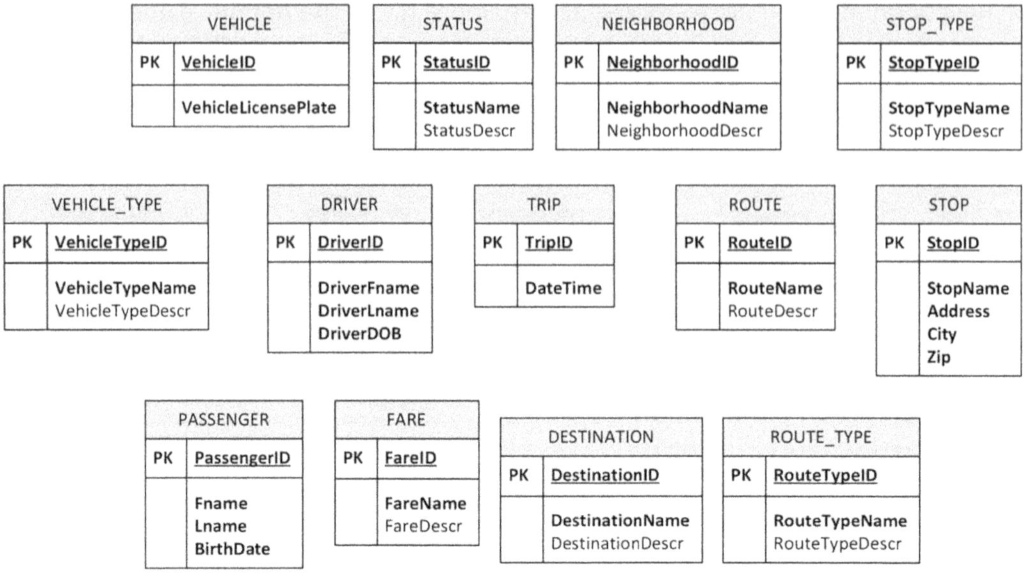

Figure 4.17: *Moving entities into common sections based on possible relationships*

A database comes together easily if the related entities are clustered nearby. While not required for functionality or performance, it helps the design process 'make sense' when relationships are ultimately defined with shorter lines that do not cross over each other. These are more elegant and easier to read.

Relationships Will Change

As the design of any new database is being fleshed out, there will be situations where the definition of a relationship will change as we learn more about data and continue the normalization process. One such example is shown here:

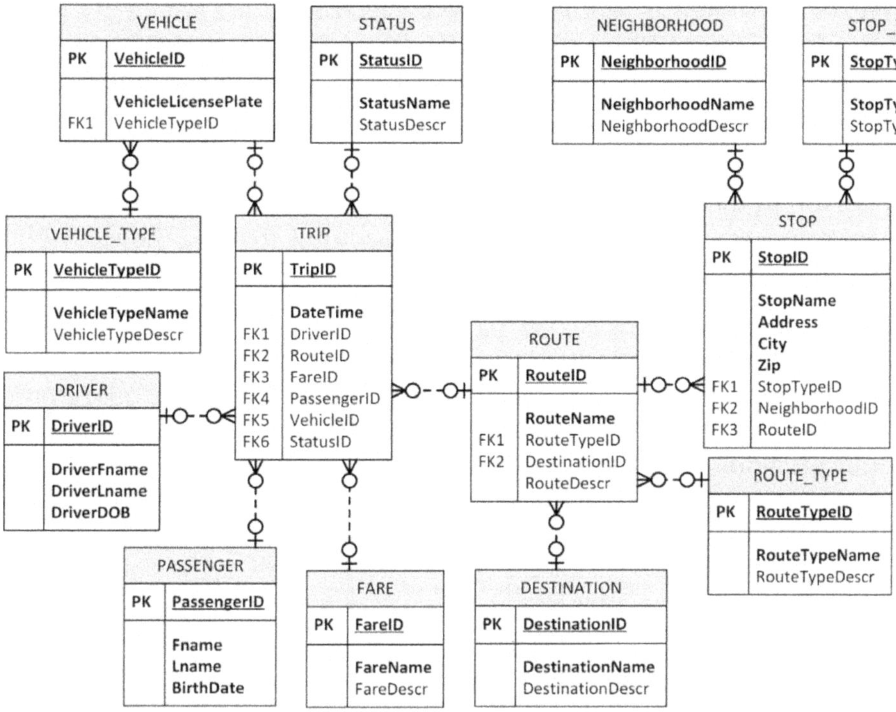

Figure 4.18: *Creating initial relationships with PK/FK*

As we continue the ironing process, we will assemble a collection of entities that will resemble the finished ERD in *Figure* 3.24 from *Chapter* 3. Let us analyze what we have obtained so far in *Figure* 4.18.

The entities at this stage of development are going to look different than the entities initially created during the 'vertical' method in *Figure* 3.24. This ironing/horizontal method is not going to be as exhaustive as the traditional or 'vertical' method where we brainstormed over all the attributes of each entity. The goal here is to follow a template of 'ID + Name + Descr' as basic attributes and quickly move on to the next object to create fragments that will be aligned into relationships in a still under-developed form.

As entities are added, we want to be aware whether they will hold 'transactional' data or whether they will be providing context to other transactional entities. In simple terms, an entity that has foreign keys will be collecting transactions while an entity that has no foreign keys will be providing context. We may call these 'look-up' entities. Most databases will have more look-up entities than transactional ones.

As was stated in earlier chapters, designing relational databases requires us to think in terms of designing for machines where each object is isolated and 'tagged' with labels as opposed to designing for people. Here, the data needs to make sense when we read it or where it is stored. An example of designing for people is a garage sale, where a group of items such as 'kitchen goods' or 'electronics' are stored in a common box or section of the garage. With a relational database design we must break that line of thinking. We will tag items with their type as opposed to lumping a particular type into a common entity.

Look at the **DRIVER** and **PASSENGER** tables. There are only factual data elements about each person in them. There are no elements about what they did, where they performed an action, or when they did it. The transactions that tell the story of their behavior or actions are recorded elsewhere.

Data is not stored on disk in any 'shape' or cluster for people to 'see as it is stored'; we will always use the SQL language to re-assemble data in a precise form to answer questions. These are different from storing data in the shape of the query on disk. This idea of having data might not be legible as it is stored. This is perhaps, the most difficult modification for new designers to tackle.

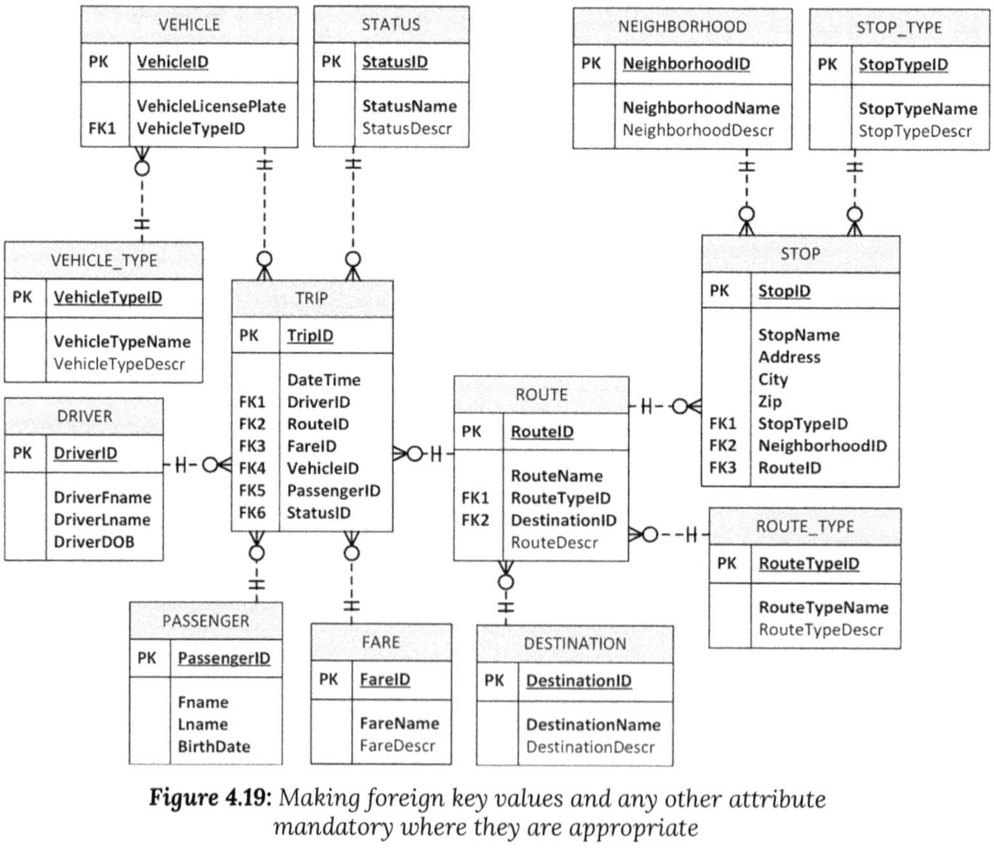

Figure 4.19: *Making foreign key values and any other attribute mandatory where they are appropriate*

Now, the initial relationships have been added with primary keys and foreign keys. We need to take a close look to determine if the foreign keys can be **NULL**; many designers argue against allowing **NULL** (empty) values if possible, but each database is going to be distinct. When the decision is made to make some or all the foreign keys mandatory, the modeling tool will make them bold as well as change the crows' foot notation from an 'O' to a 'dash'. Please refer to *Figure* 3.24 from *Chapter* 3 as a reminder (shown here):

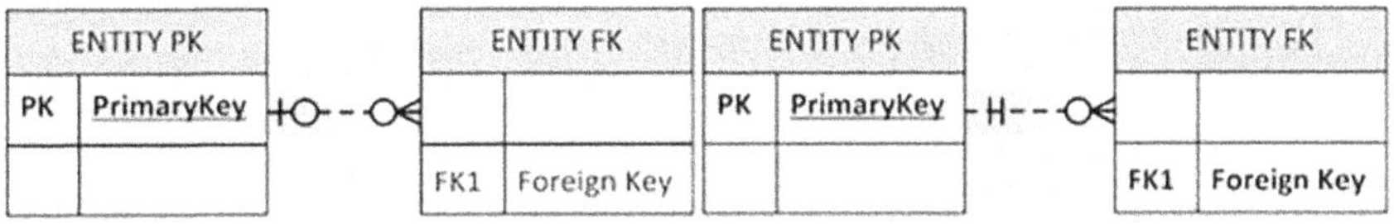

***Figure* 4.20**: *Example relationships of mandatory and optional*

Many designers consider re-reading and evaluating previously defined relationships, which might be cumbersome. However, this is an opportunity to gain intimate knowledge of the data model, which can only be obtained via thorough observation, analyses, and study.

Thus, while re-evaluating relationships, we will find that several are M:M. These include the relationship between **TRIP** and **STATUS**, **ROUTE** and **STOP**, **PASSENGER_TRIP**, and finally **ROUTE** and **DESTINATION**. In each situation of re-evaluation, we will read the relationship in both directions (left-to-right and right-to-left).

We will discover that these four relationships will need to be resolved. This means adding an 'associative entity' in between the affected entities in each relationship to create multiple 'one-to-many' relationships. These are highlighted in purple in *Figure* 4.20.

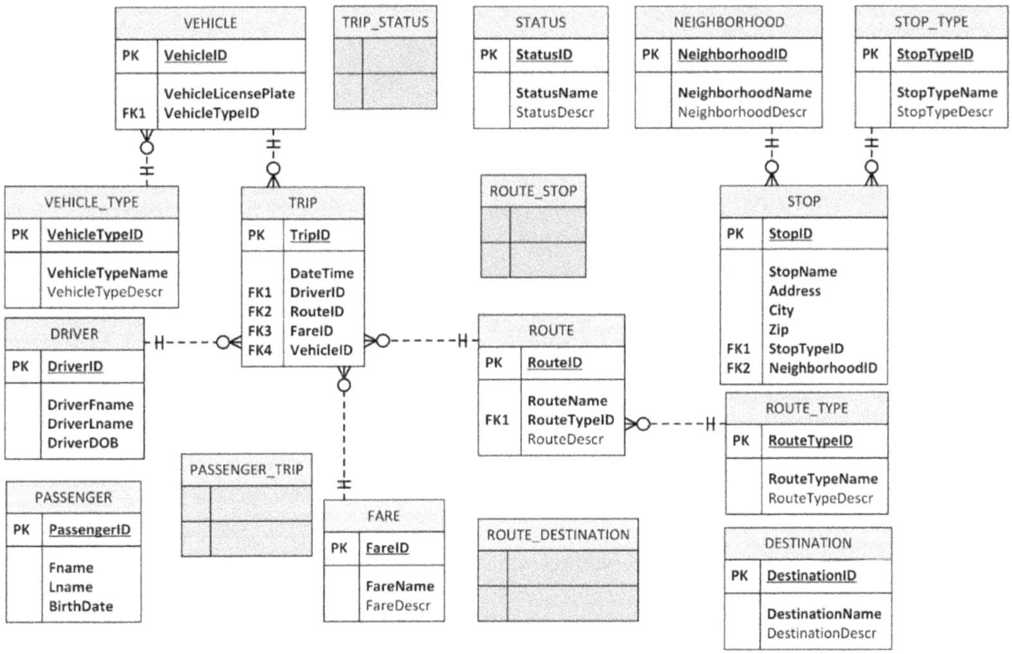

***Figure* 4.21**: *Re-evaluating each relationship looking for M:M*

After adding the initial collection of entities, we want to re-evaluate them in the context of the other entities. Our goal is to see if these new entities have changed our perception of any other relationship. Upon further evaluation, it looks like there are more M:M relationships than before, as shown here:

- **`PASSENGER : TRIP (M:M)`**
- **`TRIP : STATUS (M:M)`**
- **`ROUTE : STOP (M:M)`**
- **`ROUTE : DESTINATION (M:M)`**
- **`TRIP : FARE`**
- **`STOP : NEIGHBORHOOD (no change)`**
- **`TRIP : ROUTE? (no change)`**
- **`TRIP : DRIVER (maybe M:M)`**

The first four relationships that are re-evaluated render M:M and require resolution with a new entity. Also, after evaluating **`TRIP : FARE`**, it is becoming more apparent that a FARE does not describe a TRIP, but involves passengers.

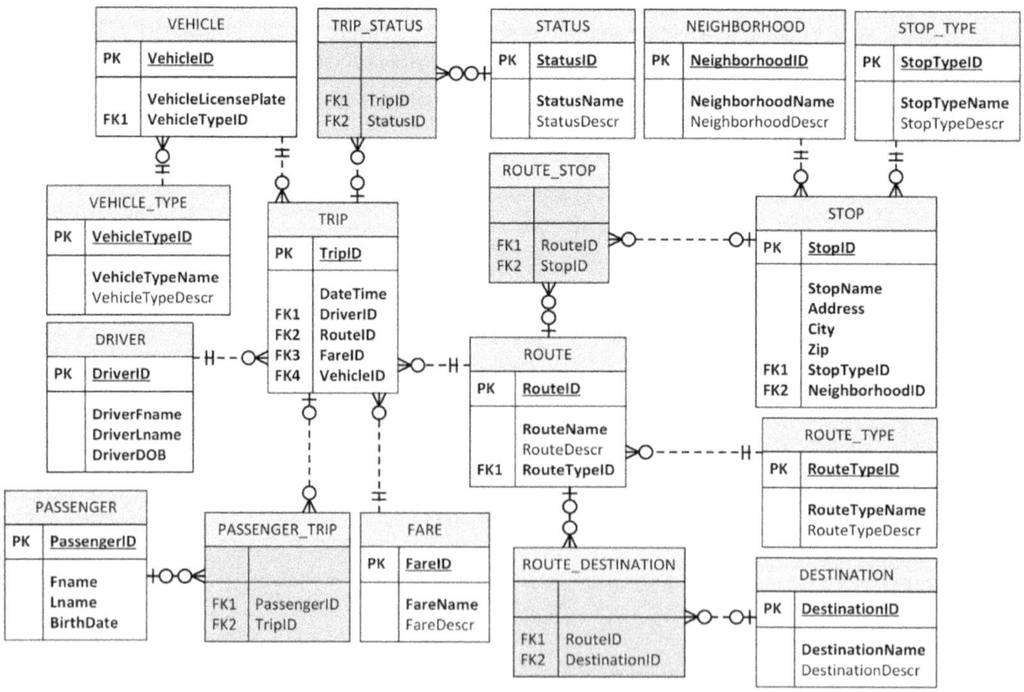

***Figure 4.22:** Resolving several M:M relationships*

The process of taking the new associative entities in *Figure 4.22* is to pull the primary keys of each participating entity inwards. Our initial option is to have composite primary keys assembled from the foreign keys, but the better choice will be to also assign a surrogate PK for these associative entities.

Resolving M:M

A good way to resolve an M:M relationship is to place an entity in between the affected entities. As a result, the forks will always point inward to the new associative entity. The foreign key will follow the fork. Therefore, we know that an M:M requires a new entity in the middle, followed by bringing in foreign keys from the affected entities, as shown in the next few examples.

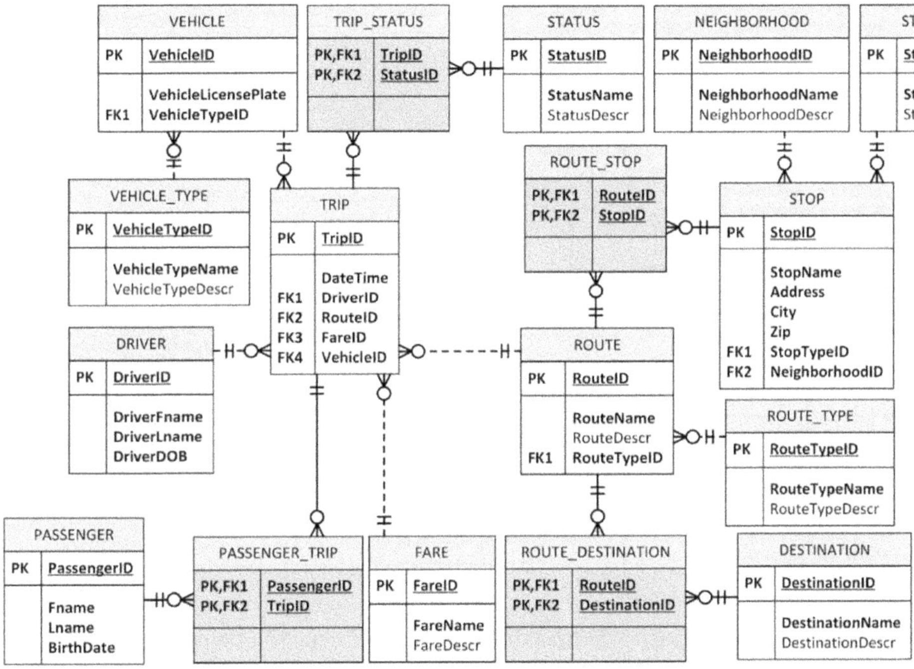

Figure 4.23: *Exploring the 1:M primary keys as composite PK*

After creating these new entities, we may want to consider a friendlier set of names for them. Often the compound nature of entity names (**PASSENGER_TRIP** for example) is created to simplify the pedantic nature of normalization. Both **PASSENGER_TRIP** and **ROUTE_STOP** should be renamed to reflect the vernacular used by primary stakeholders.

For **PASSENGER_TRIP**, a better object name is **BOARDING**, as this is a common term used by non-technical staff throughout the world. Additionally, the term **SCHEDULE** seems to be more appropriate for **ROUTE_STOP**.

SCHEDULE represents a prescribed calendar of all scheduled routes and when each is supposed to arrive at a specific stop. It encompasses the entire transportation network for the city, while representing the scheduled stops across all routes, neighborhoods and stops. As such, there may be a million rows or more. This table is also relatively static with very few updates between revisions. It may only be updated when the entire system is refreshed to accommodate slight seasonal changes.

There may be a need to change the definitions of the entities that are connected to others. Whenever changes are made to entities or relationships, we will need to review the design quickly to ensure that other relationships have not been affected.

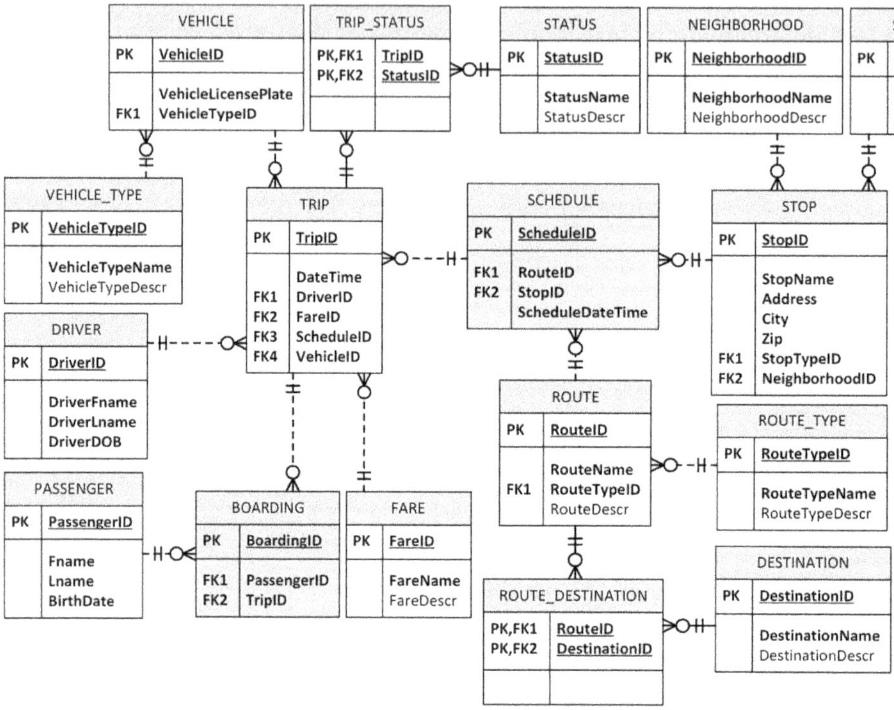

Figure 4.24: *Renamed entities `SCHEDULE` and `BOARDING` with surrogate primary keys*

As can be seen in *Figure 4.24*, the entities highlighted in purple have been re-named and have surrogate primary keys. **`SCHEDULE`** also has a new column to answer questions on when a particular trip will be made to a specific stop.

In **`METRO_TRANSIT`**, it makes sense to re-evaluate what an individual occurrence of a **`SCHEDULE`** and a **`BOARDING`** represent. It is important to make sure that the database is capturing the events in a way that aligns with business expectations and the reports generated from the database to answer specific questions.

As we re-evaluate the design, we should consider the following questions:

- Does a boarding need to include the **`StopID`** for each passenger entering the vehicle?
- Is it beneficial to include the actual time when a passenger boards a vehicle?

Let us say that it has been determined that **TRIP** needs more information about time and location than what was available with **ROUTE**. We will now change the database design to eliminate the relationship between **TRIP** and **ROUTE**, and connect the former to **SCHEDULE**.

Consider these updates shown in *Figure 4.25*:

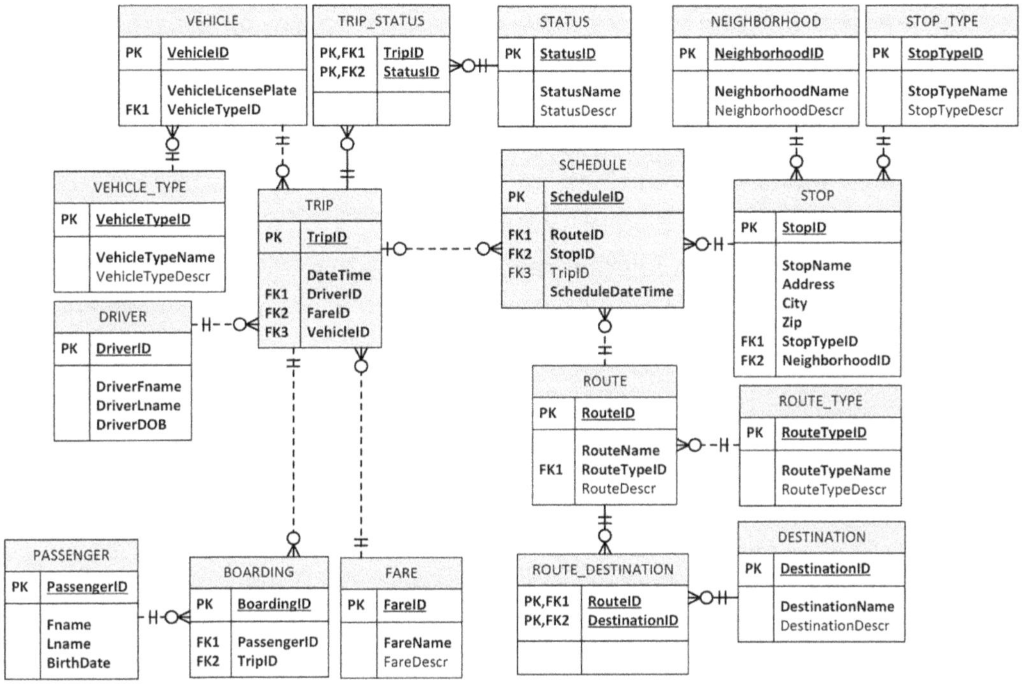

Figure 4.25: *Modifying the relationship between* **TRIP**, **ROUTE**, *and* **SCHEDULE**

In *Figure* 4.25, the revised structure of the ERD has replaced the relationship between **ROUTE** and **TRIP** with the one between **SCHEDULE** and **TRIP**. The direction of the 'fork' in the new relationship is now going toward **SCHEDULE**. This change introduces a slight challenge however, in that the **TripID** that is a foreign key in **SCHEDULE** needs to be empty ('**NULL**') when rows are first added to the table. This is because the rows in **SCHEDULE** may be initially added to the table months in advance of the day the **TripID** is created.

We have to slow down and consider the knowledge people in the system will obtain and when that knowledge will be available. In the relationship between **TRIP** and **SCHEDULE**, where a schedule is prepared and published to the world three months ahead of time, we will not be able to know which driver or exact vehicle will be on shift three months later.

Thus, by allowing the system to allow empty values for the exact **TripID**, we can communicate effectively with passengers who need to plan excursions, while also being able to update the system when a **TripID** is available. Since a single trip has a dozen or so stops and the potential to handle more than 100 passengers, it will be beneficial to record which stops have the most boardings. Previously, there was no way to know for sure where a boarding occurred.

As we evaluate the effects of the changes made in *Figure 4.24*, we want to address how it affects the entity **BOARDING**. Originally, it made sense to align a passenger to a trip; after the developments and changes made along the way, we can consider changing the definition of a **BOARDING** to be connected to **SCHEDULE**.

Now that **BOARDING** has been created, we can also change FARE to attach it to **BOARDING**. This change includes adding more columns such as **FareAmount**, **BeginDate**, and **EndDate**. Doing so allows the business to notify the public when fares increase, in addition to tracking different fares per boarding.

Consider the next rendering of **METRO_TRANSIT**, which has several changes based on re-evaluating the entities and relationships highlighted in orange, as shown here:

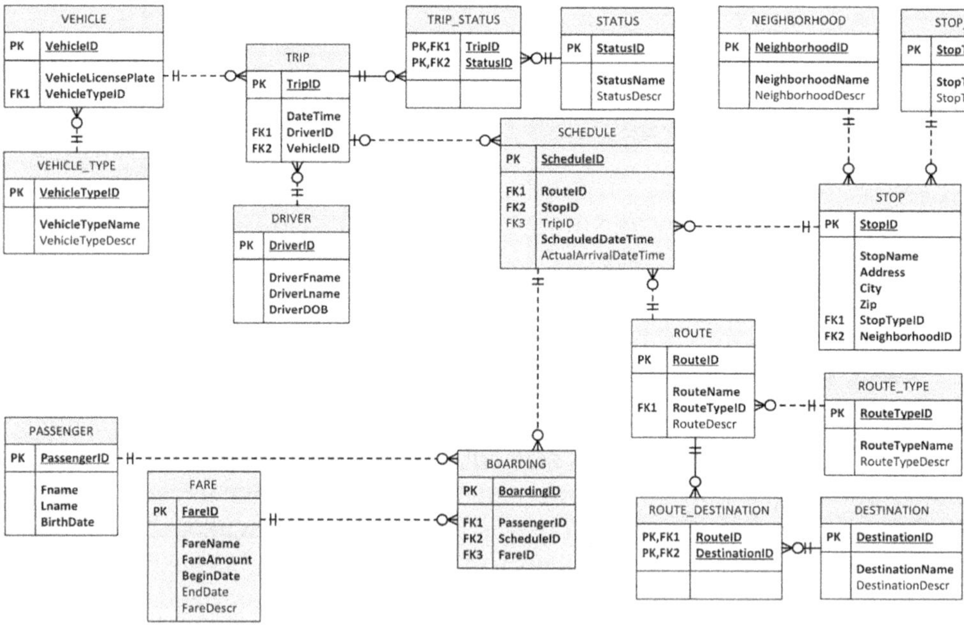

***Figure 4.26:** Re-evaluating FARE, BOARDING, and SCHEDULE*

The changes seen in *Figure* 4.26 reflect an updated and evolved interpretation of what a BOARDING is, as well as the exact data to answer future questions regarding a SCHEDULE. These updates required changing the entities that are connected to each other. In this new rendering, BOARDING is not related to TRIP anymore. Instead, it relates to SCHEDULE. At the first glance, this may be slightly confusing or simply unclear. However, the decision to make these updates is based on getting more data that informs each BOARDING. Consider the following:

- **SCHEDULE** has FK values **RouteID**, **StopID**, and **TripID**.
- Additional columns include both the **ScheduledDateTime** and **ActualDateTime**.

Since **SCHEDULE** contains these details, more questions can be answered about each **BOARDING**, including where each boarding occurred on a trip, as well as which boardings were before/after scheduled pick-up times. Ironing the design should include exploring if adding 'type' entities onto base objects will benefit the design. We should think in terms of possible categories of the base objects/entities that the business may refer to. This includes considering if the design will benefit from having a type of fare, vehicle or passenger.

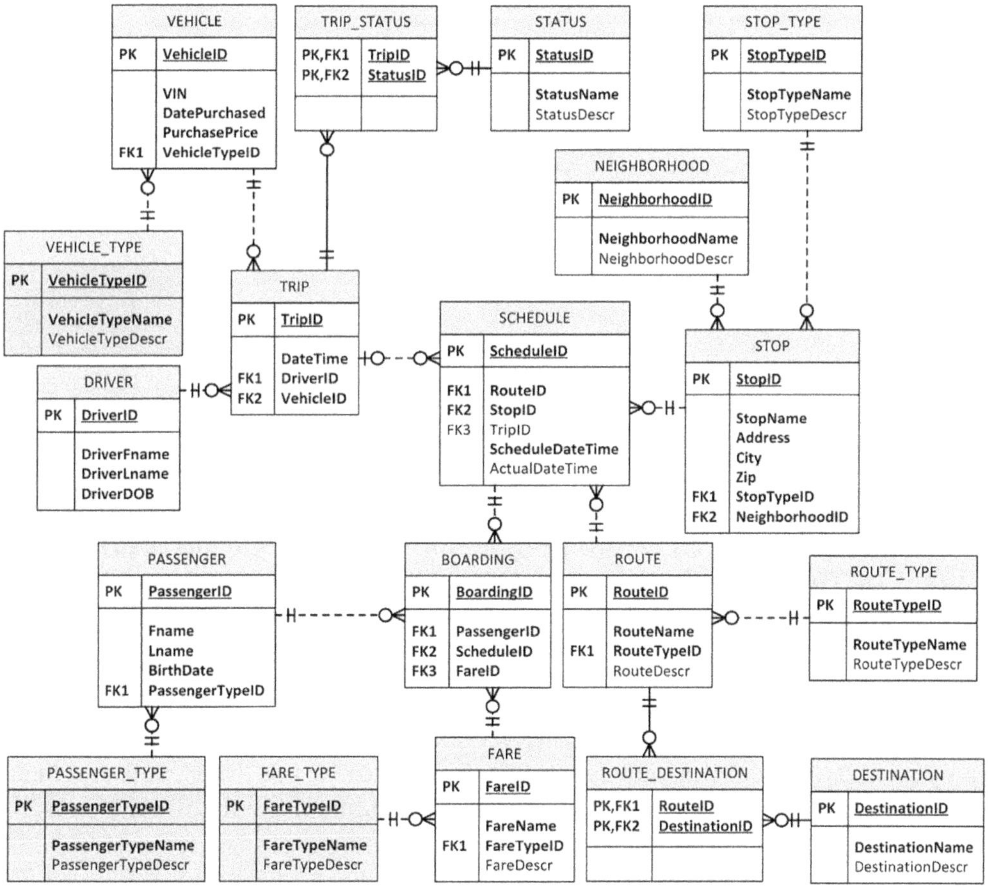

Figure 4.27: *Adding several TYPE tables to the existing entities*

In this part of database design, we will explore more attributes as we did more extensively during the 'vertical' design method. In this step, we will review the possible choices with the business side of the house and other stakeholders to validate if these additional entities are necessary. Other entities may be discovered during these check-in discussions.

See *Figure* 4.28 for potential new entities that are not included in original requirements:

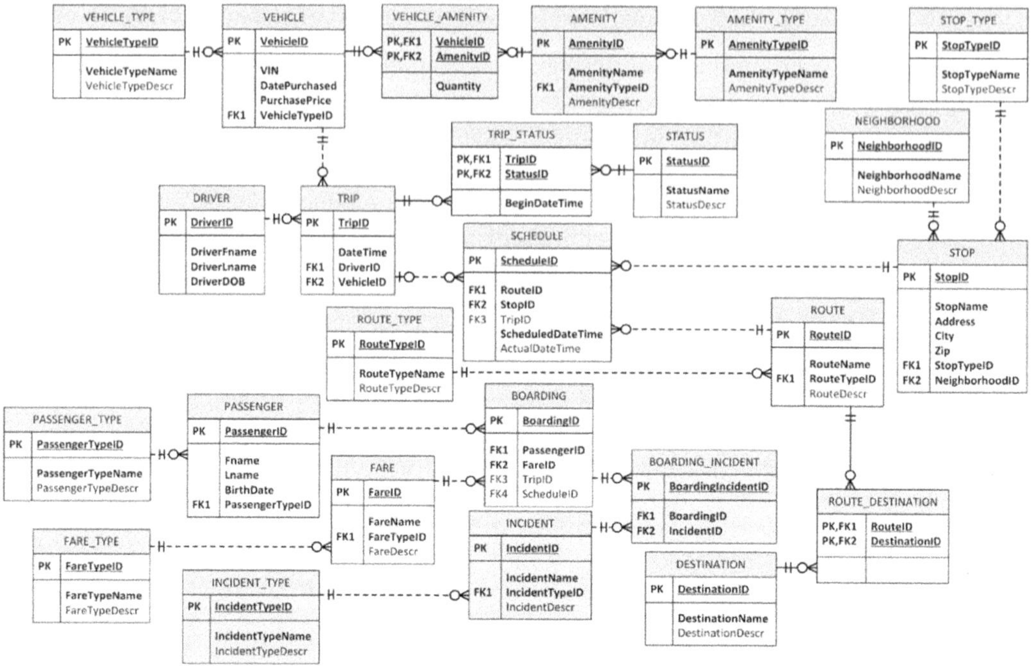

Figure 4.28: *Adding additional entities based on conversations with stakeholders*

After making these changes, we must check in with primary stakeholders to confirm the changes and get them validated by the team. There might be at least one request and/or discrepancy discovered during the meeting. For instance, it is discovered that a single **`BOARDING`** can be involved in more than a single **`INCIDENT`**, as well as the same **`INCIDENT`** can involve more than one person (which translates to more than one **`BOARDING`**). This relationship is now M:M, and can be updated as such in the design.

Highlighted in green in *Figure* 4.28 are the last few entities requested by stakeholders after reviewing the design and seeking feedback for possible improvements. These include an expansion of the data captured with **`EMPLOYEE`**, **`POSITION`**, **`JOB`**, and **`SEX`**. The final entity called **`COMMENT`** allows for unlimited tracking of the details of any recorded **`INCIDENT`**.

Several computed columns are highlighted in yellow. These provide aggregations for important calculations used in weekly reporting, perhaps for a dashboard.

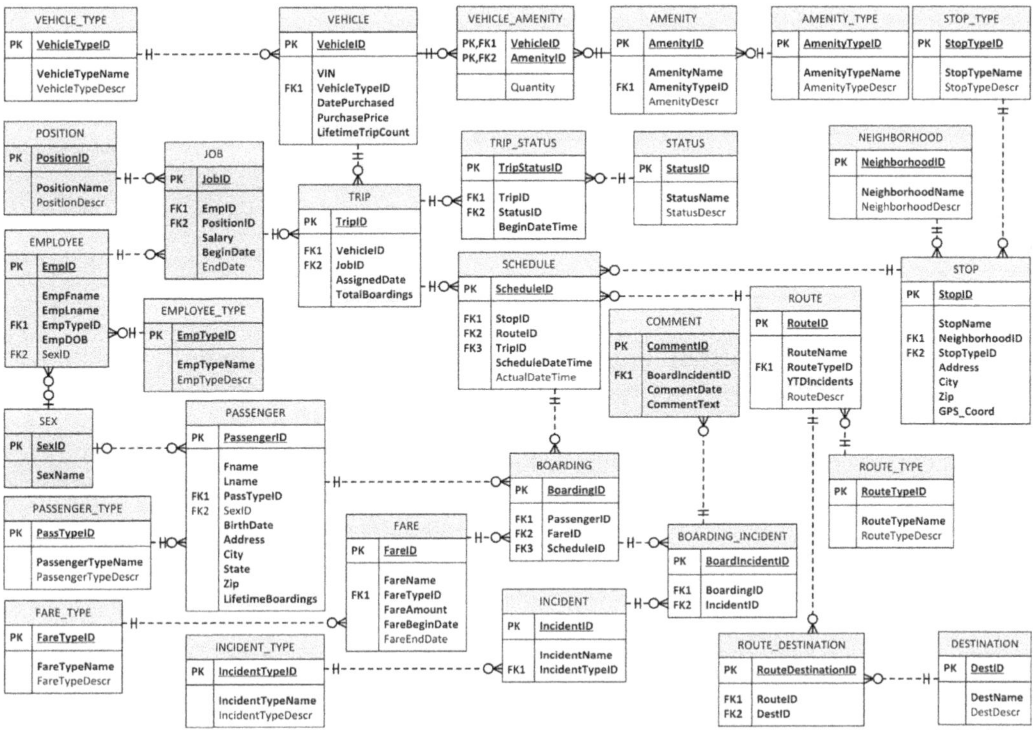

Figure 4.29: *Final few entities and reporting columns added to ERD*

The diagram in *Figure* 4.29 is arguably in 4NF and is ready to be passed along to developers to create a schema for deployment.

Common Mistakes

When conducting normalization, beginner data modelers often make the following mistakes:

- Overloading base entities
- PK/FK going in the wrong direction (often with a **TYPE** table)
- Referential loop in the design

When building out a database, it is important to recognize higher-level entities that describe each row of a lower-level entity. These higher-level entities can be thought of as a "category" or "type" entity.

In *Chapter* 3, we observed an example of an entity in *Figure* 3.5 that contained a list of products. Here is how it looked like:

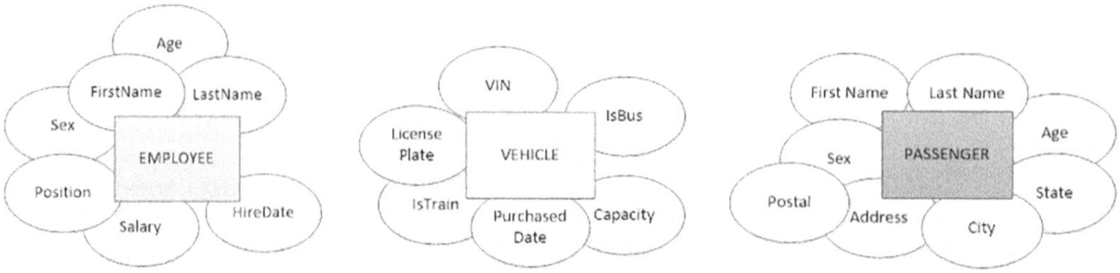

Figure 4.30: *Example of 'overloaded' entities*

It is evident that the **VEHICLE** entity in this diagram has too many columns or is overburdened as it tries to describe the kind of vehicle a single row represents. While this is important, it is an effective way to manage the data consistently and therefore allows for mistakes. Unmanaged data allows for typos and abbreviations. This is a result of the designer not exploring a higher-level category entity to take the burden off the base entity. Additionally, there are a couple of "yes/no" questions that appear as column headers (IsBus as well as IsTrain). These columns introduce chaos into the database design.

We also observed the range of values allowed under this poor design; there are unmatched values due to misspellings as well as uncontrolled checkmarks of various forms attempting to answer the yes/no questions. To better understand why this design is considered flawed, try to write a query that will account for every possible misspelling, typo, or variation of checkmark from data presented in *Figure* 3.3 with only ten rows. This process will be even more tedious when we try to prove a query while drawing data from a table with millions of rows!

These poor design choices can be quickly fixed by identifying the problem columns and creating a **VEHICLE_TYPE** entity to manage the categories. Once **VEHICLE_TYPE** has been established, there is a finite range of categories that each row in the **VEHICLE** entity must adhere to; these typos or abbreviations will not figure in the most basic query if we do so.

We tend to avoid overburdened base entities when following the 'ironing' method, but we still would like to be wary of columns when trying to answer questions that should be in a **TYPE** entity.

A second common mistake early career designers make is placing a foreign key in a 'type' table. At this point in your learning, it is safe to hold a mantra of a type table will never have a foreign key! The root of this mistake is how people classify simple household objects, like utensils in the kitchen or clothing in the closet. We tend to 'clump' these items by their type in a single location; consider that 'box of rags' in their garage or a generic 'sock drawer' many of us have. This is NOT how we organize items in a database! In a normalized database, we will assign a tag to each item with a foreign key as opposed to placing the name of the item in the associate type table. Be open to a new way of thinking as database design often requires breaking decades of learned organizational skills.

Once we have had a breakthrough by establishing a **_TYPE** entity for each base entity, it will be a mistake to place the foreign key in the wrong entity. Remember, once we bring in a foreign key, we will be limiting a row (which includes a primary key, some kind of name, and a description, most likely) to a single occurrence throughout the design.

Let us consider **STOP_TYPE** entity, and look at the different types of bus or train stops mentioned as follows:

- Covered
- Uncovered
- Elevated
- Tunnel

If we can only come up with four values, then there should never be more than four rows in this entity. This goes for any **_TYPE** entity, as these are finite categories.

Consider the following **flawed** example of an FK being placed in **STOP_TYPE** entity:

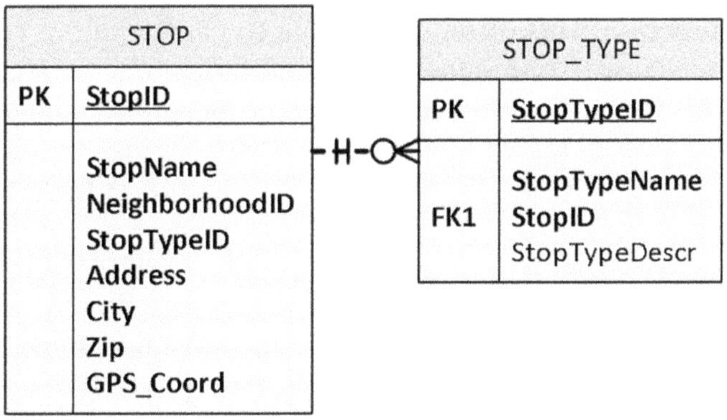

***Figure 4.31:** Example of a design mistake with a foreign key in a TYPE entity*

You must know that when we determined values for types of stops, we only came up with four; this means that there are only four rows (ever) for **STOP_TYPE**. When we incorrectly bring in a foreign key, we will encounter another challenge of keeping track of several stops throughout a large transit system in a major city.

Here, our first impulse to "connect a base entity to the type" would be backward.

A base entity does not describe a "type" (but a type does in fact describe a base value). The design in *Figure* 4.31 would require several columns in the **STOP_TYPE** entity to account for the design mistake as one additional column for each stop to align with its 'type' will be introduced.

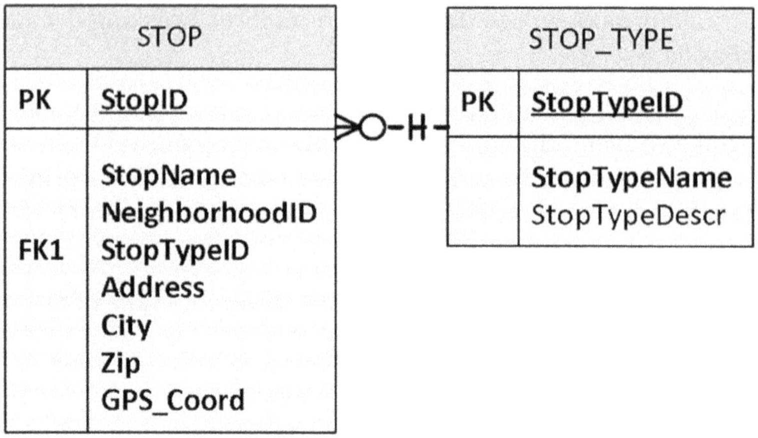

Figure 4.32: *Example of the correct design of a TYPE entity providing a foreign key to base entity*

Remembering that a type table will never have a foreign key will go a long way in recognizing patterns in relational database design and data modeling.

PK/FK Going in the Wrong Direction

Another common mistake to encounter will be when the primary and foreign keys go in the wrong direction. This often occurs due to haste and not recognizing how a foreign key can limit a row to one value over the lifetime of the database. The following figure illustrates this flawed relationship between a **PASSENGER** and **BOARDING**:

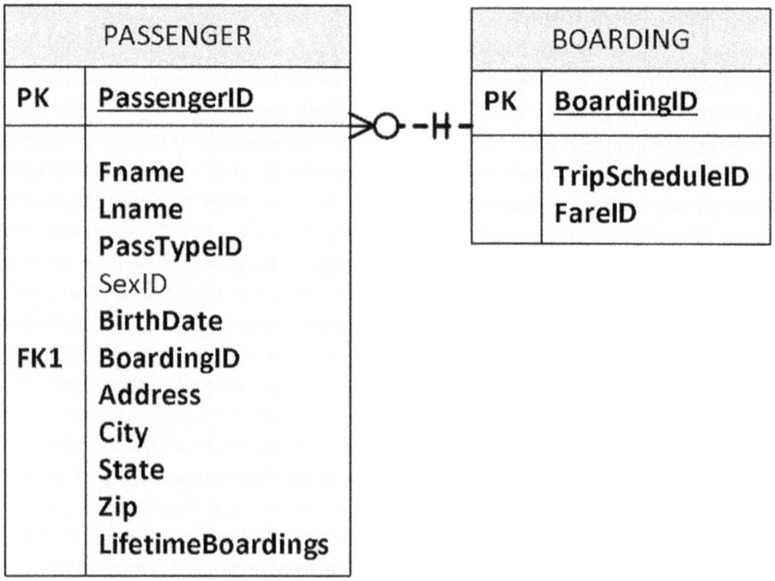

Figure 4.33: *Example of a mistake with the primary keys and foreign keys going in the wrong direction*

Let us slow down and evaluate the incorrect relationship as defined above. Since we wanted to track the **BOARDING** by the specific **PASSENGER**, we will bring in the primary key of **BOARDING** into the **PASSENGER** entity to answer this concern. Unfortunately, this is wrong. On further review, we should recognize that bringing in the **BoardingID** as an FK into the **PASSENGER** entity forever limits a passenger to one and only one boarding ever. This restriction should be eliminated as realistically, a passenger tends to board a vehicle several times over their lives.

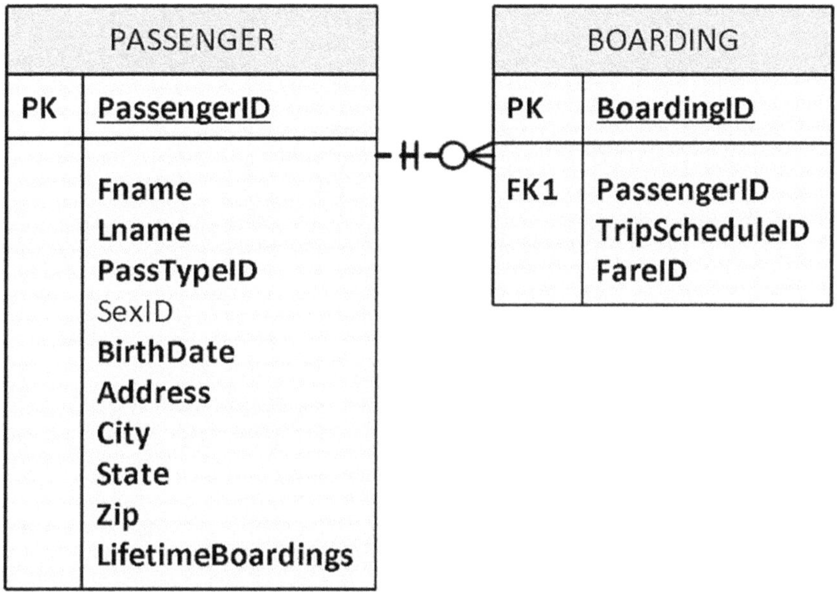

Figure 4.34: *Example of a correct design with the primary and foreign keys going in the right direction*

In *Figure* 4.34, we see a **BOARDING** is for one and only one **PASSENGER**. And that **PassengerID** goes into **BOARDING** as a foreign key. Again, if your first impulse was to assign **BoardingID** to **PASSENGER**, that would be wrong. One way to make this more clear is to remember that placing the **BoardingID** foreign key in **PASSENGER** will forever limit a passenger to one and only one boarding for their entire life!

Slow down each time assigning a foreign key to any table; visualize an actual row of data in your head and ask yourself, "Do I forever want to limit a row in this table with one and only one of these FK values for the life of the database?"

Referential Loops

A referential loop occurs when entity relationships form a closed loop. Observe the loop created between **SEX**, **EMPLOYEE**, **JOB**, **TRIP**, **TRIP_SCHEDULE**, **BOARDING** and **PASSENGER**. The '**LOOP**' occurs when users can connect all seven entities in a closed circle by traversing all the entities in multiple directions.

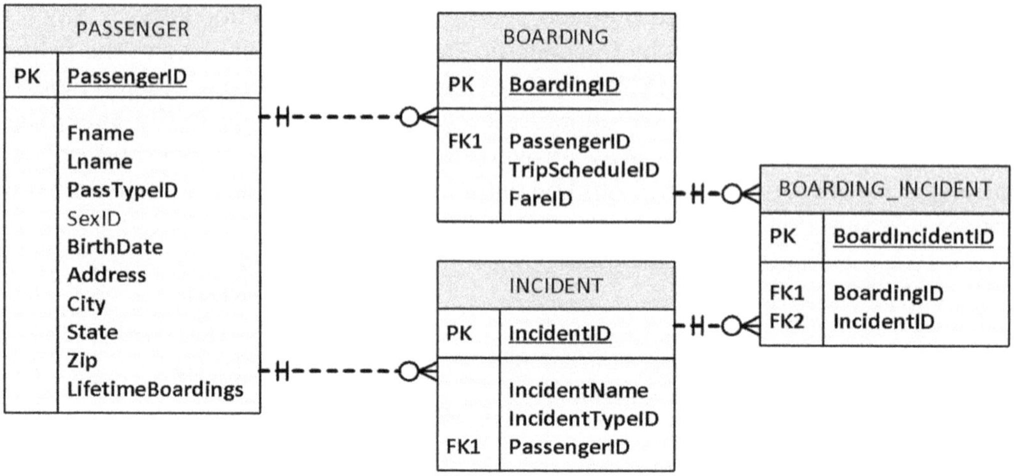

Figure 4.35: *Example of a poor design with a referential loop connecting four entities*

A referential loop places a burden on the user to ensure that the data remains consistent within the loop. For example, in the preceding design, **PassengerID** in **INCIDENT** must match with the **PassengerID** in **BOARDING** to avoid inconsistency. To determine the correct **PassengerID** and resolve the referential loop, we must locate the entity that is providing values in two directions or otherwise has both "forks pointing outwards". In *Figure* 4.34, the entity with the 'forks out' is the **PASSENGER**.

We will then determine if we can effectively answer questions regarding the **INCIDENT** (such as which passenger(s) were involved) with a single direction of relationships, instead of having a loop. In this example, if we track which **BOARDING** the **INCIDENT** occurred, we can assume that the passenger referenced in the **BOARDING** is the one involved in the **INCIDENT**. Younger developers often do not trust the database to accurately reference the passenger through **BOARDING**.

We will learn later that this becomes a problem because a database is being used by thousands of simultaneous connections. With high volume, users trying to obtain locks (known as "deadlocks") will collide and will have to make insert statements or updates, which will cause the transaction processing to come to a complete halt. Until then, it is better to avoid referential loops if possible.

Have a look at the corrected version of the referential loop with one of the **PassengerID** foreign keys removed in *Figure* 4.34:

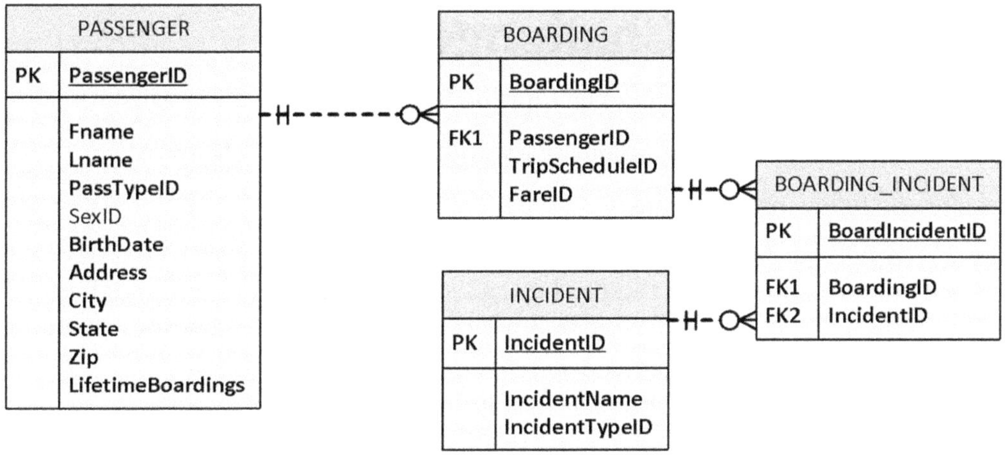

Figure 4.36: *Example of a proper design without a referential loop*

Again, designing relational databases and normalization are far from easy. Recognizing design patterns will go a long way towards enhancing your confidence in developing robust and scalable database solutions.

Conclusion

Data modeling and the normalization process are critical for building robust relational and transactional database systems. A well-defined model provides a repository of critical organizational data that is trustworthy, readily available, and secure. A fully normalized relational database also grants insights into the behavior of core company objects (often defined as 'read' activity) without intruding on the processing of capturing new transactional data (known as 'write' activity).

Ultimately, a database is intended for organizational learning that enhances the capabilities and competitive strength of an organization as it evolves. Proper analytics with truthful data allow for high-speed learning which makes companies more responsive to customer and market demands.

Knowing about these processes and methods will help you evolve into an effective design professional who can conduct their own systems without relying on others for infrastructure or transactional data.

Next up, will see how Structured Query Language (SQL) works with simple examples. SQL is the standard programming and query language in use by millions of organizations across the world to manage billions of transactions each day in addition to petabytes of cumulative data in storage. We will be exposed to the wonders of how SQL can provide exceptional insight and learning, beginning a valuable set of skills.

Post-Chapter Challenges

Based on what you have learned so far, approach the following challenges:

Track 1: Data Tourist Seeking Ancillary Awareness (THINK ~10 Minutes)

Consider the following questions:

- Why do you think that one method will align more easily with your approach? Reminder: The first method is the academic 'vertical' approach, and the second method is a 'horizontal' approach with standard column names (ID, Name, and Description).
- How many of the 'violations of a relation' can you recall?
- How has exposure to the data layer design process affected your desire to add more 'full stack' development and design skills to your existing portfolio?

Track 2: Dedicated Student or Recent Graduate (WRITE ~ 45 Minutes)

Respond to these questions and give adequate reasons for your answers:

- How would you follow the normalization process during database design? Explain it in simple words.
- Lay out the process of how a data model moves through raw brainstorming while beginning in UNF, before eventually being refined and ending up in 4NF. Also explain the importance of such a transition.

Track 3: Aspiring Professionals (BUILD ~3 Hours)

This track is for the readers aspiring to pursue a career in data science. Now that we have seen the second method of normalization, let us continue with the buildout of the database you embarked upon in the last chapter:

- Take your design to 4NF. Note any interesting discoveries you encounter or decisions you make along the way. You must retell the story of your journey after re-evaluating relationships, and resolving any M:M relationships. Explain why you make these adjustments and design tweaks.

CHAPTER 5
Beginning with SQL

Introduction

The Structured Query Language (shortened to SQL, and pronounced either by the letters 'S-Q-L' or as a word 'sequel') is the standard query and programming language that is leveraged to create databases and objects used in the database (such as tables, logins, stored procedures, and user-defined functions among others). With SQL, there is an opportunity to automate most processes that create or consume data, such as point-of-sale purchases as well as publishing reports or updating a dashboard. These are sophisticated, powerful, advanced tasks but are easy enough to learn by most college students or any learner with focus and ambition.

Being proficient in leveraging SQL is an exceptionally valuable technical skill for nearly every data-centric position. Many learners will have a bit of discomfort as we are confronted with challenges; learning a new querying and programming language will certainly have this. Keep an open mind as we explore design structures of storing data for machines and not the hierarchies that humans have organized with paper-based systems for centuries. This may seem like a revolutionary way of thinking.

Structure

In this chapter, we will explore the following topics:

- Download and Install SQL Server 2025 Express
- Data Definition Language (DDL) to build basic database schemas (CREATE and ALTER)
- Data Modification Language (DML) to populate tables (INSERT, UPDATE, and DELETE)
- Basic query structure, including SELECT statements
- Practice SQL using common operators

Download and Install SQL Server 2025 Express

Even though it may seem easier to just copy or load a file of prepared code, learning any language is best served if you take the time, and do some typing.

We must first create a database to hold the tables that will store data. For this first introduction and practice, we will use the example database for tracking a metro bus or transit system from previous chapters. We will call this new database METRO_TRANSIT. During this process, please notice the comments included within the SQL code to provide anecdotal explanations in the code that is a learning moment.

Download an SQL Development Tool

As a Fourth Generation Language (4GL), SQL is refined and has many standard keywords that simplify many tasks. This enables users to focus on the immediate analytical objectives without the stress of designing 'how' to accomplish them. SQL is intended to be a standardized language but there are slight differences across vendors. There are other very capable database products such as Oracle, MySQL, PostgreSQL, IBM DB2, and Microsoft SQL Server with very similar implementations of the SQL syntax.

This textbook is centric to Microsoft SQL Server. Unfortunately, there is not enough time or space to make a list of every slight syntax change for all these products. Please do your best to follow along if you end up using a product other than SQL Server.

There are several software tools that are ideal for students to engage the database code in this textbook to facilitate hands-on practice and deeper learning:

Tool	**Platform**	**Link**
DB Visualizer	Windows, MAC, Linux	https://www.dbvis.com/download/
Data Grip	Windows, MAC, Linux	https://www.jetbrains.com/datagrip/download
SQL Server Management Studio	Windows	https://learn.microsoft.com/en-us/ssms/install/install
SQL Server 2025 Developer	Windows, Linus	https://www.microsoft.com/en-us/sql-server/sql-server-downloads#trysql
SQL Server 2025 Express	Windows, Linux	https://www.microsoft.com/en-us/sql-server/sql-server-downloads#trysql

Table 5.1: *List of prominent development tools to engage* METRO_TRANSIT

To get started with connecting to a SQL Server database, please select one of the development tools listed above based on the type of computer or laptop you are using. For the easiest engagement, it is highly recommended to use a Windows-based machine with at least 750 MB of free storage space available with SQL Server 2025 Express. This product is free to download and has many of the same features as the fully operational commercial enterprise version.

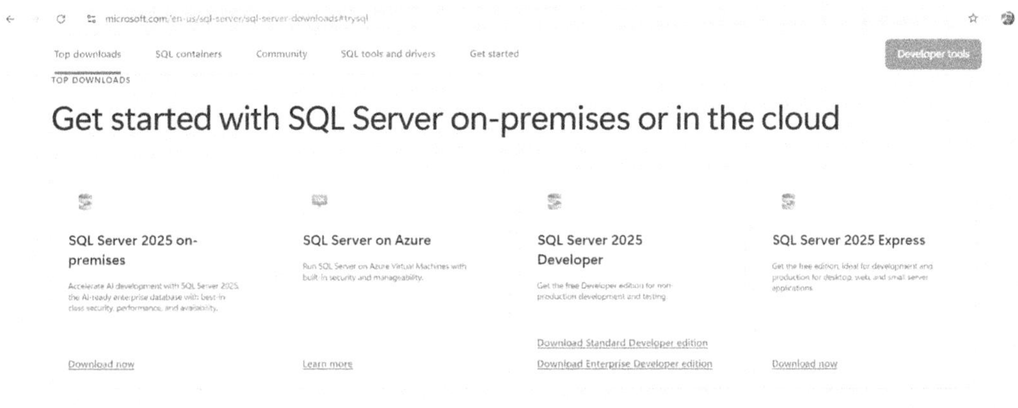

Figure 5.1: *Screenshot of location to download and install SQL Server 2025 Express*

After completing the download and initiating the installation process for SQL Server 2025 Express, consider also installing SQL Server Management Studio (SSMS). This tool allows for a standard management of the database engine that is being installed on your computer, and will mirror much of the instructions and screenshots presented in this textbook.

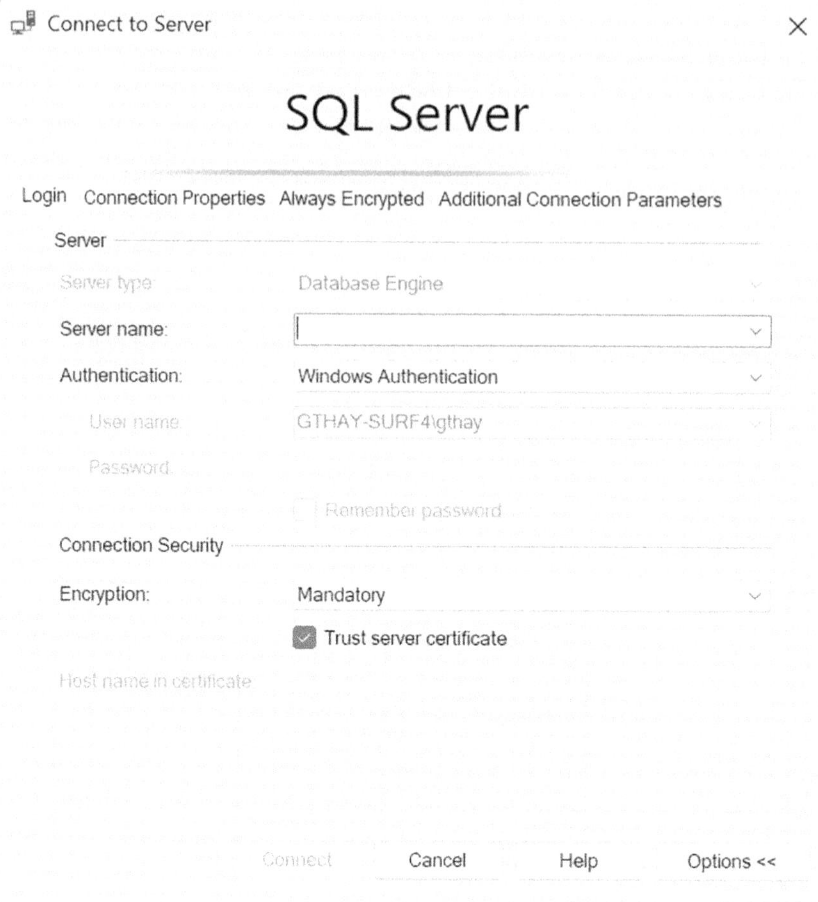

Figure 5.2: *Screenshot of launch screen for SQL Server 2025 Express*

Once SQL Server 2025 Express and SSMS has been installed, launch SQL Management Studio to connect to your SQL Server database engine. As seen in Figure 5.2, the newly-installed SQLExpress server should match the name of your laptop and automatically be visible when you click to select Server Name. Try also selecting Windows Authentication to complete the connection process.

To successfully operate SQL Server 2025 Express on a Mac, another application named Docker is required to establish something called a container. This additional work by you is required since no version of Microsoft SQL Server runs natively on any macOS. After you install Docker Desktop for Mac, pull the SQL Server image from Docker Hub and choose to run it as a container. While somewhat of a workaround, this process and configuration allows you to use SQL Server on a Mac with Apple silicon chips.

In addition to obtaining a database tool like SQL Server 2025 Express, each reader will benefit from downloading at least one sample database from the publisher's github repository. The sample databases are based on actual metro transit systems from around the globe and are intended to provide familiar context for the database concepts and objects that are presented. After establishing a database platform on a workstation or laptop, please visit the following link to peruse the list of cities that have been used as a background for **METRO_TRANSIT** databases. Download a back-up file to restore on your local machine if you are able to find a city to your liking!

Download files for METRO_TRANSIT through:

https://github.com/ava-orange-education/ultimate-SQL-for-Data-Science-and-Analytics

Structured Query Language (aka "Sequel") is the standard database language across the world. There are more positions in the data industry that seek intermediate SQL skills (beyond the basic query statement) than almost any other technical language (go to dice.com and type in 'SQL' for a keyword search and perhaps 10,000 listings will be returned). As there are literally thousands of open positions seeking skilled database programmers at this exact moment, you will benefit from having a competency in SQL as it helps clarify business objects, their relationships, and a range of typical values. Database designers often become experts of their business data through repetitive conversations with various departments and multiple layers of management, becoming increasingly more valuable to their organization.

SQL has also been the *de facto* standard database query language since the early 1980s. Essentially, all popular relational database applications have SQL as their core user-based method of engagement. However, we will skip the history of SQL and highlight its practical applications instead. If your goals are just observational, then it may be better to download the full version of **METRO_TRANSIT** from the link provided previously.

By coding the **METRO_TRANSIT** dataset in SQL, you will be able to run the queries presented in later chapters without having to download extra files.

This text will walk you through the process of building an abbreviated, sub-set of **METRO_TRANSIT** to practice Data Definition Language (DDL). Here is the seven-step process to do so:

Coding Process Sequence

1. Write the **CREATE DATABASE** statement.
2. Write the **USE** statement to begin defining the newly created database.
3. Write the **CREATE TABLE** statements with all columns, proper data types, **NULLABILITY**, and auto-increment enabled on a surrogate primary key (this is done with the **IDENTITY()** function). We will see how several keywords will be included to increase functionality and performance.

4. Write **ALTER TABLE** statements for each foreign key; this last step is different from the **CREATE TABLE** statements intentionally as the **ALTER TABLE** statement allows for the table definitions to be arranged in any order.
5. Save the script for safety as we will be re-running the script several times while exploring development options.
6. Test the **DROP** command.
7. Re-run the entire script again.

While building a unique copy of the **METRO_TRANSIT** database with SQL code in this next section, you must be aware of the sample SQL code that is structured in a different font like this:

```
example code will be provided like this and should be typed as such.
```

Let's get started by opening a new query window inside SQL Server Management Studio by typing [Ctrl + N] from the opening menu screen (there is also a New Query button on the top ribbon if that is easier):

DDL: CREATE, ALTER, and DROP

Next are the steps to systematically create a new database on your SQL Server 2025 Express installation. These steps are intended to reinforce the basic process for building a database of any size.

Step 1: Make a new copy of METRO_TRANSIT database

Type in the following code to create your personal copy of **METRO_TRANSIT**. Highlight the text in the query window and type [Ctrl + E] to execute the command (only the highlighted code will be read by SQL Server). Alternatively, there is an **Execute** button on the top ribbon as well that can be clicked to get the highlighted code to run.

```
CREATE DATABASE METRO_TRANSIT
GO
```

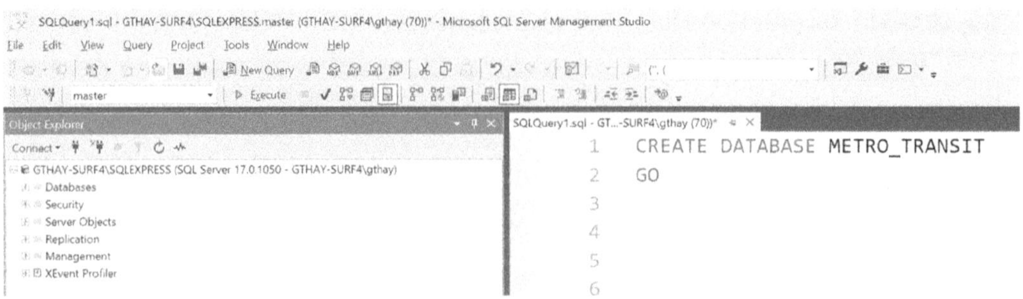

***Figure 5.3:** SQL Server Management Studio and typing SQL command to CREATE DATABASE*

Step 2: Change Context of Query Window to Newly Created Database

Next, we must change the context of the query window to be inside the newly created database of **`METRO_TRANSIT`** you just made.

```
USE METRO_TRANSIT
GO
```

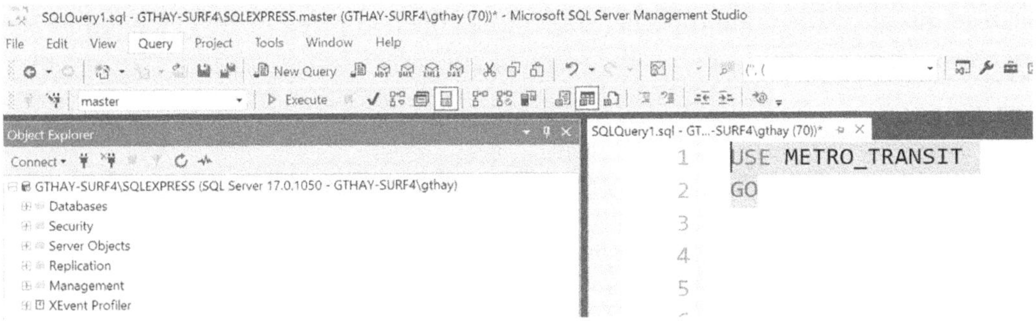

***Figure* 5.4**: *SQL Server Management Studio and typing SQL command to* USE METRO_TRANSIT

Now that we have established a new query window within the context of your brand-new database, we are ready to write SQL statements to make new tables, enter data values into these tables, and eventually write queries.

First of all, the CREATE statement is used to construct a named object with SQL; these objects include the database itself, as well as each table, column, view, stored procedure, user-defined function, login, job, and index. You can use the CREATE statement to establish pretty much anything that is named within a relational database.

Next, let us code the 13 entities that represent a simplified or basic version of the **`METRO_TRANSIT`** entity-relationship diagram from Chapter 3. This abbreviated version is intended to help readers practice writing CREATE and ALTER TABLE statements as well as preliminary insert statements without spending a lot of time. These entities include DRIVER, ROUTE_TYPE, ROUTE, VEHICLE_TYPE, VEHICLE, NEIGHBORHOOD, STOP_TYPE, STOP, ROUTE_STOP, TRIP, TRIP_STOP, CUSTOMER, and BOARDING.

Step 3: Establish Tables, Columns, and PKs with CREATE TABLE Statements

Syntax: Some organizations have a preferred naming convention; the prefix 'tbl' is included for each table here as a standard, but it is not mandatory.

Notice the following patterns when using the **`CREATE TABLE`** statement:

- Open parentheses begins and closes the column definition.
- Each line (except the final one) has a comma at the end.
- TableName + ID is great name for the surrogate primary key.
- **`IDENTITY(1,1)`** establishes auto-increment function for SQL Server databases.

- Each column has appropriate data type and length
- Every column will be mandatory or defined as '**NOT NULL**'.
- The word '**GO**' separates each table definition and allows faster execution

Now, at the beginning of the SQL code; type the next 2 pages of SQL (all the way through Step Four). Alternatively, this script is available for download from github. We will execute all of the code together after it has been entered or downloaded in Step Six.

Here we go!

```
CREATE TABLE tblDRIVER
(DriverID INTEGER IDENTITY(1,1) PRIMARY KEY,
Fname VARCHAR(25) NOT NULL,
Lname VARCHAR(25) NOT NULL,
BirthDate DATE NOT NULL,
Salary Numeric (8,2) NOT NULL,
LicenseNumber VARCHAR(35) NULL)
GO


CREATE TABLE tblROUTE_TYPE
(RouteTypeID INTEGER IDENTITY(1,1) PRIMARY KEY,
RouteTypeName VARCHAR(50) NOT NULL,
RouteTypeDescr VARCHAR(500) NULL)
GO
CREATE TABLE tblROUTE
(RouteID INTEGER IDENTITY(1,1) PRIMARY KEY,
RouteName VARCHAR(100) NOT NULL,
RouteTypeID INTEGER NOT NULL,
RouteAbbrev VARCHAR(20) NOT NULL,
RouteDescr VARCHAR(500) NULL)
GO


CREATE TABLE tblVEHICLE_TYPE
(VehicleTypeID INTEGER IDENTITY(1,1) PRIMARY KEY,
VehicleTypeName VARCHAR(100) NOT NULL,
NumSeats INTEGER NOT NULL,
TotalCapacity INTEGER NOT NULL,
VehicleTypeDescr VARCHAR(500) NULL)
GO


CREATE TABLE tblVEHICLE
(VehicleID INTEGER IDENTITY(1,1) PRIMARY KEY,
VehicleName VARCHAR(50) NOT NULL,
```

```
VehicleTypeID INTEGER NOT NULL,
PlateNumber VARCHAR(20) NOT NULL,
PurchasePrice Numeric(10,2) NOT NULL,
VehiclePurchaseDate DATE NOT NULL)
GO


CREATE TABLE tblNEIGHBORHOOD
(NeighborhoodID INTEGER IDENTITY(1,1) PRIMARY KEY,
NeighborhoodName VARCHAR(50) NOT NULL,
NeighborhoodDescr VARCHAR(500) NULL)
GO


CREATE TABLE tblSTOP_TYPE
(StopTypeID INTEGER IDENTITY(1,1) PRIMARY KEY,
StopTypeName VARCHAR(50) NOT NULL,
StopTypeDescr VARCHAR(500) NULL)
GO

CREATE TABLE tblSTOP
(StopID INTEGER IDENTITY(1,1) PRIMARY KEY,
StopName VARCHAR(50) NOT NULL,
StopTypeID INTEGER NOT NULL,
NeighborhoodID INTEGER NOT NULL,
GPS_CorOrd VARCHAR(50) NULL)
GO
CREATE TABLE tblROUTE_STOP
(RouteStopID INTEGER IDENTITY(1,1) PRIMARY KEY,
RouteID INTEGER NOT NULL,
StopID INTEGER NOT NULL,
SequenceNumber INTEGER NULL,
RevisedDate DATE NOT NULL)
GO


CREATE TABLE tblTRIP
(TripID INTEGER IDENTITY(1,1) PRIMARY KEY,
DriverID INTEGER NOT NULL,
VehicleID INTEGER NOT NULL,
RouteID INTEGER NOT NULL,
BeginDateTime DATETIME NOT NULL,
EndDateTime DATETIME NULL)
GO


CREATE TABLE tblTRIP_STOP
```

```
(TripStopID INTEGER IDENTITY(1,1) PRIMARY KEY,
TripID INTEGER NOT NULL,
StopID INTEGER NOT NULL,
TripStopDateTime DATETIME NOT NULL)
GO


CREATE TABLE tblCUSTOMER
(CustomerID INTEGER IDENTITY(1,1) PRIMARY KEY,
Fname VARCHAR(25) NOT NULL,
Mname VARCHAR (25) NULL,
Lname VARCHAR(25) Not NULL,
BirthDate DATE NULL,
CustAddress VARCHAR (100) NULL,
CustCity VARCHAR(50) NULL,
CustState VARCHAR(50) NULL,
PostalCode VARCHAR(15) NULL)
GO
```

Observe that two foreign key values are created right in the middle of the CREATE TABLE statement for **`tblBOARDING`**; this is called 'in-line' definition and is frequently used when there are only a handful of tables in a database. The source table of FK values must already exist. SQL code to create table **`tblBOARDING`** is as follows:

```
CREATE TABLE tblBOARDING
(BoardingID INTEGER IDENTITY(1,1) PRIMARY KEY,
CustomerID INTEGER FOREIGN KEY REFERENCES tblCUSTOMER
(CustomerID) NOT NULL,
TripStopID INTEGER FOREIGN KEY REFERENCES tblTRIP_STOP
(TripStopID) NOT NULL,
BoardingDateTime DATETIME NOT NULL,
Fare Numeric(5,2) NOT NULL)
GO

PRINT 'Completed CREATE TABLE statements for all tables in
abbreviated METRO_TRANSIT'
GO
```

Step 4: Establish Foreign Keys with `ALTER TABLE` Statements.

Ensure that foreign keys are coded separately from the **`CREATE TABLE`** code with **`ALTER TABLE`**. SQL code to establish foreign keys is as follows:

```
ALTER TABLE tblROUTE
ADD CONSTRAINT FK_tblROUTE_RouteTypeID
FOREIGN KEY (RouteTypeID)
REFERENCES tblROUTE_TYPE (RouteTypeID)
GO
```

```
ALTER TABLE tblVEHICLE
ADD CONSTRAINT FK_tblVEHICLE_VehicleTypeID
FOREIGN KEY (VehicleTypeID)
REFERENCES tblVEHICLE_TYPE (VehicleTypeID)
GO


ALTER TABLE tblSTOP
ADD CONSTRAINT FK_tblSTOP_StopTypeID
FOREIGN KEY (StopTypeID)
REFERENCES tblSTOP_TYPE (StopTypeID)
GO


ALTER TABLE tblSTOP
ADD CONSTRAINT FK_tblSTOP_NeighborhoodID
FOREIGN KEY (NeighborhoodID)
REFERENCES tblNEIGHBORHOOD (NeighborhoodID)
GO


ALTER TABLE tblROUTE_STOP
ADD CONSTRAINT FK_tblROUTE_STOP_StopID
FOREIGN KEY (StopID)
REFERENCES tblSTOP (StopID)
GO


ALTER TABLE tblROUTE_STOP
ADD CONSTRAINT FK_tblROUTE_STOP_RouteID
FOREIGN KEY (RouteID)
REFERENCES tblROUTE (RouteID)
GO


ALTER TABLE tblTRIP
ADD CONSTRAINT FK_tblTRIP_DriverID
FOREIGN KEY (DriverID)
REFERENCES tblDRIVER (DriverID)
GO


ALTER TABLE tblTRIP
ADD CONSTRAINT FK_tblTRIP_VehicleID
FOREIGN KEY (VehicleID)
REFERENCES tblVEHICLE (VehicleID)
```

```
GO


ALTER TABLE tblTRIP
ADD CONSTRAINT FK_tblTRIP_RouteID
FOREIGN KEY (RouteID)
REFERENCES tblROUTE (RouteID)
GO

ALTER TABLE tblTRIP_STOP
ADD CONSTRAINT FK_tblTRIP_STOP_TripID
FOREIGN KEY (TripID)
REFERENCES tblTRIP (TripID)
GO


ALTER TABLE tblTRIP_STOP
ADD CONSTRAINT FK_tblTRIP_STOP_StopID
FOREIGN KEY (StopID)
REFERENCES tblSTOP (StopID)
GO


PRINT 'Completed ALTER TABLE statements for adding foreign keys'
GO
```

This sequence of steps establishes a basic, functional database that we can code up in a single 60-minute session. Again, feel free to download the code in the previous two pages to save time, but you must know that there will be moments where you may need to know how to code the **CREATE TABLE** statements from memory without any code to download.

As we learn more, we will add more modifications to the basic script (also called 'schema'). The goal of slowly adding complexity is to inform you about the development process as well as help you type out the syntax of building each object. Next, we will see the effects of issuing a **DROP** statement.

Step 5: Save the Script as a File; We Will Need to Re-Run It in a Moment

Make sure to save your script as a .txt file as well as send an entire copy on your email to avoid losing work. If you are using Azure Data Studio or SQL Server Management Studio, hit [Ctrl+ S] to save your script on your local machine.

Step 6: Highlight and execute the execute the entire script

Running code in SQL Server Management Studio is easy as we have seen. Be sure to highlight the exact code we want to run. In this case, if you have typed in exactly what has been presented here (or downloaded the prepared file), there should be no errors.

If after running the code you receive errors, do your best to troubleshoot (this is part of being a technician, unfortunately). Some of the more common errors are as follows:

- There is a typo in the code being executed; To try and repair, double click on the red errors in the results pane and SQL Server Management Studio should bring the problem code to your attention. Review the code to see if there are mismatches between what is expected and what you typed.
- What you highlighted to run did not include all of the required code. Try running the code again, this time be extra careful to highlight what is required.
- The objects already exist. This often happens during the data definition stage and we are running **`CREATE`** table statements and only part of the script is executed or there is a tiny error. When we try to pick up where we left off, half of the tables have already been created (and throw an error as already existing). Best bet (assuming you have a saved copy of your script) is to simply drop the database and re-run the script. Oftentimes, this takes only a handful of seconds to run.

If the code continues to error, download the files again, and re-run the process. Normally, all students are in a lab environment and there are instructors present to assist. Search online with the exact error message or try to reach out via LinkedIn!

Step 7: DROP Database

This command will destroy everything we have created so far, so make sure that you have saved your script as a file or at least have copied the code out to a text editor. We will re-run the script to re-establish what we have built so far after seeing the effects of the last DDL command. Dangerous SQL code to drop a database is as follows:

```
DROP DATABASE METRO_TRANSIT
GO
```

The preceding steps can change the context of the query window to the central database (master) of the database management system, and allows us to eliminate the recently completed database.

Now that we have dropped the database, refresh the window of your database management system. Spend a brief minute and look around the environment; the **`METRO_TRANSIT`** database is nowhere to be found. Again, the **`DROP`** command is used to destroy any object we have created; we might need to start over with slight alterations during the development process and make modifications like adding a column that was previously forgotten or was defined with an incorrect data type.

Instead of spending our time using the **`ALTER TABLE`** statement, it is significantly faster to just DROP the whole database and run the coded script again to get back to the desired state. If you did not save your script, you will need to re-type the code from steps 1 through 6 all over again.

Step 8: Re-Run the Entire Database Script

If you downloaded the script from GitHub, you should be able to build the **METRO_TRANSIT** database in a matter of a few minutes.

Next we are ready to begin populating **METRO_TRANSIT** and begin writing simple queries. Please see the following ERD:

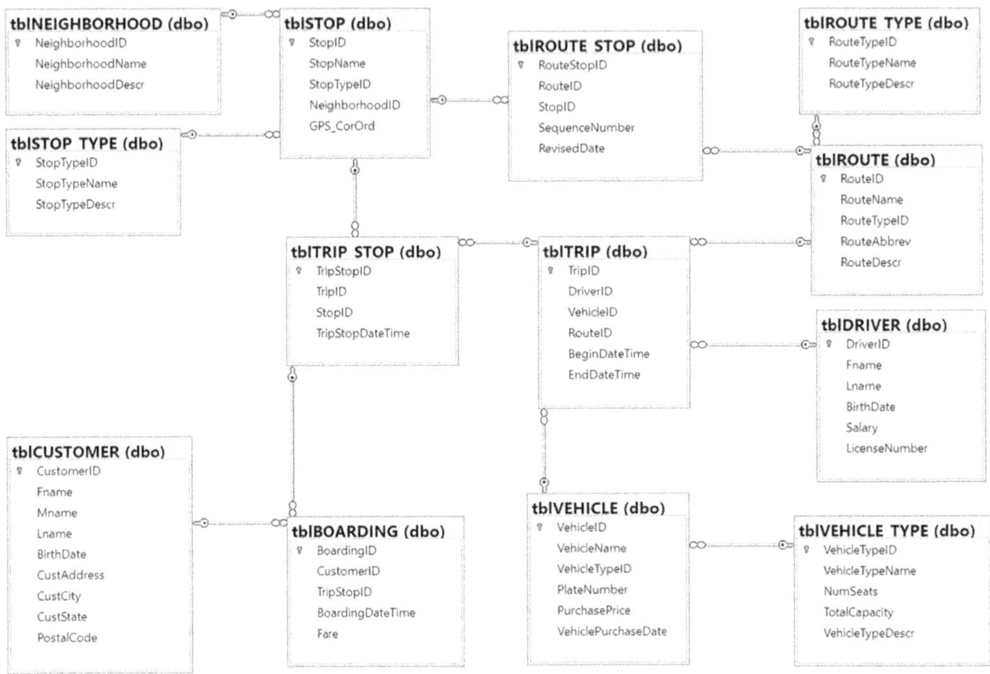

***Figure 5.5**: Simplified Entity Relationship Diagram (ERD) of METRO_TRANSIT*

Figure 5.5 shows the ERD generated from the code discussed so far in this chapter. This code represents a slightly simplified version of **METRO_TRANSIT** from the fully normalized version that has more than 40 entities.

The fully normalized schema of **METRO_TRANSIT** is too elaborate to code up a database schema manually. The more elaborate schema is available for download via: https://github.com/ava-orange-education/ultimate-SQL-for-Data-Science-and-Analytics and will prove to be valuable when more complex SQL query commands are introduced in *Chapters 6 and* 7.

DML: INSERT, UPDATE, DELETE

Now that we have the structure of a basic database, we are ready to add data using Data Modification Language, or DML. While the most-common commands and statements under DML are INSERT, UPDATE, and DELETE, there are dozens of additional key words you can use.

As we begin to populate our database, pay attention to the sequence of which tables get the data inserted. These tables are almost always the 'look-up' tables that provide foreign key values to the more transactional tables in the database.

Most relational databases will have perhaps 90% of the entire contents of data concentrated in only two or three tables. Some databases will have a look-up table with more than four values, while one of its transactional tables may have millions of rows. This design is fast and efficient in recording new data accurately in the database and getting queries returned from the largest tables. This is considered as the brilliance of relational theory.

In the **METRO_TRANSIT** database, the tables that will store the bulk of the data are **tblTRIP_STOP** and **tblBOARDING**. These are the transactional tables as they contain the details about each time a vehicle drives past a stop on a scheduled trip even if no one boards the bus. Again, a transactional table often contains multiple foreign keys that allow a connection back to the look-up tables. You must recognize that values contained under the columns in these transactional tables have no 'words'; this means that if we were to break into a database and read just the values from a transactional table, it will not be legible for a person as the numbers have no context.

All the associated context is in the look-up tables. Therefore, it can be concluded that data should be stored in relational databases for machines. Thereafter, we will write queries that connect tables together when we need to read names associated with the values stored in transactional tables.

Look-Up Tables Must be Filled First

If more than 90% data in a relational database is held in a few transactional tables that reference values in other look-up tables to obtain a detailed context via foreign keys, then the foreign key values must exist ***before*** they can be referenced. We will populate the look-up tables in the **METRO_TRANSIT** database now. Note that aside from including names of several famous people from the 1970s, these values are fabricated for illustrative purposes.

You must also remember to not populate the primary key values as the auto-increment feature will be enabled (that is what **IDENTITY(1,1)** does in the **CREATE TABLE** statement).

You can also observe that the column headers are named specifically in the **INSERT** statement; this is considered an industry best-practice as not naming them may unintentionally put values in the wrong columns. This also provides flexibility when working with various external sources of data and being tasked with importing large amounts of data (we can change how we read the data instead of changing the external source to write the data).

You may also see that several values can be included in a single **INSERT** statement. Typing it manually is important to recognize the impact of 'better code' when we create stored procedures. For now, there are several ways to bring data into a relational database; it will be important to know these methods to boost efficiency.

Code Example: INSERT Statement

```
INSERT INTO tblDRIVER (Fname, Lname, BirthDate, Salary,
LicenseNumber)
VALUES
('Jimi', 'Hendrix', 'November 27, 1942', 42590, 'JMHend3487RR'),
('Bruce', 'Lee', 'November 27, 1940', 42590, 'BTLee*2198DL'),
('Jim', 'Morrison', 'December 8, 1943', 47625, 'JPMorr7762WS'),
('Meryl', 'Streep', 'June 22, 1949', 46965, 'MDStre8121UJ')
GO
```

String data types have single quotations, while numbers (INTEGER, FLOAT, NUMERIC, DECIMAL, MONEY) do not. Date values are considered to be string data types. SQL code to insert more sample data into table **tblROUTE_TYPE** is as follows:

```
INSERT INTO tblROUTE_TYPE (RouteTypeName, RouteTypeDescr)
VALUES
('Express', 'An express route is often designed to have limited
stops during the morning and evening commute hours'),

('Special Event', 'A special event route is often scheduled for
high-attendance events at sporting venues or downtown'),

('Regular', 'A regular route is any route not identified as
express or special event'),

('Inclement Weather/Reduced Service', 'Any route affected by weath-
er')
GO
```

Most description columns (such as those ending in 'DESCR') are often defined as NULL; this means that values are not mandatory and may be left empty. Because of this, we will rarely write queries to filter across a range of values held in any description column. This means that no important data should be placed in a description field. Moreover, its intent is to provide clarification for users on a case-by-case basis only if necessary. SQL code to insert sample data into table **tblVEHICLE_TYPE** is as follows:

```
INSERT INTO tblROUTE (RouteName, RouteTypeID, RouteAbbrev, RouteDescr)
VALUES
```

```
('Sodo-Downtown Express', (SELECT RouteTypeID FROM tblROUTE_TYPE
WHERE RouteTypeName = 'Express'), '42-E', 'Express route from South
of Downtown to main stops downtown'),

('Sodo-Downtown', (SELECT RouteTypeID FROM tblROUTE_TYPE WHERE
RouteTypeName = 'Regular'), '42', 'Commuter route from South of
Downtown to main stops downtown'),

('Fremont-Downtown Express', (SELECT RouteTypeID FROM tblROUTE_TYPE
WHERE RouteTypeName = 'Express'), '78-E', 'Express route from Fre-
mont to main stops downtown'),

('Fremont-Downtown', (SELECT RouteTypeID FROM tblROUTE_TYPE WHERE
RouteTypeName = 'Regular'), '78', 'Commuter route from Fremont to
main stops downtown'),

('Fremont-Waterfront-Downtown', (SELECT RouteTypeID FROM tblROUTE_
TYPE WHERE RouteTypeName = 'Special Event'), '78-S', 'Special route
from Fremont along waterfront to main stops downtown during summer
weekend concert series'),

('Capitol Hill-Downtown', (SELECT RouteTypeID FROM tblROUTE_TYPE
WHERE RouteTypeName = 'Regular'), '32', 'Regular route from Capitol
Hill to main stops downtown')
GO


INSERT INTO tblVEHICLE_TYPE (VehicleTypeName, NumSeats,
TotalCapacity,
VehicleTypeDescr)
VALUES
('Standard Bus', 54, 76, 'Standard bus is primary use for residen-
tial neighborhoods during non-commute hours'),

('Double-Decker Bus', 96, 144, 'Double Decker bus is primary coach
on state highways between major population centers as well as for
special events'),

('Standard Light Rail Car', 58, 88, 'Standard Light Rail car is
staple for fixed-track, high-volume routes that connect suburban and
urban centers with the airport often in alignments with 4 connected
cars'),

('Heavy Rail Single Passenger Train', 40, 50, 'Heavy Rail Single
cars are placed on routes that are greater than 85 KM from major
urban centers; these often are aligned with 12 connected cars')
GO
```

The next set of **INSERT** statements will include a **SELECT** statement inside of the **INSERT** statement; this is called a 'sub-query' and is useful in leveraging the existing information to find what we do not know (which is usually the value of a required foreign key). We will spend more time on this; for now, it is enough to recognize the placement and the use of the subquery, which saves us time from having to manually look up the values. SQL code inserting sample data into tables **tblVEHICLE**, **tblNEIGHBORHOOD**, **tblSTOP_TYPE**, **tblSTOP**, **tblROUTE_STOP**, **tblCUSTOMER**, **tblTRIP**, and **tblTRIP_STOP** is as follows:

```
INSERT INTO tblVEHICLE (VehicleName, VehicleTypeID, PlateNumber,
PurchasePrice, VehiclePurchaseDate)
VALUES
('GS203', (SELECT VehicleTypeID FROM tblVEHICLE_TYPE WHERE Vehi-
cleTypeName = 'Double-Decker Bus'), 'DRE-657J',887533, 'March 3,
2019'),

('GS204', (SELECT VehicleTypeID FROM tblVEHICLE_TYPE WHERE Vehicle
TypeName = 'Double-Decker Bus'), 'GTT-7JHS',887533, 'March 3,
2019'),

('PA7', (SELECT VehicleTypeID FROM tblVEHICLE_TYPE WHERE Vehicle-
TypeName = 'Standard Bus'), 'XYW-23KJ', 566988,'July 13, 2023'),

('GS208', (SELECT VehicleTypeID FROM tblVEHICLE_TYPE WHERE Vehicle-
TypeName = 'Standard Bus'), 'TG8-99L2',604995,'August 9, 2024')
GO

INSERT INTO tblNEIGHBORHOOD (NeighborhoodName, NeighborhoodDescr)
VALUES

('Capitol Hill', 'Vibrant, colorful, and walkable neighborhood with
many shops and services'),
('Waterfront', 'Naturally scenic, tourist-focused neighborhood with
many food options'),

('Downtown', 'Urban, business-focused with many restaurants and
transit connections to entire region'),

('SoDo', 'Gritty and industrial neighborhood'),

('Fremont', 'Eccentric and organic feel with shops and restaurants
that fit a range of budgets')
GO


INSERT INTO tblSTOP_TYPE (StopTypeName, StopTypeDescr)
VALUES
```

```
('Uncovered', 'Standard stop that has a 3-person bench and garbage
can'),

('Covered', 'Upgraded 3-sided stop'),

('Tunnel Station', 'High capacity stop that has full service and
security'),

('Elevated Rail Station', 'High capacity stop that serves only
rail')
GO


INSERT INTO tblSTOP (StopName, StopTypeID, NeighborhoodID, GPS_
CorOrd)
VALUES
('Elliott Avenue and Mercer Street', (SELECT StopTypeID FROM
tblSTOP_TYPE WHERE StopTypeName = 'UnCovered'), (SELECT Neighborhood
ID FROM tblNEIGHBORHOOD WHERE NeighborhoodName = 'Waterfront'),
'47.6567° N, 122.2470° W'),

('Hwy 99-N 36th', (SELECT StopTypeID FROM tblSTOP_TYPE WHERE Stop-
TypeName = 'Covered'), (SELECT NeighborhoodID FROM tblNEIGHBORHOOD
WHERE NeighborhoodName = 'Fremont'),'47.6567° N, 122.3474° W'),

('Fourth Avenue South and Lander Street', (SELECT StopTypeID FROM
tblSTOP_TYPE WHERE StopTypeName = 'UnCovered'), (SELECT Neighborhoo-
dID FROM tblNEIGHBORHOOD WHERE NeighborhoodName = 'SoDo'),'47.0117°
N, 122.2430° W'),

('Sixth Avenue and Battery Street', (SELECT StopTypeID FROM tblSTOP_
TYPE WHERE StopTypeName = 'UnCovered'), (SELECT NeighborhoodID FROM
tblNEIGHBORHOOD WHERE NeighborhoodName = 'Downtown'),'47.6417° N,
122.3276° W'),

('Hwy 99-N 54th', (SELECT StopTypeID FROM tblSTOP_TYPE WHERE Stop-
TypeName = 'Covered'), (SELECT NeighborhoodID FROM tblNEIGHBORHOOD
WHERE NeighborhoodName = 'Fremont'),'47.6697° N, 122.3964° W'),

('Fourth Avenue and Seneca Street', (SELECT StopTypeID FROM tblSTOP_
TYPE WHERE StopTypeName = 'UnCovered'), (SELECT NeighborhoodID FROM
tblNEIGHBORHOOD WHERE NeighborhoodName = 'Downtown'),'47.6398° N,
122.3371° W'),

('Broadway Avenue and Cherry Street', (SELECT StopTypeID FROM
tblSTOP_TYPE WHERE StopTypeName = 'Covered'), (SELECT NeighborhoodID
 FROM tblNEIGHBORHOOD WHERE NeighborhoodName = 'Capitol
```

```
Hill'),'47.6317° N, 122.3383° W'),

('First Avenue and Terry Street', (SELECT StopTypeID FROM tblSTOP_
TYPE WHERE StopTypeName = 'Covered'), (SELECT NeighborhoodID FROM
tblNEIGHBORHOOD WHERE NeighborhoodName = 'SoDo'),'47.6212° N,
122.3243° W')
GO


INSERT INTO tblROUTE_STOP (RouteID, StopID, SequenceNumber, Revised-
Date)
VALUES
((SELECT RouteID FROM tblROUTE WHERE RouteName = 'Fremont-Water-
front-Downtown'), (SELECT StopID FROM tblSTOP WHERE StopName =
'Sixth Avenue and Battery Street'), 4, 'May 1, 2024'),

((SELECT RouteID FROM tblROUTE WHERE RouteName = 'Fremont-Water-
front-Downtown'), (SELECT StopID FROM tblSTOP WHERE StopName = 'Hwy
99-N 36th'), 2, 'May 1, 2024'),

((SELECT RouteID FROM tblROUTE WHERE RouteName = 'Fremont-Water-
front-Downtown'), (SELECT StopID FROM tblSTOP WHERE StopName
= 'Elliott Avenue and Mercer Street'), 3, 'May 1, 2024'),

((SELECT RouteID FROM tblROUTE WHERE RouteName = 'Fremont-Water-
front-Downtown'), (SELECT StopID FROM tblSTOP WHERE StopName
= 'First Avenue and Terry Street'), 1, 'May 1, 2024'),

((SELECT RouteID FROM tblROUTE WHERE RouteName ='Sodo-Downtown
Express'), (SELECT StopID FROM tblSTOP WHERE StopName = 'Fourth
Avenue South and Lander Street'), 1, 'May 1, 2024'),

((SELECT RouteID FROM tblROUTE WHERE RouteName ='Sodo-Downtown
Express'), (SELECT StopID FROM tblSTOP WHERE StopName = 'Sixth Ave-
nue and Battery Street'), 2, 'May 1, 2024'),

((SELECT RouteID FROM tblROUTE WHERE RouteName = 'Capitol Hill-Down-
town'), (SELECT StopID FROM tblSTOP WHERE StopName = 'Broadway
Avenue and Cherry Street'), 1, 'May 1, 2024'),

((SELECT RouteID FROM tblROUTE WHERE RouteName = 'Capitol Hill-Down-
town'), (SELECT StopID FROM tblSTOP WHERE StopName = 'Sixth Avenue
and Battery Street'), 2, 'May 1, 2024')
GO
```

```
INSERT INTO tblCUSTOMER (Fname, Lname, CustAddress, CustCity,
CustState, PostalCode, BirthDate)
VALUES
('Ivey','Hazekamp','7279 North Lavender Lake Avenue','PETRO-
LEUM','Indiana, IN','46778','1995-12-24'),

('Darcel','Eustache','6087 West Cambridge Beach
Sloop','FRUITA','Colorado, CO','81521','1995-06-11'),

('Kenyetta','Terron','6664 NW Arthur Terrace Drive','GRAND
RIVER','Ohio, OH','44045','1995-09-27'),

('Janey','Lundgren','14351 N Oak Beach Walk','CENTRALIA','Illinois,
IL','62801','1996-01-25')
GO


INSERT INTO tblTRIP (DriverID, VehicleID, RouteID, BeginDateTime,
EndDateTime)
VALUES
((SELECT DriverID FROM tblDRIVER WHERE Fname = 'Meryl' AND Lname
= 'Streep' AND BirthDate = 'June 22, 1949'), (SELECT VehicleID
FROM tblVEHICLE WHERE VehicleName = 'GS204'), (SELECT RouteID FROM
tblROUTE WHERE RouteName = 'Capitol Hill-Downtown'), '2025-04-24
06:17:00', NULL),

((SELECT DriverID FROM tblDRIVER WHERE Fname = 'Jimi' AND Lname =
'Hendrix' AND BirthDate = 'November 27, 1942'), (SELECT VehicleID
FROM tblVEHICLE WHERE VehicleName = 'GS203'), (SELECT RouteID FROM
tblROUTE WHERE RouteName = 'Fremont-Downtown Express'), '2025-04-24
06:42:55', NULL),

((SELECT DriverID FROM tblDRIVER WHERE Fname = 'Meryl' AND Lname
= 'Streep' AND BirthDate = 'June 22, 1949'), (SELECT VehicleID
FROM tblVEHICLE WHERE VehicleName = 'GS204'), (SELECT RouteID FROM
tblROUTE WHERE RouteName = 'Fremont-Waterfront-Downtown'),
'2025-04-23 07:23:00', NULL),

((SELECT DriverID FROM tblDRIVER WHERE Fname = 'Bruce' AND Lname =
'Lee' AND BirthDate = 'November 27, 1940'), (SELECT VehicleID FROM
tblVEHICLE WHERE VehicleName = 'PA7'), (SELECT RouteID FROM tblROUTE
WHERE RouteName = 'Capitol Hill-Downtown'), '2025-04-24 06:57:00',
NULL),

((SELECT DriverID FROM tblDRIVER WHERE Fname = 'Meryl' AND Lname
= 'Streep' AND BirthDate = 'June 22, 1949'), (SELECT VehicleID
FROM tblVEHICLE WHERE VehicleName = 'GS204'), (SELECT RouteID
```

```
FROM tblROUTE WHERE RouteName = 'Fremont-Downtown'), '2025-04-29
08:07:00', NULL)
GO


INSERT INTO tblTRIP_STOP (TripID, StopID, TripStopDateTime)
VALUES
((SELECT TripID FROM tblTRIP T
   JOIN tblDRIVER D ON D.DriverID = T.DriverID
   JOIN tblROUTE R ON T.RouteID = T.RouteID
WHERE D.Fname = 'Bruce' AND D.Lname = 'Lee'
AND R.RouteName = 'Capitol Hill-Downtown'
AND T.BeginDateTime = '2025-04-24 06:57:00'),
(SELECT S.StopID
FROM tblSTOP S
WHERE StopName = 'Broadway Avenue and Cherry Street'), '2025-04-24
07:06:51'),


--second value for tblTRIP_STOP
((SELECT TripID FROM tblTRIP T
   JOIN tblDRIVER D ON D.DriverID = T.DriverID
   JOIN tblROUTE R ON T.RouteID = T.RouteID
WHERE D.Fname = 'Bruce' AND D.Lname = 'Lee'
AND R.RouteName = 'Capitol Hill-Downtown'
AND T.BeginDateTime = '2025-04-24 06:57:00'),
(SELECT S.StopID FROM tblSTOP S
   WHERE StopName = 'Fourth Avenue and Seneca Street'), '2025-04-24
07:15:23'),


-- third value for tblTRIP_STOP
((SELECT TripID FROM tblTRIP T
   JOIN tblDRIVER D ON D.DriverID = T.DriverID
   JOIN tblROUTE R ON T.RouteID = T.RouteID
WHERE D.Fname = 'Jimi' AND D.Lname = 'Hendrix'
AND R.RouteName = 'Fremont-Downtown Express'
AND T.BeginDateTime = '2025-04-24 06:42:55'),
(SELECT S.StopID
FROM tblSTOP S
WHERE StopName = 'Hwy 99-N 54th'), '2025-04-24 06:43:00'),


-- fourth value for tblTRIP_STOP
((SELECT TripID FROM tblTRIP T
   JOIN tblDRIVER D ON D.DriverID = T.DriverID
   JOIN tblROUTE R ON T.RouteID = T.RouteID
```

```
WHERE D.Fname = 'Jimi' AND D.Lname = 'Hendrix'
AND R.RouteName = 'Fremont-Downtown Express'
AND T.BeginDateTime = '2025-04-24 06:42:55'),
(SELECT S.StopID
FROM tblSTOP S
WHERE StopName = 'Hwy 99-N 36th'), '2025-04-24 06:47:23'),


-- fifth value for tblTRIP_STOP
((SELECT TripID FROM tblTRIP T
   JOIN tblDRIVER D ON D.DriverID = T.DriverID
   JOIN tblROUTE R ON T.RouteID = T.RouteID
WHERE D.Fname = 'Jimi' AND D.Lname = 'Hendrix'
AND R.RouteName = 'Fremont-Downtown Express'
AND T.BeginDateTime = '2025-04-24 06:42:55'),
(SELECT S.StopID
FROM tblSTOP S
WHERE StopName = 'Elliott Avenue and Mercer Street'), '2025-04-24
06:56:34'),


-- sixth value for tblTRIP_STOP
((SELECT TripID FROM tblTRIP T
   JOIN tblDRIVER D ON D.DriverID = T.DriverID
   JOIN tblROUTE R ON T.RouteID = T.RouteID
WHERE D.Fname = 'Meryl' AND D.Lname = 'Streep'
AND R.RouteName = 'Capitol Hill-Downtown'
AND T.BeginDateTime = '2025-04-23 07:23:00'),
(SELECT S.StopID
FROM tblSTOP S
   WHERE StopName = 'Sixth Avenue and Battery Street'), '2025-04-23
07:41:06')
GO
```

The **SELECT** statement inside the **INSERT** statement is called a 'subquery' and demonstrates the power of a relational database. We do not have to manually discover the foreign key values in each of the **INSERT** statements. We can simply write the query in place of the expected value and the database engine replaces it for us automatically.

However, you need to have a data entry if you have not been able to download the data files from the following link:

https://github.com/ava-orange-education/ultimate-SQL-for-Data-Science-and-Analytics

The next section may seem arduous for those entering the data manually. While there might be easy ways to do this, practicing this exercise manually will reinforce the principles of automation and repetitive code.

As we continue populating the **METRO_TRANSIT** database, you may notice the multiple look-ups required for **tblROUTE_STOP** (one for each foreign key). It is necessary to avoid hard-coding foreign key values as constant look-ups can be tedious.

The order of columns in an **INSERT** statement can be arbitrary if they are specified; even though **BirthDate**, for example, appears in the schema as the fourth column (after **Fname**, **Mname**, and **Lname**), we can stick it at the end of the **INSERT** statement. In this case, the source of this sample data was arranged in an order that was different from this schema.

Secondly, **Mname** is not included in this **INSERT** statement. It was designed with '**NULL**' (as opposed to '**NOT NULL**'), which means that values are not mandatory. Moreover, the source of this sample data did not include a middle name.

Once the look-up tables have been populated, we can begin referencing them for context in the transactional tables. For the **METRO_TRANSIT** database, the transactional tables are the ones that have the highest frequency of new data and include **tblTRIP**, **tblTRIP_STOP**, and **tblBOARDING**. Imagine a public transportation system in a typical metropolitan center; there may be only a dozen or so types of vehicles operating over a span of fifty years. In some of the busiest transit systems, there are often over ten million boardings in a single day.

You should also recognize the difference in volatility in the number of rows affecting a look-up table versus a transactional table; one is effectively static and unchanging (also known as 'read-only') and the other is a firehose of insert activity. While ten million rows a day for **tblBOARDING** may seem like an incredible amount of data, this number is far from massive. Social media sites and email authentication easily surpass a billion rows of activity each day.

These next few INSERT statements are meant for the transactional tables of the **METRO_TRANSIT** database as we have not yet learned the structures of better efficiency and automation. Handling these statements is a cumbersome task.

Excessive typing to include subqueries in an insert statement, which is a rather clumsy method to populate these tables. However, there are more efficient methods to do this.

Code Example: INSERT statement with embedded SELECT statement

SQL code to insert 3 values into tblBOARDING is as follows:

```
INSERT INTO tblBOARDING (CustomerID, TripStopID, Fare, BoardingDate-
Time)
VALUES(
(SELECT CustomerID
FROM tblCUSTOMER
WHERE Fname = 'Ivey' AND Lname = 'Hazekamp' AND BirthDate
= '1995-12-24'),
```

```
(SELECT TripStopID FROM tblTRIP_STOP TS
   JOIN tblTRIP T ON TS.TripID = T.TripID
   JOIN tblROUTE R ON T.RouteID = T.RouteID
   JOIN tblSTOP S ON TS.StopID = S.StopID
WHERE R.RouteName = 'Capitol Hill-Downtown'
AND S.StopName = 'Sixth Avenue and Battery Street'
AND BeginDateTime = '2025-04-23 07:23:00'),
3.75, '2025-04-23 07:41:35')
GO

INSERT INTO tblBOARDING (CustomerID, TripStopID, Fare, BoardingDate-
Time)
VALUES(
(SELECT CustomerID
FROM tblCUSTOMER
WHERE Fname = 'Ivey' AND Lname = 'Hazekamp' AND BirthDate = '1995-
12-24'),

(SELECT TripStopID FROM tblTRIP_STOP TS
   JOIN tblTRIP T ON TS.TripID = T.TripID
   JOIN tblROUTE R ON T.RouteID = T.RouteID
   JOIN tblSTOP S ON TS.StopID = S.StopID
WHERE R.RouteName = 'Fremont-Downtown Express'
AND S.StopName = 'Hwy 99-N 36th'
AND BeginDateTime = '2025-04-24 06:42:55.000'),
3.75, '2025-04-24 06:47:23.000')
GO

INSERT INTO tblBOARDING (CustomerID, TripStopID, Fare, BoardingDate-
Time)
VALUES(
(SELECT CustomerID
FROM tblCUSTOMER
WHERE Fname = 'Kenyetta' AND Lname = 'Terron' AND BirthDate = '1995-
09-27'),

(SELECT TripStopID FROM tblTRIP_STOP TS
   JOIN tblTRIP T ON TS.TripID = T.TripID
   JOIN tblROUTE R ON T.RouteID = T.RouteID
   JOIN tblSTOP S ON TS.StopID = S.StopID
WHERE R.RouteName = 'Fremont-Downtown Express'
AND S.StopName = 'Hwy 99-N 36th'
AND BeginDateTime = '2025-04-24 06:42:55'),
3.25,'2025-04-24 06:47:23')
GO
```

After executing the SQL INSERT statement, the database we have been able to build is ready to engage with SQL statements.

SELECT Statement

Finally! Our database is ready to engage with SQL. These examples will provide a solid set of basic skills that can be used immediately, besides providing a strong foundation for further growth. In the METRO_TRANSIT database, there are only a few rows of data, which are small enough for you to read the data manually (called 'eyeballing'). For now, you can manually review the data to ensure that everything is accurate. To do so, you can use the SELECT statement, which is one of the most common commands in SQL. Through this, we will obtain the filtered data (called the 'result set') back to our screen.

A SELECT statement consists of at least two keywords (**SELECT** and **FROM**) but may also contain several other keywords depending on the complexity and filtering requirements of the query. The list of keywords for a basic SQL query is as follows (in this particular order):

- The SELECT statement determines the column(s) that values of data are to be retrieved.
- The FROM clause identifies the table(s) that contain the column(s) in the SELECT clause. In all cases, the keyword SELECT precedes the keyword FROM (in a later module, we will introduce subqueries where multiple SELECT statements are embedded within a single query).

Example Query 1: "What are the first and last names of people in the table **tblCUSTOMER**?"

```
SELECT Fname, Lname
FROM tblCUSTOMER
```

Next is the WHERE clause, which is not mandatory in a basic SELECT statement. It provides users the option to filter the rows of data returned from the database, while "fine-tuning" the result set to reduce clutter.

Example Query 2: "What are the first and last names of people in the CUSTOMER table who were born after June 9, 1993?"

```
SELECT Fname, Lname, BirthDate
FROM tblCUSTOMER
WHERE BirthDate > 'June 9, 1993'
```

As SQL is very flexible, a user can include more than one single conditional filter in the WHERE clause by simply adding the keyword 'AND' between each condition.

Example Query 3: "What are the first and last names of people in the passenger table who were born after June 9, 1993, who also reside in the state of California?"

```
SELECT Fname, Lname, BirthDate, CustCity, CustState
FROM tblCUSTOMER
WHERE BirthDate > 'June 9, 1993'
AND CustState = 'California, CA'
```

We should also familiarize ourselves with the following clauses:

- **SELECT**: Provides a list of column(s) to obtain data values
- **FROM**: Provides a list of tables that contain the specified column(s) in SELECT
- **WHERE**: Optional clause that provides filtering of values based on conditional logic

Most businesses have questions that require data from many tables in a single query; we will explain how to do this in the next chapter. For now, focus on building a solid understanding of the structure, the basic operators, and how they work.

Readers with prior SQL experience can skip to the challenges at the end of the chapter.

The next examples of practice queries from SQL require that the query window has the context of the database that we have recently designed, coded, and populated with a handful of values. This can be completed by choosing the database name **METRO_TRANSIT** in the navigation window, or typing and executing **USE METRO_TRANSIT**.

If you are not connected to the cloud database, then the following queries are drawing only from the data that was entered previously. Try to download the browser-based tools (either SSMS or Azure Data Studio) to engage the sample data in the proper context.

It may be a burden to manually type more than a page of data, but the ability to engage in real-time with live data is critical for those learning a programming language.

Query 1: Type the following and run in the query window:

```
SELECT VehicleID, VehicleName, VehiclePurchaseDate
FROM tblVEHICLE
WHERE VehiclePurchaseDate = 'March 3, 2019'
```

Results Messages

	VehicleID	VehicleName	VehiclePurchaseDate
1	1	GS203	2019-03-03
2	2	GS204	2019-03-03

***Figure 5.6**: Simple query using '=' with result set*

Query 2: Type the following and run in the query window:

```
SELECT VehicleID, VehicleName, VehiclePurchaseDate
FROM tblVEHICLE
WHERE VehiclePurchaseDate > 'June 1, 2018'
```

Results Messages

	VehicleID	VehicleName	VehiclePurchaseDate
1	1	GS203	2019-03-03
2	2	GS204	2019-03-03
3	3	PA7	2023-07-13
4	4	GS208	2024-08-09

Figure 5.7*: Simple query using ‘>’ with result set*

The following queries are returning data from the table **`tblVEHICLE`**, as it is the value in the FROM clause. The WHERE clause in each query has an operator that filters the returned data. These are literal and absolute filters. For example, in Query 1, the entries with an exact match with March 3, 2019 will be returned. It will not apply if you are matching the same date from a different year. A query is written to absolutely determine the values that are found.

Likewise, in Query 2, if a vehicle has a purchase date of June 1, 2018, it would not be returned because the date is equal to June 1, 2018, instead of being greater than (often symbolized as ‘>’) June 1, 2018.

There are other symbols that represent the logical operators within SQL. SQL has perhaps a dozen standard operators in common with other programming languages. These are logical symbols used for arithmetic and filtering of values. See the following table to know about them:

Operators within SQL

Symbol	**Name**	**Purpose**
+	Plus	Addition as well as concatenation with string values
-	Minus	Subtraction
*	Multiplier	Multiplication of two values
/	Divisor	Division between two values
%	Modulo	Returns the remainder value after completing division
>	Greater Than	Logical comparison of two values with first being larger
<	Less Than	Logical comparison of two values with first being smaller than the second

=	Equals	Logical comparison of two values where they match
<=	Less than/equals	Logical comparison of two values where they match, or the first value is smaller
>=	Greater than/equals	Logical comparison of two values where they match or the first larger
<>	Not equals	Logical comparison to find un-matching values
!=	Not equals	Logical comparison to find un-matching values

Table 5.2: *List of operators within SQL*

Wildcards

SQL has several characters that can be used to represent 'spaces' instead of values. These are frequently used when people know part of the value they are searching or are trying to quickly narrow a results set. Wildcards are used to save time which could have been wasted in manually typing the values.

- **%** Percent Sign: Wildcard for 'any number' of characters
- **_** Underscore: Wildcard for 1 character space only

Wildcards are very common in a WHERE clause as we filter data in a query. They work against all data types including those that are characters, numeric, and date.

The keyword LIKE immediately precedes the use of wildcards. See these examples:

- Write the SQL to return all customers with a last name beginning with letter 'L'

```
SELECT *
FROM tblCUSTOMER
WHERE Lname LIKE 'L%'
```

Results Messages

	CustomerID	Fname	Mname	Lname	BirthDate	CustAddress	CustCity	CustState	PostalCode
1	4	Janey	NULL	Lundgren	1996-01-25	14351 N Oak Beach Walk	CENTRALIA	Illinois, IL	62801

Figure 5.8: *SQL code using keyword LIKE, % wildcard, and result set*

- Return all customers with the letter 'Y' anywhere in their first name:

```
SELECT *
FROM tblCUSTOMER
WHERE Fname LIKE '%y%'
```

Results Messages

	CustomerID	Fname	Mname	Lname	BirthDate	CustAddress	CustCity	CustState	PostalCode
1	1	Ivey	NULL	Hazekamp	1995-12-24	7279 North Lavender Lake Avenue	PETROLEUM	Indiana, IN	46778
2	3	Kenyetta	NULL	Terron	1995-09-27	6664 NW Arthur Terrace Drive	GRAND RIVER	Ohio, OH	44045
3	4	Janey	NULL	Lundgren	1996-01-25	14351 N Oak Beach Walk	CENTRALIA	Illinois, IL	62801

Figure 5.9: *SQL using keyword LIKE and wildcards before and after search*

- Return all customers with the letter 'N' in the third position in their first name:

```
SELECT *
FROM tblCUSTOMER
WHERE Fname LIKE '__n%'
```

Results Messages

	CustomerID	Fname	Mname	Lname	BirthDate	CustAddress	CustCity	CustState	PostalCode
1	3	Kenyetta	NULL	Terron	1995-09-27	6664 NW Arthur Terrace Drive	GRAND RIVER	Ohio, OH	44045
2	4	Janey	NULL	Lundgren	1996-01-25	14351 N Oak Beach Walk	CENTRALIA	Illinois, IL	62801

Figure 5.10: *SQL code using keyword LIKE and two single-position wildcards ('_') to search on fixed position*

- Return all customers with number '4' in the second to last position of their postal code:

```
SELECT *
FROM tblCUSTOMER
WHERE PostalCode LIKE '%4_'
```

Results Messages

	CustomerID	Fname	Mname	Lname	BirthDate	CustAddress	CustCity	CustState	PostalCode
1	3	Kenyetta	NULL	Terron	1995-09-27	6664 NW Arthur Terrace Drive	GRAND RIVER	Ohio, OH	44045

Figure 5.11: *SQL code using both wildcards to find the character*

SELECT Statement without FROM

While many sources claim that the FROM clause is mandatory in any **SELECT** statement, the following examples prove that to be false. Type and execute them in a query window as indicated:

```
SELECT 36 * 42
GO
```

Results Messages

	(No column name)
1	1512

Figure 5.12: *SQL code example of a SELECT statement without a FROM clause*

In *Figure 5.12*, the **SELECT** statement acts like a calculator. We often will need to determine quantities, percentages, discounts, sums and many other results, which are dynamic and volatile. We want to be comfortable with SQL as a trusted partner that can reliably handle complex scenarios in a high-volume context. One such operation is indicated as follows:

```
SELECT GETDATE()
GO
```

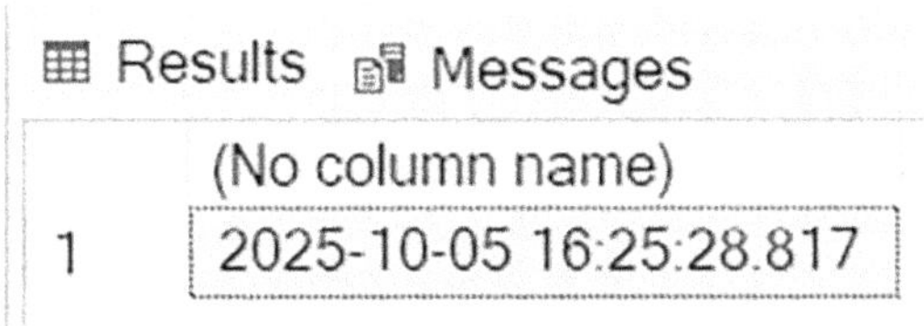

Figure 5.13: *SQL code example of the SELECT statement calling a date function with no FROM clause*

In *Figure* 5.13, the SELECT statement is calling a date function. This is a very common task and a key part of SQL. We want to programmatically obtain the date and/or time of many events such as when an order or a phone call has occurred. If people are involved, not only does it slow down processing significantly, but it also increases the scope for injecting deliberate misinformation and other mistakes. This is indicated in the following code example:

```
SELECT 'Data are cool…I am beginning to like SQL'
GO
```

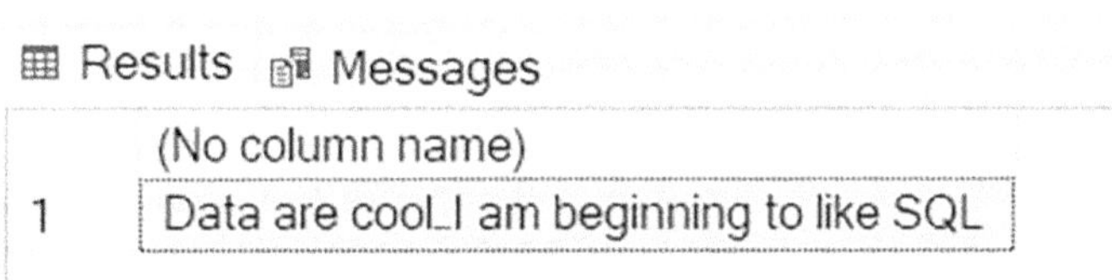

Figure 5.14: *SQL code example of SELECT statement without FROM clause*

In *Figure* 5.14, the SELECT statement returns the string value of what was presented. This will become valuable as we capture values based on queries and can then use them in other processes. Harnessing the power of database systems will significantly increase our ability to design analytical processing as opposed to doing it manually.

This is incredibly valuable as it allows for autonomous and independent learning.

Despite being familiar with the fundamentals of database design, it is not sufficient without understanding SQL as the two are mutually dependent. A person cannot engage with SQL without knowing the basics of database theory. Likewise, strictly learning about relational database theory without a context of SQL is also difficult. Therefore, it is important to learn the two simultaneously.

As we engage with SQL beyond a basic SELECT statement, we must understand some best practices before we are fully exposed to conceptual theory. The following is a brief list of SQL traps that can be intimidating for a novice professional. Not all these concepts have been fully introduced yet; however, you must understand that the theory and coding of SQL are presented in parallel and will eventually coalesce.

That being said, the following list and brief explanations will give you a heads-up on upcoming challenges. Each topic is explored from the perspective of a novice for ease of understanding.

Here, you need to be attentive about the structure and order of keywords. There will be example code snippets in future sections where you will be able to test the execution of these concepts.

NULL

Basic SQL requires a thorough understanding of what NULL is. NULL is not a number or a value. In fact, it is the absence of a value (because it was either not provided or the value is unknown). Nothing *equals* NULL, not even another NULL value.

The important part of understanding NULL is how to treat equations that happen to include it. You will have the following choices to tackle them:

- **Choice #1:** Return NULL for the results (even if only one value out of a million is NULL).
- **Choice #2:** Replace NULL values with a known value (like the average of everything else).
- **Choice #3:** Drop the NULL values from the calculation entirely.

Many scientific calculations will follow choices 1 and 2 while many business calculations will most probably follow choices 2 and 3. It all depends on how precise the measurement needs to be and the decision maker's comfort with approximate values. You must also remember that NULL does NOT equal anything, including zero.

Now that you understand the basics of SQL and writing a simple query, you can code live against a real database. The next section will provide you with a "starter code" as well as prompts to execute it; pay attention to the results and familiarize yourself with the process of engaging a database. Many complex and intricately layered questions can be answered with SQL, as it is both logical and robust. The challenge for beginners is to recognize the patterns associated with setting up answers as well as learning the various keywords and their functionalities.

You can try writing queries to reference the data model in *Figure* 5.5 from **`METRO_TRANSIT`**. This may be brand new for you, but you are encouraged to experiment by changing each query slightly to observe the impact of the results set.

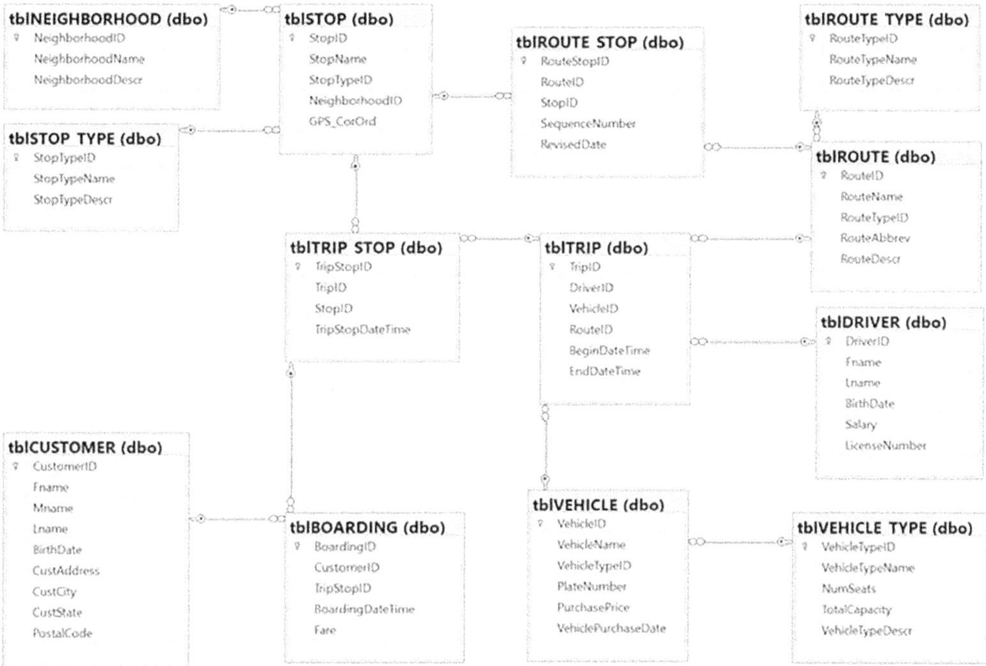

Figure 5.15: A *Simplified Entity-Relationship Diagram* (ERD) *of* `METRO_TRANSIT`

As mentioned previously, there are fully normalized versions of the **`METRO_TRANSIT`** database available for download on the publisher's github site. While these do have data that is intentionally similar to the simplified version of **`METRO_TRANSIT`** as seen in Figure 5.15, these are also significantly more complex with designs intended to represent millions of boardings by passengers across the globe. The larger databases are also intended for advanced classes at prominent universities to be able to explore the concepts of data analytics in an easy to use format.

The fully normalized ERD can be seen again in the following *Figure* 5.16:

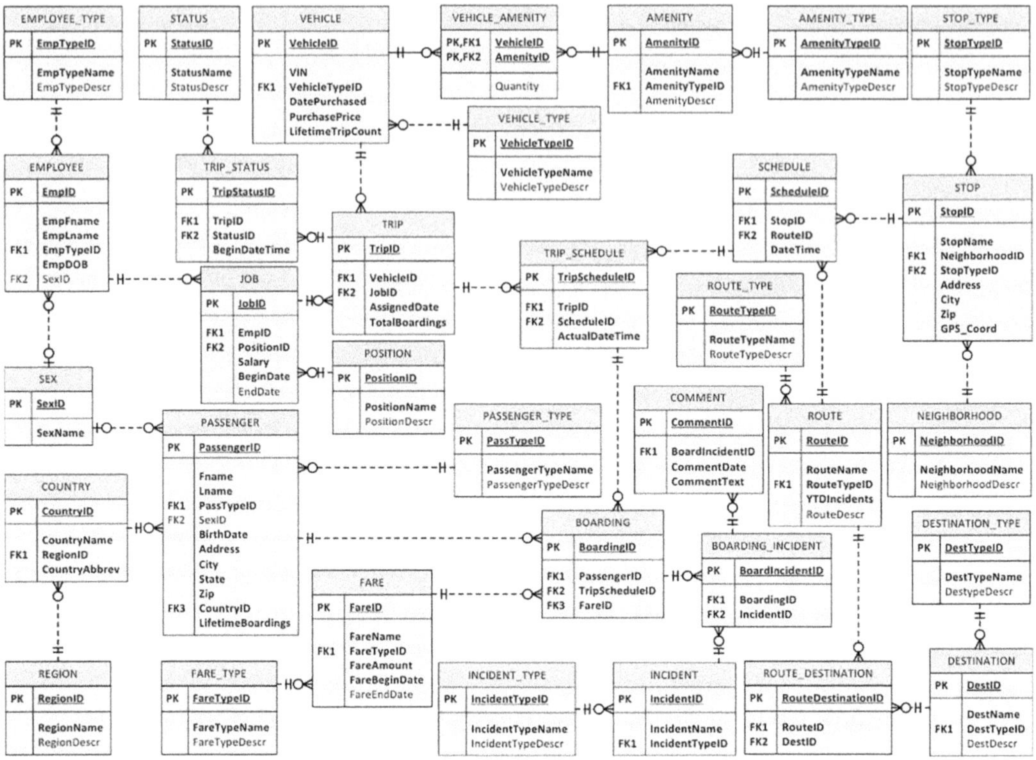

***Figure 5.16**: A fully normalized Entity-Relationship Diagram (ERD) of METRO_TRANSIT*

Practice

To tackle the following challenges, you can review the schema for the fully developed **`METRO_TRANSIT`** diagram in *Figure* 5.16.

Visit the following link to download relevant files for the coding portion of this chapter: https://github.com/ava-orange-education/ultimate-SQL-for-Data-Science-and-Analytics

Here, you will find more than eight different **`METRO_TRANSIT`** databases populated with data drawn from the transit systems serving the prominent cities listed as follows:

- New York City
- London
- Istanbul
- Dubai
- Seoul
- Delhi

- Shanghai
- Mumbai

The exciting part about this schema is that you can scrape data from real-world transit systems from around the world.

Regardless of which **METRO_TRANSIT** database you have chosen to work with, the following eight queries are based on the generic schema that is shared by all the iterations of **METRO_TRANSIT**. Each database has elements of real data pulled from a transit system, including data on routes, vehicles, neighborhoods, stops, and schedules. All data concerning passengers, drivers, boardings, and incidents is fabricated.

The purpose of these data sets is to provide a learning platform that resembles your lived experience. Additionally, METRO_TRANSIT has enough data to challenge all learners with a full range of SQL commands, while giving them a safe place to explore and practice independently without losing crucial data.

You will encounter questions that are centric to specific METRO_TRANSIT databases from various cities around the world in this chapter as well as the ones that will follow.

Conclusion

SQL is a powerful tool to answer sophisticated and nuanced questions buried within complex systems. In this chapter, we have learned to build a real database on a central server with only a fragment of starter code.

We have also executed simple queries using SELECT, FROM, and WHERE clauses; this is a solid foundation upon which great skills can be built. The various sections of this chapter highlight the importance of framing a query so that a database management system can read and decipher it easily.

In the next chapter, we will build upon SQL basics and explore the nuances of many SQL commands and functions. We will learn how to connect tables together using the JOIN command to increase the sophistication and complexity of the queries we can write. We will also be introduced to the aggregate and date functions that leverage the GROUP BY and HAVING clauses.

Questions

1. Write the SQL code to determine the customers who are from the zip code 80471.
2. Write the SQL code to determine the customers who have 'Blvd' in their address.

3. Write the SQL to determine which employees have last names that match the pattern 'F**R' (read F in position one and R in position four) and reside in either Florida or Texas.
4. Write the SQL to determine the employees who have a first name beginning with the two letters 'Ra' and live in California.
5. Write the SQL code to determine the customers who have 'Leaf' in their address and have the two letters 'ba' appearing sequentially together in any part of the city they live in.
6. Write the SQL query to determine the employees born after November 5, 1996.
7. Write the SQL to determine the vehicles that have a purchase price less than $1,250,000 and were purchased after October 1, 2019.
8. Write the SQL to return each STOP that is in the city of Bellevue in Washington state or is in the zip code '98102'.

Answers

This section will walk you through each question and reinforce SQL basics.

1.
```
SELECT *
FROM tblCUSTOMER
WHERE ZIP = '80471'
```

2.
```
SELECT *
FROM tblCUSTOMER
WHERE Address LIKE '%Blvd%'
```

2.
```
SELECT *
FROM tblEMPLOYEE
WHERE State IN ('Florida, FL', 'Texas, TX')
AND EmpLname LIKE 'F__r%'
```

3.
```
SELECT *
FROM tblEMPLOYEE
WHERE State = 'California, CA'
AND EmpFname LIKE 'Ra%'
```

4.
```
SELECT *
FROM tblCUSTOMER
WHERE Address LIKE '%leaf%'
AND City LIKE '%ba%'
```

5.
```
SELECT EmpID, EmpFname, EmpLname, EmpDOB
FROM tblEMPLOYEE
WHERE EmpDOB > 'November 5, 1996'
```

6.
```
SELECT VehicleID, VIN,DatePurchased, PurchasePrice
FROM tblVEHICLE
WHERE DatePurchased > 'October 1, 2019'
AND PurchasePrice < 1250000
```

7.
```
SELECT *
FROM tblSTOP
WHERE (City = 'Bellevue'
AND State = 'Washington, WA')
OR ZIP = '98102'
```

Post-Chapter Challenges

Approach the given challenges and respond to them on the basis of what you have learned from this chapter.

Track 1: Data Tourist Seeking Ancillary Awareness (THINK ~10 Minutes)

Review the following questions and answer them as per your understanding of the chapter:

- How is the structure of SQL makes it simple/difficult for you to remember the sequence and syntax of particular commands?
- Do you find it interesting to write queries or search through data to answer business questions? Why or why not?
- Imagine that you are explaining SQL to someone with no prior knowledge or experience with coding or databases. Which SQL advantages will you highlight for them? What are the obstacles or disadvantages of using SQL?
- What parts of your daily life might be more manageable if all of the relevant data was available in a well-designed relational database and was effectively 'one query away' from learning more about everything?

Track 2: Dedicated Student or Recent Graduate (WRITE ~ 45 Minutes)

Respond to the following questions and give reasons for your answers:

- Frame the sequence of commands and the overall structure of an example query in a few short paragraphs without referring to your notes or the data model. What are the primary or key commands found in nearly every basic query?

- What are the limitations of the basic SQL query structure from what we have seen so far? As most businesses need sophisticated analyses across a range of data and entities, what is the level of complexity we can currently address with our existing knowledge of SQL laid out in this chapter?

Track 3: Professional Aspirant (BUILD ~3 Hours)

This track targets those readers who aspire to pursue a career or seek better jobs in the realm of data science. Now that we have been introduced to SQL, let us continue coding the schema of the database you have designed based on a personal or professional interest.

- You have to code your original database from scratch! Leverage the SQL coding skills you have to create each table in your database with proper data types for each column, as well as surrogate primary keys and foreign keys.

CHAPTER 6
Intermediate SQL Part 1

Introduction

Excellent progress so far by getting engaged with SQL! This chapter builds on the **METRO_TRANSIT** database we coded previously, and continues with applying standard SQL commands within this context. Later, we will add more data in look-up tables and establish realistic-looking transactions to populate the database with 100,000's of rows of data. Completing this chapter will put you in a position to develop a stronger understanding of SQL, and accelerate through more difficult programming structures including stored procedures and user-defined functions.

Again, this chapter begins to apply the theory, and fundamentals recently acquired into the beginnings of processing data, and targeted learning through analytics. We will be introduced to system functions, subqueries, and other common commands that fill out your data toolbox. This is a fascinating journey!

Structure

In this chapter, we will explore the following topics:

- Coding Shortcuts in SQL
- JOIN statements
- GROUP BY command
- HAVING clause
- System functions

Shortcuts

So, let us begin this chapter with a reminder of the simplified version data model for the **METRO_TRANSIT** database, we built and coded by hand in the last chapter:

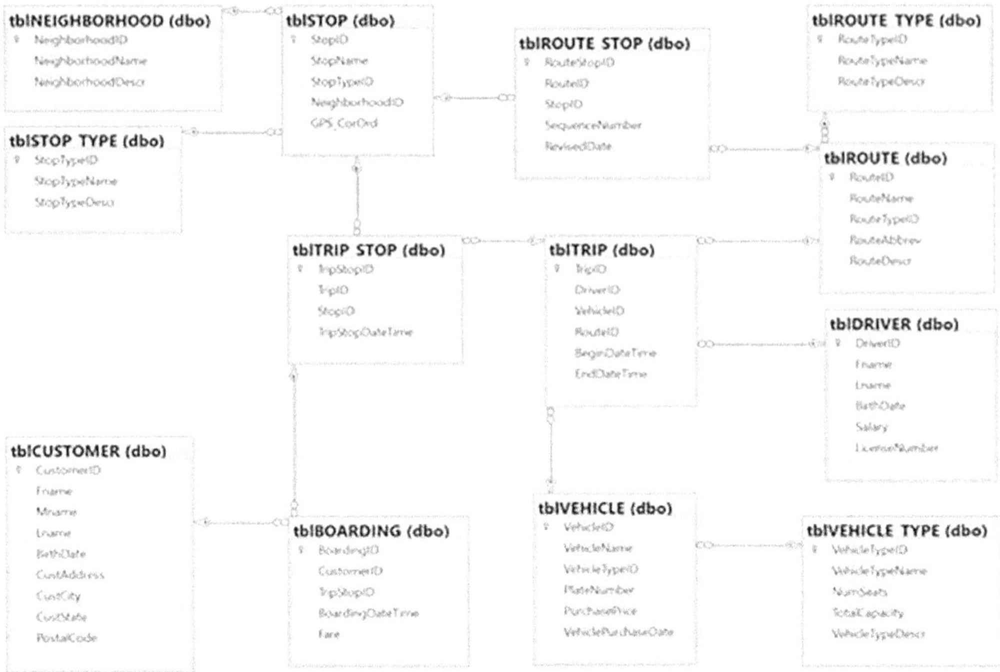

Figure 6.1: *Reminder of the simplified version of `METRO_TRANSIT` from chapter 5*

Shortcuts are part of our everyday lives, and the need for people to be more efficient. We often seek out shortcuts in many ways, such as getting to work quicker, finding the shortest line at the grocery store, or over-engineering a quicker method to get a weekend chore done at home. Programming languages, just like any spoken language, have slang; often single words that replace a bundle of others that are intended to simplify or shorten the time it takes to communicate a common practice. With SQL, it could be argued that the entire language (as a 4GL) is constructed with slang! There are already over 100 reserved keywords that have been established to replace tedious coding details for repetitive tasks.

Think about each command and statement presented so far just in this book, such as CREATE, ALTER, DROP, and SELECT. These are all technical shortcuts. This sleekness is part of the charm, beauty, and brilliance of nearly every programming language, and especially SQL. With this in mind, we have created "shortcuts on shortcuts" and added a few more keywords and symbols to further reduce the time as well as the required typing to obtain efficiency. Please review the following common shortcuts:

Open a query window and connect to the database designed in this book previously, and coded by you that was named **`METRO_TRANSIT_your_initials_3_numbers_you_chose`**.

Shortcut #1: Asterisk (*)

The asterisk (commonly referred to as 'star') is a shortcut to mean 'all columns' in the SELECT line of a query. This shortcut will return every column from all tables included in the query.

```
SELECT *
FROM tblVEHICLE
GO
```

Many times, analysts begin investigations with simplicity, and are effectively searching for any matching rows, often without concern of the minimal or filtered columns. We start with a quick query, see what gets returned, and then often narrow the search in the WHERE clause depending on what we learn from the preceding query. Eventually, we will most likely change the **SELECT** line to be a precise collection of columns that meet the needs of a recurring query.

Words of caution when using '**SELECT ***' are that it can return an overwhelming number of columns that can quickly become difficult to manage, especially when multiple tables are connected in a single query. Many organizations following industry best practices will state that '**SELECT ***' is to be avoided, particularly when queries are engaging in millions of rows of data, as an unfiltered query can clog a company's internal network with noncritical data.

Shortcut #2: SELECT..INTO

The **SELECT..INTO** sequence of SQL code makes a copy of an existing table. This includes the table definition/schema as well as potentially the entire data as well. This is a wonderful shortcut whenever we need a quick copy of a table.

```
SELECT *
INTO Test_Copy_tblVEHICLE
FROM tblVEHICLE
GO

SELECT CustomerID, Fname, Lname
INTO Test_Copy_tblCUSTOMER
FROM tblCUSTOMER
WHERE BirthDate > 'January 1, 1955'
```

The **SELECT INTO** statement also allows for the filtering of columns in the **SELECT** line as well as adding a **WHERE** clause. Creating a whole copy or just a subset of an existing table is powerful, and often takes just a few seconds.

Shortcut #3: INSERT INTO...SELECT

A great shortcut in SQL is when we want to copy data from an existing table into another. The common use cases are when we are generating a working set of data, perhaps, during an investigation of an issue or perhaps, even maintenance. Our goal, may be, is to quickly isolate a subset of data into a new table for further work. We can do this with SQL by combining a **SELECT** statement with an **INSERT** statement. The only caveat is that the destination table must already exist, which is different from a shortcut we just saw with **SELECT..INTO** which creates the destination table on the fly.

For example, let us try to obtain a subset of rows from **tblSTOP** where the stops are from two specific neighborhoods, such as 'Downtown', 'Waterfront', and 'Fremont'.

First, we must make sure that the destination table exists. For the sake of this example, we will create a new entity now, called '**Tourist_Stops**'. SQL Code to create **tblTOURIST_STOPS** is as follows:

```
CREATE TABLE tblTOURIST_STOPS
(TN_ID INTEGER IDENTITY(1,1) primary key,
NeighborhoodID INT not null,
NeighborhoodName varchar(50) not null,
StopID INT not null,
StopName varchar(50) not null,
GPS_CorOrd VARCHAR(50) NULL)
GO
```

Give the following query a try! It is important to be able to assemble copies of data when we are on a mission to conduct a deeper investigation or build one-off reports. SQL Code to insert values into **tblTOURIST_STOPS** is as follows:

```
INSERT INTO tblTOURIST_STOPS (NeighborhoodID, NeighborhoodName,
StopID, StopName, GPS_CorOrd)
SELECT N.NeighborhoodID, NeighborhoodName, S.StopID, StopName,
GPS_CorOrd
FROM tblNEIGHBORHOOD N
      JOIN tblSTOP S ON N.NeighborhoodID = S.NeighborhoodID
WHERE N.NeighborhoodName IN ('Downtown', 'Waterfront', 'Fremont')
```

Please note, the columns in the **SELECT** line (the query) must align with the columns in the **INSERT INTO** line; otherwise the query will fail or perhaps, put invalid data into your working table. Also, the WHERE clause in the preceding paragraph is using IN as a keyword to search for a collection of values.

Shortcut #4: ALIASES

Another common shortcut within programming languages (not just SQL) is substitute names. An alias in general is most often intended to reduce the number of letters needed to type. In fact, many people have abbreviations (also known as 'nicknames') of their formal or legal names. While many of us have a legal first name that is longer than what our friends and family call us. Consider the names of Michelle, Satyendra, or Gregory, which often get shortened to 'Mich', 'Sat', and 'Greg'. Perhaps, our closest friends and siblings often call us by just a single letter like just 'G'. These nicknames can be considered aliases as they simplify the naming process, communicate goodwill, and often add affection.

In SQL, the most common use of aliases is in queries where we want to replace the long names of columns or tables. In the case of replacing column names, we are converting a cryptic 'short name' to one more appropriate to human readers. An example is as follows:

```
SELECT CustomerID, Fname, Lname
FROM tblCUSTOMER
GO
```

Results Messages

	CustomerID	Fname	Lname
1	1	Ivey	Hazekamp
2	2	Darcel	Eustache
3	3	Kenyetta	Terron
4	4	Janey	Lundgren

Figure 6.2: *Example query without any alias using database METRO_TRANSIT*

Next, let us see an example query now using 2 aliases in the **SELECT** line.

```
SELECT CustomerID, Fname AS 'First', Lname AS 'Last'
FROM tblCUSTOMER
```

Results Messages

	CustomerID	First	Last
1	1	Ivey	Hazekamp
2	2	Darcel	Eustache
3	3	Kenyetta	Terron
4	4	Janey	Lundgren

Figure 6.3: *Example query with the use of two aliases ('First' and 'Last')*

Please note that the column headers in the results have been replaced by the aliases!

When used effectively, aliases cannot only reduce the typing required to execute a query but also eliminate a significant portion of the query code---thereby improving the readability for other users.

- **Hands-on Practice: query connecting tables *without* aliases**

  The following query will return data to answer the question of "Which vehicle types were driven by any person with the last name 'Lee' after June 1, 2024?"

```
SELECT tblVEHICLE_TYPE.VehicleTypeID, tblVEHICLE_TYPE.Vehicle-
TypeName, tblDRIVER.Fname, tblDRIVER.Lname
FROM tblVEHICLE_TYPE, tblVEHICLE, tblTRIP, tblDRIVER
WHERE tblVEHICLE_TYPE.VehicleTypeID = tblVEHICLE.VehicleTypeID
AND tblVEHICLE.VehicleID = tblTRIP.VehicleID
AND tblTRIP.DriverID = tblDRIVER.DriverID
      AND tblDRIVER.Lname = 'Lee'
      AND tblTRIP.BeginDateTime > 'June 1, 2024'
```

Results Messages

	VehicleTypeID	VehicleTypeName	Fname	Lname
1	1	Standard Bus	Bruce	Lee

***Figure 6.4**: Example of a busy query with no use of any aliases*

Example query connecting tables **WITH** aliases

The following query will return the same data as above, yet is substituting the names of tables with aliases:

```
SELECT VT.VehicleTypeID, VT.VehicleTypeName, D.Fname, D.Lname
FROM tblVEHICLE_TYPE VT, tblVEHICLE V, tblTRIP T, tblDRIVER D
WHERE VT.VehicleTypeID = V.VehicleTypeID
AND V.VehicleID = T.VehicleID
AND T.DriverID = D.DriverID
      AND D.Lname = 'Lee'
AND T.BeginDateTime > 'June 1, 2024'
```

Please note the first mention of each table is completely spelled out, followed by the desired alias. We do not need to include the keyword 'AS' during this process. This use of aliases not only reduces typing but also makes the reading of the code easier for people.

Also, please notice that we connect multiple tables along the primary key, and foreign key relationships. This allows for the return of the matching data that is filtered exclusively to the values we seek (in this case, just the vehicles driven by all drivers with the last name of 'Lee'). This alignment of connecting across PK/FK is called referential integrity, although we will also say 'transactional integrity'.

The above query connects several tables, beginning with **tblVEHICHLE_TYPE**, and includes **tblVEHICLE**, **tblTRIP** and **tblDRIVER**. The table **tblTRIP** records the individual travels of a bus on a route that picks up dozens of passengers over an hour or so. In this database, it may only have 100 rows of new data each week. Again, one row in **tblTRIP** represents a driver taking a bus through a scheduled route, and picking up passengers before turning around, and perhaps, conducting a second trip. When compared to other databases found in large organizations, 100 rows each week is miniscule; however, in the **METRO_TRANSIT** database we designed, it is labelled 'highly' transactional. A second table in **METRO_TRANSIT** that can be labelled 'highly transactional' is **tblTRIP_STOP**. All this really means is that the bulk of the data in the entire database (the transactional details, represented by foreign keys) will be held in these tables.

When a query includes a highly transactional table (like our query above), potentially millions of rows of data will be considered. Depending on how we frame our question, we may get results that are answering our question literally, and include details from a transactional table. Let me explain with an example from **METRO_TRANSIT**.

We must be aware whenever we write a query that includes or 'crosses through' a transactional table as it has awakened a bee's nest of details. Now, many queries may need these details, such as whenever we want to determine revenue from all customers or total trips by vehicle. If, however, we want to know which customers have boarded a specific route on a particular day, we would need to be aware the results would include duplicate names if the customer happened to meet the search criteria in two separate instances. This is a very common mistake for younger and beginning analysts! Just be thoughtful each time writing a query; is it crossing a transactional table? If the answer is yes, the next question should be, "do I want duplicate names?" that represent each matching occurrence. There are occasions where we need both answers. Just be aware, intentional, and deliberate in writing each query. Let us see how to discern between these two queries when crossing a transactional table by using the keyword, **DISTINCT**.

DISTINCT

The following query is from the **METRO_TRANSIT** database and passes through the transactional table, **tblTRIP**. The fact that the query crosses a transactional table means there will be detailed ID values for each driver, vehicle, and route. In an average week of business for **METRO_TRANSIT**, there may be dozens of rows for each driver, vehicle, and route as each participates in delivering service to the public.

Type the following code to answer the question, 'Which drivers have participated in a trip on any route that included stops in the neighborhood of Fremont during June of 2025?'

Since we do not want the names of drivers appearing multiple times, this query will benefit from the DISTINCT keyword to only return the names of drivers who meet the search criteria as opposed to *each time* they met the search criteria.

```
SELECT DISTINCT D.DriverID, D.Fname, D.Lname
FROM tblDRIVER D, tblTRIP T, tblTRIP_STOP TS, tblSTOP S,
tblNEIGHBORHOOD N
WHERE T.DriverID = D.DriverID
AND T.TripID = TS.TripID
AND TS.StopID = S.StopID
AND S.NeighborhoodID = N.NeighborhoodID
       AND N.NeighborhoodName = 'Fremont'
       AND T.BeginDateTime >'June 1, 2025'
AND T.BeginDateTime < 'July 1, 2025'
```

Results Messages

	DriverID	Fname	Lname
1	4	Meryl	Streep

Figure 6.5: *Example of a busy query with the use of DISTINCT keyword*

Just for comparison, delete the word '`DISTINCT`' from the select line, and run the query a second time; the results you receive should produce duplicate rows because the same driver has matched the search criteria two times:

Results Messages

	DriverID	Fname	Lname
1	4	Meryl	Streep
2	4	Meryl	Streep

Figure 6.6: *Example of a query without `DISTINCT` keyword showing duplicate rows*

We will learn in the very next section how to do query-writing across multiple tables using the keyword JOIN, which might be easier to construct, and has some performance benefits.

JOIN Statement

The JOIN statement is where SQL picks up speed and flexes power by broadening the reach of accessing data across an entire database. We have already learned to write queries that span multiple tables by simply including additional tables in the FROM clause. The method that we have learned already is considered 'old-school', and while flexible by allowing connections across any number of columns, the method is also a potential performance drag, if the query is poorly written.

The **JOIN** statement is often preferred as it requires comparisons (the actual 'joining' of two tables) to be between primary key and foreign relationships. This may require a few extra minutes writing a more methodical query, it will avoid wasting time on mistakes such as comparing a column with phone numbers against a column with zip codes. Another example from **METRO_TRANSIT**, is searching for a driver's last name or birthdate against a vehicle license plate number. Even if there happens to be a 'miraculous match' does it mean there is any business relationship or transactional relevance? I suppose there *might* be a situation where incorrect data needs to be located and cleaned up but for the most part, we will rarely need to join on unrelated columns.

Thus, by using the PK/FK relationships built into the database design, the JOIN statement can take advantage of default indexes, and often complete a search through 100,000's of rows in a second or two. There are a handful of JOIN statements in SQL, including **INNER**, **OUTER**, **LEFT**, **RIGHT**, **SELF**, and **SEMI**. While this may seem like a lot of options, most joins will be the default of **LEFT INNER JOIN**. Let us see these in action with some examples using Venn Diagrams as well as coding ourselves in the **METRO_ TRANSIT** database!

INNER JOIN

An **INNER JOIN** is by far the most common type of **JOIN** in SQL. In fact, when we just type JOIN, it is the default action. This default **JOIN** returns the matching rows between 2 or more tables. In the following Venn Diagram, the intersection or 'overlap' between the blue circle and the yellow circle is colored green.

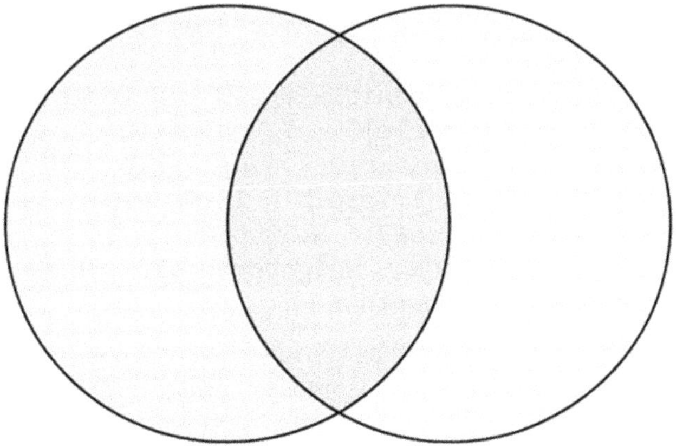

Figure 6.7: *An example Venn Diagram showing the intersection of two circles in green*

Again, there is no difference between an **INNER JOIN** and just '**JOIN**'. Many times, analysts seek the intersection between two or more tables, and gravitate to this JOIN. An example of seeking the intersection between two tables from the **METRO_TRANSIT** database is "which routes are of type express?".

```
SELECT R.RouteID, R.RouteName, RT.RouteTypeName
FROM tblROUTE_TYPE RT
      JOIN tblROUTE R ON RT.RouteTypeID = R.RouteTypeID
WHERE RT.RouteTypeName = 'Express'
```

If you are writing queries against the abbreviated **METRO_TRANSIT** database we created in the previous chapter, there are two rows returned as follows:

Results Messages

	RouteID	RouteName	RouteTypeName
1	1	Sodo-Downtown Express	Express
2	3	Fremont-Downtown Express	Express

Figure 6.8: *Example of a query with the use of JOIN keyword*

As mentioned previously, the **JOIN** statement is critical of being able to connect tables together in a relational database. This simple statement will unlock the ability to answer very complex questions with the basics of SQL that we have already covered. So, please consider it as a valuable step in your learning journey for SQL.

Multiple JOIN Statements in a Single Query

Let us see an example query that JOINs several tables from the **METRO_TRANSIT** database. The following query from the abbreviated **METRO_TRANSIT** diagram seeks to return the names of drivers, vehicles, vehicle types, as well as the **BeginDateTime** of all trips through the neighborhood of 'downtown'. There will be six **JOIN** statements:

```
SELECT VT.VehicleTypeName, VehicleName, Fname, Lname, T.BeginDateTime
FROM tblVEHICLE_TYPE VT
    JOIN tblVEHICLE V ON VT.VehicleTypeID = V.VehicleTypeID
    JOIN tblTRIP T ON V.VehicleID = T.VehicleID
    JOIN tblDRIVER D ON T.DriverID = D.DriverID
    JOIN tblTRIP_STOP TS ON T.TripID = TS.TripID
    JOIN tblSTOP S ON TS.StopID = S.StopID
    JOIN tblNEIGHBORHOOD N ON S.NeighborhoodID = N.NeighborhoodID
WHERE NeighborhoodName = 'Downtown'
```

	VehicleTypeName	VehicleName	Fname	Lname	BeginDateTime
1	Standard Bus	PA7	Bruce	Lee	2025-04-24 06:57:00.000
2	Double-Decker Bus	GS204	Meryl	Streep	2025-04-23 07:23:00.000

Figure 6.9: *Example query showing results from multiple JOIN statements*

As seen in the query for *Figure* 6.9, there is essentially no limit to the number of entities that can be joined in a single SQL query. The questions may be the following:

1. 'How do I include a table that is not directly connected to the previous table?'
2. 'Does it matter where I begin writing a query with multiple join statements?'

Great questions! First, once a table has been 'joined', it belongs in the ever-expanding base of tables the query will draw data from. Looking at the query in *Figure* 6.10, the join sequence is direct from **tblVEHICLE_TYPE**, through **tblVEHICLE**, **tblTRIP**, and reaching **tblDRIVER**. Next, the query needs to 'jump' back to **tblTRIP** to join **tblTRIP_STOP**, and continue towards **tblNEIGHBORHOOD**. This is fine!

Second, it does not matter where your query begins with multiple join statements (either left-to-right in the diagram, right-to-left, top-down, or bottom-up). That said, there is an element of elegance when *reading* a query that includes multiple join statements. The best rule for most queries is to start at an 'edge' of the diagram and join tables in the shortest stream that makes sense. The sequence of joins in the query for *Figure* 6.10 is very easy to follow in the diagram as it represents a linear or sequential connection stream from the lower right of the ERD to the upper left (with a brief jump to get driver data):

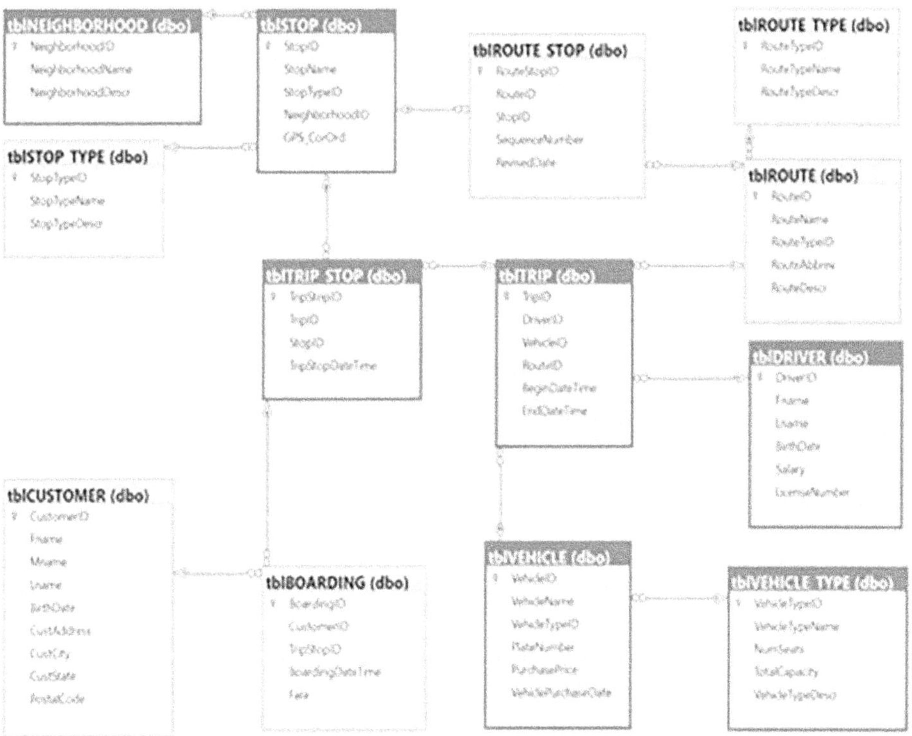

Figure 6.10: *Example query showing table connected in multiple JOIN statements*

Compare the query that was written for *Figure* 6.9 with the somewhat scattered version of the following same query:

```
SELECT VT.VehicleTypeName, VehicleName, Fname, Lname, T.BeginDateTime
FROM tblDRIVER D
    JOIN tblTRIP T ON D.DriverID = T.DriverID
    JOIN tblVEHICLE V ON T.VehicleID = V.VehicleID
    JOIN tblTRIP_STOP TS ON T.TripID = TS.TripID
    JOIN tblSTOP S ON TS.StopID = S.StopID
    JOIN tblVEHICLE_TYPE VT ON V.VehicleTypeID = VT.VehicleTypeID
    JOIN tblNEIGHBORHOOD N ON S.NeighborhoodID = N.NeighborhoodID
WHERE NeighborhoodName = 'Downtown'
```

	VehicleTypeName	VehicleName	Fname	Lname	BeginDateTime
1	Standard Bus	PA7	Bruce	Lee	2025-04-24 06:57:00.000
2	Double-Decker Bus	GS204	Meryl	Streep	2025-04-23 07:23:00.000

Figure 6.11: *Example of a query and results with a scattered approach to joining tables*

Please note the query results in Figure 6.11 are the exact same as the results from the query in Figure 6.9. The only difference between the two should be the time it takes to run as the stream-lined version in Figure 6.9 should be noticeably faster.

The key takeaway is the order by which tables are joined in a complex query with multiple join statements does not functionally matter. If each join statement connects via proper primary and foreign key relationships, the sequence of join statements does not make a difference in whether the query will parse. As for readability and performance, it is better for the join statements to be in a single direct sequence with as few jumps as possible.

OUTER JOIN

Whereas the INNER JOIN filters only the intersection of two or more tables, an OUTER JOIN returns all rows of each table regardless of whether there are matching values in the other table. The Venn diagram of all values may be rendered as follows:

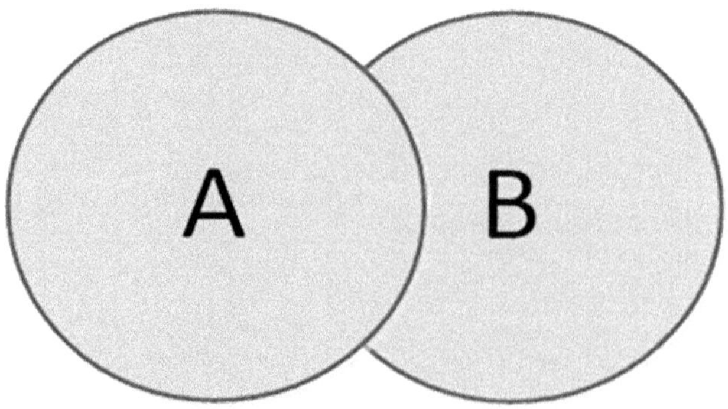

Figure 6.12: *A Venn Diagram showing the FULL OUTER JOIN with all rows returned*

Please note in Figure 6.13 that both circles (the 'entire collection') are colored in green; this reflects that all values in both entities are returned in a **FULL OUTER JOIN**.

```
SELECT V.VehicleID, V.VehicleName, T.RouteID, T.BeginDateTime
FROM tblVEHICLE V
LEFT OUTER JOIN tblTRIP T ON V.VehicleID = T.VehicleID
```

	VehicleID	VehicleName	RouteID	BeginDateTime
1	1	GS203	6	2025-06-22 06:42:00.000
2	2	GS204	6	2025-06-22 06:17:00.000
3	2	GS204	5	2025-06-23 07:23:00.000
4	2	GS204	4	2025-06-29 08:07:00.000
5	3	PA7	6	2025-06-22 06:57:00.000
6	4	GS208	NULL	NULL

***Figure 6.13**: Example query showing results from LEFT OUTER JOIN with all rows returned, including NULL values from non-matching rows*

The results from the query in *Figure* 6.13 show all rows from **tblVEHICLE** and all rows from **tblTRIP**, including row 6 in the results set that have **NULL** (highlighted in blue). The reason there are NULL values is because **VEHICLE** with **VehicleID** of 4 and **VehicleName** 'GS208', has not yet been assigned a TRIP.

Also, please notice there are three rows of values that match 2 under the column of **VehicleID**, and three matches for value of 'GS204' under column **VehicleName**. This reflects that this vehicle has been assigned three separate trips. These should not be considered 'duplicates' as the **TripID**, **RouteID**, and therefore, **BeginDateTimes** are different. Let us see essentially the same exact query with the substitution of '**RIGHT**' in place of the word **LEFT** from the query we just saw in *Figure* 6.14:

```
SELECT V.VehicleID, V.VehicleName, T.RouteID, T.BeginDateTime
FROM tblVEHICLE V
      RIGHT OUTER JOIN tblTRIP T ON V.VehicleID = T.VehicleID
```

Results | Messages

	VehicleID	VehicleName	RouteID	BeginDateTime
1	2	GS204	6	2025-04-24 06:17:00.000
2	1	GS203	3	2025-04-24 06:42:55.000
3	2	GS204	5	2025-04-23 07:23:00.000
4	3	PA7	6	2025-04-24 06:57:00.000
5	2	GS204	4	2025-04-29 08:07:00.000

***Figure 6.14**: Example query showing results from RIGHT OUTER JOIN*

The query from *Figure* 6.14 represents a substitution of the word '**LEFT**' with the word

'**RIGHT**'. With this change, the results are now only 5 rows as the table on the '**RIGHT**' in the query (which is **tblTRIP**) has no **NULL** values for **VehicleID** or **RouteID**.

Experiment with **LEFT OUTER JOIN** and **RIGHT OUTER JOIN** in a few queries on your own with the limited data set we have hand-typed from *Chapter 5, Beginning with SQL*; this process will make this concept clearer as we progress through the introduction of other JOIN terms.

LEFT JOIN

A **LEFT JOIN** is the same thing as a **LEFT OUTER JOIN** with less typing!

LEFT JOIN returns all rows from the first table and the matching values from the second table; if there is a row in the first table, and no matching values in the second table, then a **NULL** is returned.

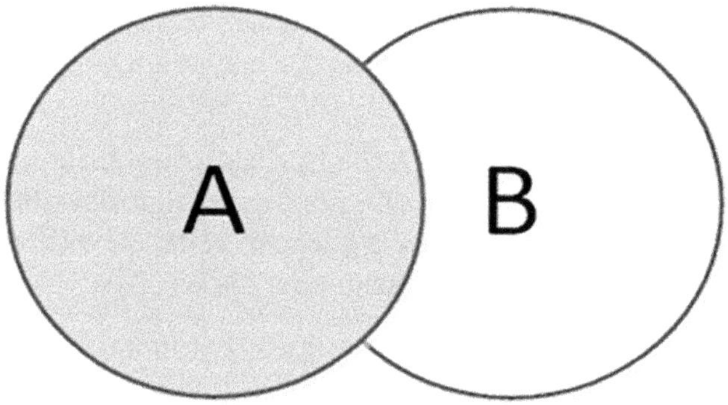

***Figure 6.15**: A Venn Diagram showing a LEFT JOIN with all rows returned from table A on the left and NULL values for any rows not matching from table B on the right*

```
SELECT RT.RouteTypeName, R.RouteName
FROM tblROUTE_TYPE RT
     LEFT JOIN tblROUTE R ON RT.RouteTypeID = R.RouteTypeID
```

Results | Messages

	RouteTypeName	RouteName
1	Express	Sodo-Downtown Express
2	Express	Fremont-Downtown Express
3	Special Event	Fremont-Waterfront-Downtown
4	Regular	Sodo-Downtown Commuter
5	Regular	Fremont-Downtown Commuter
6	Regular	Capitol Hill-Downtown
7	Inclement Weather/Reduced Service	NULL

***Figure 6.16**: An example result of LEFT JOIN returning NULL value for non-matching row*

Now, most of the time there will be a route somewhere that matches every route type. In fact, the query results we have in the database return a **NULL** value for **RouteTypeName** matching 'Inclement Weather/Reduced Service' because no route has yet to be assigned this specific route type. Every other RouteTypeName has at least one matching row in the **ROUTE** table. Let us add one more row to see another example with an **INSERT**.

Consider for a moment, that the administration of **METRO_TRANSIT** is adding a new route type of 'Waterfront Bypass' due to some sort of emergency construction. For the time that the new route type name of 'waterfront bypass' is entered into the system until specific routes have been assigned this associated **RouteTypeID**, the above query will return a **NULL** value for 'Waterfront Bypass'.

```
INSERT INTO tblROUTE_TYPE (RouteTypeName, RouteTypeDescr)
VALUES ('Waterfront Bypass', 'Routes that are in place during
construction of new seawall barrier along waterfront')
```

Now, re-run the earlier query with **LEFT JOIN**

```
SELECT RT.RouteTypeName, R.RouteName
FROM tblROUTE_TYPE RT
     LEFT JOIN tblROUTE R ON RT.RouteTypeID = R.RouteTypeID
```

Results Messages

	RouteTypeName	RouteName
1	Express	Sodo-Downtown Express
2	Express	Fremont-Downtown Express
3	Special Event	Fremont-Waterfront-Downtown
4	Regular	Sodo-Downtown Commuter
5	Regular	Fremont-Downtown Commuter
6	Regular	Capitol Hill-Downtown
7	Inclement Weather/Reduced Service	NULL
8	Waterfront Bypass	NULL

***Figure 6.17**: An example result of LEFT JOIN returning NULL value for non-matching rows*

We see the addition of one more row in the **LEFT** table (which is **tblROUTE_TYPE**) and a corresponding **NULL** value when joined to **tblROUTE**. The reason for this is for a moment, no routes have been created to have **RouteTypeID** that aligns with 'Waterfront Bypass'.

RIGHT JOIN

A **RIGHT JOIN** is the same thing as a **RIGHT OUTER JOIN** with less typing.

RIGHT JOIN is effectively the opposite of a **LEFT JOIN** in that it returns all rows from the second table (Table B below) and the matching values from the first table (Table A below). This means if there is a row in the second table and no matching values in the first table, then a NULL is returned in place of a value for the first table.

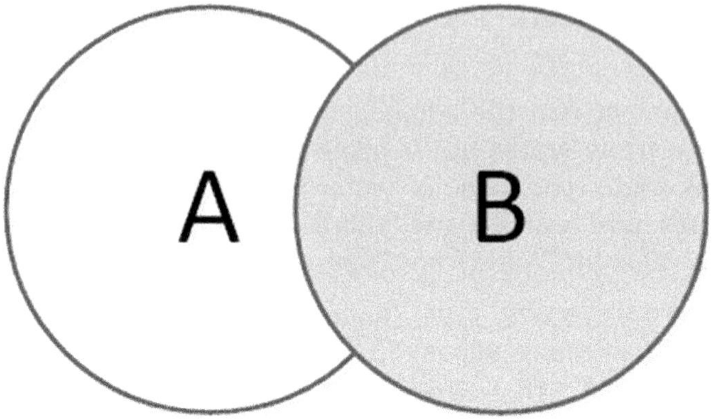

***Figure 6.18**: A Venn Diagram showing a RIGHT JOIN with all rows returned from table B on the right and NULL values for any rows not matching from table A on the left*

Let us explore the **RIGHT JOIN** with another example query from **METRO_TRANSIT**. This time we want to return every row from the **NEIGHBORHOOD** table as well as every row from **STOP**. If there happens to be a Neighborhood that currently does not have any stops assigned, then those rows will still be returned, however, there will be **NULL** values instead of the name of a stop. Be sure to put **tblNEIGHBORHOOD** as the second table!

```
SELECT S.StopID, S.StopName, N.NeighborhoodName
FROM tblSTOP S
      RIGHT JOIN tblNEIGHBORHOOD N
            ON S.NeighborhoodID = N.NeighborhoodID
```

Results Messages

	StopID	StopName	NeighborhoodName
1	6	Broadway Avenue and Cherry Street	Capitol Hill
2	3	Elliott Avenue and Mercer Street	Waterfront
3	4	Sixth Avenue and Battery Street	Downtown
4	5	Fourth Avenue and Seneca Street	Downtown
5	7	First Avenue and Terry Street	SoDo
6	1	Hwy 99-N 54th	Fremont
7	2	Hwy 99-N 36th	Fremont

***Figure 6.19**: An example query result from a RIGHT JOIN*

Now, let us add a new neighborhood to prove how the **RIGHT JOIN** will behave.

```
INSERT INTO tblNEIGHBORHOOD (NeighborhoodName, NeighborhoodDescr)
VALUES ('Richmond Highlands', 'Smaller neighborhood with a mix of
shops, light industry, and schools West of Highway 99 in Shoreline')
```

Please re-run the previous query with the recently added row of a new neighborhood:

```
SELECT S.StopID, S.StopName, N.NeighborhoodName
FROM tblSTOP S
      RIGHT JOIN tblNEIGHBORHOOD N ON S.NeighborhoodID
      = N.NeighborhoodID
```

Results Messages

	StopID	StopName	NeighborhoodName
1	6	Broadway Avenue and Cherry Street	Capitol Hill
2	3	Elliott Avenue and Mercer Street	Waterfront
3	4	Sixth Avenue and Battery Street	Downtown
4	5	Fourth Avenue and Seneca Street	Downtown
5	7	First Avenue and Terry Street	SoDo
6	1	Hwy 99-N 54th	Fremont
7	2	Hwy 99-N 36th	Fremont
8	NULL	NULL	Richmond Highlands

Figure 6.20: *An example query result from a RIGHT JOIN with a NULL value*

The results set have returned 1 row with a **NULL** value for the recently added row in **tblNEIGHBORHOOD** because no stops have been assigned the **NeighborhoodID** of 'Richmond Highlands'.

SELF JOIN

A self-join is used when trying to locate data from a table that equals other data from the same table. A very common example of this is an **EMPLOYEE** table that has a primary key of the EmpID column for each employee but also a second EmpID for tracking the employee's manager. The second EmpID tracking the manager is a foreign key back to the primary key in the same table. At first glance, this seems weird.

When we want to write a query to return the list of employees and their managers, we will need to join two instances of the same table. Nothing needs to change in the process of writing our query as we just make sure to have different aliases for the following each instance:

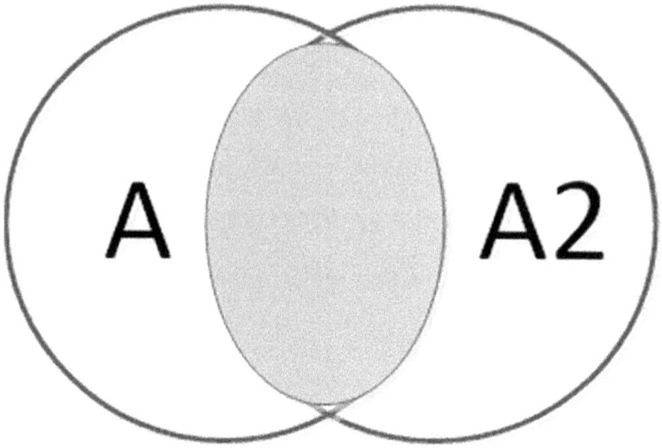

***Figure 6.21**: A Venn diagram showing a SELF JOIN*

Again, a **SELF** Join returns the intersection of rows from a query drawing data from two separate instances of one table (same table...joined to itself with different aliases).

To see a self-join example, we will need to make a slight change to the schema of **METRO_TRANSIT**. Imagine in **METRO_TRANSIT** that each driver is now required to have another driver (who might be slightly older or more experienced) assigned to them as a mentor. How might we track this assignment in our database? As it is currently designed, we have no column for tracking a mentor. So, let us fix this!

The following query will add a new column **MentorID** to the **tblDRIVER** table as well as making the primary key (**DriverID**) a foreign key in the same table!

SQL code to **ALTER tblDRIVER** to add column MentorID is as follows:

```
ALTER TABLE tblDRIVER
ADD MentorID INT
FOREIGN KEY
REFERENCES tblDRIVER (DriverID)
```

Next, let us update a few rows to reflect potential mentoring relationships. The SQL code to **INSERT** values into **tblDRIVER** for **MentorID** is as follows:

```
UPDATE tblDRIVER
SET MentorID =
      (SELECT DriverID
      FROM tblDRIVER
      WHERE Fname = 'Bruce' and Lname = 'Lee')
WHERE DriverID =
      (SELECT DriverID
      FROM tblDRIVER
      WHERE Fname = 'Jimi' and Lname = 'Hendrix')
```

```
GO

UPDATE tblDRIVER
SET MentorID =
       (SELECT DriverID
       FROM tblDRIVER
       WHERE Fname = 'Jimi' and Lname = 'Hendrix')
WHERE DriverID =
       (SELECT DriverID
       FROM tblDRIVER
       WHERE Fname = 'Meryl' and Lname = 'Streep')
GO
```

Now, we have added these values into our database, we can write a self-join to return the values in the context of a report.

```
SELECT D1.Fname AS Driver_First, D1.Lname AS Driver_Last,
D2.Fname AS Mentor_First, D2.Lname AS Mentor_Last
FROM tblDRIVER D1
       JOIN tblDRIVER D2 ON D1.DriverID = D2.MentorID
```

Results Messages

	Driver_First	Driver_Last	Mentor_First	Mentor_Last
1	Bruce	Lee	Jimi	Hendrix
2	Jimi	Hendrix	Meryl	Streep

Figure 6.22: *A query result from a Self-Join with DRIVER joining itself*

Please note that the query results in *Figure 6.22* is drawing data from two copies of **tblDRIVER** (labeled as D1 and D2). The results show the driver and their respective mentor. Self joins are not very common, but when there is a need to layer queries, knowing how to connect two copies of a single together is invaluable.

CROSS JOIN

A cross join returns a Cartesian product of each row in one table and every single matching combination from another table. While this kind of query can result in an overwhelming number of rows, there are some situations where it may be the only way to answer a question. In the **METRO_TRANSIT** database, it might be important to see each trip that every driver has ever been assigned. Let us use round numbers for simplicity.

If **METRO_TRANSIT** was used by a medium-sized city, it may have perhaps 500 drivers in the database. If each driver is assigned 100 trips a month, after 5 years (obviously 60 months) there may be over 1 million rows of data. Since it would be nearly impossible for a person to read this much data, the use of **CROSS JOIN** is probably limited to capturing data for feeding another application for analyses or perhaps, archival or historical purposes.

Let us see this example from **METRO_TRANSIT** first with a simple JOIN s a comparison:

```
SELECT *
FROM tblDRIVER D
        JOIN tblTRIP T ON D.DriverID = T.DriverID
```

Results | Messages

	DriverID	Fname	Lname	BirthDate	Salary	LicenseNumber	MentorID	TripID	DriverID	VehicleID	RouteID	BeginDateTime	EndDateTime
1	4	Meryl	Streep	1949-06-22	46965.00	MDStre8121UJ	1	1	4	2	6	2025-06-22 06:17:00.000	2025-06-22 06:50:00.000
2	1	Jimi	Hendrix	1942-11-27	42590.00	JMHend3487RR	2	2	1	1	6	2025-06-22 06:42:00.000	2025-06-22 07:29:00.000
3	4	Meryl	Streep	1949-06-22	46965.00	MDStre8121UJ	1	3	4	2	5	2025-06-23 07:23:00.000	2025-06-23 08:17:00.000
4	2	Bruce	Lee	1940-11-27	42590.00	BTLee*2198DL	NULL	4	2	3	6	2025-06-22 06:57:00.000	2025-06-22 07:48:00.000
5	4	Meryl	Streep	1949-06-22	46965.00	MDStre8121UJ	1	5	4	2	4	2025-06-29 08:07:00.000	2025-06-29 08:48:00.000

Figure 6.23: *A query result from a standard* JOIN

A standard **JOIN** returns 5 rows from the **METRO_TRANSIT** database as it only returns values that match across primary and foreign key relationships. Now, compare to a **CROSS JOIN** without any restrictions:

```
SELECT *
FROM tblDRIVER D
        CROSS JOIN tblTRIP T
```

Results | Messages

	DriverID	Fname	Lname	BirthDate	Salary	LicenseNumber	MentorID	TripID	DriverID	VehicleID	RouteID	BeginDateTime	EndDateTime
1	1	Jimi	Hendrix	1942-11-27	42590.00	JMHend3487RR	2	1	4	2	6	2025-06-22 06:17:00.000	2025-06-22 06:50:00.000
2	1	Jimi	Hendrix	1942-11-27	42590.00	JMHend3487RR	2	2	1	1	6	2025-06-22 06:42:00.000	2025-06-22 07:29:00.000
3	1	Jimi	Hendrix	1942-11-27	42590.00	JMHend3487RR	2	3	4	2	5	2025-06-23 07:23:00.000	2025-06-23 08:17:00.000
4	1	Jimi	Hendrix	1942-11-27	42590.00	JMHend3487RR	2	4	2	3	6	2025-06-22 06:57:00.000	2025-06-22 07:48:00.000
5	1	Jimi	Hendrix	1942-11-27	42590.00	JMHend3487RR	2	5	4	2	4	2025-06-29 08:07:00.000	2025-06-29 08:48:00.000
6	2	Bruce	Lee	1940-11-27	42590.00	BTLee*2198DL	NULL	1	4	2	6	2025-06-22 06:17:00.000	2025-06-22 06:50:00.000
7	2	Bruce	Lee	1940-11-27	42590.00	BTLee*2198DL	NULL	2	1	1	6	2025-06-22 06:42:00.000	2025-06-22 07:29:00.000
8	2	Bruce	Lee	1940-11-27	42590.00	BTLee*2198DL	NULL	3	4	2	5	2025-06-23 07:23:00.000	2025-06-23 08:17:00.000
9	2	Bruce	Lee	1940-11-27	42590.00	BTLee*2198DL	NULL	4	2	3	6	2025-06-22 06:57:00.000	2025-06-22 07:48:00.000
10	2	Bruce	Lee	1940-11-27	42590.00	BTLee*2198DL	NULL	5	4	2	4	2025-06-29 08:07:00.000	2025-06-29 08:48:00.000
11	3	Jim	Morrison	1943-12-08	47625.00	JPMorr7762WS	NULL	1	4	2	6	2025-06-22 06:17:00.000	2025-06-22 06:50:00.000
12	3	Jim	Morrison	1943-12-08	47625.00	JPMorr7762WS	NULL	2	1	1	6	2025-06-22 06:42:00.000	2025-06-22 07:29:00.000
13	3	Jim	Morrison	1943-12-08	47625.00	JPMorr7762WS	NULL	3	4	2	5	2025-06-23 07:23:00.000	2025-06-23 08:17:00.000
14	3	Jim	Morrison	1943-12-08	47625.00	JPMorr7762WS	NULL	4	2	3	6	2025-06-22 06:57:00.000	2025-06-22 07:48:00.000
15	3	Jim	Morrison	1943-12-08	47625.00	JPMorr7762WS	NULL	5	4	2	4	2025-06-29 08:07:00.000	2025-06-29 08:48:00.000
16	4	Meryl	Streep	1949-06-22	46965.00	MDStre8121UJ	1	1	4	2	6	2025-06-22 06:17:00.000	2025-06-22 06:50:00.000
17	4	Meryl	Streep	1949-06-22	46965.00	MDStre8121UJ	1	2	1	1	6	2025-06-22 06:42:00.000	2025-06-22 07:29:00.000
18	4	Meryl	Streep	1949-06-22	46965.00	MDStre8121UJ	1	3	4	2	5	2025-06-23 07:23:00.000	2025-06-23 08:17:00.000
19	4	Meryl	Streep	1949-06-22	46965.00	MDStre8121UJ	1	4	2	3	6	2025-06-22 06:57:00.000	2025-06-22 07:48:00.000
20	4	Meryl	Streep	1949-06-22	46965.00	MDStre8121UJ	1	5	4	2	4	2025-06-29 08:07:00.000	2025-06-29 08:48:00.000

Figure 6.24: *A query result from a* CROSS JOIN

A **CROSS JOIN** produces a cartesian product, and in this case returns 20 rows. In the preceding image, also note the NULL values for MentorID for Bruce Lee and Jim Morrison, since they were not yet assigned mentors. Bruce did not get a mentor because, well, he did not need one and Jim did not get one because he refused to listen to anyone.

Multiple Conditions in JOIN

One last set of examples with JOIN statements needs to include multiple filters. In the following example, we are adding a JOIN filter to determine if the driver is completing the trip during the month of their birthday.

Note: **`MONTH()`** *is a date function, and will be explored in greater detail with other Date functions soon!*

```
SELECT D.DriverID, Fname, Lname, BirthDate, T.TripID, BeginDateTime
FROM tblDRIVER D
   JOIN tblTRIP T ON D.DriverID = T.DriverID
   AND MONTH(D.BirthDate) = MONTH(T.BeginDateTime)
```

Results Messages

	DriverID	Fname	Lname	BirthDate	TripID	BeginDateTime
1	4	Meryl	Streep	1949-06-22	1	2025-06-22 06:17:00.000
2	4	Meryl	Streep	1949-06-22	3	2025-06-23 07:23:00.000
3	4	Meryl	Streep	1949-06-22	5	2025-06-29 08:07:00.000

***Figure 6.25**: A query result with multiple JOIN conditions*

Please note that June matches both the month that Meryl Streep was born as well as when the trips were operated (satisfying the conditions of the query). The preceding query could quite easily be written with the second condition in a separate **`WHERE`** clause, but this method may perform faster, depending on the number of rows in the table.

Functions

Functions are beautiful! Functions are intended to save time, and reduce errors on repetitive tasks, such as getting the current time of day or perhaps total up the bill for an order. A function is simply a pre-written block of code that is named, saved, and ready to run whenever called. There are several different types of functions, including system functions, numeric, string, NULL, aggregate, date, and ranking functions as well as those we can design and code ourselves (called user-defined functions). Most database systems will include more than 100 functions built-in when the system is installed. As mentioned, functions may be the most beautiful item in all programming, not just SQL. We save time in three instances when using functions which can be categorized as before, during, and after runtime (runtime is when the function is called or used in processing).

Efficiencies gained before runtime include not having to write the code again or reinventing a process. While all code must be written the first time, after the testing is completed and the code is released, we try to put that baby to bed and walk away quietly. This is often the first (and only) answer I receive from students when asked, “how do we gain efficiency from pre-written code?” Efficiency in not having to re-write code may only represent 10% of all efficiencies gained.

Efficiencies gained during runtime are perhaps a bit obscure. When any code is submitted to be processed, it must first be compiled into a digital form that machines and processors can understand (appropriately called 'machine language'). This is called being 'compiled' and may take only a fraction of a second. Additionally, each piece of compiled code includes what is called an 'Execution Plan' which acts like a navigator in a car and basically tells the query how to get to the destination where the data lives inside the database. Again, the savings per query may be only a second or two for simple tasks but may be significantly more for more complex code. If we build functions, these blocks of code are compiled the first time they are used and then rarely if ever need to be re-compiled again. This may not seem like a big deal but imagine a process (such logging-in to email) that occurs billions of times a day, and then we can see that every fraction of a second matters.

Later in your journey to acquire advanced database design skills, there will be more to learn about the advantages gained during runtime (including parallel processing, index optimization, proper error-handling, and avoiding cascading rollbacks). These are significant but well beyond the scope of this textbook.

Efficiencies gained after runtime are theoretical and only able to be estimated. These estimates include events and errors that NEVER HAPPENED. Think about it; How many people did not die because they never started smoking as teenagers? We can postulate an approximate number based on statistics, but we will never know in absolute terms. It is theoretical. The same is true when trying to measure the efficiencies gained from using pre-written code like functions. How many disasters did not happen because the code was pre-written, tested, validated and included proper error-handling? We will never know in absolute terms either.

The best organized technology companies have very strict processes and rules regarding the use of repetitive code, no short cuts. The idea is to spend the extra time building something correctly the first time to avoid the pain and confusion of having to fix the same issue many more times in the future.

Let us explore the different kinds of functions included with most SQL systems:

- String
- Numeric
- NULL
- Aggregate
- Date

String Functions

Many (if not most) queries need a little bit of minor tweaks when trying to match the nuance of a business question. We have dozens of keywords that help adjust not only the asking of the question driving the query but also formatting the results set of data returned to be better able to be read and understood by people.

Please review the following incomplete list of the most common string functions:

Name	**Purpose**
CONCAT	Returns a string that is the result of combining multiple strings together end-to-end
CAST	Changes the data type of a column during query execution
LEFT	Returns the characters from far LEFT of string (counting left to right)
LEN	Returns the number of characters in a string, ignoring blanks at the end
LOWER	Returns a string with all characters in LOWERCASE
LTRIM	Returns the characters remaining from a string after trimming leading blanks
REPLACE	Replaces all occurrences of specified string with a second specified replacement
RIGHT	Returns the characters from far RIGHT of string (counting right to left)
RTRIM	Returns the string after trimming trailing blanks
STR	Returns character data converted from numeric data
SUBSTRING	Chops out string when provided a beginning point and desired number of characters
TRIM	Removes specified characters from beginning and ending of string (often blank spaces)
UPPER	Returns a string with all characters in UPPERCASE

Table 6.1: *A list of common string functions*

The above string functions are a subset of a larger list of string functions. These are considered basic and essential to most data scenarios for those being introduced to relational databases and SQL. Please search online for a more exhaustive list.

CONCAT()

There are many times characters and results from queries that need to be combined or concatenated for easier reading. This can be accomplished without the use of a function as follows, using simple plus sign and quoted blank spaces:

```
SELECT 'Jimi ' + 'Hendrix ' + 'was a great musician') AS Homage_Jimi
```

	Homage_to_Jimi
1	Jimi Hendrix was a great musician

Figure 6.26: *An example query combining characters without a function*

CONCAT() happens to be a string function to make the process of combining strings together more programmatic and directly tied to a query result. See the following:

```
SELECT CONCAT('Jimi', ' ', 'Hendrix', ' ','was a great musician') AS
Homage_to_Jimi_2
```

	Homage_to_Jimi_2
1	Jimi Hendrix was a great musician

Figure 6.27*: An example query combining characters with CONCAT()*

Next, please see **CONCAT()** returning data from columns in **tblDRIVER**:

```
SELECT CONCAT(fname,' ', Lname, ' ', 'was a great musician')
AS Homage_to_Jimi_3
FROM tblDRIVER
    WHERE fname = 'Jimi'
```

	Homage_to_Jimi_3
1	Jimi Hendrix was a great musician

Figure 6.28*: An example query combining characters pulled from a table with CONCAT()*

Similar to other SQL commands, **CONCAT()** can be combined with several other functions to extend its reach and power.

LEFT() and RIGHT()

LEFT() is a function that can cut a specified number of characters from a string, reading from left to right. **RIGHT()** is going to be exactly opposite (backwards?) by cutting a specified number of characters from a string reading from right to left.

```
SELECT LEFT(CONCAT(fname, Lname), 6) AS Left_6_Characters
FROM tblDRIVER
```

	Left_6_Characters
1	JimiHe
2	BruceL
3	JimMor
4	MerylS

Figure 6.29*: An example query with LEFT() and CONCAT()*

```
SELECT RIGHT(CONCAT(fname, Lname), 6) AS Right_6_Characters
FROM tblDRIVER
```

	Right_6_Characters
1	endrix
2	uceLee
3	rrison
4	Streep

Figure 6.30: *Example query with RIGHT() and CONCAT() returning the last 6 characters*

The results from *Figure* 6.30 may not be obviously useful at this point; when will anyone need to know the last 6 characters of a combined first and the last name? Readers need to be aware of the capabilities of the most common functions, so when the process of cleaning data obtained from a web scrape or a third-party vendor gets dropped on us!

LEN()

LEN() is a function that allows a user to determine the number of characters (or **LENGTH**) of a string. This knowledge can then help us as we programmatically extract data from the string with other functions such as **LEFT()** and **RIGHT()** among others we shall see shortly.

```
SELECT Fname, Lname, LEN(Lname) AS Number_Characters_Lname
FROM tblDRIVER
    WHERE fname = 'Bruce'
```

	Fname	Lname	Number_Characters_Lname
1	Bruce	Lee	3

Figure 6.31: *An example query with LEN() to determine the number of characters*

The query in *Figure* 6.31 produces a result of 3 for the value of the aliased column (**Number_Characters_Lname**) when provided the **fname** value of '**Bruce**'. This makes sense as the only driver with the first name of 'Bruce' is Bruce Lee. There are 3 characters in 'Lee'.

LOWER() and UPPER()

The next two functions are going to be a valuable part when presenting data to others as part of a formal dashboard or other reporting requirements. Frequently, data results will need to be displayed in a pattern of consistently upper or lower case.

```
SELECT LOWER(CONCAT(Fname,' ', Lname)) AS lower_Fname_Lname
FROM tblDRIVER
```

	lower_Fname_Lname
1	jimi hendrix
2	bruce lee
3	jim morrison
4	meryl streep

***Figure 6.32**: An example query with LOWER() to affect readability*

```
SELECT UPPER(CONCAT(Fname,' ', Lname)) AS UPPER_Fname_Lname
FROM tblDRIVER
```

	UPPER_Fname_Lname
1	JIMI HENDRIX
2	BRUCE LEE
3	JIM MORRISON
4	MERYL STREEP

***Figure 6.33**: An example query with UPPER() to affect readability*

TRIM(), LTRIM(), and RTRIM()

While scraping data from various locations on the web or because of extracting data from multiple resources, we may need to deal with unnecessary blank spaces either at the beginning or end of values. The string functions **`TRIM()`**, **`LTRIM()`**, and **`RTRIM()`** can cut out these blank spaces!

`TRIM()` will remove blanks both in front as well as at the end. See as follows with a string with an initial length of 30 characters (including the two blanks at the beginning and 2 more at the end):

```
SELECT TRIM('  2 blanks in front and back  ') AS TRIM_Gets_Front_and_
Back
```

	TRIM_Gets_Front_and_Back
1	2 blanks in front and back

***Figure 6.34**: An example query with TRIM()*

Do not simply take my word that **`TRIM()`** removed the empty spaces in the example found in *Figure* 6.34. Please see the following query that uses **`LEN()`** to measure the number of characters remaining after **`TRIM()`** runs:

```
SELECT LEN(TRIM('  2 blanks in front and back  ')) AS TRIM_Gets_
Front_and_Back
```

	Length_After_TRIM
1	26

***Figure 6.35**: An example query with TRIM() removing blank spaces in front and back*

Next, let us see the use of both **`LTRIM()`** and **`RTRIM()`** with the same string and validation queries to drop the blank spaces, one at a time.

```
SELECT LTRIM('  2 blanks in front and back  ') AS LTRIM_Gets_Front
SELECT LEN(LTRIM('  2 blanks in front and back  ')) AS LTRIM_Gets_
Front
```

	LTRIM_Gets_Front
1	2 blanks in front and back

	LTRIM_Gets_Front
1	28

***Figure 6.36**: An example query with `LTRIM()` removing blank spaces in front*

Next, let us see a similar example using **`RTRIM()`** to drop blank characters from the end of a string and then validate the results with another query using **`LEN()`**.

```
SELECT RTRIM('  2 blanks in front and back  ') AS RTRIM_Gets_Only_End
SELECT LEN(RTRIM('  2 blanks in front and back  ')) AS Number_Of_
Characters_from_30
```

	RTRIM_Gets_Only_End
1	2 blanks in front and back

	Number_Of_Characters_from_30
1	28

***Figure 6.37**: An example query with `RTRIM()` removing blank spaces in back*

There may be a need for dropping leading characters that are not blank spaces. From

METRO_TRANSIT, see the example in *Figure* 6.37 where the first two characters (which are '19') are dropped from each birthdate value in the results set.

```
SELECT Fname, Lname, BirthDate, LTRIM(BirthDate, 19) AS NonBlank_
LTRIM
FROM tblDRIVER
```

	Fname	Lname	BirthDate	NonBlank_LTRIM
1	Jimi	Hendrix	1942-11-27	42-11-27
2	Bruce	Lee	1940-11-27	40-11-27
3	Jim	Morrison	1943-12-08	43-12-08
4	Meryl	Streep	1949-06-22	49-06-22

Figure 6.38: *An example query with `LTRIM()` removing specific characters*

Consider product data from a supplier or industry partner that we are trying to import to conduct analyses. Maybe, all we really want are the names and prices of the products they sell to our organization, yet this external data has 'over-loaded' values with proprietary productid, or product category names mixed in the name values. **LTRIM()** might be the perfect function to drop leading characters that all have the same pattern.

REPLACE()

REPLACE() is a string function that substitutes one new string that overwrites another. It has the following syntax with 3 inputs:

```
REPLACE (full_string, substring_to_be_replaced, new_substring)
```

An example from **METRO_TRANSIT** includes re-writing the description for some values in **tblNEIGHBORHOOD**. Consider wanting to replace 'restaurant' with 'retail and award-winning restaurants' for the sake of a single query:

```
SELECT NeighborhoodDescr, REPLACE(NeighborhoodDescr, 'restaurants',
'retail and award-winning restaurants') AS Updated_Changes
FROM tblNEIGHBORHOOD
```

	NeighborhoodDescr	Updated_Changes
1	Vibrant, colorful, and walkable neighborhood with many shops and services	Vibrant, colorful, and walkable neighborhood with many shops and services
2	Naturally scenic, tourist-focused neighborhood with many food options	Naturally scenic, tourist-focused neighborhood with many food options
3	Urban, business-focused with many restaurants and transit connections to entire region	Urban, business-focused with many retail and award-winning restaurants and transit connections to entire region
4	Gritty and industrial neighborhood	Gritty and industrial neighborhood
5	Eccentric and organic feel with shops and restaurants that fit a range of budgets	Eccentric and organic feel with shops and retail and award-winning restaurants that fit a range of budgets

Figure 6.39: *An example query with `REPLACE()` swapping a string with a second string*

The values returned in *Figure* 6.39 include only 2 rows that were modified with the **REPLACE()** function (rows 3 and 5). The unaffected values are those that did not have the substring 'restaurants' already.

Please note, the data stored in the column NeighborhoodDescr in the table **tblNEIGHBORHOOD** are NOT permanently changed; the **REPLACE()** function only returns changes for a single query. We would need to execute an UPDATE command to make permanent changes to the database.

STR()

STR() is a function that takes a number value and makes it a string. This conversion helps integrate the data with other string data, perhaps a longer document where the numbered data is being presented in its final form, and is no longer going to be involved in math.

The **STR()** function has several inputs including the following:

- Number (required)
- Length (optional)
- Decimals (optional)

The **STR()** function is flexible but be cautious when using; this function will round to the nearest whole number if the decimals option is not specified.

```
SELECT Fname, Lname, BoardingDateTime, Fare, STR(Fare) AS Amount_
Fare_Default_STR
FROM tblBOARDING B
    JOIN tblCUSTOMER C ON B.CustomerID = C.CustomerID
```

	Fname	Lname	BoardingDateTime	Fare	Amount_Fare_Default_STR
1	Ivey	Hazekamp	2025-04-23 07:41:35.000	3.75	4
2	Kenyetta	Terron	2025-04-24 06:47:23.000	3.25	3
3	Ivey	Hazekamp	2025-04-24 06:47:23.000	3.75	4

Figure 6.40: *An example query with STR() returning numeric data as string*

The last column in *Figure* 6.40 is a string value drawn from the numeric data type. Even though the value has 2 decimal places (as seen in the second to last column 'Fare'), the **STR()** default rounds to the nearest whole number.

The following optional inputs will provide greater accuracy with **STR()**:

```
SELECT Fname, Lname, BoardingDateTime, Fare, STR(Fare, 8, 2) AS
Amount_Fare_STR_Decimals
FROM tblBOARDING B
    JOIN tblCUSTOMER C ON B.CustomerID = C.CustomerID
```

	Fname	Lname	BoardingDateTime	Fare	Amount_Fare_STR_Decimals
1	Ivey	Hazekamp	2025-04-23 07:41:35.000	3.75	3.75
2	Kenyetta	Terron	2025-04-24 06:47:23.000	3.25	3.25
3	Ivey	Hazekamp	2025-04-24 06:47:23.000	3.75	3.75

Figure 6.41: *An example query with STR() including input options*

SUBSTRING()

One of the most powerful and important string functions must be **SUBSTRING()**. This function enables an analyst to take any string value and extract a portion (hence the name 'sub-string'). This takes several inputs including the entire string, the starting point of the extraction, and the total number of characters to extract.

The syntax of **substring()** is: `SUBSTRING(string, starting position, length)`

```
SELECT SUBSTRING('this is an example text', 6, 11) AS SUBSTRING_
EXAMPLE
```

	SUBSTRING_EXAMPLE
1	is an examp

Figure 6.42: *An example query with SUBSTRING()*

In a typical organization, there is a frequent need to extract data from string values. Consider trying to clean up a block of text from a spreadsheet or large text file where a set length of data is buried within other undesirable text. Having a command like **substring()** will make the process of data analyses much more convenient.

CAST()

Many times, when working with data we will want to present the data in reports or a dashboard with a different data type from how the data is stored in the database. The function that is best used for this task is **CAST()** (technically **CAST()** is not a string function but it is included in this section as it will be required in future sections).

The most common switches in data types are changing numbers and character/ string (in both directions), as well as modifying date and time formats. Without affecting the data stored within the database, we can change how the data is returned or presented on the fly during a query execution by using **CAST()**.

The syntax for this function is: `CAST (expression AS target_type [ ( length ) ] )`

Consider wanting to change the data type of **tblDRIVER.salary** from NUMERIC(8,2) to INTEGER for aesthetic reasons like dropping decimal places.

```
SELECT fname, Lname, Salary, CAST(Salary AS INTEGER) AS Salary_INT
FROM tblDRIVER
```

	fname	Lname	Salary	Salary_INT
1	Jimi	Hendrix	42590.00	42590
2	Bruce	Lee	42590.00	42590
3	Jim	Morrison	47625.00	47625
4	Meryl	Streep	46965.00	46965

Figure 6.43: *An example query with `CAST()` changing data type NUMERIC to INTEGER*

Other data types are frequently changed during queries, like dates to character.

```
SELECT fname, Lname, BirthDate, CAST(BirthDate AS varchar(10)) AS
BIRTH_VARCHAR
FROM tblDRIVER
```

	fname	Lname	BirthDate	BIRTH_VARCHAR
1	Jimi	Hendrix	1942-11-27	1942-11-27
2	Bruce	Lee	1940-11-27	1940-11-27
3	Jim	Morrison	1943-12-08	1943-12-08
4	Meryl	Streep	1949-06-22	1949-06-22

Figure 6.44: *An example query with `CAST()` changing data type DATE to VARCHAR(10)*

Figure 6.44 shows a query result with the column Birthdate as both a date data type as well as cast to varchar(10). These results are indistinguishable! We are better able to integrate character data types with other strings when aiming for a consistent format or readability.

Numeric Functions

The following functions are some of the more common when working with numerical data:

Name	**Purpose**
ABS	Determines the absolute value of a number
CEILING	Determines the smallest integer value greater than or equal to a number
FLOOR	Determines the largest integer value less than or equal to a number
MOD	Determines Modulo or Remainder
ISNUMERIC	Tests whether an expression is numeric
POWER	Returns the value of a number raised to the power of another number
RAND	Returns a random number that is between 0 and 1 (16 digits)

ROUND	Rounds a number to a specified number of decimal places
SQRT	Returns the square root of a number
SQUARE	Returns the square of a number

Table 6.2: *A list of 10 basic numeric functions in SQL*

Now, let us take a closer look at the more basic numeric functions from *Table6.2*. As with many languages, there are more numeric functions than are listed here, the goal of this book is to provide a foundational understanding of SQL and relational databases. Moreover, as your skills and interest grows with analytics and SQL, there will be opportunities to expand your knowledge beyond the basic introduction of functions found here.

Please feel free to type along with these examples and experiment with your own data to get a feel for how these are used and the results generated.

ABS()

This function is used in evaluations often when seeking to measure distance in variation from an expected value (without regard to positive or negative).

```
SELECT ABS (-43.87) AS Example_ABS
```

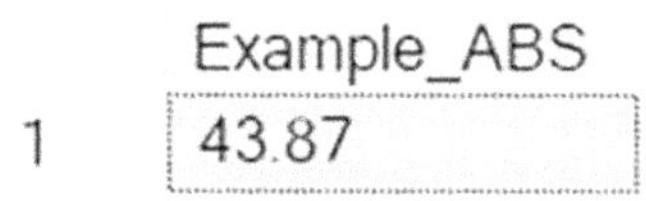

Figure 6.45: *Example queries using numeric function ABS (Absolute Value)*

```
SELECT ABS (54 * -43.87) AS Example2_ABS
```

Figure 6.46: *Example queries using numeric function ABS (Absolute Value)*

`Ceiling()` and **`FLOOR()`** are great functions to be familiar with as they simplify a result set by returning the whole number that is either larger or smaller than the calculated results. **`CEILING()`** will round UP to the nearest whole number while **`FLOOR()`** will round **DOWN**.

```
SELECT CEILING(26.768 * 13.923) AS CEILING_BasicMath
```

Figure 6.47: *Example queries using numeric function* `CEILING()`

```
SELECT FLOOR(26.768 * 13.923) AS FLOOR_BasicMath
```

	FLOOR_BasicMath
1	372

Figure 6.48: *Example queries using numeric function and* `FLOOR()`

These functions are consistent with negative results as well. Change the sign on one of the numbers in the equations and review the results:

```
SELECT CEILING(26.768 * -13.923) AS CEILING_BasicMath_Negative
```

	CEILING_BasicMath_Negative
1	-372

Figure 6.49: *Example query of CEILING_BasicMath_Negative*

```
SELECT FLOOR(26.768 * -13.923) AS FLOOR_BasicMath_Negative
```

	FLOOR_BasicMath_Negative
1	-373

Figure 6.50: *Example query of FLOOR_BasicMath_Negative*

We will see aggregate functions in greater detail a moment, however, please consider that **`AVG()`** will calculate the average across many values as follows:

```
SELECT AVG(SALARY) AS AVG_Salary
FROM tblDRIVER
```

	AVG_Salary
1	44942.500000

Figure 6.51: *Example query showing results from AVG() aggregate function*

Next, please see that **`CEILING()`** and **`FLOOR()`** can be layered over **`AVG()`** to round the results to the nearest whole number:

```
SELECT CEILING(AVG(SALARY)) AS CEILING_AVG_Salary
FROM tblDRIVER
```

	CEILING_AVG_Salary
1	44943

Figure 6.52: *Example query showing results with multiple functions*

```
SELECT FLOOR(AVG(SALARY)) AS FLOOR_AVG_Salary
FROM tblDRIVER
```

	FLOOR_AVG_Salary
1	44942

Figure 6.53: *Example queries showing results from* `CEILING()` *and* `FLOOR()` *over* `AVG()`

Both **`CEILING()`** and **`FLOOR()`** are great functions to be familiar with when investigating a set of data. These can help quickly establish the boundaries of the range of values contained in a column with a numeric data type as well as gaining a comprehensive understanding of an entire data ecosystem when applied in conjunction with other functions and formulas.

ISNUMERIC()

Occasionally, when working with a vast amount of tabular data, there will be a need to determine whether a column (or a value) contains numeric data. The good news is SQL has a function to determine this! **`ISNUMERIC()`** will return a value of '1' (positive) if the input parameter it evaluates is a numeric value. Conversely, **`ISNUMERIC()`** will return a value of '0' (negative) if the input parameter it evaluates is NOT a numeric value.

The first example will be against a string as follows:

```
SELECT ISNUMERIC(lname) AS Testing_For_Numeric_1
FROM tblDRIVER
      WHERE Fname = 'Meryl'
```

	Testing_For_Numeric_1
1	0

Figure 6.54: *Example query using `ISNUMERIC()`*

There should be no surprise from the resulting value of '0' from *Figure* 6.54 as the string value 'Streep' is evaluated as the input to the function is not numeric.

Let us try passing other inputs, such as salary from the same table in addition to an obvious math equation:

```
SELECT ISNUMERIC(salary) AS Testing_For_Numeric_2
FROM tblDRIVER
WHERE Fname = 'meryl'
```

	Testing_For_Numeric_2
1	1

Figure 6.55: *Example query using ISNUMERIC() against column 'salary'*

```
SELECT ISNUMERIC(23.67 * 32) AS Testing_For_Numeric_3
```

	Testing_For_Numeric_3
1	1

Figure 6.56: *Example query using `ISNUMERIC()` against a math equation*

The third example shown in *Figure* 6.56 above is against a math equation and returns the value of 1. What should be returned if the exact same equation is placed between quotes?

```
SELECT ISNUMERIC('23.67 * 32') AS Testing_For_Numeric_4
```

	Testing_For_Numeric_4
1	0

Figure 6.57: *Example query using* `ISNUMERIC()` *against a string of math equation*

The fourth example shown in *Figure* 6.57 above returns a value of 0 because once the quotes are placed around the math equation, it becomes a string.

`ISNUMERIC()` is quite useful when trying to quickly understand the results of a data set and whether other math functions are going to be effective. We will see how to process thousands (if not millions) of rows automatically later in our learning. Being able to have conditional logic that decides to include a value in math without people being involved will prove to be very important.

`MOD()` and %

There are situations when working with data that we may need to determine the remaining value after an equation that includes division. This is known as the remainder or modulus. Many database products that comply with standard SQL syntax use a function **`MOD()`** to determine the modulus. SQL Server does not use the **`MOD()`** function and instead uses the single percentage sign ('%') to perform the same functionality as **`MOD()`**. Please see the following syntax that divides 49 by 32 and returns the remaining balance:

```
SELECT 49 % 32 AS Example_Modulus
```

	Example_Modulus
1	17

Figure 6.58: *Example query showing results from division using modulus %*

Many of us should be able to conduct simple math in *Figure* 6.58 in our head to see the result after dividing 49 by 32 is 17. A common need for finding the modulus is when we want to determine whether a value is even or odd; when the base number is divided by 2, even numbers will have a remainder/modulus = 0 while any odd number will have the value of 1.

`SQUARE()`, `SQRT()` and `POWER()`

Working with data in many forms occasionally requires us to calculate any number of exponential values when provided a base number. The most common are the square, square root and a raised power (the number of times to multiply the base number to itself). Standard SQL functions are provided to address these concerns, including **SQUARE()**, **SQRT()** and **POWER()**. Consider the following examples:

```
SELECT SQUARE(5) AS Example_SQUARE
```

Figure 6.59: *Example query showing results from using* `SQUARE(5)`

Figure 6.59 provides an example use of **SQUARE()** by returning the value 25 (which is the result of 5 * 5 or the base value of 5 squared). The **SQUARE()** function also works with decimals! See the following example and try other numbers for yourself:

```
SELECT SQUARE(5.44) AS Example_SQUARE_with_Decimals
```

Figure 6.60: *Example query showing results of* `SQUARE()` *with input number decimals*

Another important exponential command that is common when working with data includes square root or **SQRT()**. This function takes one input parameter (which can include decimals) and then returns the square root as shown:

```
SELECT SQRT(5) AS Example_SQUARE_ROOT
```

Figure 6.61: *Example query showing results from using* `SQRT(5)`

One last exponential command in SQL that is useful is **POWER()**. This function takes two input parameters, including the base number as well as the desired exponent:

```
SELECT POWER(3, 4) AS Example_POWER
```

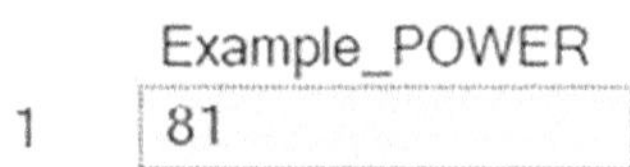

Figure 6.62: *Example query showing results from* `POWER(3,4)`

The function **POWER()** provides significant math ability inside a programming environment while reading and processing potentially millions of rows of data.

Being able to program the calculation of complex math on data without people having to do the work is incredible for two big reasons:

- People are slow by factors of millions compared to machines.
- People make mistakes!

RAND()

There are situations when testing code, like stored procedures, where we will be better able to manage repetitive executions by generating a random 16-digit number between 0 and 1. SQL provides a numeric function **RAND()** to address this need.

While there will be an entire chapter devoted to testing database objects and something called synthetic transactions in an advanced book on data analytics, these topics are beyond the scope of this first book introducing the foundational commands of SQL. Be comfortable in seeing how to generate a random number at this point in your learning and know that we will have more context with additional use cases in the future.

```
SELECT RAND() AS Random_16_digit_Number
```

Figure 6.63: *Example query showing 16-digit results from RAND() between 0 and 1*

As we will see later, there are ways to use **RAND()** to find random primary key values to automatically call stored procedures and test the effectiveness of an application and infrastructure platform. This eventually saves us time and money. For now, let's just see how the basic use of **RAND()** works. Try this code on your own as many times; there will never be the same number twice!

The following examples generate random numbers larger than 0:

```
SELECT RAND() * 10000 AS Random_16_digit_Number
```

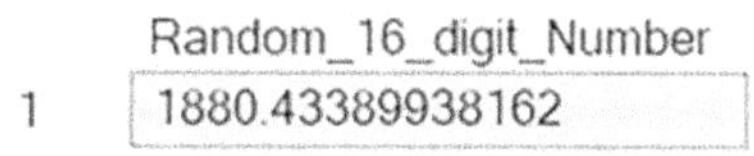

Figure 6.64: *Example query showing 16-digit results from RAND() greater than 0*

The first example in *Figure* 6.64 generates a random number that is still 16 digits in length that is larger than 0. All that has really occurred here is moving the decimal place.

Next, let's see a cleaner method without any decimal places by using the **CAST()** function to make the output a whole number:

```
SELECT CAST(RAND() * 10000 AS INT) AS Random_Number_Larger_Than_1
```

Figure 6.65: *Example query showing results from RAND() with a 3- or 4-digit number*

`ROUND()` will be the last numeric function found in SQL that we will explore in this section. Simply, this function provides the ability to determine the number of decimals that are rounded on numeric value. Let us see two examples:

```
SELECT ROUND(RAND() * 10000, 3) AS ROUND_Random_Number_3_decimals
```

	ROUND_Random_Number_3_decimals
1	1905.259

Figure 6.66: *Example query showing results from `ROUND()` to 3 decimals*

The results in *Figure* 6.66 would normally return to 16 digits, however, the **`ROUND()`** function rounds the results to a specified number of digits.

```
SELECT ROUND(23.9834, 0) AS Example_ROUND
```

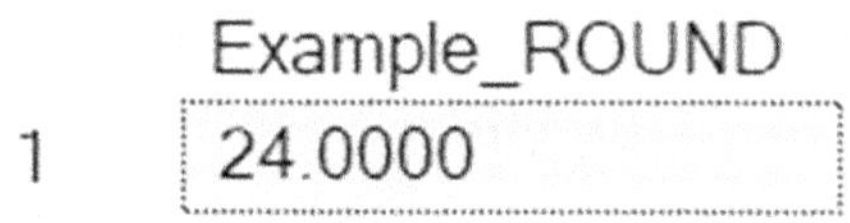

	Example_ROUND
1	24.0000

Figure 6.67: *Example query showing results from `ROUND()` to 0 decimals*

Please note that **`ROUND()`** will in fact round up or down to the specified number of decimals, however, there will still be the total number of decimals in the output as was in the calculation. If there is an interest in dropping the decimals entirely at a certain place, then we will need to use **`CAST()`** again.

```
SELECT CAST(ROUND(23.9834, 0) AS INT) AS Example_CAST_ROUND
```

	Example_CAST_ROUND
1	24

Figure 6.68: *Example query showing results from `ROUND()`*

NULL Functions

Remember please that **`NULL`** is a value that is unknown; it does not equal zero or any other value (not even another **`NULL`**).

Standard SQL includes several functions that allow users to affect how the system treats empty, missing, or otherwise unknown values. These are known as NULL functions and include the following:

- `ISNULL()`
- `COALESCE()`
- `IFNULL()`
- `NVL()`

Of the four NULL functions listed here, only **ISNULL()** and **COALESCE()** work with SQL Server and the **METRO_TRANSIT** example we have constructed. The other two are listed in case you are working with another relational database management system like Oracle or MySQL. Let us see the use of **ISNULL()** and **COALESCE()** as they are effectively identical.

```
SELECT ISNULL(NULL, 'Mary') AS Example_ISNULL
```

	Example_ISNULL
1	Mary

Figure 6.69: *Example query results with ISNULL() function*

```
SELECT COALESCE(NULL, 'had a little lamb') AS Example_COALESCE
```

	Example_COALESCE
1	had a little lamb

Figure 6.70: *Example query showing results from `ISNULL()` and `COALESCE()`*

Please note the output of the **NULL** functions in *Figures* 6.69 *and* 6.70 are interchangeable and provide the same functionality.

One last example of these **NULL** functions can be seen with revisiting an example from earlier (*Figure* 6.17) where we were drawing data on **tblROUTE_TYPE** while demonstrating the use of **LEFT JOIN**:

```
SELECT RT.RouteTypeName, R.RouteName
FROM tblROUTE_TYPE RT
      LEFT JOIN tblROUTE R ON RT.RouteTypeID = R.RouteTypeID
```

Results | Messages

	RouteTypeName	RouteName
1	Express	Sodo-Downtown Express
2	Express	Fremont-Downtown Express
3	Special Event	Fremont-Waterfront-Downtown
4	Regular	Sodo-Downtown Commuter
5	Regular	Fremont-Downtown Commuter
6	Regular	Capitol Hill-Downtown
7	Inclement Weather/Reduced Service	NULL
8	Waterfront Bypass	NULL

Figure 6.71: *Review of previous query from Figure 6.18*

Re-writing this query slightly to include different words as opposed to NULL may look like the following:

```
SELECT RT.RouteTypeName, ISNULL(R.RouteName, 'No Route currently as-
signed') AS RouteName
```

```
FROM tblROUTE_TYPE RT
LEFT JOIN tblROUTE R ON RT.RouteTypeID = R.RouteTypeID
```

	RouteTypeName	RouteName
1	Express	Sodo-Downtown Express
2	Express	Fremont-Downtown Express
3	Special Event	Fremont-Waterfront-Downtown
4	Regular	Sodo-Downtown
5	Regular	Fremont-Downtown
6	Regular	Capitol Hill-Downtown
7	Inclement Weather/Reduced Service	No Route currently assigned
8	Waterfront Bypass	No Route currently assigned

Figure 6.72: *Example query showing results from `ISNULL()` when applied to previous query from Figure 6.18 earlier in chapter*

Please note in *Figure* 6.72 that the column name RouteName has to be replaced with an alias once the function **`ISNULL()`** is applied. The values in rows 7 and 8 are originally NULL, but are substituted with the input values 'No Route currently assigned' passed into the function **`ISNULL()`**.

Aggregate Functions

Aggregate functions are very powerful and save an incredible amount of time when conducting data analyses. These should become very familiar and trusted in your toolbox of SQL chops. Some of these are self-explanatory, but it makes sense to introduce the context and best use for each as some common mistakes occur with beginning analysts.

For the time being, these functions will be demonstrated without GROUP BY and HAVING clauses. After first understanding how these functions behave, then we can expand their use and include the broader application of GROUP BY. While there are roughly ten functions that are labeled as aggregate functions, the following are the most common within SQL:

- `AVG()`
- `COUNT()`
- `MAX()`
- `MIN()`
- `SUM()`

This section of the textbook will explore the five most common aggregate functions;

later, in the advanced SQL chapter, we will include additional aggregate functions related to data analysis as we conduct a deeper dive with additional knowledge.

AVG()

There are many times we desire to determine the average value of some items while analyzing data. For example, we may want to become aware of the average income, number of years of work experience, or age of people. The average rating of customer satisfaction or reliability is important when shopping for cars. When we become aware of the average value, we can then evaluate the relative position of other values as being either 'above or below average'. While important in the world of statistics, average is just one calculation and should be considered suspect.

By itself, any value of average can often be misinterpreted if the sample is insufficient in size, is subject to significant variance or has uninvestigated outliers. That said, **AVG()** is a critical aggregate function; let's give it a try inside the **METRO_TRANSIT** database!

```
SELECT AVG(Salary) AS Average_Salary
FROM tblDRIVER
```

Figure 6.73: *A query result from aggregate function* `AVG()`

Please note in the above query returns a value of 44942.500000. Let us update our query quickly to fix it!

```
SELECT CAST(AVG(Salary) AS Numeric(8,2)) AS Average_DriverSalary
FROM tblDRIVER
```

Figure 6.74: *A query result from aggregate function* `AVG()` *with* `CAST()` *and an alias*

The results from the query now have a label and a reduced number of decimal spaces.

MAX()

What are the boundaries of any value? This is important when investigating data in a database for the first time. Instead of returning the average driver salary, let us see the most. We can use the aggregate function **MAX()** for this.

```
SELECT CAST(MAX(Salary) AS Numeric(8,2)) AS MAX_DriverSalary
FROM tblDRIVER
```

Results Messages

	MAX_DriverSalary
1	47625.00

Figure 6.75: *A query result from aggregate function* `MAX()` *and* `CAST()`

Once again, be comfortable changing the results with the **`CAST()`** function to reduce the number of decimal places as well as using an alias to add a column header.

While we are here, let us make a quick side query and see if we can leverage the **`MAX()`** function to find the driver(s) that earn this salary. How might we write this?

```
SELECT DriverID, Fname, Lname, CAST(Salary AS Numeric(8,2)) AS SALARY
FROM tblDRIVER
WHERE Salary = (SELECT MAX(Salary) FROM tblDRIVER)
```

	DriverID	Fname	Lname	SALARY
1	3	Jim	Morrison	47625.00

Figure 6.76: *A query result from aggregate function* `MAX()` *and* `CAST()` *and subquery*

Be careful! Many beginning SQL query-writers do not see this question as including a subquery; often beginners want to have **`MAX(Salary)`** in the **`SELECT`** line and do not get the results they seek. Get comfortable obtaining the value we seek to include in a logical filter through a calculation by writing an entirely separate query and then sticking it inside the other query (more on subqueries is coming up).

MIN()

The **`MIN()`** aggregate function is obviously very similar to what we have just seen with **`MAX()`**. Let us see a few more examples:

```
SELECT MIN(Fare) AS Smallest_Fare
FROM tblBOARDING
WHERE BoardingDateTime > 'August 5, 2018'
```

	Smallest_Fare
1	3.25

Figure 6.77: *A query result from aggregate function* `MIN()`

Aggregate functions can also be used together to do additional calculations. Consider the following query that determines the difference between the highest (**MAX()**) and lowest (**MIN()**) fares collected during the month of June 2025:

```
SELECT MAX(fare) AS Highest, MIN(fare) AS Lowest,(SELECT MAX(fare)-
MIN(fare)) AS Fare_Difference
FROM tblBOARDING
WHERE BoardingDateTime > 'June 1, 2025'
      AND BoardingDateTime < 'July 1, 2025'
```

	Highest	Lowest	Fare_Difference
1	3.75	3.25	0.50

Figure 6.78: *A query result of multiple aggregate functions MAX(), MIN() with calculation*

Aggregate functions **MAX()** and **MIN()** can also work on other data types besides numeric, including varchar and dates columns.

```
SELECT MAX(BirthDate) as Youngest_DriverBirthDate
FROM tblDRIVER
```

	Youngest_DriverBirthDate
1	1949-06-22

Figure 6.79: *A query result from aggregate function* **MAX()** *against a date column*

Please note how the largest/maximum value for a birthdate returns the YOUNGEST person! This is because the largest birthdate value according to the database logic is closest to present day, thus yielding the shortest lifespan.

The **MIN()** and **MAX()** aggregate functions can also be run against a datatype of varchar, such as tblDRIVER.lname.

```
SELECT MIN(Lname) AS Min_Lname
FROM tblDRIVER
```

	Min_Lname
1	Hendrix

Figure 6.80: *A query result from aggregate function* **MIN()** *against a character column*

By itself, this query result does not provide much learning opportunity. It can be argued that it might be cool to know that **MIN()/MAX()** functions can be run against character data types, the questions we are trying to address may be better answered in other ways. Please see the following query that may provide better understanding of relative ages of drivers:

```
SELECT TOP 5 D.DriverID, D.Fname, D.Lname, D.BirthDate
FROM tblDRIVER
ORDER BY BirthDate DESC
```

Results | Messages

	DriverID	Fname	Lname	BirthDate
1	4	Meryl	Streep	1949-06-22
2	3	Jim	Morrison	1943-12-08
3	1	Jimi	Hendrix	1942-11-27
4	2	Bruce	Lee	1940-11-27

Figure 6.81: *A query result using TOP command and ORDER BY clause*

Please note that data on all drivers are returned in a sorted order of youngest to oldest using the ORDER BY clause. This *may* provide a better answer than trying to use either **MIN()** or **MAX()** against a birthdate.

COUNT()

The aggregate function **COUNT()** may be the most frequently used aggregate function. Being able to know how many rows match a certain condition is the guts of what writing a query with SQL is all about, especially when conducting a high-level initial investigation.

There are several quick concerns to be aware of when writing a query where we seek to know the number of matching rows using the aggregate function **COUNT()**:

- Do NOT confuse **COUNT()** with **SUM()**
- Use the keyword DISTINCT when the query JOINs a transactional table

COUNT() versus SUM()

Many times, in introductory database classes, my students will make a mistake and try to 'count' the results of columns containing money values when the proper aggregate function is **SUM()**. This mistake is fixed early in an engineer's career (usually right after a failing grade on their first midterm). Also, we can use **COUNT()** with a specific input parameter either a primary key or a foreign key in the parentheses, as follows:

```
SELECT COUNT(TripID) AS NumberOfTrips
FROM tblTRIP
```

	NumberOfTrips
1	5

Figure 6.82: *Query with COUNT() aggregate function with primary key as input parameter*

```
SELECT COUNT(T.VehicleID) AS NumberOfTrips
FROM tblVEHICLE V
      JOIN tblTRIP T ON V.VehicleID = T.VehicleID
WHERE V.VehicleName = 'GS204'
```

	NumberOfTrips
1	3

Figure 6.83: *Query with* `COUNT()` *aggregate function with foreign key as input parameter*

The results in *Figures* 6.80 and 6.81 are based on different questions. The first returns the result for the question 'how many trips have occurred?' The second query narrows the first question and filters on the foreign key value in **`tblTRIP`** to find the number of trips assigned to just a single vehicle, which has the name of 'GS204'. Many times, analysts are seeking the results of a filtered query based on the results of another previous query, narrowing each subsequent query as more is learned.

While having a PK or FK as input parameters is more precise, they can be replaced with the asterisk ('*') without losing functionality (go ahead and try it!).

```
SELECT COUNT(*) AS NumberOfTrips
FROM tblTRIP
```

	NumberOfTrips
1	5

Figure 6.84: *Query with* `COUNT()` *aggregate function with asterisk(*) as input parameter*

Please note that the substitution of the asterisk ('*') as an input parameter for the aggregate function queries does not change the results. This is often used during informal investigations where the analyst is conducting a quick perusal of data, and not sticking to explicit reporting nomenclature.

SUM()

Whenever we are 'doing math', we need to read the values inside of each cell as opposed to just counting rows that match the filtering criteria we specify in the WHERE clause. Examples may include determining the amount of money a single passenger has spent on boarding fares, the total amount of money spent on vehicles of a certain type, as well as annual salaries for all drivers. First, in *Figure* 6.83, we can remind ourselves of the simplified **`METRO_TRANSIT`** diagram.

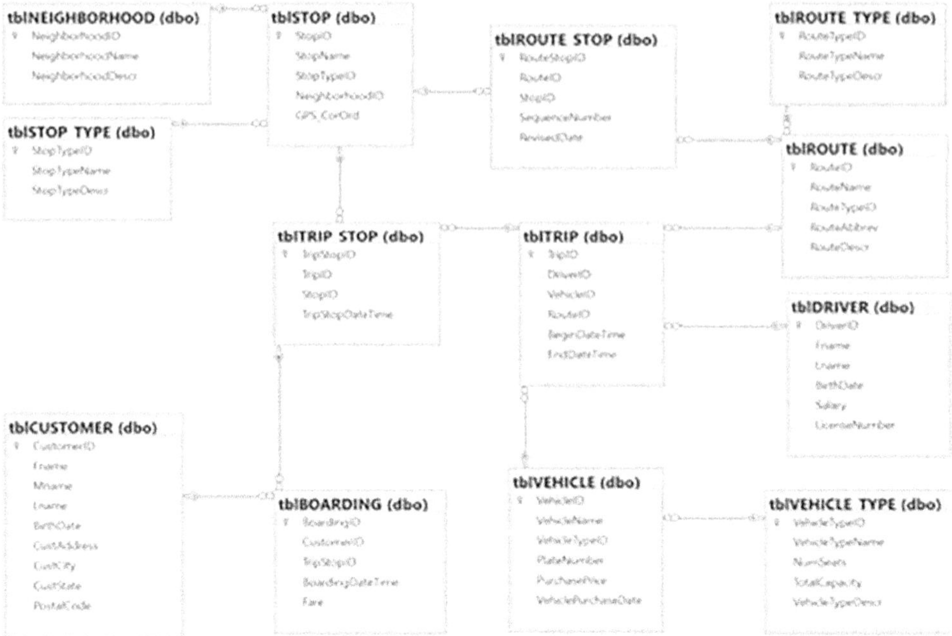

Figure 6.85: *Reminder of simplified Entity-Relationship diagram of METRO_TRANSIT*

From the preceding *Figure* 6.85, the following queries are posed as example challenges to incorporate aggregate function of **SUM()**:

- Write the SQL to determine the total boarding fares from customer Ivey Hazekamp.

```
SELECT SUM(Fare) AS TotalFareAmount
FROM tblCUSTOMER C
      JOIN tblBOARDING B ON C.CustomerID = B.CustomerID
WHERE Fname = 'Ivey'
      AND Lname = 'Hazekamp'
```

	TotalFareAmount
1	7.50

Figure 6.86: *Example query using aggregate function SUM()*

- Write the SQL code to determine the total amount of money spent on vehicles of type 'Double-Decker Bus'.

```
SELECT SUM(PurchasePrice) AS TotalExpenditure
FROM tblVEHICLE V
      JOIN tblVEHICLE_TYPE VT ON V.VehicleTypeID = VT.Vehicle
TypeID
WHERE VT.VehicleTypeName = 'Double-Decker Bus'
```

	TotalExpenditure
1	1775066.00

Figure 6.87: *Example query with aggregate function SUM()*

- Write the SQL code to determine the total annual salaries for all drivers.

```
SELECT SUM(Salary) AS TotalSalaries
FROM tblDRIVER
```

	TotalSalaries
1	179770.00

Figure 6.88: *Example queries using `SUM()` aggregate function*

The preceding queries and results in *Figure* 6.88 are simple as they are aggregating a column from a single column. We will see in a moment how to expand this function and apply the function against many rows.

Common Mistake with `SUM()`

Occasionally, students will confuse **`COUNT()`** and **`SUM()`** when being introduced to aggregate functions for the first time. This mistake is passing the primary key value as the parameter to be included in the math equation, as we may get comfortable passing in primary key values with **`COUNT()`** and think these are interchangeable.

Consider the following 'mistake' query:

```
SELECT SUM(DriverID) AS TotalMistake
FROM tblDRIVER
```

	TotalMistake
1	10

Figure 6.89: *Example mistake(!!) query of `SUM()` function against a primary key value*

The math equation of adding unique identifiers together may not seem like a mistake at this moment (especially if these functions are new for you). Consider in slow-motion the act of adding these values together; even though a value has been returned by the database system, does the value (in this case '10') even make sense? This result is from adding up each unique identifier from the primary key column (1 + 2 + 3 + 4):

DriverID	Fname	Lname
1	Jimi	Hendrix
2	Bruce	Lee
3	Jim	Morrison
4	Meryl	Streep

Figure 6.90: *Primary key and name values of all drivers showing common mistaken use of `SUM()` function against a primary key value*

This accident has no business value in the same way that adding every driver's phone numbers or home house number together; just because the system returns a value does not alleviate the mistake! Avoid using **`SUM()`** against primary key or foreign key values.

Other Aggregate Functions

There are other SQL commands that are considered aggregate functions; however, they have limited use in the scope of this textbook. Please be aware the following aggregate functions exist, and explore them in further detail on your own if you see fit:

- `BINARY_CHECKSUM()`
- `CHECKSUM()`
- `CHECKSUM_AGG()`
- `GROUPING()`
- `GROUPING_ID()`

Great job getting through the material here in Chapter 6: *Intermediate* SQL! This content is considered difficult for many learners, and getting this far is a very strong indicator of your dedication and focus.

Conclusion

The basic query structures used to draw data out of a database can be a difficult pattern of words, if we try to simply memorize them. There is the basic sequence of 'SELECT, FROM and WHERE' and then dozens of keywords called functions. Approaching this data retrieval language as a method of learning may make the onboarding process a bit easier.

Learning in the modern economy involves being able to analyze data, often found in massive relational databases. The basic language used by millions of companies is SQL;

being comfortable writing intermediate queries across dozens of tables is a valuable skill that will allow you to become more independent as an analyst and critical thinker pursuing innovation and opportunities for improving efficiency and optimization across an organization. If you can get an original database established (designed, normalized, coded, and populated) you will have joined the top 5% of developers in the world!

So, you have done a fantastic job so far getting through the first 6 chapters and on-boarding SQL beyond a basic level of competency! Do not slow down just yet as there is a small amount of additional learning required with SQL. The next chapter is #7, *Intermediate SQL Part 2*, which includes ground-changing skills of GROUP BY, date functions, and subqueries in greater detail. Keep rolling!

Post-Chapter Challenges

Based on your objectives and intentions on learnings from this book, please approach the following challenges as appropriate.

Track 1: Data Tourist Seeking Ancillary Awareness (THINK ~10 minutes)

Please spend a solid 10 minutes reviewing the following questions, exploring your thoughts. These questions and your responses cut to the essence of this chapter:

- Which of the shortcuts and functions intended to simplify the coding process resonate with you after finishing the reading? Why?
- Consider the ability you now possess to write sophisticated and complex queries by adding the JOIN statement, aggregate functions, and GROUP BY command. JOIN allows you the ability to draw data from across an unlimited number of entities, and do math against millions of rows of data! How powerful is that?
- How might data analytical skills with SQL allow you to be more effective, impactful, or otherwise 'do a better job' for any position you may pursue as a career?

Track 2: Dedicated Student or Recent Graduate (WRITE ~ 45 minutes)

Based on your completion of this chapter, WRITE several paragraphs in response to each question; explore these as if you are being asked a similar question during a job interview!

- Write the INSERT statements to populate another 5 rows of data into the following 'look-up' entities:
    - **`tblCUSTOMER`**
    - **`tblEMPLOYEE`**
    - **`tblDRIVER`**

    - `tblROUTE`
    - `tblVEHICLE`
- Write the INSERT statements to populate another 10 rows of data into the following transactional entities:
    - `tblTRIP`
    - `tblTRIP_STOP`
    - `tblBOARDING`

Writing INSERT statements to populate transactional entities can be considered advanced! It is important to see the struggle of managing multiple foreign key values. Hopefully, your journey will eventually include how to insert data with automated code and 'stored procedures'. For now, try to get the data in with INSERT statements.

Track 3: Full Speed Learner Seeking Job (BUILD ~3 hours)

This track targets readers of this book who want to develop professional skills working with data to launch a career or obtain a more satisfying job. Now that we have seen more of what SQL can do, let us continue with the building of your new database by adding the data:

- Take your database from Chapter 5, *Beginning with SQL*, and write the INSERT statements to populate all the entities with at least 5 rows of data. Remember to start with the tables that do not have any foreign keys. Save your script!

CHAPTER 7
Intermediate SQL Part 2

Introduction

A reader finishing chapter 6, *Intermediate* SQL *Part 1*, is nearly ready for industry projects and paid internships, based on their understanding of database design, normalization, and SQL query writing. This chapter continues the journey through the swath of more intermediate SQL concepts, including GROUP BY and HAVING clauses, which will expand the capabilities of many of the functions learned previously. Additional functions that will be introduced in this chapter include date and time functions.

Completing this chapter will put you in a position to develop a stronger understanding of SQL and accelerate through more difficult programming structures including stored procedures and user-defined functions. Again, this chapter begins to apply the theory, and fundamentals recently acquired into the beginnings of processing data and targeted learning through analytics. We will be introduced to system functions, subqueries, and other common commands that fill out your data toolbox. This is a fascinating journey!

Structure

In this chapter, we will explore the following topics:

- `GROUP BY` command
- `HAVING` clause
- Date functions
- Subqueries
- Temporary objects

GROUP BY Command

The **GROUP BY** command is a tremendously powerful query tool as it effectively runs the aggregate function against each row of the columns included in the **SELECT** statement. With **GROUP BY**, we can apply the aggregate functions against individual rows like vehicles or drivers, and see the number of trips each has been assigned all with a single query (as opposed to having to re-run the same query for each vehicle or driver). This command allows us to take any of the aggregate functions we have just learned, and apply them across a significantly larger range of data, often tens of millions of rows!

Knowing how to apply GROUP BY and its relevant commands marks the beginning of being a professional data analyst. So, let us see an example question that uses **GROUP BY**:

- Write the SQL to determine the vehicles of type 'Double-Decker Bus' that has made the most trips

```
SELECT V.VehicleID, VehicleName, COUNT(*) AS NumberOfTrips
FROM tblVEHICLE V
      JOIN tblTRIP T ON V.VehicleID = T.VehicleID
      JOIN tblVEHICLE_TYPE VT ON V.VehicleTypeID = VT.Vehicle
TypeID
WHERE VT.VehicleTypeName = 'Double-Decker Bus'
GROUP BY V.VehicleID, VehicleName
```

	VehicleID	VehicleName	NumberOfTrips
1	1	GS203	1
2	2	GS204	3

***Figure 7.1:** Example Query with GROUP BY command applying COUNT(*) across all vehicles of type 'Double-Decker Bus'*

Please note the query in *Figure 7.1* executes the query command of **COUNT()** against every row that matches the filtering logic in the **WHERE** clause, of which there are two.

Let us see another example of using an aggregate function across many rows with the following question:

- Write the SQL to determine the number of seats, total capacity of each vehicle as well as 'fleet capacity' by all vehicles currently in the system of each vehicle type.

```
SELECT VT.VehicleTypeName, NumSeats, TotalCapacity, COUNT
(VehicleID) AS NumberOfVehicles, TotalCapacity * COUNT(VehicleID)
AS FleetCapacity
FROM tblVEHICLE_TYPE VT
```

```
        LEFT OUTER JOIN tblVEHICLE V ON VT.VehicleTypeID
= V.VehicleTypeID
GROUP BY VT.VehicleTypeName, NumSeats, TotalCapacity
```

	VehicleTypeName	NumSeats	TotalCapacity	NumberOfVehicles	FleetCapacity
1	Double-Decker Bus	96	144	2	288
2	Heavy Rail Single Passenger Train	40	50	0	0
3	Standard Bus	54	76	2	152
4	Standard Light Rail Car	58	88	0	0

***Figure 7.2**: Example query with GROUP BY affecting multiple columns*

The query in *Figure* 7.2 is a bit tricky! Let us break down this query:

- The returning of columns, **NumSeats** and **TotalCapacity** in the **SELECT** line are not tricky.
- The aggregate function **COUNT()** is used to determine the **NumberOfVehicles** in the system (somewhat tricky if you are new to writing SQL).
- Determining '**FleetCapacity**' is tricky because we are involving the aggregated results from **COUNT(VehicleID)** to immediately participate in a math problem! Look at row 1 to see **2 Vehicles * TotalCapacity** of 144 for **FleetCapacity** of 288.
- Also, tricky is deciding to use **LEFT OUTER JOIN** to observe the VehicleTypeNames that currently have 0 vehicles in the fleet.

Next, let us see some of the options with **GROUP BY**, including **HAVING**, **ROLLUP**, **CUBE**, and **GROUPING SETS**.

HAVING

The **HAVING** clause works directly with **GROUP BY** command, and acts like a second **WHERE** clause by applying a filter to the results of the **GROUP BY**. **HAVING** is therefore a post-**GROUP BY** filter, while the **WHERE** clause is used to filter data pre-**GROUP BY**. Our first example adds the **HAVING** clause to the most recent query, we just ran with a filter in the **HAVING** clause to return only the vehicles with a count of more than 1 trip:

```
SELECT V.VehicleID, VehicleName, COUNT(*) AS NumberOfTrips
FROM tblVEHICLE V
        JOIN tblTRIP T ON V.VehicleID = T.VehicleID
        JOIN tblVEHICLE_TYPE VT ON V.VehicleTypeID
= VT.VehicleTypeID
WHERE VT.VehicleTypeName = 'Double-Decker Bus'
GROUP BY V.VehicleID, VehicleName
HAVING COUNT(*) > 1
```

	VehicleID	VehicleName	NumberOfTrips
1	2	GS204	3

Figure 7.3: *Example query with HAVING applied to GROUP BY*

Please note that the aggregate function is repeated in the **HAVING** clause; unfortunately, we are unable to take advantage of the alias '**NumberOfTrips**' that was established in the **SELECT** line. The reason the alias is not able to be referenced in the **HAVING** clause is the query engine is not yet aware that it has been created! The order of processing creates the alias after the data has been aggregated in the GROUP BY clause, and then filtered in the **HAVING** clause.

In *Figure* 7.3, the **HAVING** clause eliminates the row for vehicle name 'GS203' as it did not meet the criteria for having more than one trip. While there are very few rows in our limited data set generated by hand in earlier chapters, please explore these commands in the larger data sets available from the publisher at the same link referenced earlier in chapter 5, *Beginning with* SQL to get a feel of how powerful the **GROUP BY/HAVING** combination is at returning the insightful data. It is repeated here for convenience:

`https://github.com/ava-orange-education/ultimate-SQL-for-Data-Science-and-Analytics`

Let us see a few more examples of the **GROUP BY** and **HAVING** commands working together on some basic queries from the abbreviated **METRO_TRANSIT**.

ROLLUP

Rollup is another option that extends the capabilities of the **GROUP BY** command. In the same way that the **GROUP BY** command saves a user from having to re-run the aggregate function against each value in a table (potentially hundreds or thousands of times), the **ROLLUP** option also saves a user from having to re-run the same query against each row.

Consider the following query that seeks to explore the boardings by neighborhood, stop and route:

```
SELECT NeighborhoodName, StopName, RouteName, COUNT(BoardingID)
AS NumberOfBoardings
FROM tblNEIGHBORHOOD N
      JOIN tblSTOP S ON N.NeighborhoodID = S.NeighborhoodID
      JOIN tblTRIP_STOP TS ON S.StopID = TS.StopID
      JOIN tblBOARDING B ON TS.TripStopID = B.TripStopID
      JOIN tblTRIP T ON TS.TripID = T.TripID
      JOIN tblROUTE R ON T.RouteID = R.RouteID
GROUP BY
ROLLUP (NeighborhoodName, StopName, RouteName)
```

	NeighborhoodName	StopName	RouteName	NumberOfBoardings
1	Downtown	Sixth Avenue and Battery Street	Fremont-Waterfront-Downtown	1
2	Downtown	Sixth Avenue and Battery Street	NULL	1
3	Downtown	NULL	NULL	1
4	Fremont	Hwy 99-N 36th	Fremont-Downtown Express	2
5	Fremont	Hwy 99-N 36th	NULL	2
6	Fremont	NULL	NULL	2
7	NULL	NULL	NULL	3

Figure 7.4: *Example query with ROLLUP applied to GROUP BY*

As seen in *Figure* 7.4, the **ROLLUP** command executes the **GROUP BY** command and **COUNT()** aggregate function against the combinations of **NeighborhoodName**, **StopName**, and RouteName. With the limited data in the abbreviated **METRO_TRANSIT** database, there are only 3 total boardings which occurred at only 2 stops (named 'Sixth Avenue and Battery Street' as well as 'Hwy 99- N 36th').

Please note that rows 1 through 3 in *Figure* 7.4 provide a summary of each combination of columns! Row 1 has the **NumberOfBoardings** for the combination of **NeighborhoodName**, **StopName**, and **RouteName**, while row 2 has the combination of just **NeighborhoodName** and **StopName**. Finally, in row 3, just the summary of boardings for the neighborhood of 'Downtown' is provided. The 'NULL' values highlighted in yellow indicate that these columns are not part of the aggregated total under **NumberOfBoardings**.

Similarly, rows 4 through 6 reveal the number of boardings for the next combination of **neighborhoodname**, **stopname**, and **routename**. The final calculation found in row 7 is for all boardings across the entire table. Again, there are only 3 boardings in the abbreviated data set because we manually entered the data; there are additional data sets with significantly more data available from the more complete data sets available from the publisher.

The number of combinations in a transactional table such as **tblBOARDING** can be quite large, with potentially millions of rows after a year or so. The key takeaway for the use of ROLLUP is this will be a great command to know when you need to break down the list of transactions into greater details with distinct combinations of columns. While the number of rows returned by the ROLLUP command may appear to be large, next we will see the CUBE command, which applies the aggregate function against EVERY possible combination of columns from the query. This is essentially a cartesian product.

CUBE

CUBE is a third option that provides additional capabilities to the **GROUP BY** command. As evident in *Figure* 7.5, the **CUBE** command makes additional calculations beyond the

ROLLUP command, and returns a cartesian product of all columns aggregated against each other in all possible combinations.

```
SELECT NeighborhoodName, StopName, RouteName, COUNT(BoardingID)
AS NumberOfBoardings
FROM tblNEIGHBORHOOD N
      JOIN tblSTOP S ON N.NeighborhoodID = S.NeighborhoodID
      JOIN tblTRIP_STOP TS ON S.StopID = TS.StopID
      JOIN tblBOARDING B ON TS.TripStopID = B.TripStopID
      JOIN tblTRIP T ON TS.TripID = T.TripID
      JOIN tblROUTE R ON T.RouteID = R.RouteID
GROUP BY
CUBE (NeighborhoodName, StopName, RouteName)
```

	NeighborhoodName	StopName	RouteName	NumberOfBoardings
1	Fremont	Hwy 99 N 36th	Fremont-Downtown Express	2
2	NULL	Hwy 99 N 36th	Fremont-Downtown Express	2
3	NULL	NULL	Fremont-Downtown Express	2
4	Downtown	Sixth Avenue and Battery Street	Fremont-Waterfront-Downtown	1
5	NULL	Sixth Avenue and Battery Street	Fremont-Waterfront-Downtown	1
6	NULL	NULL	Fremont-Waterfront-Downtown	1
7	NULL	NULL	NULL	3
8	Downtown	NULL	Fremont-Waterfront-Downtown	1
9	Downtown	NULL	NULL	1
10	Fremont	NULL	Fremont-Downtown Express	2
11	Fremont	NULL	NULL	2
12	Fremont	Hwy 99 N 36th	NULL	2
13	NULL	Hwy 99 N 36th	NULL	2
14	Downtown	Sixth Avenue and Battery Street	NULL	1
15	NULL	Sixth Avenue and Battery Street	NULL	1

***Figure 7.5**: The CUBE option applied to GROUP BY to return a Cartesian Product*

Please note in *Figure* 7.5, the **CUBE** command now returns 15 rows as opposed to the 7 from ROLLUP. The combinations aggregated in the column, '**NumberOfBoardings**' include columns by themselves as well as with each other. Be careful! While the level of detail obtained from CUBE can be precise, the number of rows returned can be tremendous.

GROUPING SETS

GROUPING SETS is one last option that extends the functionality of the **GROUP BY** command by allowing a user to establish custom groupings of columns to be included in the **GROUP BY** command. This effectively allows each analyst to engage the data with improvised combinations of columns as they explore the data. As we will learn, data analyses often include a lengthy exploration of how the data changes when compared to other elements or columns. When we have control of the combinations to explore, we can be much more effective in finding anomalies or trends in the data collection.

Consider the following query showing the use of **GROUP BY** with **GROUPING SET**:

```
SELECT NeighborhoodName, StopName, RouteName, COUNT(BoardingID)
AS NumberOfBoardings
FROM tblNEIGHBORHOOD N
      JOIN tblSTOP S ON N.NeighborhoodID = S.NeighborhoodID
      JOIN tblTRIP_STOP TS ON S.StopID = TS.StopID
      JOIN tblBOARDING B ON TS.TripStopID = B.TripStopID
      JOIN tblTRIP T ON TS.TripID = T.TripID
      JOIN tblROUTE R ON T.RouteID = R.RouteID
GROUP BY GROUPING SETS (
(NeighborhoodName),
(StopName, RouteName),
(StopName),
(NeighborhoodName, StopName, RouteName),
()
)
```

	NeighborhoodName	StopName	RouteName	NumberOfBoardings
1	Fremont	Hwy 99-N 36th	Fremont-Downtown Express	2
2	NULL	Hwy 99-N 36th	Fremont-Downtown Express	2
3	NULL	Hwy 99-N 36th	NULL	2
4	Downtown	Sixth Avenue and Battery Street	Fremont-Waterfront-Downtown	1
5	NULL	Sixth Avenue and Battery Street	Fremont-Waterfront-Downtown	1
6	NULL	Sixth Avenue and Battery Street	NULL	1
7	NULL	NULL	NULL	3
8	Downtown	NULL	NULL	1
9	Fremont	NULL	NULL	2

Figure 7.6: *Example query with GROUPING SETS applied to GROUP BY*

Without the inclusion of the **GROUPING SETS** command, **GROUP BY** will apply an aggregate function against the one collection of columns specified. The use of **GROUPING SETS** extends the **GROUP BY** command to be applied against multiple combinations of columns, thus providing a quick return of data to either validate or repudiate hunches that the analyst is investigating.

In *Figure 7.6* there is a more condensed version of aggregations than when using **ROLLUP** or **CUBE**; the user has complete control of the exact collection of columns that **GROUP BY** applies the aggregate function against. Becoming comfortable with the **GROUP BY** command will take a bit of practice! I have found that this is essentially the beginning of real data analysis, and therefore, should be highlighted as a target skill to acquire.

CAUTION: Incorrect Interpretation of Query Results

When seeking the number of matching rows for a particular query, we sometimes are too focused on connecting the 'right' entities, and getting our understanding of the 'correct' logic in the WHERE clause that we forget to consider whether the query is counting the foreign key value more than once. When a query includes or 'crosses' a transactional table, there may be many occurrences of a foreign key value meeting the conditions set forth in the WHERE clause. If the query writer is not acutely aware of the multiple occurrences, this will lead to an incorrect interpretation of the query results!

Consider the next 2 queries trying to answer the simple question of 'how many people boarded a vehicle after March 1, 2023':

```
SELECT COUNT(*) AS NumberOfBoardings
FROM tblBOARDING
WHERE BoardingDateTime > 'March 1, 2023'
```

	NumberOfBoardings
1	3

Figure 7.7: *Example query with possible mis-interpreted data*

While the answer of 3 for this query is technically correct, many times, younger analysts do not recognize the difference between boardings and distinct customers. Depending on which is preferred, the analyst writing this query will need to decide whether duplicate values of customers should be counted.

Let us refine our query slightly:

```
SELECT Fname, Lname, BirthDate, PostalCode
FROM tblCUSTOMER C
      JOIN tblBOARDING B ON C.CustomerID = B.CustomerID
WHERE B.BoardingDateTime > 'March 1, 2023'
```

	Fname	Lname	BirthDate	PostalCode
1	Ivey	Hazekamp	1995-12-24	46778
2	Kenyetta	Terron	1995-09-27	44045
3	Ivey	Hazekamp	1995-12-24	46778

Figure 7.8: *Query that passes through a transactional table creates duplicate values*

Be careful! Maybe, you want to know the total number of boardings across all customers (counting the boardings by people with multiple boardings). Other times, we just want to know the names of the people who met the criteria of our query, regardless of the number of times that met these conditions.

```
SELECT DISTINCT C.CustomerID, Fname, Lname, BirthDate, PostalCode
FROM tblCUSTOMER C
      JOIN tblBOARDING B ON C.CustomerID = B.CustomerID
WHERE B.BoardingDateTime > 'March 1, 2023'
```

	CustomerID	Fname	Lname	BirthDate	PostalCode
1	1	Ivey	Hazekamp	1995-12-24	46778
2	3	Kenyetta	Terron	1995-09-27	44045

Figure 7.9: *Query that passes through a transactional table WITHOUT duplicate values*

Quick reminder about the use of the keyword, **DISTINCT** when we are aware that our query passed through a transactional table, and our results should **NOT** have multiple copies of one of our columns. Be deliberate in your queries, and ask yourself, 'is it okay to return multiple copies or duplicates of some of these values?' Be certain to include **DISTINCT** whenever there is a need to restrict duplicates.

DATE Functions

We saw a detailed explanation of date-based data types, way back in *Chapter 2, Brief Overview of Relational Model* that introduced the various different ways to store date values in SQL Server. It may help the reading of this section on Date Functions with reviewing that portion of the textbook.

As mentioned previously, some of the most important elements of transactional data (the core of relational databases) have a significant dependence on time. This includes not only 'when' a transaction occurs, but also perhaps, the number of similar events during the past month, quarter, 90 days, or some other period. Because there is such an emphasis on time, we need to become familiar with the functions that enable us as analysts to quickly establish parameters around dates and times that are either absolute or relative.

Absolute versus Relative Dates

Absolute dates and times are those that are identified exactly by a specific value like 'March 14, 2003' or 2:38 PM. We will often call these 'hard-coded'. Many data analyses intend to find matches based on transactions occurring on, before or after exact or absolute dates. Examples from **METRO_TRANSIT** include a query to determine the people who have had a boarding since January 1, 2025.

A relative date is based on when the query is executed. There are many reports based on 'the past X number of days', such as number of orders, number of incidents, revenue generated, and so on. We will code the queries used in such reports with relative logic, so that we can avoid having to figure out in our head the date that equals 90 days ago, and hard code the query. If we write the query correctly, it will always refer to a calculated date relative to when it is being executed. Brilliant!

The most important date functions I believe, are as follows:

- `DAY()`
- `MONTH()`

- `YEAR()`
- `CURRENT_TIMESTAMP`
- `CURRENT_DATE`
- `SYSDATETIME()`
- `GETDATE()`
- `DATENAME()`
- `DATEADD()`
- `DATEDIFF()`
- `DATEPART()`
- `DATEFROMPARTS()`

DAY(), MONTH(), YEAR()

The date functions **`DAY()`**, **`MONTH()`**, and **`YEAR()`** can be useful when searching for a range of values to see which ones match a particular part of a date value we seek to filter in the WHERE clause. Another case might be when we first find a row based on other criteria (for example, the name of an event, or of a person) then we seek the date value.

These functions (**`DAY()`**, **`MONTH()`**, and **`YEAR()`**) each read the entire date value and parse out only the numeric portion that is identified to their name. Please see the following:

```
SELECT Fname, Lname, NeighborhoodName, StopName, BoardingDateTime
FROM tblCUSTOMER C
      JOIN tblBOARDING B ON C.CustomerID = B.CustomerID
      JOIN tblTRIP_STOP TS ON B.TripStopID = TS.TripStopID
      JOIN tblSTOP S ON TS.StopID = S.StopID
      JOIN tblNEIGHBORHOOD N ON S.NeighborhoodID
= N.NeighborhoodID
WHERE DAY(BoardingDateTime) = 24
```

	Fname	Lname	NeighborhoodName	StopName	BoardingDateTime
1	Kenyetta	Terron	Fremont	Hwy 99-N 36th	2025-04-24 06:47:23.000
2	Ivey	Hazekamp	Fremont	Hwy 99-N 36th	2025-04-24 06:47:23.000

***Figure 7.10**: Example query showing use of Date Function Day () in Where clause*

It is common to conduct a search using date functions in the WHERE clause as we peruse the data during an investigation. Occasionally, there may be a reason to filter on other criteria (such as names) to identify the parts of a date value that may have relevance to an incident or other business need.

```
SELECT DAY(BirthDate) AS Day_From_BirthDate
FROM tblCUSTOMER
WHERE Fname = 'Ivey'
      AND Lname = 'Hazekamp'
```

	Day_From_BirthDate
1	24

Figure 7.11: *Example Query Showing Use of Date Function* `DAY()` *in SELECT Line*

Multiple date functions can be included in a single query, for example, if two parts of an event date are desired to be filtered. Consider the following query in *Figure* 7.12 where both the **`MONTH()`** and **`YEAR()`** functions are applied to find customers:

```
SELECT Fname, Lname, NeighborhoodName, StopName, BoardingDateTime
FROM tblCUSTOMER C
      JOIN tblBOARDING B ON C.CustomerID = B.CustomerID
      JOIN tblTRIP_STOP TS ON B.TripStopID = TS.TripStopID
      JOIN tblSTOP S ON TS.StopID = S.StopID
      JOIN tblNEIGHBORHOOD N ON S.NeighborhoodID
= N.NeighborhoodID
WHERE MONTH(BoardingDateTime) = 4
      AND YEAR(BoardingDateTime) = 2025
```

	Fname	Lname	NeighborhoodName	StopName	BoardingDateTime
1	Ivey	Hazekamp	Downtown	Sixth Avenue and Battery Street	2025-04-23 07:41:35.000
2	Kenyetta	Terron	Fremont	Hwy 99-N 36th	2025-04-24 06:47:23.000
3	Ivey	Hazekamp	Fremont	Hwy 99-N 36th	2025-04-24 06:47:23.000

Figure 7.12: *Example Query Showing Use of 2 Date Functions* `MONTH()` *and* `YEAR()`

There are several commands and functions in SQL Server that can be used to calculate the immediate date and time, which are frequently used for dashboard and other reports. These include the following:

- `CURRENT_TIMESTAMP`
- `SYSDATETIME()`
- `GETDATE()`
- `CURRENT_DATE`

Let us see how each of these commands work with the commands to return a complete date and time value:

```
SELECT CURRENT_TIMESTAMP AS Time_Right_Now
SELECT GETDATE() AS MACHINE_DATETIME
SELECT SYSDATETIME() AS Date_and_Time_Right_Now_Nano_Seconds;
```

	Time_Right_Now
1	2025-07-04 05:08:17.907

	MACHINE_DATETIME
1	2025-07-04 05:08:17.907

	Date_and_Time_Right_Now_Nano_Seconds
1	2025-07-04 05:08:17.9080127

Figure 7.13: *Example Queries Showing Use of Date Functions* `CURRENT_TIMESTAMP`, `GETDATE()`, *and* `SYSDATETIME()`

The date functions **`CURRENT_TIMESTAMP`**, **`GETDATE()`**, and **`SYSDATETIME()`** are functions that will return a complete date and time value from the moment the query is executed. The only difference is the number of sub-second digits or level of precision.

`CURRENT_TIMESTAMP` and **`GETDATE()`** are interchangeable, and return the exact same data down to the hundredths of a second. **`SYSDATETIME`** has greater precision and returns a seven digits underneath the measurement of a second. This equals precision all the way down to 100 nanoseconds (useful for tracking volume of events that number in millions per minute).

JUST THE DATE!

When the query does not need to return any data regarding time, a user has several options including using a combination of commands.

```
SELECT CURRENT_DATE AS DATE_RIGHT_NOW
```

	Date_Right_Now
1	2025-07-04

Figure 7.14: *Example Query Showing Use of Date Function* `CURRENT_DATE`

First, as seen in *Figure* 7.14, can execute **`CURRENT_DATE`** to receive a simple date value from the system in a format of YYY-MM-DD. Alternatively, a user can use the **`CAST()`** or **`CONVERT()`** functions to change the value to eliminate the time.

```
SELECT CAST(GETDATE() AS DATE) AS DATE_ONLY_CAST_GETDATE
SELECT CONVERT(DATE, GETDATE()) AS DATE_ONLY_CONVERT_GETDATE
```

	DATE_ONLY_CAST_GETDATE
1	2025-07-04

	DATE_ONLY_CONVERT_GETDATE
1	2025-07-04

Figure 7.15: *Example Queries Showing Use of `CAST()` and `CONVERT()` with `GETDATE()`*

Functions are fantastic tools for helping generate the specific shape of data we are seeking. As seen in *Figure* 7.15, a combination of functions can be used to prepare data to be in a format that makes sense when only the date is desired, without any reference to time. In the same vein, there are additional functions that allow the presentation of time-specific data without reference to date:

JUST THE TIME!

```
SELECT CAST(GETDATE() AS TIME) AS TIME_CAST_GETDATE
SELECT CONVERT(TIME, GETDATE()) AS TIME_CONVERT_GETDATE
SELECT CAST(CURRENT_TIMESTAMP AS TIME) AS TIME_CAST_TIMESTAMP
```

	TIME_CAST_GETDATE
1	05:44:39.4500000

	TIME_CONVERT_GETDATE
1	05:44:39.4500000

	TIME_CAST_TIMESTAMP
1	05:44:39.4500000

Figure 7.16: *More Example Queries Showing Use of `CAST()` and `CONVERT()` with `GETDATE()`*

Consider a web-based dashboard for **`METRO_TRANSIT`**. Many queries need to be aware of the current date or time when they are executed to return the desired data. Examples from **`METRO_TRANSIT`** may include queries that return the number of boardings, fare revenue, or number of trips ‘in the last 16 hours’. Each query written to support such a dashboard will most likely include one of the date functions explained above.

More on Relative **Date** functions

As mentioned previously, we need to be able to distinguish between absolute and relative dates. Absolute dates are fixed and precise, while relative dates 'move' and are often calculated as part of the execution of the query. There are several very common date functions that are critical to writing queries for reports that rely on relative dates, including the following:

- `DateAdd()`
- `DateDiff()`
- `DatePart()`

DATEADD()

`DateAdd()` is a very flexible and powerful function that can automatically calculate a date value based on a date part (like day, week, or month), a specified number and then an original or 'beginning' date. These 3 parameters 'do math' collectively.

The best use for **`DATEADD()`** is when the third input value of the original or beginning date is not hard-coded and is calculated when the query is executed.

```
SELECT DATEADD(MONTH, 1, '12/22/2025') AS DateAdd_Ex1
```

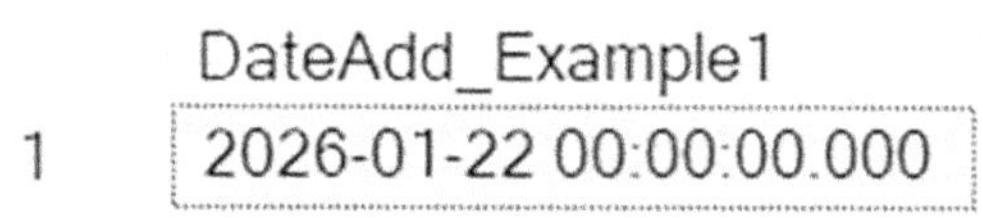

Figure 7.17: *Example Query Using DATEADD() with a Fixed Date*

The example in *Figure* 7.17 shows a hard-coded ('fixed') date of December 22, 2025, and then calculating a date exactly 1 month into the future. There are also 9 zeros that seem to add a bit of clutter to the value. Let us see if we can use the **`CAST()`** function to eliminate the zeros in place for time that is not needed:

```
SELECT CAST(DATEADD(YEAR, -6, '12/22/2025') AS DATE) AS DateAdd_Ex2
```

Figure 7.18: *Example Query Using `DATEADD()` with Negative Number and `CAST()`*

Figure 7.18 shows a query that uses **`CAST()`** to change the return data type to DATE as well as showing that negative numbers can be passed in to calculate a day 6 years prior.

```
SELECT DATEADD(DAY, -120, GetDate()) AS DateAdd_Ex3
```

	DateAdd_Ex3
1	2025-03-06 08:24:34.633

Figure 7.19: *Example Query Using* `DATEADD()` *with Negative Number and* `GETDATE()`

Figure 7.19 is an example query that uses **`GETDATE()`** function to create the input or beginning original date. Additionally, the query shows a negative number being passed in to count backwards whenever the query is executed. This is therefore a relative date.

Next, let us see a query from **`METTRO_TRANSIT`** that may be part of a continuous dashboard, showing boardings of the past 90 days from whenever the query is executed:

```
SELECT Fname, Name, BoardingDate
FROM tblBOARDING B
      JOIN tblCUSTOMER C ON B.CustomerID = C.CustomerID
WHERE BoardingDateTime > DATEADD(MONTH, -90, GETDATE())
```

	Fname	Lname	BoardingDateTime
1	Ivey	Hazekamp	2025-04-23 07:41:35.000
2	Kenyetta	Terron	2025-04-24 06:47:23.000
3	Ivey	Hazekamp	2025-04-24 06:47:23.000

Figure 7.20: *Example Query Relative Date Calculated from* `GETDATE()` *Using* `DATEADD()`

One real quick comment on **`DATEADD()`** in *Figure* 7.20 is the math to determine the date is calculated only a single time, even if the query compares the value against thousands of rows or more. This means the speed by which **`DATEADD()`** executes is considered fast.

DATEDIFF()

`DATEDIFF()` is a wonderful function to determine the distance between two known dates or times. This function can be used to determine the age of people or the time, since an event or incident has occurred. Please see the following example:

```
SELECT Fname, Lname, DATEDIFF(YEAR, BirthDate, GetDate()) AS Years
SinceBirth
FROM tblDRIVER
```

	Fname	Lname	YearsSinceBirth
1	Jimi	Hendrix	83
2	Bruce	Lee	85
3	Jim	Morrison	82
4	Meryl	Streep	76

Figure 7.21: *Example Query Showing Use of Date Function* `DATEDIFF()` *to Calculate the Number of Years since Birth*

Be careful as **`DateDiff()`** is misused frequently! This function calculates the difference between two dates for each row it encounters based on the WHERE clause.

For example, if there are 2 million passengers in the **`METRO_TRANSIT`** database, and we want to find only those YOUNGER than 30, we do NOT want to make 2 million calculations with **`DATEDIFF()`**. The better choice is to use **`DATEADD()`**, and make one calculation 30 years ago from today to then compare against birthdates. See the following query:

```
SELECT Fname, Name, BirthDate
FROM tblCUSTOMER
WHERE BirthDate > DATEADD(YEAR, -30, GETDATE())
```

	Fname	Lname	BoardingDateTime
1	Ivey	Hazekamp	2025-04-23 07:41:35.000
2	Kenyetta	Terron	2025-04-24 06:47:23.000
3	Ivey	Hazekamp	2025-04-24 06:47:23.000

Figure 7.22: *Example Query Showing Use of Date Function* `DATEADD()` *Instead of* `DATEDIFF()` *to Calculate which Customers are Younger Than 30 Years Old*

Please be aware that there is only one single calculation required to determine the date exactly 30 years ago from today. This saves a significant amount of computing cycles on the CPU when we can avoid calculating the dates between today and a customer's birthdate, and then seeing if it is less than 30.

DATEPART()

`DatePart()` allows for detailed dissecting of dates by ANY of the parts exposed for either date or time (big or small). Please consider the following list for all the options associated with **`DATEPART()`** and other functions:

DatePart Name	Abbreviation
NANOSECOND	Ns

MICROSOECOND	Mcs
MILLISECOND	Ms
SECOND	ss, s
MINUTE	mi, n
HOUR	Hh
DAY	dd, d
DayOfYear	dy, y
WEEKDAY	dw, w
WEEK	ww, wk
MONTH	mm, m
QUARTER	qq, q
YEAR	yyyy, yy

Table 7.1: *Table of Date Parts Available to Use with* `DATEPART()` *Function*

```
SELECT *
FROM tblDRIVER
WHERE DATEPART(WEEKDAY, BIRTHDATE) = 6
```

	DriverID	Fname	Lname	BirthDate	Salary	LicenseNumber
1	1	Jimi	Hendrix	1942-11-27	42590.00	JMHend3487RR

Figure 7.23: *Example Query with* `DATEPART()` *Function Based on Being Born on a Saturday*

`DATEPART()` is very flexible as well as powerful; we can use it multiple times in a single query (or more) to narrow the number of rows being returned. Please see *Figure 7.25*:

```
SELECT Fname, Name, BoardingDateTime
FROM tblCUSTOMER C
      JOIN tblBOARDING B ON C.CustomerID = B.CustomerID
WHERE DATEPART(HOUR, BoardingDateTime) < 12
      AND DATEPART (MINUTE, BoardingDateTime) > 30
```

	Fname	Lname	BoardingDateTime
1	Ivey	Hazekamp	2025-04-23 07:41:35.000
2	Kenyetta	Terron	2025-04-24 06:47:23.000
3	Ivey	Hazekamp	2025-04-24 06:47:23.000

Figure 7.24: *Example Query Using* `DATEPART()` *Function Two Times*

DATENAME()

Occasionally, users desire to see the words from a date value as opposed to numbers.

Lucky for us, there is another **DATENAME()** is a date function that allows for just this use.

```
SELECT DATENAME (WEEKDAY, '6/19/1966') AS DAY_OF_WEEK_BROTHER_DAN_BORN
SELECT DATENAME (MONTH, '6/19/1966') AS MONTH_BROTHER_DAN_BORN
SELECT DATENAME (QUARTER, '6/19/1966') AS QUARTER_BROTHER_DAN_BORN
SELECT DATENAME (DAYOFYEAR, '6/19/1966') AS DAY_YEAR_BROTHER_DAN_BORN
SELECT DATENAME (WEEK, '6/19/1966') AS WEEK_YEAR_BROTHER_DAN_BORN
```

***Figure 7.25**: Example queries using DATENAME function*

	DAY_OF_WEEK_BROTHER_DAN_BORN
1	Sunday

	MONTH_BROTHER_DAN_BORN
1	June

	QUARTER_BROTHER_DAN_BORN
1	2

	DAY_YEAR_BROTHER_DAN_BORN
1	170

	WEEK_YEAR_BROTHER_DAN_BORN
1	26

***Figure 7.26**: Example Queries Showing Use of Date Function `DATENAME()`*

One last date function that is useful is **DATEFROMPART()** which is sort of a Frankenstein assembly of values that can be thrown together to make a date value. This often occurs when the data being assembled is drawn from external sources, or is otherwise being converted from a column, not properly labeled as a date value. Consider the following example that constructs an output that is from hard-coded numbers:

```
SELECT DATEFROMPARTS(2025, 11, 28) AS Date_From_Parts
```

	Date_From_Parts
1	2025-11-28

***Figure 7.27**: Example Query Showing Use of Date Function `DATEFROMPARTS()`*

There will be many opportunities to practice date functions in the addendum code.

Take effort to become proficient with their use as well as the best use scenario of each.

Subqueries

A subquery executes inside another, and provides a fast and efficient method of providing complex logic to process as well as return massive amounts of data. SQL is brilliant in its ability to conduct bulk processing. This means that people write a few lines of code with a set of logical conditions to filter data, and then the relational system retrieves all rows that match the query logic. This may include millions and millions of rows generated as the output of one query becoming subsequent input data for a second, or even third query in a seamless and simultaneous execution. Let us take a closer look at how subqueries work by understanding the relationship between an inner and outer query.

Correlated Subqueries

A correlated subquery is when an inner query refers to the resulting values produced from the processing of an outer query operating simultaneously. This dynamic processing is on a row-by-row basis. The number of iterations of the inner query is wholly dependent on the number of rows produced by the outer query and has a 1:1 relationship. Again, the output values from the outer query become the dependent input values for the inner query.

Due to the 1:1 row-dependency between the inner query and the outer query, the correlated (inner) subquery cannot be executed by itself independent from the outer query. Additionally, the 1:1 row dependency means the inner correlated subquery is executed repeatedly (1 time for each row evaluated by the outer query).

See the following example where the inner query calculates the maximum purchase price for each vehicle type, and then feeds that price into the outer query to find the vehicles that have a matching value:

```
SELECT VehicleName, PurchasePrice, VehicleTypeName
FROM tblVEHICLE V1
   JOIN tblVEHICLE_TYPE VT ON V1.VehicleTypeID = VT.VehicleTypeID
WHERE
    PurchasePrice IN (SELECT MAX(V2.PurchasePrice)
                       FROM tblVEHICLE V2
                       WHERE V2.VehicleTypeID = V1.VehicleTypeID
                       GROUP BY V2.VehicleTypeID)
ORDER BY VehicleName, PurchasePrice, VehicleTypeName
```

	VehicleName	PurchasePrice	VehicleTypeName
1	GS203	887533.00	Double-Decker Bus
2	GS204	887533.00	Double-Decker Bus
3	GS208	604995.00	Standard Bus

Figure 7.28: *Example of Correlated Subquery with 1:1 Dependency between Inner and Outer Queries*

Not every query will have this inter-dependency found in *Figure* 7.28.

We will take a closer look at the power of subqueries as they blow open the ability of analysts to engage complex problems. As with many tools, there are multiple methods and approaches that can be applied to render the correct results. The method chosen to implement can vary based on the data available at the time as well as how we visualize the problem. We will see different approaches to writing correlated and non-correlated subqueries, including those that appear in the following locations of a query:

- `SELECT`
- `WHERE`
- `FROM`
- '`ABC`' method

Subquery in `SELECT` line

The following query returns each vehicle from **`METRO_TRANSIT`** by name as well as the purchase price paid. Additionally, the overall average price of all vehicles is also returned as a comparison. This is an example of having two non-correlated queries in the select line.

```
SELECT VehicleName, PurchasePrice,
      (SELECT AVG(PurchasePrice) FROM tblVEHICLE) AS Average_Price
FROM tblVEHICLE
GROUP BY VehicleName, PurchasePrice
```

	VehicleName	PurchasePrice	Average_Price
1	GS203	887533.00	736762.250000
2	GS204	887533.00	736762.250000
3	GS208	604995.00	736762.250000
4	PA7	566988.00	736762.250000

Figure 7.29: *Example of Non-correlated Subquery in SELECT Line*

While somewhat uncommon, there are times when unrelated data like what is in *Figure* 7.29 is desired. Just be aware that we can return values with separate queries in **`SELECT`**.

Subquery in **WHERE** Clause

More common is the need to filter rows of data based on criteria that affects many rows or perhaps may also include an aggregate function and **GROUP BY** just in the conditional logic. This can often be addressed with a subquery placed in the WHERE clause. An example may be as follows:

Write the query to determine the neighborhoods that had at least 2 boardings in April 2025 ***that also*** had more than 3 boardings in July of 2024. As the queries used for examples here have limited data because we entered the data manually). First, write the query to determine the neighborhoods that had at least 2 boardings in April 2025 as follows:

```
SELECT NeighborhoodName, COUNT(*) AS NumBoardings_Apr2025
FROM tblNEIGHBORHOOD N
      JOIN tblSTOP S ON N.NeighborhoodID = S.NeighborhoodID
      JOIN tblTRIP_STOP TS ON S.StopID = TS.StopID
      JOIN tblBOARDING B ON TS.TripStopID = B.TripStopID
WHERE MONTH(B.BoardingDateTime) = 4
      AND YEAR(B.BoardingDateTime) = 2025
GROUP BY NeighborhoodName
HAVING COUNT(*) > 1
ORDER BY NumBoardings DESC
```

	NeighborhoodName	NumBoardings
1	Fremont	2

Figure 7.30: *Example of Building Non-correlated Subquery in WHERE Clause*

Next step, write the query to determine the neighborhoods that meet the other condition of at least three boardings in July 2024:

```
SELECT NeighborhoodName, COUNT(*) AS NumBoardings_July2024
FROM tblNEIGHBORHOOD N
      JOIN tblSTOP S ON N.NeighborhoodID = S.NeighborhoodID
      JOIN tblTRIP_STOP TS ON S.StopID = TS.StopID
      JOIN tblBOARDING B ON TS.TripStopID = B.TripStopID
WHERE MONTH(B.BoardingDateTime) = 7
      AND YEAR(B.BoardingDateTime) = 2024
GROUP BY NeighborhoodName
HAVING COUNT(*) >= 3
ORDER BY NumBoardings DESC
```

The last step is to combine these two queries in the **WHERE** clause of one! Please note that it does not matter which of these queries is positioned in the **WHERE** clause of the other.

```
SELECT N.NeighborhoodID, NeighborhoodName, COUNT(*) AS Num
Boardings_Apr2025
FROM tblNEIGHBORHOOD N
      JOIN tblSTOP S ON N.NeighborhoodID = S.NeighborhoodID
      JOIN tblTRIP_STOP TS ON S.StopID = TS.StopID
      JOIN tblBOARDING B ON TS.TripStopID = B.TripStopID
WHERE MONTH(B.BoardingDateTime) = 4
      AND YEAR(B.BoardingDateTime) = 2025
      AND N.NeighborhoodID IN (
SELECT N2.NeighborhoodID
FROM tblNEIGHBORHOOD N2
      JOIN tblSTOP S ON N.NeighborhoodID = S.NeighborhoodID
      JOIN tblTRIP_STOP TS ON S.StopID = TS.StopID
      JOIN tblBOARDING B ON TS.TripStopID = B.TripStopID
WHERE MONTH(B.BoardingDateTime) = 7
      AND YEAR(B.BoardingDateTime) = 2024
GROUP BY N2.NeighborhoodID
HAVING COUNT(*) >= 3)

GROUP BY N.NeighborhoodID, NeighborhoodName
HAVING COUNT(*) > 1
ORDER BY NumBoardings_Apr2025 DESC
```

Several notes regarding the use of non-correlated subqueries in the WHERE clause:

- Only one column can be included in the **SELECT** line of the inner query! This is required because we are using IN as a condition to match rows between the two queries, and returning more than one value will break the logic.
- This means the aggregate function for the inner query is not returned to the outer query (we will need to run the query independently to verify we like the results and then we trim the query).
- The **ORDER BY** clause must also be dropped from the inner query as the order of the results set is immaterial to the logic.

Based on these required modifications here, placing the subquery in the **WHERE** clause is **NOT** frequently the first choice for data analysts. Often, analysts prefer greater flexibility in the data that is returned in the outer query, and like to see all aggregated data. The functionality is presented here as a FYI as it may be the easiest method to write a complex query using the **WHERE** clause someday.

Next, let us see the same query essentially, except for connecting the two queries in the **FROM** clause. Hint: this is often a preferable choice because we can return the aggregate values from both queries (the inner query and the outer query):

```
SELECT NeighborhoodID, NeighborhoodName, NumBoardings_July2025,
COUNT(*) AS NumBoardings_Apr2025
FROM tblNEIGHBORHOOD N
      JOIN tblSTOP S ON N.NeighborhoodID = S.NeighborhoodID
      JOIN tblTRIP_STOP TS ON S.StopID = TS.StopID
      JOIN tblBOARDING B ON TS.TripStopID = B.TripStopID

      JOIN
            (SELECT NeighborhoodID, NeighborhoodName, COUNT(*)
            AS NumBoardings_July2025
            FROM tblNEIGHBORHOOD N
                  JOIN tblSTOP S ON N.NeighborhoodID
            = S.NeighborhoodID
                  JOIN tblTRIP_STOP TS ON S.StopID = TS.StopID
                  JOIN tblBOARDING B ON TS.TripStopID
            = B.TripStopID
            WHERE MONTH(B.BoardingDateTime) = 7
                  AND YEAR(B.BoardingDateTime) = 2024
            GROUP BY NeighborhoodName
            HAVING COUNT(*) >= 3) AS subquery1 ON N.Neighbor
            hoodID = subquery1.NeighborhoodID

WHERE MONTH(B.BoardingDateTime) = 4
AND YEAR(B.BoardingDateTime) = 2025
GROUP BY NeighborhoodID, NeighborhoodName, NumBoardings_July2025
HAVING COUNT(*) > 1
ORDER BY NumBoardings_Apr2025 DESC
```

Notes from the subquery design in the above code:

- The structure of the query is **JOINing** to the subquery just like any other table! This requires including the primary key value from **tblNEIGHBORHOOD** so we can connect from the inner query to the outer query.
- The query results returned to the screen can include all aggregate functions (this is a good thing); we must add the alias of the inner aggregate function to **BOTH** the outer query **SELECT** line and the outer **GROUP BY** clause to accomplish this.

One final example for now on writing a subquery is what I have named the 'ABC method' as we will name each query with a letter ('A' for the first query, 'B' for the second, 'C' if there is a third query and so on for however many queries are included). Let us see the above query converted to this method:

```
SELECT A.*, B.NumBoardings_July2025
FROM
(SELECT NeighborhoodID, NeighborhoodName, COUNT(*) AS NumBoard-
ings_Apr2025
FROM tblNEIGHBORHOOD N
```

```
        JOIN tblSTOP S ON N.NeighborhoodID = S.NeighborhoodID
        JOIN tblTRIP_STOP TS ON S.StopID = TS.StopID
        JOIN tblBOARDING B ON TS.TripStopID = B.TripStopID
WHERE MONTH(B.BoardingDateTime) = 4
        AND YEAR(B.BoardingDateTime) = 2025
GROUP BY NeighborhoodID, NeighborhoodName
HAVING COUNT(*) > 1) A,

(SELECT NeighborhoodID, NeighborhoodName, COUNT(*) AS NumBoard-
ings_July2025
FROM tblNEIGHBORHOOD N
JOIN tblSTOP S ON N.NeighborhoodID = S.NeighborhoodID
JOIN tblTRIP_STOP TS ON S.StopID = TS.StopID
JOIN tblBOARDING B ON TS.TripStopID = B.TripStopID
WHERE MONTH(B.BoardingDateTime) = 7
AND YEAR(B.BoardingDateTime) = 2024
GROUP BY NeighborhoodName
HAVING COUNT(*) >= 3) B

WHERE A.NeighborhoodID = B.NeighborhoodID
```

Notes from the subquery design in the above code:

- Each subquery is bounded by parentheses, and named with a sequential letter.
- There needs to be an 'old-school' connection of a **WHERE** clause (highlighted in yellow above) that establishes the transactional integrity across the queries.
- There needs to be a new **SELECT** line at the very top of the queries to determine the exact columns to be returned. In this code, this is **A.***, **B.NumBoardings_July2025** (highlighted in green). It eliminates duplicates and is very easy to remember.
- This format of writing subqueries is by far the most popular among the thousands of students due to the simplicity and ease of adding an unlimited number of queries (80%+ of all homework, labs/quizzes, and exams follow this method).

Subqueries are very powerful and provide several ways to tackle increasingly complex problems with not-so-difficult queries. Each of the methods presented in this section are considered valid ways of solving problems with data; do not feel as though one method is superior. While eventually you may find a favorite or preferred method from the examples above that aligns with how you 'see' the problem, please practice all methods to become more effective, and skilled in writing a range of queries.

Basic Temporary Objects

Temporary objects are commonplace when working with larger volumes of data. Often during maintenance tasks or simply while conducting normal operations, there are several needs to capture subsets of data for extra attention or processing. Like most occupations, there is a tool for every need.

Derived Table

A derived table is essentially any result set from a query. It lives in memory as opposed to being a permanent table on disk or part of the database structure. We tend to identify result sets as 'tables' because it helps frame how we can work with them. A derived table can be captured, filtered, and stored just like any other table. Just as a reminder of what we are referencing here, please observe the query as well as the results below (again, formally called a derived table):

```
SELECT *
FROM tblDRIVER D
      JOIN tblTRIP T ON D.DriverID = T.DriverID
```

	DriverID	Fname	Lname	BirthDate	Salary	LicenseNumber	TripID	DriverID	VehicleID	RouteID	BeginDateTime	EndDateTime
1	4	Meryl	Streep	1949-06-22	46965.00	MDStre8121UJ	1	4	2	6	2025-04-24 06:17:00.000	NULL
2	1	Jimi	Hendrix	1942-11-27	42590.00	JMHend3487RR	2	1	1	3	2025-04-24 06:42:55.000	NULL
3	4	Meryl	Streep	1949-06-22	46965.00	MDStre8121UJ	3	4	2	5	2025-04-23 07:23:00.000	NULL
4	2	Bruce	Lee	1940-11-27	42590.00	BTLee'2198DL	4	2	3	6	2025-04-24 06:57:00.000	NULL
5	4	Meryl	Streep	1949-06-22	46965.00	MDStre8121UJ	5	4	2	4	2025-04-29 08:07:00.000	NULL

Figure 7.31: *Example Derived Table Generated from a Simple Query*

Again, a derived table is the ephemeral results set returned after executing any query. These values are structured within rows and columns and live in memory which means they are not stored on a disk drive somewhere in the same shape. The source data that is brought into the results set during the execution of a query must live somewhere within the database obviously but not in the shape that we see on our computer screen.

A derived table can participate in other larger queries, and even be included in a subquery (basically JOINing to other derived tables and queries).

View

Views are essential to most data environments! Views are almost identical to a derived table in that it can produce the results from a complex query (something that might include 12 join statements and 3 subqueries). The difference is a view can be named, which has several benefits: First, a view looks, smells, and acts like a table, which allows engineers to mask data drawn from around their environment without having to expose the design of the environment to casual users. This abstraction improves security by limiting what people can read as well as modify directly.

Second, a complex query that may have taken a dozen hours to write perfectly can be saved as a view. This means the query does not ever have to be re-engineered in the future. In the 'old days', engineers would have to save the code in a text file or send it to us as an attachment in an email.

Third, a view is essentially indistinguishable from a permanent table when participating in a complex query and often users will not even be aware they are connecting to a view if the name of it does not make it apparent. This allows engineers flexibility when designing dashboards for decision-makers with various technical sophistication.

The downside of using views is related to potential poor performance. Even though views can often reside in memory, are frequently pre-compiled, and have an execution plan, they must go collect the data at runtime. The 'saved' query must be executed as a **SELECT** statement each time the view is called. Some database environments have unfortunately relied on views (that joined to other views) that were called thousands of times every minute. This is often painful to unravel and expensive to try and re-engineer.

So, let us see how a view is coded. Take any **SELECT** statement we made earlier:

Using the example from *Figure* 7.28 (must eliminate the **ORDER BY** line):

```
CREATE VIEW vw_Example1
AS
SELECT VehicleName, PurchasePrice, VehicleTypeName
FROM tblVEHICLE V1
JOIN tblVEHICLE_TYPE VT ON V1.VehicleTypeID = VT.VehicleTypeID
WHERE
    PurchasePrice IN (SELECT MAX(V2.PurchasePrice)
                      FROM tblVEHICLE V2
                      WHERE V2.VehicleTypeID = V1.VehicleTypeID
                      GROUP BY V2.VehicleTypeID)
```

Now, let us see the process of retrieving data from this view. Remember, it is essentially a table (even though it is a saved query that has been given a name). We will access this view the same way, we access tables by using a select statement as follows:

```
SELECT *
FROM vw_Example1
```

	VehicleName	PurchasePrice	VehicleTypeName
1	GS203	887533.00	Double-Decker Bus
2	GS204	887533.00	Double-Decker Bus
3	GS208	604995.00	Standard Bus

Figure 7.32: *Example of View* `vw_Example1` *Treated Like a Virtual Table*

Notes regarding views:

- A view behaves like a table; this means we can JOIN to a view with other views as well as other tables.
- Views are great in moderation; there are at their core a named **SELECT** statement and therefore must be executed when called; this means performance could suffer across the data environment if the volume is too high.
- Be careful! Too many data environments struggle with a rat's nest of overlapping views. Be prudent and only use views sparingly like feeding a dashboard.

#Table (read 'temp table')

Another common temporary object we want to be familiar with is called a temp table. A temp table is designated with a 'pound sign' (aka 'hash-tag') and creates a permanent table on disk (yes...this seems odd that a **#table** is permanently on disk). Side work such as assembling reports is a common use case for **#tables**.

A quick history lesson is in order. Back in the early days of modern computing (early 1970's), random access memory (RAM) was incredibly expensive. I remember 4-megabyte RAM sticks (not a misstatement: MB instead of GB) cost over $1,000 when a full semester of college tuition was $300 (additionally, brand new cars went for $4,000- and 3-bedroom houses in Seattle were about $80,000). Meaning, a full year of tuition at the University of Washington (and probably elsewhere) was cheaper than 4 MB of memory! Because memory was so very expensive in the early days, temporary tables played the role of additional workspace outside the database where we could assemble data, do side processing or otherwise capture data for various purposes such as for reporting without having to spend tens of thousands of dollars on memory.

Let us see an example use of **#TempTable** by using the same code from **vw_Example1**:

```
SELECT VehicleName, PurchasePrice, VehicleTypeName
INTO #TempTable_1
FROM tblVEHICLE V1
      JOIN tblVEHICLE_TYPE VT ON V1.VehicleTypeID = VT.VehicleTypeID
WHERE PurchasePrice IN (SELECT MAX(V2.PurchasePrice)
                        FROM tblVEHICLE V2
                        WHERE V2.VehicleTypeID = V1.VehicleTypeID
                        GROUP BY V2.VehicleTypeID)
```

Once the #table has been created and populated, it will live as a permanent table on disk under the system database TempDB. Again, this is a shared workspace outside the security and resource group of the database we may have intended to capture data or prepare reports for, so please be aware. Best practices include dropping temp tables as soon as they are no longer needed (which is often within hours of creation).

These behave as regular tables. See the following query:

```
SELECT *
FROM #TempTable_1
```

	VehicleName	PurchasePrice	VehicleTypeName
1	GS203	887533.00	Double-Decker Bus
2	GS204	887533.00	Double-Decker Bus
3	GS208	604995.00	Standard Bus

Figure 7.33: *Example of Querying Data from Temporary Table #TempTable_1*

Like temporary tables on disk, there are temporary tables in memory. These are written as **`@Table`** and are named "table variables". As mentioned previously, **`TempTables`** on disk were designed to be on permanent drives because random access memory was prohibitively expensive. Over the 40 years since, technological advances have reduced the cost of RAM significantly (as well as with Solid State Drives or SSD which can mimic/rival RAM), there is no longer the stigma of writing temp objects to memory. Depending on the type and volume of data, as well as the frequency of updates, table variables can perform exceptionally well.

The only confusing part for many people used to working with temporary tables on disk is the data in table variables disappears completely at the end of the query. It lasts less than a microsecond or two and then is gone. This behavior is no different than any other variable used in coding, but it seems to be a sticking point for many beginning analysts.

We will see parameters and variables after more experience as these are considered advanced SQL objects, so this will be a brief introduction at best. Variables are temporary containers that last only for the life of a query (again, think microseconds). We use the word DECLARE to establish them, frequently within repeatable code managing specific processes that hit a database (like logging in to a social media account or buying something from Amazon).

```
DECLARE @Table1 Table
(TID INT IDENTITY(1,1) primary key,
Tname varchar(30) not null,
TDate datetime not null)

INSERT INTO @Table1 (Tname, Tdate)
VALUES
('Coffee', 'May 4, 2025 11:35:45'),
('Mug', 'May 8, 2025 07:22:16'),
('Hammer', 'May 10, 2025 08:52:06')

SELECT * FROM @Table1
```

	TID	Tname	TDate
1	1	Coffee	2025-05-04 11:35:45.000
2	2	Mug	2025-05-08 07:22:16.000
3	3	Hammer	2025-05-10 08:52:06.000

Figure 7.34: *Example of Creation of a Table Variable Named @Table1*

As can be seen in *Figure* 7.34, there is a moment of time where the data in the script is placed in a temporary object named **`@Table1`**. It behaves briefly like a table as users can write queries the same way as a regular table. The only difference is the object disappears (including all the data and any work conducted) as soon as the query completes.

See the same query run a minute or so later:

```
Msg 1087, Level 15, State 2, Line 53
Must declare the table variable "@Table".

Completion time: 2025-07-16T13:28:23.2022430+05:00
```

Figure 7.35: *Example of error received after table variable has evaporated*

Notes regarding **`@Table`** variables:

- We love table variables! They are quick to build, are flexible, and easy to clean-up.

Conclusion

Great job! You now have intermediate chops working with SQL! Both chapter 6 (*Intermediate SQL: Part 1*) and this chapter cover significant material that is critical to being a well-rounded data analyst. This includes the foundational concepts of JOIN statement, bringing together data across multiple tables, while maintaining transactional integrity, system functions, GROUP BY (and all its variations) as well as subqueries and temporary objects. This is quite a bit of material.

While your knowledge and understanding of this content may be best described as 'emerging', do not discount what you have absorbed so far; the only difference between the position you are in right now, and someone who has ten years' experience is simply hands-on practice.

Chapter 8, *Putting it All Together*, essentially the core of designing a fully normalized relational database schema based on a set of user requirements. The goal of the final chapter is to cement the foundational concepts that each reader has obtained so far, and to enable each person to construct an original database application. Fewer than 20% of all professional information technology technicians with a focus or concentration on data analysis have achieved this objective!

Post-Chapter Challenges

Based on your objectives and intentions on learnings from this book, please approach the following challenges as appropriate.

Track 1: Data Tourist Seeking Ancillary Awareness (THINK ~10 minutes)

Please spend a solid 10 minutes reviewing the following questions, exploring your thoughts. These questions and your responses cut to the essence of this chapter:

- How does the GROUP BY and HAVING clauses expand the power of SQL?
- Consider the combination of functions demonstrated in this chapter regarding determining absolute and approximate dates and times; again, reflect on the ability you have to create very precise date and time ranges that make sense to people.
- How might you explain the use and function of temporary objects (like views) as well as subqueries to a non-technical person, and convince them that these are substantial concepts critical to databases?

Track 2: Dedicated Student or Recent Graduate (WRITE ~ 45 minutes)

Based on your completion of this chapter, WRITE several paragraphs in response to each question; explore these as if you are being asked a similar question during a job interview!

- Write 10 basic queries that include the learnings of this chapter out of the `METRO_TRANSIT` database. Include the following:
    - `Aggregate functions`
    - `Date functions`
    - `GROUP BY / HAVING`
    - `Views`
    - `Subqueries`

Track 3: Full Speed Learner Seeking Job (BUILD ~3 hours)

This track targets readers of this book who want to develop professional skills working with data to launch a career or obtain a more satisfying job. Now that we have seen more of what SQL can do, let us continue with the building of your new database by adding data:

- After populating a dozen or so rows in each table of your project database, establish a set of queries that provide immediate value to a typical user of your database.
- Show off what you have learned! Include in your queries some of the following objects:
  - `Functions (aggregate, date, string, numeric)`
  - `GROUP BY/HAVING`
  - `Subqueries`
- Examples include the following:
  - `Number of units sold in the past 90 days`
  - `Total dollars received from sales in the past 30 days`
  - `Number of new customers (by state) that have registered in past year`

Chapter 8
Putting it All Together

Introduction

Congrats, this is the last chapter! Hopefully, the material so far has resonated as more than just a slot-filler for your academic schedule (that is how my accidental technology career started back in 1985). The next steps recommended for your learning journey depend on the momentum you have with the material presented in chapters 1 through 7. Only you know for sure whether the material found in this book is interesting enough for you to be worth a further investment of your time and energy. Now, most likely the current semester is wrapping up, and the last thing on most people's minds is doing more work. Improving the number of industry opportunities can happen if you develop these skills. It can be suggested that right now is the perfect time to leverage the work you have recently completed, and hammer out one more cycle of designing, building, and populating an original database. It could be the most valuable assignment you have ever completed.

Not only will a second database design-build project cement your understanding of everything presented in this book so far, but it will help you determine whether data analysis, data engineering, and project management are true passions. Additionally, completing an original project with purpose will provide a tangible set of experiences that will forever be able to be referenced in your resume and future job interviews not only for the important tangible hard coding skills but also for intangible soft skills like grit, determination, and tenacity that many employers seek.

If the material in the first seven chapters has been unremarkable in generating a career-like passion for you, completing a second project now while the knowledge is fresh may be enough to make it so! You have made it this far; trust that the very best students have all taken extra work to define their skills more robustly as well as distinguishing themselves as an emerging professional ready to work. Competition for internships and early career jobs is fierce; there is no other way to become attractive to employers than proving that you are willing to do what it takes to become excellent!

Structure

In this chapter, we will explore the following topics:

- Industry Challenge: Retail Coffee Shop
- Steps for Establishing a Fully Normalized Database
- Read Case Study (found in the addendum)
- Conduct Additional Research
- Select a Perspective
- Establish User Requirements
- Create Data Flow Diagram
- Create Conceptual Database Diagram
- Create a Logical Database Design
- Create Physical Database Design
- Manually Populate Database
- Run the Entire Script as Single Executable

Industry Challenge: Retail Coffee Shop

Completing an industry project requires several factors to align well for even a chance for achieving success. These aligning factors include executives agreeing that a problem exists, that it is worthwhile investing limited funds, and that it has priority over other pressing needs. Additionally, there needs to be competent front-line leadership who cannot only break down the project into concise sequential tasks, hire effective technical personnel but also communicate urgent timelines, and manage odd personalities, all the while maintaining motivation and morale across a diverse team.

Many people argue the only way to get good at anything (such as playing an instrument, driving a car, speaking a new language, or even cooking) is to dive in and get busy as best we know how. This means we will be making many mistakes! If we take notes, reflect honestly on what went wrong, and how to do things better the next time, there is very little downside to 'learning by doing'. Not only will practical experience build confidence that we belong, but the skills we acquire during an independent project are also the exact skills that are expected for many positions we hope to get hired for.

By the end of this chapter, you will have a deeper appreciation of the systems development lifecycle, defining customer requirements, and ultimately the process of designing software by completing a rapid development of an original database based on an established commercial organization.

The challenge in this chapter has been designed to behave exactly like an industry project (not quite an internship, but that would be the next step after finishing one more design). As with any authentic industry project, your challenge includes applying the skills gleaned from the following:

- Practicing "*Organize or Die*" traits, while following all five phases of the SDLC
- Completing fundamental research on your target company and its associated industry, while defining appropriate user requirements
- Producing several official Project Management artifacts including executive summary, data flow diagram, user stories, personas, project charter, and Gantt chart
- Creating all documentation for the DESIGN phase of SDLC, including conceptual, logical, and physical database designs
- Deploying a physical database model into cloud environment with SQL script
- Coding **`SQL INSERT`** statements to populate look-up and transactional tables
- Writing **`SELECT`** statements in SQL to retrieve data as defined in data flow diagram

The completion of this challenge will put each reader in a position to gain employment in the technology industry because they will have relevant project experience. My goal is for each reader to review their existing hobbies, personal interests or perhaps, the various industries they seek to join someday soon. This chapter challenge will be much more rewarding, if you choose a company that is close to your heart!

Upon completing the industry project (or during), feel free to join the software design community at **`smash.technology`** (it is free). This site is a place I have created to help younger developers from around the world build a network with others who share the passion for learning technology. There are opportunities to participate in live office hours, find additional industry projects, connect with seasoned industry mentors, as well as join hackathons and learn about exclusive internships from our corporate sponsors.

So, let us get started with a hands-on project to solidify the concepts that have been covered so far, and allow you to enter the realm of extreme learning. The rest of this chapter will be a step-by-step guide to complete a database design on a new topic.

Steps for Establishing a Fully Normalized Database

The following steps will be presented in sequence to walk a reader through a database design project from needs analysis, through brainstorming objects, data modeling (including normalization), as well as coding the final design and populating the schema with realistic-look data. In all, it is estimated that this project will take between 15 to 25 hours (doable in about 4 weeks) to complete. Please begin by reviewing the following outline:

1. Read through the provided case study (or make your own!)
2. Augment your knowledge of the case study business with additional research
3. Choose a user perspective for design (customer, management, supplier or staff)
4. Establish a Gantt Chart to organize tasks for project completion as well as tracking deliverables while practicing project management skills
5. Write a concise set of user requirements to support your chosen perspective
6. Construct a dataflow diagram
7. Create conceptual database diagram of perhaps 15 entities
8. Develop a logical database design and normalize the conceptual diagram
9. Write the SQL CREATE statements to code the physical database schema
10. Write the SQL INSERT statements to populate a dozen rows for each table
11. Run the entire script as single executable on a student cloud drive
12. Write ten SQL SELECT queries to generate useful/functional user reports

While these steps are rudimentary, they are intended to reflect the level of skill for a person who has nearly completed a single introductory college-level class on database design and SQL. If you continue with a career in technology (or perhaps, have already begun one, and are adding to a burgeoning skill set with this textbook), you will eventually recognize that many projects will be far more complex than what is presented here. For most people, this may be their first real industry project, and reinforcing the basic concepts is exactly what is most beneficial.

For this challenge, things are very easy to get started by including an 18-page summary overview on the quick-serve retail coffee market that can loosely be referred to as a case study. The primary example profile in this overview is Starbucks Corporation. Starbucks and coffee retailing was chosen as an example for the same reason public transportation, and **`METRO_TRANSIT`** was presented throughout this book. Many readers will have familiarity with the coffee business, and be able to focus on the application of their recent knowledge as opposed to having to gain a better understanding of how coffee shops operate. The hope is coffee shops are so common to most readers that they can do their best work quickly.

If for whatever reason, conducting a database design project on the **`COFFEE_SHOP`** case study is NOT interesting, that is totally fine; another 25 or so case studies across more than a dozen other industries have been prepared, and are available for download at the publisher's GitHub repository as well as **Smash.Technology**.

https://github.com/ava-orange-education/ultimate-SQL-for-Data-Science-and-Analytics

Most readers should find one that resonates with a range of hobbies, interests or lifestyle. Please find one that can hold your focus for the 4 weeks or so this industry project will take to finish. Consider making a 'case study' on your own by conducting primary research with interviews, observations, and personal insight that you already possess. Creating an original document demonstrates tremendous passion, commitment, leadership, and diligence as well as being something to show off during interviews. It would be a hit!

Read Case Study

As we saw earlier in the textbook, preparing to design a database requires learning as much as we can about the organization as well as the perceived problem space. We need to be able to answer the two big questions:

- Who is going to use the database?
- What decisions are they going to make?

Follow-up research may be required to refine our answers to include revelations around the exact data required to support these decisions. This includes knowing how frequently the necessary data needs to be captured, and how many minutes it is fresh and relevant.

Whether engaging in the Coffee Shop study or another topic, make sure to spend enough time reading the summary overview (as well as additional independent research as needed) to be fluent in the data needs of the organization.

While reading the case study, take notes and write down all questions where our knowledge is thin or our understanding is ambiguous. This may mean having to re-read entire sections several times! The notes taken during reading will be the foundation of not only the base knowledge required to go through this project but also, they will help direct many of the intricate design choices that will make this experience truly memorable.

Conduct Additional Research

Rarely, is a project clearly defined or thoroughly understood by everyone in the design and development team. Many times, even the project sponsor or company executives are not in agreement with the goals, objectives, or priorities of a project!

Any effort put in to provide better understanding will go a long way towards a better resulting design.

Aim to get a well-rounded understanding of the enterprise. This includes being able to articulate the motivations and data needs for each of the following perspectives:

- Customer
- Corporate Management/Executives
- Third-Party Suppliers (the providers of paper cups, beans, straws, and so on)
- Employees

The details of a database for any company will change dramatically based on the perspective of the primary users; be sure to consider the data needs and decision-making demands for all perspectives, if possible.

If there is a coffee shop in a neighborhood nearby, consider visiting the shop and speaking to an employee or manager about their data needs. This hands-on data gathering is the type of behavior that not only builds confidence but also shines in job interviews.

Select a Perspective

In real life, we will often be directed to solve a specific problem that has been defined by others. In the absence of being handed a directive to focus on a narrow problem, the choice is open for us to find the perspective within the case study that is most interesting or best aligned to our career goals. If we have put in the due diligence, and have acquired an adequate depth of knowledge on our subject, there is no wrong answer. Also, in this situation, we are not stuck in any single perspective, so we can easily pivot efforts to a different one, if the first proves to be a bad fit. Cherish this opportunity!

As mentioned already, the choices of perspective include the customer, corporate management, third-party suppliers, as well as employees.

Establish User Requirements

After selecting a perspective, the next set of tasks includes defining the user requirements. In real life, there will be an exhaustive set of artifacts intended to help solidify the collective understanding of the project, including the minimum mandatory features, available budget, as well as the timelines for delivery.

As mentioned earlier in this book, there are dozens of standard artifacts for a typical project that are intended to define the objective clearly, communicate progress, and inform people about changes, among others. There is an entire association of professionals dedicated to elevating the roles and responsibilities of project management, called the Project Management Institute (PMI). They have a very handy body of knowledge called PMBOK that can be searched online in much greater detail than will be provided here. For more information, please see the list of defined documentation promoted by PMI at their website: https://www.projectengineer.net/the-pmboks-project-management-documents/.

For the sake of keeping this project simple, just be aware of the following artifacts to be in a better position to appreciate their function during another project in your future (or perhaps, an interview):

- Project charter
- Gantt chart
- Scrum check-ins/status updates

Defining user requirements for this project does not have to be too elaborate or even formal. For now, simply create a list of perhaps five (5) decisions that will be made by the user perspective you have selected, while including the associated data elements required to support the decisions. Additional elements to include with this list are the frequency of the decisions, as well as how long the data can go without being refreshed.

As presented earlier in this book, try and think along the lines of the transactions that will be generated by the applications connected to this new database. This may be the most difficult part of developing user requirements, especially early in a career. This will not be perfect, so it is okay to be frustrated!

Customers are perhaps the most obvious users of data in a business. Many of us are frequent patrons of coffee shops, and can simply think of the decisions we make when we choose to stop for a cup or two with friends. What data helps us to decide where and when to visit a store? The customer goals and objectives within the scenario of a coffee shop may include the following:

- List of Products
- Prices
- Hours of operation
- Ratings of previous customers
- Location of the nearest store
- Special events
- Discounts from membership

The perspective of corporate management may also be easy to generalize, as they are responsible for high-level guidance and strategy for operations and marketing. The goals they prioritize may include the following:

- Year over year growth in sales revenue
- Cost of goods
- Most/least reliable suppliers
- Employee turnover
- Most effective marketing campaigns
- Best/least-selling products
- Highest/Lowest performing stores

The user perspective of employees in a coffee shop may not be too difficult to evaluate, as many of us have a job (or if not yet in the workforce, know someone who has a job). Some of the goals and data elements to support employee decisions may include the following:

- Salary/Pay rate (if part-time or hourly)
- Exact job duties
- Menu items
- Shift assignments
- Customer satisfaction
- Manager/peer feedback
- Internal job opportunities
- Employee benefits
- Incident report procedures

The perspective of suppliers may not be obvious for many database designers. Many Business-to-Business (B2B) applications are hidden from most users, and require special permission to access. As a result, many people have never been exposed to the use case of gathering data in this space.

The goals and elements to support the decisions made by suppliers in the space of the coffee shop case study may include the following:

- Historical price received per item
- Volume of units provided
- Items returned from stores
- Best/worst-selling items
- Seasonal demand for each product type by number of units ordered

- Current lead time from order to delivery
- Manufacturing costs per item
- Satisfaction feedback from store management

Create Data Flow Diagram

While still in the process of defining user requirements, it may prove to be helpful to create a Data Flow Diagram (DFD). A DFD helps to frame the sequence of events as well as the people involved when data are created and processed. This includes the key points that decisions are being made throughout the environment.

A DFD can help all the people involved to gain a better understanding of exactly where data issues exist, potential vulnerabilities, as well as how to become more secure, resilient, and efficient with design improvements. While this is an optional step, many organizations frequently seek good visual diagrams with project documentation. It makes sense to build a skill set or basic competency, if there is an interest in being competitive.

Create Conceptual Database Diagram

With a foundational understanding of the perspective, we have selected a coffee shop, and we are ready to embark on the tangible construction of the database. As we saw back in *Chapter 2, Brief Overview of Relational Model* and *Chapter 3, Data Modeling*, the conceptual design phase is a bit abstract. We may be a bit unsteady still, but that is why we have taken on this extra assignment.

The biggest exercise of creating a conceptual database diagram is brainstorming the objects involved. While not experts, we have seen this already, and so it should not be brand new. Go back and review the content in the previous chapters as necessary.

If we gain a solid understanding of the perspective we have selected, it should be possible to make a few attempts at writing down our thoughts. Consider working with another person (they do not even have to be a student learning this material). The brainstorming process should produce between 10 and 30 objects. These can also be called the 'nouns' of business as most objects we write down should be a person, place, or thing. Remember, there are no wrong answers here!

After the initial brainstorming (and taking a break), review and consolidate the list by eliminating those objects that are out of scope, duplicated, or more appropriately placed as an attribute. While not always enjoyable, conceptual diagraming is a great skill to practice, refine, and become competent at; not enough people are good at this process. Those that are skilled with this tend to get noticed and included with higher-level projects earlier in their careers than others. See this as a head start on a wonderful journey!

Create a Logical Database Design

Once the conceptual database design phase has been completed, we are ready to go through the normalization process, and refine the design into something tangible. Again, this was covered extensively earlier in this book, so feel comfortable reviewing the material in previous chapters. No one is born as an accomplished 'normalization' engineer, so the only way to get good is to practice. What Fun!

Set a goal to follow the foundational basics presented earlier; these steps are conserved safe and allow for different approaches. Try both methods as mentioned in *Chapter 3, Data Modeling* to get a better idea of which is aligned best to your thinking, and the way of problem-solving.

Also, it will benefit your future to find a diagramming tool that makes sense. Consider Draw.io (free), or MS Visio (might be free, depending on if you have an Office 365 subscription) as very simple and basic tools. Set a goal to get comfortable enough to be able to lead a demonstration with a diagramming tool during a job interview! Also, set a target of getting your design into 3NF (if not 4NF). Hit me up on LinkedIn (find me at https://www.linkedIn.com/in/greg-hay-bba9363) and I will even give live feedback over zoom on any completed design!

Create Physical Database Design

The physical design phase might be the easiest of all three! Get to the point where you have a well-designed (fully normalized database ERD), and creating the schema can be done in less than an hour (ok maybe 2). A fully complete schema includes the following characteristics:

- Surrogate primary keys.
- Auto-increment primary keys.
- Appropriate selection of data types.
- Definition of foreign keys with ALTER TABLE statements (avoids sequential dependencies of the associated CREATE TABLE statements).
- Save your script!

This Data Definition Language (DDL) was covered extensively in *Chapter 4, Beginning SQL Review* as necessary with the intent of being able to write the required statements without the need of a phone, neighbor, or ChatGPT (same conditions as a job interview). This is perhaps the best time and place to cement these skills!

Manually Populate Database

To complete this second database design project, include the SQL code to populate the schema. This will most likely be through **`INSERT INTO`** statements (beginning with type tables first). These statements can be separate from the **`CREATE TABLE`** script completed earlier, or they can be combined into a single larger script.

Additional characteristics to follow:

- Avoid hard-coding primary or foreign key values (write subqueries!)
- Target roughly 5 rows or so for each look-up entity
- Follow-up with populating transactional tables with ~15 rows of data

Eventually, there will be opportunities to learn about automating the transaction management process with stored procedures and functions. Be good with concepts and material presented so far, and it will be very easy to learn the advanced skills and concepts soon enough.

Run the Entire Script as Single Executable

There should be free student accounts available for your favorite database management system, while you are engaging in this skill-building process. This includes products from Oracle, IBM, Google, and Microsoft. The publisher of this textbook has committed to making much of the material available in a download to facilitate the practicing of the SQL commands. Search their links for the material associated with this book as there should be several example scripts to help every student understand this process.

Once the script for your project has been created, it will be guaranteed to have more than a few typos or errors (big and small). The process of running the script, watching it fail, followed by hunting down the error to fix will get old quickly. It will, however, give you something interesting to discuss in a job interview, and make you a more viable candidate.

Take notes during this process! Where did your code fail? Were there any patterns to your code that were consistently wrong? Every developer goes through this process!

Write Initial REPORTING Queries

This step will effectively represent the finishing touches on your project! Even though there may only be a handful of rows of data in your database, the ability to write the relevant queries required for the target users is critical. Completing this task means that you have joined the select few professionals (maybe 20%) who have designed a database from scratch to deployment. This is your chance to show off; anything completed here should be forever referenced in your resume, and brought up in job interviews as independent industry project experience.

Additional Characteristics to Follow When Coding These Queries:

- Make sure that the queries are aligned with the chosen perspective.
- Include a range of functions presented in Chapters 6 and 7 *Intermediate* SQL
  - Aggregate
  - Date
  - Numeric
  - String
  - `GROUP BY` / `HAVING`
  - Subqueries

Conclusion

Congrats on finishing a difficult and challenging book! So, whether this has been forced upon you to complete a degree or certificate, or you sought this text out based on a trusted recommendation (and maybe, even enjoyed it), hopefully this has been a rewarding experience that has helped open your eyes to not only what the world of data engineering has to offer, but also your capabilities and interest in going deeper into this industry.

Reflect on this experience; which tasks or steps were the easiest or most difficult? Which areas of the SDLC might hold an interest for you? Anytime, we reflect on recent experiences, we learn about ourselves, what our strengths and weaknesses are as well as build confidence. Even if this was a loathsome experience (hopefully not), at least, there was the learning of what parts of industry for you to avoid in the future!

Recognize the aspects of this process you enjoyed, or at least found interesting (again, this will help decide career paths in the future). If you are considering 'stepping on the gas' and want more challenges or real industry opportunities, find me on LinkedIn or visit me at Smash.technology (no 'com' at the end) as there is more to learn if this has your interest. More than 3,000 students just like you have taken this exact material, and gone headfirst (with a shove) into some very interesting and rewarding positions throughout the world.

Finally, thank you for taking the time and energy required to finish! It was not easy.

Post-Chapter Challenges

Based on your objectives and intentions on the learnings from this book, please approach the following challenges as appropriate.

Track 1: Data Tourist Seeking Ancillary Awareness (THINK ~10 minutes)

Please spend a solid 10 minutes reviewing the following questions, exploring your thoughts. These questions and your responses cut to the essence of this chapter:

- Reflect on the journey you have made through this textbook. How have your ambitions on a future career changed, if at all?
- What perspectives do you have now on the application build process after observing or even participating in the design and construction of a database?

Track 2: Dedicated Student or Recent Graduate (WRITE ~ 45 minutes)

Based on your completion of this chapter, WRITE several paragraphs in response to each question; explore these as if you are being asked a similar question during a job interview!

- Write out a set of 3 test questions for each chapter (big challenge!).
- After creating the test questions, go back and answer them completely!

Track 3: Full Speed Learner Seeking Job (BUILD ~3 hours)

This track targets readers of this book who want to develop professional skills working with data to launch a career or obtain a more satisfying job. Now that we have a fantastic foundation on SQL, data modeling, and normalization, keep the momentum going with perhaps, one more database project:

- Tackle one more project start-to-finish! If you relied on one of the case studies (there are more than 20 to be found at the publisher's website), consider conducting an absolute self-driven database build project on a personal hobby, or something you find interesting.
- If you have already done a personal/professional project, consider doing one of the established case studies. These are prepared for independent learners like yourself to provide quick background and objectives for the construction of a database.

ADDENDUM

Case Study: Quick-Serve Retail Coffee Shop

Introduction

This addendum contains a case study on a large chain of retail coffee shops that has more than 35,000 stores worldwide. The goal of this case study is to provide a near real-life project for readers to address and apply their newly learned database design skills. The challenge for designing any database is gaining a full understanding of the data problem! This addendum is intentionally broad to reflect the frequent gaps in data, and emphasizes the additional research required to fully appreciate what a valid solution will need to provide. Many technicians in most projects will have a general understanding of the business, and not enough of the specific problem space or user perspective. Hopefully, you will take the challenge here to engage in this coffee shop case study (or perhaps, one of the other 25 or so prepared on the publisher's website).

The following case study on the retail coffee industry is brief, and intended to provide a general understanding of the market as well as unique challenges faced by many companies and individuals operating in the market space. Specific attention is placed on Starbucks Corporation as they have a global presence, and represent many standards and practices that lead to success.

Structure

In this chapter, we will explore the following topics:

- Industry Overview
- Business Challenges
- Employee Burnout in the Retail Industry

- Data Needs
- Major Companies
- Market Size
- Popular Products and Merchandise
- Profile of a Typical Customer
- Typical Jobs
- Significant Innovations
- Future of Coffee Industry
- Overview of Starbucks Coffee
- Mission Statement of Starbucks
- Reasons Behind Starbucks' Success
- Data Needs of Starbucks
- Challenges and Goals of Starbucks
- Pleasing Starbucks Investors
- Employee Relationship Challenges
- Starbucks Global Supply Chain Challenges
- Additional Resources

Industry Overview

Retail coffee stores are businesses that sell coffee and related products to consumers in a retail setting. These stores range from small independent shops to large chains with hundreds of locations worldwide. They offer a variety of coffee drinks, including brewed coffee, espresso-based drinks, and specialty drinks like lattes, cappuccinos, and mochas.

Retail coffee stores also typically offer a range of baked goods, snacks, and other food items to complement their coffee offerings. Many coffee shops also sell coffee beans and brewing equipment for customers to use at home.

The retail coffee industry is highly competitive, with many different players vying for market share. Some of the largest and most well-known retail coffee chains include *Starbucks, Dunkin' Donuts, and Tim Hortons*, among others.

In recent years, there has been a growing trend toward specialty coffee shops, which focus on high-quality, artisanal coffee, and often serve as community gathering places. These shops may offer single-origin coffee, specialty brewing methods, and unique flavor profiles that set them apart from more mainstream coffee chains.

Overall, the retail coffee industry continues to grow and evolve, driven by consumer demand for convenient, high-quality coffee experiences.

Business Challenges

Operating a retail coffee store comes with several unique business challenges. Some of the key challenges include:

- **Intense competition:** The retail coffee industry is highly competitive, with many different players vying for market share. This can make it difficult for new businesses to gain attraction, and establish a loyal customer base.
- **Changing consumer preferences:** Consumer preferences for coffee and related products can shift quickly, and businesses need to be able to adapt in order to stay relevant. This can require significant investments in research and development, as well as marketing and advertising.
- **Rising costs:** Retail coffee stores often face significant costs related to rent, labor, equipment, and ingredients. As costs continue to rise, businesses may need to find new ways to operate more efficiently, and cut costs to maintain profitability.
- **Staffing challenges:** Finding and retaining skilled baristas and other staff members can be a challenge for many retail coffee businesses. This is especially true in areas where there is high demand for skilled workers, and a limited pool of available talent.
- **Operational complexity:** Running a successful retail coffee store requires careful management of many different operational elements, including inventory management, equipment maintenance, and customer service. This can be difficult to manage, particularly for new or inexperienced business owners.

Employee Burnout in the Retail Industry

Employee burnout in the retail industry can be attributed to several key factors:

- **High workload:** Retail employees often face demanding schedules, especially during peak seasons, leading to physical and mental exhaustion.
- **Long hours and irregular schedules:** Many retail jobs require long hours and unpredictable shifts, making it difficult for employees to maintain a work-life balance.
- **Customer interaction:** Constant interaction with customers can be emotionally taxing, especially when dealing with difficult or demanding individuals.

- **Lack of support:** Employees may feel unsupported by management, particularly if they lack resources or assistance during busy periods.
- **Low pay and benefits:** Inadequate compensation can lead to frustration and dissatisfaction, contributing to feelings of burnout.
- **Limited career advancement:** Lack of opportunities for growth and development can leave employees feeling stagnant and unmotivated.
- **Work environment:** High-pressure sales targets and a stressful workplace culture can exacerbate feelings of burnout among retail workers.
- **Job insecurity:** Economic fluctuations and changes in consumer behavior can lead to instability in retail jobs, creating anxiety among employees.

Overall, operating a successful retail coffee store requires a combination of strategic planning, careful management, and a deep understanding of the unique challenges and opportunities in the industry.

Data Needs

Operating a retail coffee company involves collecting, analyzing, and using a variety of data to make informed business decisions. Some of the key data needs for a retail coffee company include:

- **Sales data:** Retail coffee companies need to track the sales data to understand how their products are performing, and identify trends over time. This includes data on the number of drinks sold, the average ticket price, and the overall sales by product category.
- **Inventory data:** Keeping track of inventory is critical for retail coffee companies to ensure that they have enough supplies on hand to meet customer demand. This includes data on the quantity of coffee beans, milk, syrups, and other ingredients that are in stock.
- **Customer data:** Retail coffee companies need to collect the data on their customers to understand their preferences, and tailor their offerings to meet their needs. This includes data on customer demographics, purchase history, and feedback.
- **Operational data:** Retail coffee companies need to track operational data to ensure that their stores are running smoothly and efficiently. This includes data on equipment maintenance, staffing levels, and store traffic patterns.
- **Market data:** Retail coffee companies need to stay up-to-date on market trends and competitive landscape to stay relevant and competitive. This includes data on industry benchmarks, customer preferences, and competitor pricing.

Overall, the data needs of a retail coffee company are diverse and complex, and require a robust data management system as well as analytical tools to make informed business decisions.

Major Companies

The retail coffee space is highly competitive, and there are several large operators that dominate the market. The biggest operators in the retail coffee space include:

- **Starbucks:** With over 30,000 locations worldwide, Starbucks is the largest coffee chain in the world. Known for its premium coffee and upscale atmosphere, Starbucks is a global brand that has become synonymous with the retail coffee experience.
- **Dunkin' Brands:** Dunkin' Brands operates more than 12,000 locations worldwide under the Dunkin' and Baskin-Robbins brands. While Dunkin' offers a wide range of coffee drinks and baked goods, it is perhaps best known for its coffee and donuts.
- **Costa Coffee:** Costa Coffee is a UK-based coffee chain that operates at more than 3,000 locations in more than 32 countries. Known for its high-quality coffee and welcoming atmosphere, Costa Coffee is a popular choice for coffee lovers around the world.
- **Tim Hortons:** Tim Hortons is a Canadian-based coffee chain that operates in more than 4,000 locations worldwide. Known for its coffee and donuts, Tim Hortons is a beloved brand in Canada, and has a growing presence in other countries around the world.
- **McDonald's:** While not exclusively a coffee chain, McDonald's is one of the largest coffee sellers in the world. With more than 38,000 locations worldwide, McDonald's serves a wide range of coffee drinks, and is known for its affordable prices and convenient locations.

Overall, the retail coffee space is dominated by a handful of large players that have established strong brands and loyal customer bases over many years of operation.

Market Size

The retail coffee market is a large and growing industry that encompasses a wide range of products and services. While specific figures can vary depending on the source and the definition of the market, here are some general estimates of the size of the retail coffee market:

- **Global coffee market size:** The global coffee market was valued at about $102.15 billion in 2020, and is expected to reach about $155.64 billion by 2027, with a

Compound Annual Growth Rate (CAGR) of 6.5% from 2020 to 2027 (source: Fortune Business Insights).

- **US coffee market size:** The US coffee market was valued at $45.1 billion in 2020, and is expected to reach $62.1 billion by 2027, with a CAGR of 4.3% from 2020 to 2027 (source: Grand View Research).
- **Global coffee shop market size:** The global coffee shop market was valued at $201.92 billion in 2020, and is expected to reach $342.69 billion by 2028, with a CAGR of 6.4% from 2021 to 2028 (source: Research And Markets).
- **US coffee shop market size:** The US coffee shop market was valued at $47.5 billion in 2020, and is expected to reach $66.6 billion by 2027, with a CAGR of 4.5% from 2020 to 2027 (source: Allied Market Research).

The number of retail coffee shops worldwide is difficult to estimate, as the coffee shop market is highly fragmented, with many small independent coffee shops alongside large chains. However, here are some statistics on the number of retail coffee shops in certain regions:

- **United States:** As of 2021, there were approximately 36,000 coffee shops in the United States, including large chains such as Starbucks and Dunkin' Donuts, as well as independent coffee shops.
- **Europe:** As of 2020, there were approximately 34,000 coffee shops in Europe, with the largest markets being the United Kingdom, Germany, and France.
- **Asia-Pacific:** As of 2020, there were approximately 66,000 coffee shops in the Asia-Pacific region, with the largest markets being China, Japan, and South Korea.
- **Latin America:** As of 2020, there were approximately 29,000 coffee shops in Latin America, with the largest markets being Brazil and Mexico.

Overall, the retail coffee shop market is a growing industry, with increasing demand for specialty coffee, convenience, and a unique in-store experience.

Popular Products and Merchandise

Coffee culture has evolved over the years, and there are many popular coffee drinks available today. Here are some of the most popular coffee drinks:

- **Espresso:** A concentrated shot of coffee made by forcing hot water through finely grounded coffee beans.
- **Latte:** Made with espresso and steamed milk, topped with a small amount of foam.
- **Cappuccino:** Made with equal parts of espresso, steamed milk, and foam.
- **Americano:** Made by adding hot water to espresso.

- **Macchiato:** A shot of espresso with a small amount of steamed milk added on top.
- **Mocha:** Made with espresso, steamed milk, chocolate syrup, and topped with whipped cream.
- **Frappuccino:** A blended coffee drink made with ice, milk, and flavored syrups.
- **Cold brew:** A coffee drink made by steeping coffee grounds in cold water for several hours, resulting in a smooth and less acidic taste.
- **Nitro cold brew:** Cold brew coffee infused with nitrogen to give it a creamy texture and a smooth, velvety mouthfeel.
- **Pour-over coffee:** A manually brewed coffee drink made by pouring hot water over coffee grounds in a filter.

These are just a few examples of the most popular coffee drinks, but there are many variations and combinations that can be customized to individual preferences.

The most popular food items available at a coffee shop can vary depending on the region and the coffee shop's menu. However, here are some of the most found food items at coffee shops:

- **Pastries:** Pastries such as croissants, muffins, scones, and danishes are popular options for a quick breakfast or snack.
- **Bagels:** Bagels with cream cheese, jam, or butter are a popular breakfast option.
- **Sandwiches:** Sandwiches, such as egg and cheese or turkey and avocado, are often served for breakfast or lunch.
- **Wraps:** Healthy wraps filled with fresh vegetables, hummus, or chicken are a popular choice for a quick and light meal.
- **Salads:** Many coffee shops now offer fresh salads with ingredients like mixed greens, chicken, and avocado.
- **Granola bars:** Granola bars and energy bars are a popular snack option that are often sold at coffee shops.
- **Cookies:** A sweet treat to pair with coffee, cookies are often available in a variety of flavors.
- **Yogurt:** Yogurt, granola, and fruit parfaits are a healthy and filling option for breakfast or a snack.
- **Fruits:** Fresh fruits such as bananas, apples, and oranges are often sold at coffee shops.

Overall, coffee shops offer a variety of food options to cater to different tastes and dietary preferences. Many coffee shops are now also catering to the increasing demand for healthy and plant-based options, including vegan and gluten-free options.

Profile of a Typical Customer

The profile of a typical customer of a coffee shop can vary depending on the location and the specific coffee shop. However, here are some common characteristics of coffee shop customers:

- **Age:** Coffee shop customers are often young adults or professionals, although people of all ages enjoy coffee.
- **Income:** Coffee shop customers typically have a disposable income, and are willing to pay a premium price for specialty coffee and food items.
- **Education:** Coffee shop customers tend to have higher levels of education, with many being college graduates or working in knowledge-based professions.
- **Urban location:** Coffee shops are often found in urban areas, and their customers are predominantly city residents or workers.
- **Social:** Many coffee shop customers see the coffee shop as a social space, where they can meet with friends or colleagues, work remotely, or simply relax.
- **Health-conscious:** In recent years, there has been a growing demand for healthier food and beverage options, and many coffee shop customers are interested in plant-based, organic, or gluten-free options.

Hence, there are many reasons why customers visit coffee shops, and these reasons may vary depending on the individual. However, here are some common attractions that draw customers to coffee shops:

- **Quality coffee:** One of the primary attractions of a coffee shop is the quality of the coffee. Customers are often willing to pay a premium price for specialty drinks that are made with high-quality, freshly roasted coffee beans.
- **Social atmosphere:** Many customers visit coffee shops as a place to socialize with friends, colleagues, or their community. The coffee shop provides a welcoming and comfortable environment where people can relax and connect with others.
- **Work or study space:** Coffee shops are often seen as a convenient place to work or study, with free Wi-Fi, comfortable seating, and access to coffee and food, particularly snacks.
- **Food options:** In addition to coffee, many coffee shops offer a variety of food options, from pastries and baked goods to sandwiches and salads. This makes them a popular destination for breakfast, lunch, or a quick snack.
- **Convenience:** Coffee shops are often located in high-traffic areas such as downtown districts, shopping centers, or near public transportation. This makes them a convenient stop for customers who are on-the-go.

- **Ambiance:** Many coffee shops have a unique and appealing ambiance, with cozy seating, soft lighting, and music. This can create a relaxing and welcoming atmosphere that encourages customers to spend time in the coffee shop.

Overall, coffee shops provide a unique combination of quality coffee, social atmosphere, convenience, and ambiance that appeals to a wide range of customers.

Typical Jobs

The coffee industry offers a variety of job opportunities across different sectors, including production, roasting, retail, as well as wholesale and distribution. Some of the different jobs in the coffee industry include:

- **Coffee farmer:** Coffee farmers are responsible for growing coffee plants, harvesting coffee cherries, and processing beans. This is a physically demanding job that requires knowledge of farming techniques, coffee plant cultivation, as well as harvesting, packaging, and storing methods.
- **Roaster:** Coffee roasters are responsible for roasting coffee beans to the desired level of roast, which can vary depending on the type of coffee and the intended flavor profile. This job requires knowledge of coffee roasting equipment, bean sourcing, and flavor profiles.
- **Barista:** Baristas work in coffee shops and cafes, where they prepare and serve coffee drinks to customers. This job requires knowledge of coffee brewing techniques, drink preparation, and customer service.
- **Coffee shop manager:** Coffee shop managers oversee the operations of a coffee shop, including managing staff, ordering supplies, and maintaining the store. This job requires knowledge of coffee shop operations, customer service, and management techniques.
- **Coffee trader:** Coffee traders work in the wholesale coffee market, buying and selling coffee beans for commercial use. This job requires knowledge of coffee pricing, quality control, and supply chain management.
- **Coffee equipment technician:** Coffee equipment technicians are responsible for maintaining and repairing coffee equipment, including espresso machines, grinders, and brewers. This job requires knowledge of coffee equipment maintenance and repair, as well as customer service skills.

Thus, the coffee industry offers a variety of job opportunities for people with different interests and skill sets, from farming and production to retail and wholesale operations.

Significant Innovations

The history of coffee shops dates back to the 16th century, and since then, there have been many significant innovations and changes in this industry. Here are some of the most notable innovations over the recent history of coffee retail production:

- **Espresso machines:** The invention of the espresso machine in the early 20th century revolutionized the coffee industry, making it possible to produce high-quality espresso drinks quickly and efficiently.
- **Automatic coffee makers:** The development of automatic drip coffee makers in the mid-20th century made it possible for coffee shops to produce large quantities of coffee quickly and consistently.
- **Specialty coffee:** In the 1980s and 1990s, the concept of specialty coffee emerged, with a focus on high-quality, freshly roasted beans and unique brewing methods such as pour-over and French press.
- **Internet and digital technology:** With the rise of the internet and digital technology, coffee shops have been able to offer free Wi-Fi to customers and to implement mobile ordering and loyalty programs.
- **Cold brew and nitro coffee:** In recent years, cold brew and nitro coffee have become popular alternatives to traditional hot coffee, offering unique flavor profiles and a different drinking experience.
- **Sustainable practices:** In response to growing concern about the environmental and social impact of coffee production, many coffee shops have implemented sustainable practices such as using compostable packaging, and supporting fair trade practices.

Overall, the coffee industry has evolved significantly since the inception of coffee shops, with new technologies, brewing methods, and sustainability practices. These innovations have helped to create a diverse and dynamic industry that continues to attract customers around the world.

Future of the Coffee Industry

The outlook for businesses in the coffee industry is positive, with continued growth and opportunities for innovation and expansion. Here are some of the key trends and factors that are shaping the future of the coffee industry:

- **Growing demand for specialty coffee:** Consumers are increasingly interested in high-quality, specialty coffee, which offers unique flavor profiles and brewing methods. This trend is driving demand for single-origin coffee, cold brew, nitro coffee, and other specialty drinks.
- **Emphasis on sustainability:** Consumers are becoming more aware of the environmental and social impacts of coffee production, and are seeking out companies that prioritize sustainability. This includes using environmentally

friendly packaging, supporting fair trade practices, and investing in sustainable farming methods.

- **Digital transformation:** Coffee companies are investing in technology to improve customer experience, streamline operations, and expand their reach. This includes mobile ordering, loyalty programs, and digital marketing.
- **Health and wellness:** Consumers are increasingly interested in healthier food and beverage options, and coffee companies are responding with low-calorie, plant-based, and functional drinks.
- **Convenience and innovation:** Coffee companies are exploring new ways to deliver coffee to consumers, through vending machines, delivery services, and mobile pop-up shops. They are also experimenting with new flavors, ingredients, and brewing methods to keep up with the changing consumer preferences.

Overall, the coffee industry is expected to continue to grow and evolve in response to the changing consumer preferences and market trends. Companies that can innovate, prioritize sustainability, and deliver high-quality customer experience are likely to succeed in this dynamic and competitive industry.

Overview of Starbucks Coffee

Starbucks is a multinational coffee company that was founded in Seattle, Washington in 1971. **Today, Starbucks operates over 30,000 stores in 80 countries around the world, making it the largest coffeehouse chain in the world.**

Starbucks is known for its high-quality coffee, as well as its commitment to ethical sourcing and sustainability. The company sources its coffee beans from over 30 countries, and has developed partnerships with coffee farmers and cooperatives around the world to ensure fair prices and sustainable practices.

In addition to coffee, Starbucks offers a variety of food and beverage options, including tea, pastries, sandwiches, and other snacks. The company has also developed a range of branded merchandise, including mugs, tumblers, and other coffee-related accessories.

Starbucks stores are designed to provide a welcoming and comfortable atmosphere for customers, with comfortable seating, free Wi-Fi, and a variety of music and entertainment options. The company also offers a mobile app that allows customers to order and pay for their drinks ahead of time, as well as a rewards program that offers discounts and other perks to loyal customers.

Overall, Starbucks has become a global icon and a cultural phenomenon, with millions of loyal customers around the world who rely on the company for their daily dose of coffee and community.

Starbucks headquarters, also known as the Starbucks Support Center, is in Seattle, Washington and is home to a wide range of job functions across different departments. Some of the jobs at Starbucks headquarters include:

- **Corporate leadership:** This includes executives, directors, and managers who oversee the overall strategy and operations of the company.
- **Finance:** The finance team is responsible for managing the financial operations of the company, including accounting, budgeting, and financial planning.
- **Human resources:** The human resources team is responsible for managing employee relations, recruitment, benefits, and training and development programs.
- **Marketing:** The marketing team is responsible for developing and executing marketing strategies to promote Starbucks products and brand.
- **Supply chain and logistics:** The supply chain and logistics team is responsible for managing the sourcing, manufacturing, and distribution of Starbucks products, including coffee beans, equipment, and other supplies.
- **Information technology:** The IT team is responsible for developing and maintaining the technology infrastructure used by Starbucks employees and customers, including point-of-sale systems, mobile apps, and e-commerce platforms.
- **Legal:** The legal team is responsible for providing legal counsel and support to the company, including contract negotiations, intellectual property protection, and compliance with regulatory requirements.
- **Corporate social responsibility:** The CSR team is responsible for developing and implementing sustainability and social responsibility programs, including ethical sourcing, community outreach, and environmental sustainability.

Thus, Starbucks headquarters offers a wide range of job opportunities across different departments and functions, allowing employees to contribute to the company's mission of creating a positive impact on the world through coffee.

Mission Statement of Starbucks

The mission statement of Starbucks is: "*To inspire and nurture the human spirit – one person, one cup and one neighborhood at a time.*"

This mission statement emphasizes Starbucks' commitment to creating a positive impact on individuals, communities, and the environment. The company aims to achieve this mission by providing high-quality coffee, promoting ethical sourcing practices, creating a positive work environment for its employees, and supporting community-based programs and initiatives. The statement also emphasizes the importance of personal connections, and the role that Starbucks plays in bringing people together in a welcoming environment.

Reasons behind Starbucks' Success

There are many reasons why Starbucks has been so successful over the years, but here are some of the key factors:

- **Strong brand:** Starbucks has built a strong and recognizable brand that is associated with quality coffee, a comfortable atmosphere, and a welcoming community.
- **Consistent customer experience:** Starbucks is known for providing consistent customer experience across all of its locations, with high-quality coffee, comfortable seating, and friendly customer service.
- **Innovation:** Starbucks has been at the forefront of innovation in the coffee industry, introducing new products and services such as mobile ordering, reward programs, and unique drink flavors.
- **Marketing and advertising:** Starbucks has invested heavily in marketing and advertising, using social media, promotions, and creative campaigns to attract and retain customers.
- **Employee training and development:** Starbucks places a strong emphasis on employee training and development, with a comprehensive program that focuses on customer service, coffee knowledge, and leadership skills.
- **Community involvement:** Starbucks has a long history of supporting local communities, with initiatives such as sourcing coffee beans from small-scale farmers, supporting local nonprofits, and encouraging employee volunteerism.

Overall, Starbucks has been successful because it has built a strong brand, provided consistent customer experience, innovated in the coffee industry, invested in marketing and advertising, emphasized employee training and development, and engaged closely with local communities.

Starbucks has distinguished itself from its competitors in several ways, including:

- **Focus on customer experience:** Starbucks places a strong emphasis on providing a welcoming and comfortable atmosphere for customers, with comfortable seating, high-quality coffee, and friendly customer service.
- **Branding:** Starbucks has built a strong and recognizable brand that is associated with quality coffee, a welcoming atmosphere, and a sense of community.
- **Innovation:** Starbucks has been at the forefront of innovation in the coffee industry, introducing new products and services such as mobile ordering, reward programs, and unique drink flavors.

- **Sustainable practices:** Starbucks has been a leader in implementing sustainable practices in the coffee industry, such as sourcing coffee beans from small-scale farmers, supporting ethical sourcing practices, and investing in renewable energy.
- **Social responsibility:** Starbucks has a long history of supporting local communities and social causes, such as hiring refugees, providing healthcare benefits to employees, and supporting local nonprofits.
- **Employee development:** Starbucks places a strong emphasis on employee training and development, with a comprehensive program that focuses on customer service, coffee knowledge, and leadership skills.

Thus, Starbucks has distinguished itself from its competitors through its focus on customer experience, branding, innovation, sustainable practices, social responsibility, and employee development. These factors have helped to create a unique and successful coffee brand that is recognized around the world.

Data Needs of Starbucks

As a large and complex organization, Starbucks leaders have a range of data needs to help them make informed decisions, and drive business growth. Some of the key data needs of leaders at Starbucks include:

- **Sales and revenue data:** Leaders need access to data on sales and revenue trends to track performance, identify areas of growth, and develop strategies to increase revenue.
- **Customer data:** Starbucks collects a wealth of customer data through its rewards program, mobile app, and other channels. Leaders need access to this data to understand customer behavior, preferences, and trends, and to develop marketing and customer engagement strategies.
- **Product and inventory data:** Leaders need access to data on product sales, inventory levels, and supply chain performance to manage product offerings, optimize inventory levels, and ensure timely delivery of products to stores.
- **Operational data:** Leaders need data on operational performance, including store traffic, staffing levels, and supply chain performance, to identify areas of improvement and optimize operations.
- **Financial data:** Leaders need access to financial data on expenses, budgets, and profitability to manage finances, and make informed decisions around investments, cost savings, and other financial matters.
- **Market data:** Leaders need data on market trends, competition, and consumer behavior to stay informed about industry developments, and identify new opportunities for growth.

Thus, leaders at Starbucks rely on a wide range of data to help them make informed decisions, and drive business growth across different functions and departments. The company invests heavily in data analytics and business intelligence tools to ensure that leaders have access to the data they need to make strategic decisions.

Challenges and Goals of Starbucks

Starbucks, like any other business, faces various challenges, and has set specific goals for itself. Here are some of the challenges and goals of Starbucks:

Challenges:

- **Competition:** Starbucks faces stiff competition from other coffee shops and food retailers, both large chains and small independent stores.
- **Market saturation:** Starbucks has reached a point of market saturation in some areas, which makes it challenging to grow sales and attract new customers.
- **Evolving consumer preferences:** Consumers are becoming more health-conscious, and are seeking out healthier food and beverage options, which may challenge Starbucks to adjust its menu and offerings.
- **Investor relations:** As with any large public company, Starbucks must balance a myriad of conflicting interests, between short-term and long-term measurements. These include internal employees, customers, and institutional investors.
- **Employee relations:** While Starbucks has a large loyal workforce, some of the unique challenges they face are having steady relationships with their retail employees who seek greater pay, more flexible and predictable schedules as well as other benefits.
- **Supply chain management:** Starbucks must manage its supply chain effectively to ensure a steady supply of high-quality coffee beans, and to address issues such as climate change, drought, and deforestation.

Goals:

- **Growth:** Starbucks is focused on expanding its presence in new markets, and increasing its sales and profitability.
- **Sustainability:** Starbucks has set a goal to reduce its environmental footprint by sourcing coffee sustainably, reducing waste, and conserving energy.
- **Innovation:** Starbucks is committed to innovation, and is exploring new technologies, products, and services to enhance customer experience, and drive growth.
- **Social responsibility:** Starbucks is committed to social responsibility, and has set goals to hire more veterans and refugees, provide healthcare benefits to all employees, and support local communities.

- **Customer experience:** Starbucks aims to continue providing consistent and high-quality customer experience, with friendly customer service, comfortable seating, and high-quality coffee.

Pleasing Starbucks Investors

- **Sustainable Growth:** Investors expect consistent revenue growth. Starbucks must balance expansion efforts with maintaining profitability, particularly in saturated markets with a high number of existing stores.
- **Market Competition:** The coffee and beverage market is highly competitive, with numerous players vying consumer attention. Starbucks needs to differentiate itself, while meeting investor expectations for market share growth.
- **Global Economic Fluctuations:** Economic downturns or fluctuations can affect consumer spending on premium products. Starbucks must demonstrate resilience in various economic conditions to reassure investors.
- **Employee Relations:** As labor issues and unionization efforts arise, managing employee relations effectively is crucial. Investors may be concerned about how these challenges impact profitability and brand image.
- **Supply Chain Stability:** Disruptions in the supply chain can impact product availability and costs. Investors are looking for assurance that Starbucks can manage these risks effectively.
- **Innovation and Product Development:** Staying relevant requires continuous innovation in products and services. Investors expect Starbucks to deliver new offerings that resonate with consumers, while maintaining quality.
- **Sustainability Initiatives:** As consumer preference shifts toward sustainability, investors expect Starbucks to lead in ethical sourcing and environmental practices, without sacrificing profit margins.
- **Return on Investment:** Investors want to see a strong return on their investment, which requires Starbucks to manage costs effectively, while pursuing growth opportunities.

Employee Relationship Challenges

Starbucks has faced several challenges with employee relations, including:

- **Unionization Efforts:** Recently, there has been a significant push for unionization among Starbucks employees, particularly in response to working conditions and pay. The company has had to navigate negotiations and potential conflicts arising from this movement.

- **Wage and Benefits Disputes:** Employees have raised concerns about wages, benefits, and job security. Balancing employee compensation with company profitability can lead to tensions.
- **Workplace Culture:** Maintaining a positive workplace culture is crucial for employee satisfaction. Issues such as burnout, high turnover rates, and employee morale can impact the overall relations.
- **Diversity and Inclusion:** Ensuring that the company is truly diverse and inclusive has been a challenge. Employees often call for better representation and support for marginalized groups within the workforce.
- **Management Practices**: There can be discrepancies between corporate policies and the experiences of employees at the store level, leading to dissatisfaction and distrust among the staff.

Starbucks Global Supply Chain Challenges

Starbucks faces several specific challenges in managing its global supply chain:

- **Sourcing Quality Ingredients:** Ensuring a consistent supply of high-quality coffee beans and other ingredients from various countries can be difficult due to varying agricultural conditions and quality standards.
- **Sustainability Practices:** Balancing profitability with sustainable sourcing and ethical practices is crucial. Starbucks must navigate the complexities of sustainable agriculture and fair trade, which can impact sourcing decisions.
- **Logistical Complexities:** Coordinating the transportation and distribution of products across different regions involves navigating various regulations, tariffs, and logistics challenges, which can lead to delays and increased costs.
- **Market Variability:** Fluctuations in demand across different markets require flexibility in the supply chain. Adapting to local preferences, while maintaining global standards can be challenging.
- **Supplier Relationships:** Building and maintaining strong relationships with suppliers is essential but can be complicated due to geopolitical issues, economic instability, and changing market conditions.
- **Technological Integration:** Implementing and maintaining technological solutions for supply chain management can be challenging, particularly across diverse global operations.
- **Risk Management:** Natural disasters, political instability, and economic changes in sourcing regions can disrupt supply chains, necessitating robust risk management strategies.

- **Consumer Expectations:** Increasing consumer demand for transparency and ethical sourcing requires Starbucks to provide clear information about its supply chain practices, which can be challenging to manage globally.

Addressing these challenges requires strategic planning, strong supplier relationships, and a commitment to sustainability and quality.

Additional Resources

There are many articles and online resources available to help students learn about the coffee industry. Here are some suggestions:

- **Specialty Coffee Association of America (SCAA) website:** The SCAA is a non-profit organization dedicated to promoting specialty coffee. Their website offers a wealth of information on coffee, including articles, research papers, and industry news.
- **National Coffee Association (NCA) website:** The NCA is a trade organization that represents the U.S. coffee industry. Their website provides news, research, and statistics on the coffee industry.
- **Roast Magazine:** *Roast Magazine* is a trade publication that focuses on the specialty coffee industry. It offers in-depth coverage of coffee roasting, brewing, and other related topics.
- **Perfect Daily Grind**: Perfect Daily Grind is an online coffee magazine that offers news, analysis, and educational resources on the coffee industry.
- **Daily Coffee News:** Daily Coffee News is an online news source that covers the coffee industry, with a focus on business and technology.
- **Coffee & Conservation:** This is a **blog** that explores the intersection of coffee production and environmental conservation.
- ***The Coffee Roaster's Companion* by Scott Rao:** This book provides an in-depth look at coffee roasting, including techniques, equipment, and industry trends.
- **God in a Cup: *The Obsessive Quest for the Perfect Coffee* by Michaele Weissman:** This book provides a fascinating look at the specialty coffee industry, including the journey of three coffee professionals searching for the world's best coffee beans.
- ***The World Atlas of Coffee* by James Hoffmann:** This book provides a comprehensive overview of the world of coffee, including history, production, and flavor profiles.

These resources can provide a solid foundation for students looking to learn more about the coffee industry, and can help them stay informed about industry trends as well as the ongoing or future developments.

Conclusion

This case study is intended to provide a foundation of understanding of the retail coffee industry as well as a deeper exploration into the dominant company for you to possibly prepare an original database design. This case study was chosen precisely because many readers already have more than a passing knowledge of retail coffee (some may even be reading this in a coffee shop) and will have momentum taking the next step into applying their newly-gained technical database knowledge into a project building, a database focused on an aspect of the retail coffee business.

Take the next step!

Thus, the work that is done right now will significantly impact your learning, and embed the hard-fought skills in SQL and data modeling into your 'forever memory'. Good luck!

Index

T

U

V

W

www.ingramcontent.com/pod-product-compliance
Ingram Content Group UK Ltd.
Pitfield, Milton Keynes, MK11 3LW, UK
UKHW051447290926
15471UKWH00008B/1069